*New Beacon Bible Commentary

1 & 2 SAMUEL
A Commentary in the Wesleyan Tradition

Kevin J. Mellish

BEACON HILL PRESS
OF KANSAS CITY

Copyright 2012
by Beacon Hill Press of Kansas City

ISBN 978-0-8341-2721-0

Printed in the United States of America

Cover Design: J.R. Caines
Interior Design: Sharon Page

Unless otherwise indicated all Scripture quotations are from the *Holy Bible, New International Version*® (NIV®). Copyright © 1973, 1978, 1984 by Biblica, Inc.™ Used by permission of Zondervan. All rights reserved worldwide. www.zondervan.com.

King James Version (KJV).

Young's Literal Translation (YLT).

The following copyrighted versions of the Bible are used by permission.

The *Good News Translation* (*Today's English Version*)—*Second Edition* (GNT). Copyright © 1992 by American Bible Society.

The *New American Standard Bible*® (NASB®), © copyright The Lockman Foundation 1960, 1962, 1963, 1968, 1971, 1972, 1973, 1975, 1977, 1995.

The *New Revised Standard Version* (NRSV) of the Bible, copyright 1989 by the Division of Christian Education of the National Council of the Churches of Christ in the USA. All rights reserved.

The *Revised Standard Version* (RSV) of the Bible, copyright 1946, 1952, 1971 by the Division of Christian Education of the National Council of the Churches of Christ in the USA.

The Message: The Bible in Contemporary Language (TM), copyright 2002 by Eugene Peterson. All rights reserved.

Library of Congress Cataloging-in-Publication Data

Mellish, Kevin, 1968-
 1 & 2 Samuel / Kevin Mellish.
   pages cm — (New Beacon Bible commentary)
 Includes bibliographical references.
 ISBN 978-0-8341-2721-0 (pbk.)
 1. Bible. O.T. Samuel—Commentaries. I. Title. II. Title: First and Second Samuel.
 BS1325.53.M45 2012
 222'.407—dc22

2011048897

COMMENTARY EDITORS

General Editors

Alex Varughese
    Ph.D., Drew University
    Professor of Biblical Literature
    Mount Vernon Nazarene University
    Mount Vernon, Ohio

Roger Hahn
    Ph.D., Duke University
    Dean of the Faculty
    Professor of New Testament
    Nazarene Theological Seminary
    Kansas City, Missouri

George Lyons
    Ph.D., Emory University
    Professor of New Testament
    Northwest Nazarene University
    Nampa, Idaho

Section Editors

Joseph Coleson
    Ph.D., Brandeis University
    Professor of Old Testament
    Nazarene Theological Seminary
    Kansas City, Missouri

Robert Branson
    Ph.D., Boston University
    Professor of Biblical Literature
        Emeritus
    Olivet Nazarene University
    Bourbonnais, Illinois

Alex Varughese
    Ph.D., Drew University
    Professor of Biblical Literature
    Mount Vernon Nazarene University
    Mount Vernon, Ohio

Jim Edlin
    Ph.D., Southern Baptist Theological
        Seminary
    Professor of Biblical Literature and
        Languages
    Chair, Division of Religion and
        Philosophy
    MidAmerica Nazarene University
    Olathe, Kansas

Kent Brower
    Ph.D., The University of Manchester
    Vice Principal
    Senior Lecturer in Biblical Studies
    Nazarene Theological College
    Manchester, England

George Lyons
    Ph.D., Emory University
    Professor of New Testament
    Northwest Nazarene University
    Nampa, Idaho

CONTENTS

General Editors' Preface	9
Author's Preface	11
Abbreviations	12
Bibliography	15

INTRODUCTION — 19
   A. Canonical Arrangement — 19
   B. Textual History — 20
   C. History of Composition — 21
      1. Traditional View of Authorship — 21
      2. Modern Theories Regarding Authorship — 21
      3. The Deuteronomistic History — 24
      4. The Books of Samuel — 26
         a. The Story of Samuel — 27
         b. The Ark Narrative — 27
         c. The Saulide Traditions — 27
         d. The History of David's Rise — 29
         e. The Succession Narrative — 33
         f. The Appendices — 34
   D. Theological Themes — 34
      1. Leadership — 35
         a. The Monarchy — 35
         b. The Failure of Saulide Leadership — 36
         c. The Success of Davidic Leadership — 36
         d. The Rise of the Prophets — 37
      2. Reversal of Fortune — 37
      3. Reward-Punishment Theology — 38

COMMENTARY — 39

FIRST SAMUEL — 39

   I. The Premonarchical Period in Israel: Samuel and the Ark Narratives (1:1—7:17) — 39
      A. The Birth of Samuel (1:1-28; 2:11) — 39
         1. Prologue (1:1-3) — 41
         2. Elkanah's Family at Shiloh (1:4-8) — 43
         3. Hannah's Vow to Yahweh (1:9-11) — 44
         4. Eli and Hannah at the Sanctuary (1:12-18) — 46
         5. Samuel Is Presented to Yahweh (1:19-28; 2:11) — 47
      B. Hannah's Song of Thanksgiving (2:1-10) — 50
      C. Eli and His Sons (2:12—3:1a) — 53

			1. Eli's Sons in Action (2:12-26)	54
			2. Condemnation of the House of Eli (2:27-36; 3:1a)	57
		D.	Samuel's Dream Theophany (3:1b—4:1a)	60
			1. The Religious Situation at Shiloh (3:1b-3)	60
			2. Yahweh's Word to Samuel (3:4-9)	61
			3. Yahweh's Message to Samuel (3:10-21; 4:1a)	62
		E.	The Capture of the Ark of the Covenant (4:1b—7:1)	64
			1. The Setting of the Ark's Capture (4:1b-4)	65
			2. The Capture of the Ark (4:5-11)	66
			3. Report of the Capture of the Ark (4:12-18)	67
			4. The Report of a Child's Birth (4:19-22)	69
			5. The Ark Is Taken into Captivity by the Philistines (5:1-12)	69
			6. The Philistines Prepare to Move the Ark (6:1-9)	71
			7. The Ark Returns to Beth Shemesh (6:10—7:1)	72
		F.	Samuel as Judge (7:2-17)	75
			1. Samuel Presides over Israel's Repentance (7:2-4)	76
			2. The Assembly at Mizpah and Philistine Defeat (7:5-14)	77
			3. Samuel as Judge (7:15-17)	79
II.	The Emergence of the Monarchy in Israel: Saul, Israel's First King (8:1—15:35)			81
	A.	Israel Asks for a King (8:1-22)		81
		1.	The Setting (8:1-3)	82
		2.	The Request for a King (8:4-22)	83
	B.	Saul Chosen as King (9:1—10:27)		85
		1.	Saul's Introduction (9:1-2)	86
		2.	Saul Chosen and Anointed (9:3—10:16)	87
		3.	The People Select Saul (10:17-27)	90
	C.	Saul Defeats the Ammonites (11:1-15)		93
		1.	Saul Versus the Ammonites (11:1-13)	93
		2.	The Renewal of Kingship at Gilgal (11:14-15)	94
	D.	Samuel's Farewell Address (12:1-25)		95
		1.	Samuel's Opening Remarks (12:1-5)	96
		2.	Samuel Addresses the People (12:6-25)	96
	E.	Saul's Shortcomings and Downfall (13:1—15:35)		98
		1.	Saul's Introduction (13:1)	99
		2.	Saul Attacks the Philistines (13:2-7a)	99
		3.	Saul Makes an Inappropriate Sacrifice (13:7b-15a)	101
		4.	Saul's Battle with the Philistines Continued (13:15b-23)	102
		5.	Jonathan and the Philistines (14:1-23a)	103
		6.	Saul's Rash Oath (14:23b-46)	105
		7.	Miscellaneous Reports About Saul's Battles and Household (14:47-52)	107
		8.	A Divine Command (15:1-3)	108
		9.	The Battle Against Amalek (15:4-9)	110
		10.	Samuel Confronts Saul (15:10-35)	110

III. David's Rise to Kingship (1 Samuel 16:1—2 Samuel 8:18)	115
A. David's Anointing and David at Saul's Court (16:1-23)	115
1. Samuel Instructed to Anoint David (16:1-5)	116
2. David Is Anointed (16:6-13)	117
3. David Is Introduced to Saul's Court (16:14-23)	118
B. David and Goliath (17:1-58)	119
1. The Introduction of Goliath (17:1-11)	120
2. David and the Flock (17:12-30)	121
3. David and Saul (17:31-40)	122
4. The Battle with Goliath (17:41-54)	123
5. Saul Meets David a Second Time (17:55-58)	124
C. David and Saul's Household (18:1—20:42)	126
1. David, Favorable with Jonathan and Saul (18:1-9)	127
2. Saul Tries to Kill David (18:10-16)	129
3. David and Michal (18:17-29)	130
4. Closing Statement (18:30)	131
5. Jonathan Intercedes for David (19:1-7)	131
6. Michal Saves David from Saul (19:8-17)	132
7. David Flees to Ramah (19:18-24)	133
8. Jonathan and David Again (20:1-42)	134
D. David's Flight from Saul (21:1—23:29)	138
1. David Escapes to Nob (21:1-9)	139
2. David Flees to Gath (21:10-15)	141
3. David at Adullam (22:1-5)	142
4. Saul and the Priests of Nob (22:6-23)	144
5. David Saves Keilah (23:1-14)	145
6. David Eludes Saul in the Wilderness (23:15-29)	147
E. David Encounters Saul in the Wilderness (24:1—26:25)	149
1. David at En Gedi (24:1-22)	151
2. David and Nabal (25:1-44)	153
3. David Spares Saul's Life Again (26:1-25)	157
F. David Among the Philistines (27:1—30:31)	160
1. David and Achish (27:1-12)	161
2. Saul Consults a Medium (28:1-25)	162
3. The Philistines Reject David (29:1-11)	165
4. David Avenges the Destruction of Ziklag (30:1-31)	167
G. The Death of King Saul and Jonathan (31:1-13)	172
SECOND SAMUEL	177
H. The Second Report of the Death of Saul and David's Lament over the Death of Saul and Jonathan (2 Samuel 1:1-27)	177
1. An Amalekite Reports Saul's Death (1:1-16)	178
2. David's Song of Lament (1:17-27)	181
I. David as Ruler over Judah (2:1—4:12)	183
1. David Anointed as King over Judah (2:1-7)	183
2. Ish-Bosheth Established as King over Israel (2:8-11)	185

		3.	The Battle at Gibeon (2:12-32)	186
		4.	David at Hebron (3:1-5)	188
		5.	Abner Defects to David (3:6-39)	188
		6.	The Death of Ish-Bosheth (4:1-12)	192
	J.		David Becomes King over Israel (5:1-25)	195
		1.	The Israelite Tribes Make David King (5:1-5)	196
		2.	David Captures Jerusalem (5:6-16)	197
		3.	David and the Philistines (5:17-25)	200
	K.		David and the Ark of the Covenant (6:1-23)	203
	L.		God Makes a Covenant with David (7:1-29)	210
		1.	Nathan's Oracle to David (7:1-17)	210
		2.	The Prayer of David (7:18-29)	213
	M.		David's Wars and Administration (8:1-18)	215
		1.	Report of David's Wars (8:1-14)	215
		2.	David's Administration (8:15-18)	217
IV.			The Succession to the Throne of David (9:1—20:26)	219
	A.		David's Dealings with the House of Saul (9:1-13)	219
	B.		David and Hanun (10:1-19)	222
	C.		David and Bathsheba (11:1—12:31)	226
		1.	David's Adultery and Murder (11:1-13)	227
		2.	David Has Uriah Murdered (11:14-27)	230
		3.	Nathan Confronts David (12:1-15a)	231
		4.	The Death of One Child, the Birth of Another (12:15b-25)	233
		5.	The War Against Ammon (12:26-31)	235
	D.		The Rape of Tamar and Murder of Amnon (13:1—14:33)	237
		1.	The Opening Scene (13:1-5)	238
		2.	Amnon Rapes Tamar (13:6-22)	239
		3.	Absalom's Revenge (13:23-39)	242
		4.	Absalom Returns to Jerusalem (14:1-24)	243
		5.	David Forgives Absalom (14:25-33)	244
	E.		David's Flight from Jerusalem and His Return (15:1—19:43)	246
		1.	Absalom Usurps the Throne (15:1-37)	247
		2.	David's Adversaries (16:1-23)	250
		3.	The Counsel of Hushai (17:1-29)	253
		4.	The Death of Absalom (18:1-33)	255
		5.	David Returns to Jerusalem (19:1-43)	258
	F.		The Revolt of Sheba (20:1-26)	264
V.			The Appendices (21:1—24:25)	269
		1.	David and the Gibeonites (21:1-14)	272
		2.	David's Men (21:15-22)	275
		3.	David's Song of Thanksgiving (22:1-51)	276
		4.	David's Last Words (23:1-7)	278
		5.	The Mighty Men of David (23:8-39)	278
		6.	David's Census, the Plague, and the Threshing Floor (24:1-25)	280

GENERAL EDITORS' PREFACE

The purpose of the New Beacon Bible Commentary is to make available to pastors and students in the twenty-first century a biblical commentary that reflects the best scholarship in the Wesleyan theological tradition. The commentary project aims to make this scholarship accessible to a wider audience to assist them in their understanding and proclamation of Scripture as God's Word.

Writers of the volumes in this series not only are scholars within the Wesleyan theological tradition and experts in their field but also have special interest in the books assigned to them. Their task is to communicate clearly the critical consensus and the full range of other credible voices who have commented on the Scriptures. Though scholarship and scholarly contribution to the understanding of the Scriptures are key concerns of this series, it is not intended as an academic dialogue within the scholarly community. Commentators of this series constantly aim to demonstrate in their work the significance of the Bible as the church's book and the contemporary relevance and application of the biblical message. The project's overall goal is to make available to the church and for her service the fruits of the labors of scholars who are committed to their Christian faith.

The *New International Version* (NIV) is the reference version of the Bible used in this series; however, the focus of exegetical study and comments is the biblical text in its original language. When the commentary uses the NIV, it is printed in bold. The text printed in bold italics is the translation of the author. Commentators also refer to other translations where the text may be difficult or ambiguous.

The structure and organization of the commentaries in this series seeks to facilitate the study of the biblical text in a systematic and methodical way. Study of each biblical book begins with an ***Introduction*** section that gives an overview of authorship, date, provenance, audience, occasion, purpose, sociological/cultural issues, textual history, literary features, hermeneutical issues, and theological themes necessary to understand the book. This section also includes a brief outline of the book and a list of general works and standard commentaries.

The commentary section for each biblical book follows the outline of the book presented in the introduction. In some volumes, readers will find section ***overviews*** of large portions of scripture with general comments on their overall literary structure and other literary features. A consistent feature of the commentary is the paragraph-by-paragraph study of biblical texts. This section has three parts: ***Behind the Text***, ***In the Text***, and ***From the Text***.

The goal of the ***Behind the Text*** section is to provide the reader with all the relevant information necessary to understand the text. This includes specific historical situations reflected in the text, the literary context of the text, sociological and cultural issues, and literary features of the text.

In the Text explores what the text says, following its verse-by-verse structure. This section includes a discussion of grammatical details, word studies, and the connectedness of the text to other biblical books/passages or other parts of the book being studied (the canonical relationship). This section provides transliterations of key words in Hebrew and Greek and their literal meanings. The goal here is to explain what the author would have meant and/or what the audience would have understood as the meaning of the text. This is the largest section of the commentary.

The ***From the Text*** section examines the text in relation to the following areas: theological significance, intertextuality, the history of interpretation, use of the Old Testament scriptures in the New Testament, interpretation in later church history, actualization, and application.

The commentary provides ***sidebars*** on topics of interest that are important but not necessarily part of an explanation of the biblical text. These topics are informational items and may cover archaeological, historical, literary, cultural, and theological matters that have relevance to the biblical text. Occasionally, longer detailed discussions of special topics are included as ***excurses.***

We offer this series with our hope and prayer that readers will find it a valuable resource for their understanding of God's Word and an indispensable tool for their critical engagement with the biblical texts.

Roger Hahn, Centennial Initiative General Editor
Alex Varughese, General Editor (Old Testament)
George Lyons, General Editor (New Testament)

AUTHOR'S PREFACE

Writing a commentary is a tremendous undertaking, one that could not have been accomplished without the help and support of many wonderful individuals. I would like to first of all thank my friend and colleague, Dr. Robert Branson, for inviting me to participate in the commentary project and for serving as my section editor. Bob carefully and tirelessly read through several drafts of the commentary and offered helpful, productive feedback along the journey. Bob's patient and caring style made it a joy to work with him.

I also owe a debt of gratitude to Dr. Alex Varughese and the good folks at Nazarene Publishing House. They graciously granted me a writing extension when my dad's sickness and death made it difficult to work on the commentary. I will always be grateful for the concern and understanding they bestowed upon me and my family as we walked through a difficult time.

I would also like to thank my dean at Olivet Nazarene University, Dr. Carl Leth, for adjusting my teaching schedule so that I could have extra time for research and writing. Dr. Leth's willingness to grant a research load proved to be invaluable, and I will always be grateful for the personal and administrative support he extended to me along the way.

I would like to acknowledge my students who have taken both my Deuteronomistic history class and Hebrew exegesis course on 1 Samuel. Their enthusiasm for learning the text, their careful observations on the grammar and syntax of 1 Samuel, and the interesting conversations they sparked over the books of Samuel in general have been refreshing and inspiring. I have learned much from them, and many of their comments and insights have found their way into the commentary.

Finally, I would like to thank my wife, Jeanine, for her patience and understanding as I worked through this writing process. There were many times I stayed late at work, came into the office on weekends, or brought my work home with me. Through it all, she never complained. I would also like to acknowledge my children, Dakota, Delaney, and Lacie, as they had to "share" their dad with my research and writing. Now that it is over, I look forward to devoting my full attention to them once again.

ABBREVIATIONS

With a few exceptions, these abbreviations follow those in *The SBL Handbook of Style* (Alexander 1999).

General

A.D.	anno Domini (precedes date) (equivalent to C.E.)
B.C.	before Christ (follows date) (equivalent to B.C.E.)
B.C.E.	before the Common Era
ca.	circa
C.E.	Common Era
cf.	compare
ch	chapter
chs	chapters
DtrH	Deuteronomistic History
Dtr	Deuteronomistic Historian(s)
e.g.	*exempli gratia*, for example
esp.	especially
etc.	*et cetera*, and the rest
f(f).	and the following one(s)
i.e.	*id est*, that is
lit.	literally
LXX	Septuagint
MS	manuscript
MSS	manuscripts
MT	Masoretic Text (of the OT)
n.	note
n.d.	no date
n.p.	no place; no publisher; no page
nn.	notes
NT	New Testament
OT	Old Testament
s.v.	*sub verbo*, under the word
v	verse
vv	verses

Modern English Versions

GNT	Good News Translation
JPS	Jewish Publication Society
KJV	King James Version
NASB	New American Standard Bible
NIV	New International Version
NRSV	New Revised Standard Version
RSV	Revised Standard Version
TM	The Message
YLT	Young's Literal Translation

Print Conventions for Translations

Bold font	NIV (bold without quotation marks in the text under study; elsewhere in the regular font, with quotation marks and no further identification)
Bold italic font	Author's translation (without quotation marks)
Behind the Text:	Literary or historical background information average readers might not know from reading the biblical text alone
In the Text:	Comments on the biblical text, words, phrases, grammar, and so forth
From the Text:	The use of the text by later interpreters, contemporary relevance, theological and ethical implications of the text, with particular emphasis on Wesleyan concerns

Old Testament

Gen	Genesis	Dan	Daniel		
Exod	Exodus	Hos	Hosea		
Lev	Leviticus	Joel	Joel		
Num	Numbers	Amos	Amos		
Deut	Deuteronomy	Obad	Obadiah		
Josh	Joshua	Jonah	Jonah		
Judg	Judges	Mic	Micah		
Ruth	Ruth	Nah	Nahum		
1–2 Sam	1–2 Samuel	Hab	Habakkuk		
1–2 Kgs	1–2 Kings	Zeph	Zephaniah		
1–2 Chr	1–2 Chronicles	Hag	Haggai		
Ezra	Ezra	Zech	Zechariah		
Neh	Nehemiah	Mal	Malachi		
Esth	Esther				
Job	Job				
Ps/Pss	Psalm/Psalms				
Prov	Proverbs				
Eccl	Ecclesiastes				
Song	Song of Songs / Song of Solomon				
Isa	Isaiah				
Jer	Jeremiah				
Lam	Lamentations				
Ezek	Ezekiel				

(Note: Chapter and verse numbering in the MT and LXX often differ compared to those in English Bibles. To avoid confusion, all biblical references follow the chapter and verse numbering in English translations, even when the text in the MT and LXX is under discussion.)

New Testament

Matt	Matthew
Mark	Mark
Luke	Luke
John	John
Acts	Acts
Rom	Romans
1–2 Cor	1–2 Corinthians
Gal	Galatians
Eph	Ephesians
Phil	Philippians
Col	Colossians
1–2 Thess	1–2 Thessalonians
1–2 Tim	1–2 Timothy
Titus	Titus
Phlm	Philemon
Heb	Hebrews
Jas	James
1–2 Pet	1–2 Peter
1–2–3 John	1–2–3 John
Jude	Jude
Rev	Revelation

Dead Sea Scrolls

4QSam^a Samuel^a
4QSam^b Samuel^b
4QSam^c Samuel^c

Josephus

Ant. *Jewish Antiquities*

Church Fathers

Hist. eccl. Eusebius, *Ecclesiastical History*

Rabbinic Literature

B. Bat. *Baba Batra*

Greek Transliteration

Greek	Letter	English
α	alpha	a
β	bēta	b
γ	gamma	g
γ	gamma nasal	n (before γ, κ, ξ, χ)
δ	delta	d
ε	epsilon	e
ζ	zēta	z
η	ēta	ē
θ	thēta	th
ι	iōta	i
κ	kappa	k
λ	lambda	l
μ	mu	m
ν	nu	n
ξ	xi	x
ο	omicron	o
π	pi	p
ρ	rhō	r
ρ	initial rhō	rh
σ/ς	sigma	s
τ	tau	t
υ	upsilon	y
υ	upsilon	u (in diphthongs: au, eu, ēu, ou, ui)
φ	phi	ph
χ	chi	ch
ψ	psi	ps
ω	ōmega	ō
ʽ	rough breathing	h (before initial vowels or diphthongs)

Hebrew Consonant Transliteration

Hebrew/Aramaic	Letter	English
א	alef	ʾ
ב	bet	b
ג	gimel	g
ד	dalet	d
ה	he	h
ו	vav	v or w
ז	zayin	z
ח	khet	ḥ
ט	tet	ṭ
י	yod	y
כ/ך	kaf	k
ל	lamed	l
מ/ם	mem	m
נ/ן	nun	n
ס	samek	s
ע	ayin	ʿ
פ/ף	pe	p; f (spirant)
צ/ץ	tsade	ṣ
ק	qof	q
ר	resh	r
שׂ	sin	ś
שׁ	shin	š
ת	tav	t; th (spirant)

BIBLIOGRAPHY

Ackroyd, Peter R. 1971. *The First Book of Samuel*. The Cambridge Bible Commentary. Cambridge: Cambridge University Press.
_____. 1975. "The Verb 'Love'—²*aheb* in the David-Jonathan Narratives: A Footnote." *Vetus Testamentum* 25. Pp. 213-14.
Ahlstrom, G. 1961. "Der Prophet Nathan und Der Templbau." *Vetus Testamentum* 11. Pp. 113-27.
Albright, W. F. 1920-21. "A Colony of Cretan Mercenaries on the Coast of the Negev." *Journal of the Palestinian Oriental Society* 1. Pp. 187-94.
Alter, Robert. 1999. *The David Story: A Translation with Commentary of 1 and 2 Samuel*. New York: W. W. Norton.
Anderson, A. A. 1989. *II Samuel*. Word Biblical Commentary 11. Waco, Tex.: Word.
Arnold, B. T. 2005. "Samuel, Books of." *The Dictionary of the Historical Books*. Edited by Bill T. Arnold and H. G. M. Williamson. Downers Grove, Ill.: InterVarsity Press. Pp. 866-77.
Baldwin, Joyce C. 1988. *1 and 2 Samuel: An Introduction and Commentary*. The Tyndale Old Testament Commentaries. Downers Grove, Ill.: InterVarsity Press.
Biran, A., and J. Naveh. 1993. "An Aramaic Stele Fragment from Dan." *Israel Exploration Journal* 43. Pp. 81-93.
Birch, B. 1971. "The Development of the Tradition on the Anointing of Saul in 1 Sam 9:1-10:16." *Journal of Biblical Literature* 90. Pp. 55-68.
_____. 1998. "The First and Second Books of Samuel." *The New Interpreter's Bible*. Edited by L. Keck, et al. Nashville: Abingdon. Pp. 949-1383.
Branson, Robert. 2009. *Judges*. New Beacon Bible Commentary. Kansas City: Beacon Hill Press of Kansas City.
Bright, John. 1981. *A History of Israel*. Philadelphia: Westminster.
Brueggemann, W. 1988. "2 Samuel 21-24: An Appendix of Deconstruction." *Catholic Biblical Quarterly* 50. Pp. 387-97.
_____. 1990. *First and Second Samuel*. Intrepretation. Louisville, Ky.: John Knox Press.
Budde, K. D. 1902. *Die Bucher Samuel*. Tübingen: J. C. B. Mohr.
Caird, G. B. 1953. "The First and Second Books of Samuel." *The Interpreter's Bible*. Edited by G. A. Buttrick. Nashville: Abingdon. Pp. 854-1176.
Campbell, A., and M. O'Brien. 2000. *Unfolding the Deuteronomistic History: Origins, Upgrades, Present Text*. Minneapolis: Fortress.
Campbell, Antony F. 1986. *Of Prophets and Kings: A Late Ninth-Century Document*. Washington, D.C.: Catholic Biblical Association.
_____. 2003. *1 Samuel*. The Forms of Old Testament Literature 7. Edited by Rolf P. Knierim, Gene M. Tucker, and Marvin A. Sweeney. Grand Rapids: Eerdmans.
_____. 2005. *2 Samuel*. The Forms of Old Testament Literature 8. Edited by Rolf P. Knierim, Gene M. Tucker, and Marvin A. Sweeney. Grand Rapids: Eerdmans.
Caquot, A., and P. de Robert. 1994. *Le Livres de Samuel*. Geneva: Labor Et Fides.
Carlson, R. A. 1964. *David, the Chosen King: A Traditio-Historical Approach to the Second Book of Samuel*. Translated by E. J. Sharpe and S. Rudman. Stockholm: Almqvist & Wiksell.
Chankin-Gould, J. D'ror. 2008. "The Sanctified Adulteress: Bath-sheba's Bath and Self-Consecration in 2 Samuel 11." *Journal for the Study of the Old Testament* 32. Pp. 339-52.
Childs, Brevard. 1979. *Introduction to the Old Testament as Scripture*. Philadelphia: Fortress.
Cook, E. M. 1988. "Weights and Measures." *The International Standard Biblical Encyclopedia*. Vol. 4. Edited by G. W. Bromiley. Grand Rapids: Eerdmans. Pp. 1053-54.
Cross, F. M. 1973. "The Themes of the Book of Kings and the Structure of the Deuteronomistic History." *Canaanite Myth and Hebrew Epic*. Cambridge: Harvard University Press. Pp. 274-89.
Dietrich, W. 1972. *Prophetie und Geschichte: Ein Redactionsgeschichtliche Untersuchung zum Deuteronmistichen Geshcichtwerk*. Gottingen: Vandenhoeck & Ruprecht.
_____. 1977. "David in Uberlieferung und Geschichte." *Verkundigung und Forshcung* 22. Pp. 44-64.
Driver, S. R. 1966. *Notes on the Hebrew Text and the Topography of the Books of Samuel*. Oxford: Clarendon Press.

Ehrman, Bart D. 2008. *The New Testament: A Historical Introduction to the Early Christian Writings.* 4th ed. New York: Oxford University Press.

Eslinger, L. 1985. *Kingship of God in Crisis: A Close Reading of 1 Samuel 1—2.* Bible and Literature Series. Sheffield: Almond.

Evans, Mary J. 2003. *1 and 2 Samuel.* New International Biblical Commentary. Edited by Robert L. Hubbard and Robert K. Johnston. Peabody, Mass.: Hendrickson.

Fensham, F. Charles. 1964. "The Treaty between Israel and the Gibeonites." *The Biblical Archaeologist* 37. Pp. 96-100.

Finlay, T. D. 2005. *The Birth Report Genre in the Hebrew Bible.* Tübingen: Mohr (Siebeck).

Flanagan, James W. 1992. "Samuel, Book of 1-2." *The Anchor Bible Dictionary.* Vol. 5. Edited by D. N. Freedman. New York: Doubleday. Pp. 957-65.

Fokkelman, J. P. 1986. *Narrative Art and Poetry in the Books of Samuel.* Vol. 2, *The Crossing Fates (I Sam. 13-31 and II Sam. 1).* Studia Semitica Neerlandica 23. Assen: Van Gorcum.

———. 1993. *Narrative Art and Poetry in the Books of Samuel.* Vol. 4, *Vow and Desire (1 Sam. 1-12).* Studia Semitica Neerlandica 31. Assen: Van Gorcum.

Frank, John R., and Thomas C. Oden. 2005. *Joshua, Judges, Ruth, 1—2 Samuel.* Ancient Christian Commentary on Scripture. Downers Grove, Ill.: InterVarsity Press.

Friedman, Richard E. 1981. "From Egypt to Egypt: dtr (1) and dtr (2)." *Traditions in Transformation: Turning Points in Israel's Faith.* Edited by Baruch Halpern and Jon D. Levenson. Winona Lake, Ind.: Eisenbrauns. Pp. 167-92.

Fritz, V. 1993. "Where Is David's Ziklag?" *Biblical Archaeological Review* 19. Pp. 58-61, 76.

Frolov, Serge. 2002. "1 Samuel 1-7 in Synchronic and Diachronic Perspectives." PhD diss., Claremont Graduate University.

Gnuse, R. 1978. "A Reconsideration of the Form-Critical Structure in 1 Samuel 3: An Ancient Near Eastern Dream Theophany." *Abstracts.* SBL Annual Meeting. Missoula, Mont.: Scholars Press.

Gordon, Robert P. 1986. *I and II Samuel: A Commentary.* Grand Rapids: Zondervan.

Halpern, Baruch. 1992. "Shiloh." *The Anchor Bible Dictionary.* Vol. 5. Edited by D. N. Freedman. New York: Doubleday. Pp. 1213-15.

———. 2001. *David's Secret Demons: Messiah, Murderer, Traitor, King.* Grand Rapids: Eerdmans.

Hamilton, Victor P. 2004. *Handbook on the Historical Books.* Grand Rapids: Baker.

Harrison, R. K. 1969. *Introduction to the Old Testament.* Grand Rapids: Eerdmans.

Hartley, J. E. "New Moon." 1988. *The International Standard Biblical Encyclopedia.* Vol. 3. Edited by G. W. Bromiley. Grand Rapids: Eerdmans. Pp. 527-28.

Hertzberg, H. W. 1964. *I and II Samuel: A Commentary.* Translated by J. S. Bowden. Old Testament Library. Philadelphia: Westminster.

Higginbotham, Carolyn R. 2005. "Amarna Letters." *The New Interpreter's Dictionary of the Bible.* Vol. 1. Edited by K. Sakenfeld. Nashville: Abingdon. Pp. 123-24.

Hoffman, H. D. 1980. *Reform und Reformen: Untersuchungen zu einem Grundthema der deuteronomistichen Geschichtsschrieibung.* Zurich: Theologischer Verlag.

Hoffner, Harry A. 1973. "The Hittites and Hurrians." *Peoples of Old Testament Times.* Edited by D. J. Wiseman. Oxford: Clarendon Press. Pp. 197-228.

———. 1975. "Propaganda and Political Justification in Hittite Historiography." *Unity and Diversity Essays in the History, Literature, and Religion of the Ancient Near East.* Edited by Hans Goedicke and J. J. M. Roberts. Baltimore: Johns Hopkins University Press. Pp. 49-62.

Isbell, C. D. 1977. "A Note on Amos 1:1." *Journal of Near Eastern Studies* 36. Pp. 213-14.

Kapelrud, A. H. 1955. "King and Fertility. A Discussion of II Sam 21:1-14." *Norsk Teologisk Tidsskrift* 56. Pp. 113-22.

———. 1959. "King David and the Sons of Saul." *The Sacral Kingship.* Leiden: Brill. Pp. 294-301.

Keil, C. F., and F. Delitzsch. 1967. *Samuel.* Commentary on the Old Testament in Ten Volumes. Grand Rapids: Eerdmans.

Klein, Ralph W. 1979. "Samuel, Books of." *The International Standard Biblical Encyclopedia.* Edited by G. W. Bromiley. Vol. 4. Grand Rapids: Eerdmans. Pp. 312-20.

———. 1983. *1 Samuel.* Word Biblical Commentary 10. Waco, Tex.: Word.

Koch, K. 1969. *The Growth of the Biblical Tradition: The Form Critical Method.* New York: Scribner's Sons.

Lemaire, A. 1986. "Vers l'histoire de la redaction des livres des Rois." *Zeitschrift für die Alttestamentliche Wissenschaft* 98. Pp. 221-36.

Levenson, J. D., and B. Halpern. 1980. "The Political Import of David's Marriages." *Journal of Biblical Literature* 99. Pp. 507-18.

Lewis, Theodore J. 1992. "Dead, Abode of the." *The Anchor Bible Dictionary*. Vol. 2. Edited by David N. Freedman. 6 vols. New York: Doubleday. Pp. 101-5.

Mauchline, John. 1971. *1 and 2 Samuel*. New Century Bible. Edited by Ronald E. Clements. Greenwood, S.C.: Attic Press.

Mazar, A. 1992. *Archaeology of the Land of the Bible: 10,000-586 B.C.E.* New York: Doubleday.

McCarter, P. K. 1980a. "The Apology of David." *Journal of Biblical Literature* 99. Pp. 489-506.

———. 1980b. *I Samuel: A New Translation with Introduction, Notes, Commentary*. Anchor Bible 8. Garden City, N.Y.: Doubleday.

———. 1984. *II Samuel: A New Translation with Introduction, Notes, Commentary*. Anchor Bible 9. Garden City, N.Y.: Doubleday.

———. 1988. "Teraphim." *The International Standard Biblical Encyclopedia*. Vol. 4. Edited by G. W. Bromiley. Grand Rapids: Eerdmans. P. 793.

McKane, William. 1963. *I and II Samuel: Introduction and Commentary*. Torch Bible Commentaries. London: S.C.M. Press.

Mellish, Kevin. 2006. "David and Solomon in a Foreign Context: Foreign Influence on the United Monarchy." PhD diss., Claremont Graduate University.

———. 2009. "Creation as Social and Political Order in Ancient Thought and the Hebrew Bible." *Wesleyan Theological Journal* 44:1. Pp. 157-79.

Mendenhall, G. E. 1973. *The Tenth Generation: The Origins of the Biblical Tradition*. Baltimore: Johns Hopkins University Press.

———. 1975. "The Monarchy." *Interpretation* 29. Pp. 155-70.

Mettinger, T. N. 1971. D. *Solomonic State Officials: A Study of the Civil Government Officials of the Israelite Monarchy*. Lund: Gleerup.

Miller, J. M. Maxwell. 1975. "Geba/Gibeah of Benjamin." *Vetus Testamentum* 25. Pp. 145-66.

Miller, Patrick D., and J. J. M. Roberts. 1977. *The Hand of the Lord: A Reassessment of the "Ark Narrative" of 1 Samuel*. Baltimore: Johns Hopkins University Press.

Montgomery, J. A. 1951. *A Critical and Exegetical Commentary on the Books of Kings*. International Critical Commentary. Edinburgh: Clark.

Nelson, R. 1981. *The Double Redaction of the Book of Kings*. Sheffield: JSOT Press.

Niditch, S. 1993. *War in the Hebrew Bible*. Oxford: Oxford University Press.

Noth, M. 1991. *The Deuteronomistic History*. 2nd ed. Sheffield: JSOT Press. Translation of *Uberlieferungsgeschichtliche Studien. Die sammelnden und bearbeitenden Geshichtswerk im alten Testament*. Tubingen: Max Niemeyer, 1943.

O'Brien, Mark. 1989. *The Deuteronomistic Hypothesis: A Reassessment*. Gottingen: Vandenhoeck & Ruprecht.

Payne, David F. 1982. *I & II Samuel*. The Daily Bible Studies Series. Edited by John C. L. Gibson. Philadelphia: Westminster Press.

Person, Raymond F. 2002. *The Deuteronomic School: History, Social Setting, and Literature*. Atlanta: Society of Biblical Literature.

Pfeiffer, R. H. 1941. *Introduction to the Old Testament*. New York: Harper & Brothers.

Polzin, Robert. 1989. *Samuel and the Deuteronomist: A Literary Study of the Deuteronomistic History*. San Francisco: Harper and Row.

Provin, I. W. 1988. *Hezekiah and the Book of Kings*. New York: W. de Gruyter.

Rost, L. 1982. *The Succession to the Throne of David*. Translated by M. D. Rutter and D. M. Gunn. Sheffield: Almond Press. Translation of *Uberlieferung von der Thronnachfolge Davids*. BWANT III, 6. Stuttgart: W. Kohlhammer, 1926.

Rowley, H. H. 1939. "Zadok and Nehushtan." *Journal of Biblical Literature* 58. Pp. 113-41.

Rupprecht, K. 1977. *Der Tempel Von Jerusalem: Grundung Salomos Oder Jebusitisches Erbe?* Berlin: Walter de Gruyter.

Schmid, H. H. 1970. "Der Templbau Salomos in Religiousgeschichtlicher Sicht." *Archaologie und Alten Testament, est. Für K Galling*. Edited by A. Kuschke and E. Kutsch. Tübingen: Mohr. Pp. 241-50.

Schneider, Tammi J. 2004. *Sarah: Mother of Nations*. New York: Continuum.

Schniedewind, W. 1999. *Society and the Promise to David*. New York: Oxford University Press.

Schwally, F. 1892. "Zur Quellenkritik der historischen Bucher." *Zeitschrift für die Alttestamentliche Wissenschaft* 12. Pp. 155-56.

Seow, C. L. 1989. *Myth, Drama and the Politics of David's Dance*. Harvard Semitic Monograph 44. Atlanta: Scholars Press.

Shanks, H. 1999. "Rewriting Jerusalem's History: I Climbed Warren's Shaft (But Joab Never Did)." *Biblical Archaeological Review* 25. Pp. 30-35.
Smend, R. 1971. "Die Gezetz und Völker: Ein Beitrage zur Deuteronomischen Redaktiongeschichte." *Probleme Biblischer Theologie*. Edited by H. W. Wolff. Munich: Chr. Kaiser. Pp. 494-509.
Smith, H. P. 1929. *A Critical and Exegetical Commentary on the Books of Samuel*. International Critical Commentary on the Holy Scriptures. New York: Charles Scribner's Sons.
Stolz, F. 1981. *Das erst und zweite Buch Samuel*. Zurich: Theologischer Verlag.
Sweeney, Marvin A. 2007. *First and Second Kings*. Old Testament Library. Louisville, Ky.: Westminster John Knox Press.
Szikszai, S. 1962. "Samuel, I and II." *The Interpreter's Dictionary of the Bible*. Vol. 4. Edited by G. A. Buttrick. 4 vols. Nashville: Abingdon. Pp. 202-9.
Tov, Emanuel. 1985. "The Composition of 1 Samuel 16-18 in Light of the Septuagint Version." *Empirical Models for Biblical Criticism*. Edited by Jeffrey H. Tigay. Philadelphia: University of Pennsylvania Press. Pp. 97-130.
Tsumura, David Toshio. 2007. *The First Book of Samuel*. New International Commentary on the Old Testament. Grand Rapids: Eerdmans.
Tucker, G. 1966. "The Legal Background of Genesis 23." *Journal of Biblical Literature* 85. Pp. 77-84.
Ulrich, Eugene C. 1999. *The Dead Sea Scrolls and the Origins of the Bible*. Grand Rapids: Eerdmans.
Van der Toorn, K., and C. Houtman. 1994. "David and the Ark." *Journal of Biblical Literature* 113. Pp. 209-31.
Van Seters, J. 1983. *In Search of History: Historiography in the Ancient World and the Origins of Biblical History*. New Haven, Conn.: Yale University Press.
Veijola, T. 1975. *Die ewige Dynastie: David und die Entstehung of Seiner Dynasties nach der deuteronomistichen Darstellung*. AASF B. 193. Helsinki: Soumalainen Tiedeakatemia.
Von Rad, G. 1953. *Studies in Deuteronomy*. London: SCM.
———. 1962. *Old Testament Theology*, Vol. 1: *The Theology of Israel's Historical Traditions*. Translated by D. M. Stalker. San Francisco: Harper.
Walton, John H. 2000. *The IVP Background Commentary: The Old Testament*. Downers Grove, Ill.: InterVarsity Press.
Weinfeld, M. 1972. *Deuteronomy and the Deuteronomistic School*. Oxford: Clarendon.
Weippert, H. 1972. "Die deuteronomistischen Beurteilungen der Konige von Israel und Juda und das Problem der Redaktion der Konigsbucher." *Biblica* 53. Pp. 301-39.
Weiser, A. 1966. "Die Legitimation des King Davids." *Vetus Testamentum* 16. Pp. 325-54.
Willis, J. T. 1971. "An Anti-Elide Narrative Tradition from a Prophetic Circle at the Ramah Sanctuary." *Journal of Biblical Literature* 90. Pp. 288-308.
Wolff, H. W. 1975. "The Kerygma of the Deuteronomistic Historical Work." *The Vitality of the Old Testament Traditions*. Edited by W. Brueggeman and H. W. Wolff. Atlanta: John Knox. Pp. 83-100.
Wurthwein, E. 1974. *Die Erzahlung von der Thronfolge Davids—Theologische oder politische Geschichtsschreibung?* Zurich: Theologischer Verlag.
Yarchin, W. 2000. "Text Criticism, Text Composition, and Text Concept in 2 Sam 23-24." *Reading the Hebrew Bible for a New Millennium: Form, Concept, and Theological Perspective*. Edited by W. Kim. Harrisburg, Pa.: Trinity Press International. Pp. 326-57.
Youngblood, Ronald F. 1992. "1, 2 Samuel." *The Expositor's Bible Commentary*. Edited by Frank E. Gaebelein. Grand Rapids: Zondervan. Pp. 553-1104.

INTRODUCTION

A. Canonical Arrangement

In the Hebrew or Jewish Bible, the books of 1 and 2 Samuel belong to the section known as the Former Prophets and in the Christian OT they are a part of the collection known as the Historical Books. The books of Samuel also constitute an important part of the larger literary work that extends from Joshua through Kings, which modern scholars refer to as the Deuteronomistic History (DtrH). Based upon their relationship to the other books located within the OT/Hebrew canon, the books of Samuel provide a vital literary and historical link in the Bible's overall presentation of Israel's past. On the one hand, the events in Samuel are predicated upon Israel's exodus from Egypt and the establishment of the Mosaic covenant at Mount Sinai (Exodus and Deuteronomy), the conquest and settlement of the land of Canaan/Palestine (Joshua), and the era of the judges (Judges). On the other hand, the books of Samuel represent a formal end or break with the period of the judges (1 Samuel), and they report on the emergence of the prophet/priest Samuel as well as the inception of the Israelite monarchy under King Saul. Moreover, the books of Samuel look beyond Saul's monarchy to the establishment of David's throne and his dynasty (1 Sam 16—2 Sam 7), the expansion of the kingdom of Israel under David's leadership (2 Sam 8), and, ultimately, anticipate the struggle for the throne among David's sons following the king's death (1 Kgs 1—2). Thus, if one takes into consideration the broader canonical structure of the OT/Hebrew Bible, the books of Samuel are intimately connected with the early history of the people of Israel and the formation of the Israelite kingdom, yet they serve as a fitting preface to the account of Solomon's reign (1 Kgs 1—11), the history of the divided kingdom following Solomon's death (1 Kgs 12—2 Kgs 16), and the destruction and exile of the kingdoms of Israel in 721 B.C. and Judah in 586 B.C. (2 Kgs 17—25).

B. Textual History

In ancient times the books of Samuel were originally one book. The earliest Hebrew manuscripts indicate that 1 and 2 Samuel were not divided into separate parts. The Samuel scroll from Qumran (4QSam^a), for example, includes both books under the title Samuel, the Talmud regularly makes reference to the "Book of Samuel," and the Masoretic notes at the end of 2 Samuel report that Samuel contains a total of 1,506 verses with 1 Sam 28:24 marking the middle verse of the entire book. Early church fathers such as Jerome and the church historian Eusebius were also aware of the book of Samuel in this original form (*Hist. eccl.* 7.25.2).

The decision to divide the book of Samuel into two sections extends back to classical antiquity when books were written on scrolls of fixed length. The book of Samuel, which is slightly longer than Kings and Chronicles, became too unwieldy to handle on one scroll and thus it was divided (along with Kings and Chronicles) into two major parts in the early manuscripts of the Septuagint (LXX) or Greek Bible. The Septuagint translators titled the books of Samuel *Basileion* A and B (1 and 2 Kingdoms or 1 and 2 Reigns). These translators subsequently grouped the books of Samuel, based upon common themes and concerns, with the two books of Kings (*Basileion* C and D) and referred to them as *Bibloi Basileion* (Books of Kingdoms). The church father Jerome later modified this title slightly to *Libri Regum* (Books of Kings) so that Samuel and Kings became known as 1, 2, 3, and 4 Kings respectively. Today, Catholic scholars and commentators still refer to the books of Samuel according to their Greek titles (1 and 2 Kings), but Jewish and Protestant communities refer to the books by their ancient Hebrew name.

According to modern biblical scholars the rational for dividing the books of Samuel at their present juncture conformed to the ancient custom of concluding a biblical book with the death of a major figure (i.e., Jacob and Joseph at the end of Genesis; Moses in the closing scene of Deuteronomy; Joshua at the conclusion of his farewell speech; and Saul at the end of 1 Samuel) (McCarter 1980b, 3). Other authoritative translations such as the Vulgate, the ancient Latin translation of the Hebrew text, continued the tradition of the Greek translators by including both books of Samuel in its canon and the practice of making reference to two books of Samuel, a practice that has carried forward into modern times. The first reference to the books of 1 and 2 Samuel in an actual Hebrew text is attested in a handwritten manuscript in 1448, and the practice of listing the books of Samuel independently became more official in the Rabbinic Bible of 1516-17 edited by Felix Pratensis (Klein 1979, 313; Szikszai 1962, 203). That the division between 1 and 2 Samuel received a type of formal sanction in the Jewish community is further evidenced by the fact that the second Rabbinic Bible of 1524-25 listed them separately as well (Flanagan 1992, 957).

C. History of Composition

1. Traditional View of Authorship

The books of Samuel take their name from the great prophet who serves as the leading figure in the beginning section of 1 Samuel (chs 3—8, 12, 15—16). With regard to the title, ancient Jewish commentators first claimed that Samuel had actually written Judges and a large portion of Samuel. The Babylonian Talmud specifically states that "Samuel wrote the book that bears his name" (*B. Bat.* 14b). However, the same Talmud makes the explicit qualification that Samuel was responsible for only the first twenty-four chapters (since 1 Sam 25:1 reports his death) and the rest of the Samuel corpus was ascribed to the prophets Nathan and Gad (*B. Bat.* 15a). The writers of the Talmud maintained this position because much of 1 and 2 Samuel is narrated from a decidedly prophetic point of view. Moreover, the Jewish scribes took seriously the reference in 1 Chr 29:29 that states: "As for the events of King David's reign, from beginning to end, they are written in the records of Samuel the seer, the records of Nathan the prophet and the records of Gad the seer." Throughout history, other candidates for authorship have been put forth, such as the priests Ahimaaz (2 Sam 15:27, 36; 17:17, 20; 18:19, 22-23, 27-29) and Zabud (1 Kgs 4:5). In spite of these efforts to try and account for the authorship of Samuel along traditional lines, a lack of firm evidence to support these claims has failed to convince modern scholars.

2. Modern Theories Regarding Authorship

Old Testament scholars today do not adhere to the traditional view that the books of Samuel were composed by prophets such as Samuel, Gad, and Nathan nor are they convinced that the priests Ahimaaz or Zabud had a hand in writing them. Rather, modern exegetes would posit that the final composition of the books of Samuel should be attributed to anonymous authors or editors who compiled a series of independent traditions (first transmitted in oral form and then written down) about Samuel, the ark, Saul and David, for instance, into a holistic text (Arnold 2005, 870). Based upon the merits of contemporary scholarship and the critical questions it has raised about the text, modern scholars posit that the books of Samuel are best seen as the byproduct of a long history of editorial or redactional activity. Through the employment of various critical disciplines (such as literary analysis, historical and archaeological investigation, and textual, form, redaction criticism, etc.) scholars have uncovered evidence that would lend great support to this notion.

First, a critical observation or evaluation of the text of Samuel clearly shows that these books are "not among the most aptly named in the Old Testament" (Gordon 1986, 19). Although Samuel takes precedence as the leading religious and political figure in several of the opening chapters of 1 Samuel (1—3, 7—12, 13, 15—16), his appearance is extremely limited in narrative contexts following the tradition regarding David's anointing (16:6-16). A brief reference to Samuel turns up in a notice about his death in 25:1, and he also speaks briefly in a posthumous appearance to King Saul at the end of 1 Samuel (28:12-19). Taken as a whole, then, the total number of narrative sections covering the figure Samuel are relatively small when compared to the amount of material devoted to the ark traditions (chs 4—6) and Saul's monarchy (chs 9—31), for instance. Moreover, Samuel is completely overshadowed by the figure of David who receives no less than forty chapters of literary coverage in both books (1 Sam 16—2 Sam 24). The fact that these books are named after Samuel, even though he is not the dominant character in them, simply confirms the ancient custom of Jewish interpreters who titled biblical books after prominent figures from Israel's history.

Second, noticeable parallel accounts, incongruities, and tensions within the text provide solid evidence that the books of Samuel are the result of the compilation of independent traditions over an extended period of time (Harrison 1969, 696). The English scholar R. H. Pfeiffer, for example, listed several examples of textual discrepancies in his introductory text (1941, 340): the announcement concerning the end of Eli and his house on two occasions (1 Sam 2:13 ff.; 3:11 ff.); the secret anointing of Saul (9:26—10:1), followed later by two public ceremonies in which Saul is selected (10:21; 11:15); two occasions in which Samuel rejected Saul as king (13:14; 15:23); two introductions of David to Saul (16:21; 17:58); two escapes of David from the court of Saul (19:12; 20:42); two occasions when David spared Saul's life (24:3; 26:5); three different covenants between David and Jonathan (18:3; 20:16, 42; 23:18); two flights by David to Gath (21:10; 27:1), and the perplexing tradition regarding the killing of Goliath by David and later by a warrior named Elhanan (1 Sam 17:51; 2 Sam 21:19).

In addition to the aforementioned examples, sharp differences in the religious outlook of several portions of Samuel can be detected (Szikszai 1962, 204). Within 1 Sam 7—12, for example, there are conflicting or shifting views regarding the development of the monarchy in Israel's society. On the one hand, there are places in the text when the monarchy is condemned by God as an apostasy (8:17-18) but other occasions where monarchy is acceptable (12:13-14) and even commendable (9:16-17). The same assertions can be made with regard to the Saul and David traditions. There are occasions when Saul is portrayed in a positive light and God is supportive of him (9:1—10:16; 11:1-13; 14:47-48) while at other times he is depicted as an abysmal failure whom God regrets making king (15:11). David, likewise, is presented as God's choice as king (16:6-13), a person of great faith (ch 17) and merciful (chs 24; 26), which contrasts markedly from the portrayal of him as a brutal and calculating murderer God has to chastise (2 Sam 11—12) or as a weak father and commander (chs 14—19).

Third, textual analysis has convincingly demonstrated that the received MT of Samuel, on which our modern English translations are based, is in rather "poor repair" and has suffered more in scribal transmission than any other OT book (McCarter 1980b, 5). The MT of 1 and 2 Samuel is plagued extensively from haplography; that is, from scribal omission of words and phrases brought on by repeated sequences of letters (most often at the ends of words) and from various other copying errors. Moreover, the Hebrew text of these books is shorter than the ancient Greek translation of the Hebrew Bible and other ancient versions such as the Latin Vulgate, the Aramaic Targums, and the Peshitta (Birch 1998, 950). Until recent times, scholars assumed that the Greek translators had simply added traditions to their manuscripts and thus expanded the overall text. This is a view that has been modified based on careful textual analysis.

In order to make sense of the corruptions and shortcomings of the Hebrew text and in an effort to reconstruct the most reliable edition of the Hebrew text, scholars have been forced to systematically compare and contrast the Hebrew text of Samuel with the source material of Chronicles and other ancient translations such as the Septuagint (LXX). Close readings and careful evaluation of the various ancient textual witnesses to the books of Samuel by textual critics such as Thenius, Wellhausen, and Driver from the nineteenth century revealed that the differences between the Greek text of Samuel and the Hebrew text are due to more than simple editorial traditions and minor interpolations. Text critics explained that the reason why the Greek and Hebrew texts of Samuel diverge to such an extent was due to the fact that that the Septuagint translators based their work on a Hebrew text (a vorlage) that preceded the MT and is no longer available to us.

Research on the Hebrew text of Samuel has also been greatly enhanced within the last sixty years due to the discovery of the Dead Sea Scrolls (DSS). Within the ancient library of the Qumran sect three Samuel manuscripts were discovered (Ulrich 1999). The most important of these, 4QSam^a, dates to 50-25 B.C. and contains large portions of 1 and 2 Samuel in a well-preserved condition. The second, 4QSam^b, which dates from the mid-third century B.C., contains a badly preserved portion of 1 Samuel. The third, 4QSam^c, is from the early first century B.C. and contains fragments of 1 Sam 25 and 2 Sam 14—15. Comparisons of the Hebrew text with the Qumran literature seem to confirm the proximity of an early Hebrew tradition to the vorlage of the LXX. Textual critics have determined more specifically that the Qumran texts read more closely with the Lucianic manuscripts (LXX^L) than to Codex Vaticanus (LXX^B) (Klein 1979, 314). This would suggest that that the Lucianic tradition represents a move toward a Palestinian Hebrew text tradition that is represented by the Qumran literature (Flanagan 1992, 958).

3. The Deuteronomistic History

In addition to the work of textual critics, knowledge about the development of the books of Samuel was greatly enhanced by the publication of Martin Noth's monograph on the Deuteronomistic History (Noth 1991). Prior to Noth's publication, scholars at the end of the nineteenth century and into the early twentieth century attempted to explain the composition of the books extending from Joshua to Kings in light of pentateuchal source criticism. This method of investigation proved to be unsuccessful, as source critical scholars could not agree as to what pentateuchal sources actually continued into the historical books nor could they agree as to where the sources stopped and historical or archival material began. Noth's work addressed this issue by arguing that the books of Joshua through Kings were not the product of the sources that comprised the Pentateuch but they came about through a different transmission process (see also Branson 2009, 26-30, for summary).

Noth basically contended that the books of Joshua through Kings were the product of a single author/redactor whom he labeled "Dtr." Noth argued that this author/editor was both a compiler/arranger of older source materials *and* a creative author. Noth claimed that Dtr had composed important speeches at critical junctures in Israel's story (Josh 1, 23; 1 Sam 12; 1 Kgs 8:14 ff.) and provided summarizing reflections (Josh 12; Judg 2:11 ff.; 2 Kgs 17:7 ff.) that helped bring a sense of cohesion to disparate source materials. Thus, according to Noth, Dtr's theological/ideological agenda could be ascertained not only in the manner in which he organized the documents he had available at his disposal but also in the speeches and summary statements that he composed.

Noth also posited that Dtr provided a theological and ideological evaluation of Israel's past. Dtr recounted Israel's history and evaluated the people of Israel and Israel's leaders in light of the laws expressed in Deuteronomy. Thus the term "Deuteronomistic" History was coined. Noth maintained that the DtrH primarily explained why the exiles of 721 B.C. and 586 B.C. occurred. According to Dtr, the people of Israel went into exile because they consistently and repeatedly disobeyed God's instruction as set forth in the laws of Deuteronomy. Thus, the DtrH demonstrated that the exile was a just punishment executed by God for Israel's sin. Noth also contended that because the laws of Deuteronomy provided the theological lens by which Dtr judged Israel's past, it functioned as a preface to Joshua through Kings and should not be included as part of the Pentateuch.

Since the publication of Noth's work, there have been many reactions and objections to his initial thesis regarding the compositional history of the historical books. In North America, Frank M. Cross of Harvard posited that the DtrH was composed of two major sources and not the work of just one author/editor. The first edition of the DtrH, which he called Dtr 1, was a preexilic document that pointed to and supported the reforms of King Josiah (2 Kgs

22—23). The second edition, labeled Dtr 2, was an exilic work that updated the last section of Kings (2 Kgs 24—25) and turned Dtr 1 into a sermon for the exilic community and promised the hope of restoration (1973, 274-89). A number of scholars, primarily from North America, have found Cross's two redactional theory view persuasive and have articulated it in various forms (Nelson 1981; Friedman 1981, 167-92).

European scholars have provided a counterpart to Cross's main thesis regarding the composition of the DtrH. Researchers from the Gottingen School, in particular, have proposed a model that suggests the DtrH is a thoroughly exilic work. Unlike Noth, however, who argued that the DtrH was the product of one individual, members of the Gottingen School proposed that the DtrH was comprised of three specific layers of exilic redaction (Dietrich 1972; Smend 1971, 494-509; Veijola 1975). The first layer served as the basic story line or historical record (the Grundschrift) of Israel's past, which they labeled DtrG (580 B.C.). After DtrG another layer of redaction was included that underscored the role of the prophets in the DtrH (i.e., 1 Kgs 14:7-11; 16:1-4; 21:20*b*-24; 22:38; 2 Kgs 9:6-10, 36; 10:17; 21:10-16; 24:2), which was labeled DtrP and attributed to prophetic circles (561 B.C.). A final redactional layer was included by an editor who showed concern for the Law or Torah of Moses and stressed obedience to it (i.e., 1 Kgs 3:4-15; 9:1-9). They labeled this editor DtrN (560 B.C.) or the nomistic editor (nomistic = law).

Over the last several decades scholars have proposed other theoretical models to account for the development of the DtrH that have both incorporated elements of the above theories and moved in other directions. The following provides a basic list summarizing the methodological trends within DtrH research over the last sixty years:

    a. The DtrH was constantly being revised throughout Israel's history so that it is comprised of various preexilic editions (pre-Hezekian, Hezekian, Josianic) that included exilic updates (Friedman 1981; Lemaire 1986, 221-36; Provin 1988; Weippert 1972, 301-39; Sweeney 2007, 1-32).

    b. The DtrH was the product of a "prophetic" record that extended from 1 Sam 1—2 Kgs 10, included a Josianic edition as well as exilic updates (Campbell 1986; O'Brien 1989).

    c. The DtrH is the product of a creative writer who lived during the exilic period (Hoffman 1980; Van Seters 1983).

    d. The DtrH was composed by writers/editors of a Deuteronomistic school. This school was based in the wisdom tradition of the ancient Near East (Weinfeld 1972) or was part of a reform movement that existed in the exilic and postexilic period (Person 2002).

As the reader can see, modern theories of the composition of the DtrH are complex and take many forms. It is not likely that a consensus will be found in the near future. The most recent trend in biblical scholarship includes studying the historical books within the overall structure of Genesis through Kings. Scholars now refer to Genesis through Kings as the Enneateuch, because they believe that historical books share a genetic relationship with the first five books of the OT.

Scholars have also disagreed with Noth over the purpose the DtrH served in the life of the Israelite community. Noth contended that the DtrH primarily explained the reason why the exile occurred and did not provide a word about the future or what the Israelites should do once the exile occurred. Thus, in his judgment, the DtrH remained closed and rather pessimistic. Other scholars, however, contended that the DtrH provided a measure of hope for the exilic community and beyond. Gerhard Von Rad, for example, took notice of God's promise to David to establish an eternal dynasty and traced how God had preserved the dynasty through Israel's history. The notice at the end of 2 Kings regarding the release of Jehoiachin from prison stood as proof positive that God had kept his word, even in the exile. Thus, for Von Rad, a note of grace permeated the pages of the history and Israel's history remained open-ended (1953, 74-96). In addition to Von Rad, H. W. Wolff studied the DtrH and noticed that a rebellion-punishment-repentance-restoration schema could be detected in it. Wolff argued that the DtrH pointed out that when Israel "returned" to God in repentance God would extend forgiveness and healing to the community. Wolff believed, then, that the DtrH was actually a kerygma or message to the people who lived in exile in that it presented a model of what they were supposed to do when they faced punishment. The exiles needed to understand that they were in the second stage of the cycle and thus "return" to God in repentance (Wolff 1975, 83-100).

4. The Books of Samuel

Old Testament scholars have devised a number of theories and ideas over the past several decades to address the difficult issues that are raised in the text as well as explain the origins and composition of the books of 1 and 2 Samuel. The books of Samuel present their own unique challenges as it relates to their compositional history. The books of Samuel show little of the Deuteronomistic language and editing techniques that the books of Kings demonstrate, for instance. This fact has caused scholars to argue that the books of Samuel are the compilation of "blocks" of materials/traditions that were assembled together over a period of time. Noth, for example, did allow for some Deuteronomistic editing, which he argued could be detected in the following passages (Baldwin 1988, 25):

1. 1 Sam 7:2*b*, the chronological note, "a long time passed, some twenty years" (NRSV).
2. 1 Sam 7:7-14, Noth connected with Judg 13:1.
3. 1 Sam 13:1, the chronological note regarding Saul's reign.
4. 2 Sam 2:10-11, the chronological reigns of Ish-Bosheth and David.

5. 1 Sam 8 and 12, Dtr's disapproval of the establishment of the monarchy.
6. 2 Sam 5:4-5, the chronology of David's reign, and 5:6-12, David's conquest of Jerusalem.
7. 2 Sam 7:7a, 22-24, editorial notes regarding the prohibition of the temple and the promise concerning the institution of the Davidic monarchy.

Noth, overall, considered these editorial insertions and compositions to be relatively minor considering the overall length of the books of Samuel. The bulk of the source material within Samuel derived from older, written traditions that Dtr had at his disposal. Within the books of Samuel, several independent units of tradition have been identified by Noth and others:

a. The Story of Samuel

The materials related to the life of Samuel are concentrated within chs 1—3, 7—8, 12, 15 in particular. In these texts, Samuel is presented as the faithful priest/prophet/judge who replaces Eli and his corrupted household at the sanctuary at Shiloh. Samuel was the product of a Nazirite vow who led the community of faith in the proper worship of Yahweh and whom the people came to recognize as a "trustworthy" prophet. Samuel was also instrumental during this period of transition in Israel's society in that he became the individual responsible for anointing Saul, first, and then David as kings of Israel. His role was essential in solidifying the people's request for a king (1 Kgs 8; 12). Even though Samuel played a critical role within the transition from the period of the judges to the monarchy, his importance to the remaining portions of Israel's story is limited.

b. The Ark Narrative

Within the books of Samuel, the Ark Narrative is located in two sections: 1 Sam 4:1b—7:1 and 2 Sam 6. In the first part of the Ark Narrative, the ark was captured by the Philistines, taken from the land of Israel, and brought back to Philistine territory. The Philistines, however, suffered great and terrible calamities because of the ark and realized that they must return it to Israelite territory. The ark is mysteriously absent throughout the remainder of 1 Samuel and only reappears in a short episode after David becomes king. David retrieved the ark from the territory of Kiriath Jearim, where it had been sitting for many years, and transported it to the newly established capital of Jerusalem. The ark remained in Jerusalem and was eventually installed in the temple by Solomon (1 Kgs 8:3-4). References to the ark never appear after 1 Kgs 8, but it probably was taken or destroyed during the Babylonian exile.

c. The Saulide Traditions

The emergence of Saul as the first king over the nation of Israel and his rejection dominate chs 9—15. Various independent traditions about Saul and how he became king have been combined by the Deuteronomistic editor(s) (9:1—10:16; 10:17-27; 11:14-15) and joined together with the material related to Saul's battles with the Ammonites (11:1-13), the Philistines (13:1—14:46), and the Amalekites (15:1-34) to round out this unit. Moreover, a short summary statement regarding Saul's exploits and family appear at the end of 1 Sam 14 (vv 47-51).

The manner in which these traditions have been situated paint a very complicated and confusing portrait of Saul. They result in a perspective of King Saul that is both positive and negative. Scholars have been quick to point out that from the standpoint of its canonical arrangement, chs 8—12, especially, provide contrasting portraits of Saul's monarchy (Childs 1979, 277-78). Chapters 8 and 12 generally critique the people's request for a king as a rejection of Yahweh's leadership and thus the institution of kingship is understood to be less than ideal. Yahweh, however, allowed the people to have a king but with certain stipulations. The material in 10:17-27 portrays Saul as a timid, almost reluctant, candidate for kingship who appears unlikely to inspire hope and courage among the Israelites. This becomes the central issue in ch 13, in particular, when Saul failed to lead the people in a time of crisis and let the peoples' fears about the Philistines influence him into disobeying Samuel's command. Sandwiched among these uncomplimentary reports about kingship and Saul are complementary reports on Israel's first king. First Samuel 9:1—10:16 offers a favorable view of Saul in that God selected him to be a vessel by which the Israelites were liberated from Philistine oppression (9:16). In this situation, Saul appears very much like one of the judges from the previous era that God raised up at opportune times to rescue his people. In the same vein, ch 11 presents Saul as a military hero who rescued the people of Jabesh Gilead from Ammonite oppression. As in the case of 9:16, Saul appears as a heroic figure who liberated God's people. Thus, within the canonical setting of chs 8—12, two favorable reports about Saul are bounded by three unflattering portraits of the king. This would indicate that the biblical writers had mixed views on Saul and on kingship in general, with the overriding view being negative.

The remaining narratives about Saul in chs 13—15 highlight the shortcomings of his monarchy. Saul was a timid leader who disobeyed the word of Samuel as it related to sacrifice (ch 13). Saul also failed in his mission as a military commander in that he was unable to defeat the Philistines. The text goes to great lengths to show that he was actually a barrier to success in Israel's wars against them (chs 13—14). Saul also failed to obey God's command as it related to the war with the Amalekites in that he spared some of the spoils of the battle (ch 15). By ch 15 God was sorry that he had selected Saul as king and sent Samuel to bring word of Saul's demise (vv 26-28). The remaining portion of 1 Samuel (16—31) is devoted to Saul's downfall.

d. The History of David's Rise

Leonard Rost was one of the first scholars to divide the story of David in the books of Samuel into two distinct sections: the history of David's rise (1 Sam 16—2 Sam 5) and the Succession Narrative (2 Sam 9—20; 1 Kgs 1—2) (1982). The history of David's rise follows David's meteoric rise to kingship, beginning with his anointing by Samuel (1 Sam 16) and concluding with David established as the king over all the tribes of Israel (2 Sam 5). Within the material related to David's rise to kingship, the text portrays David in very favorable, almost idealistic, terms. God was with David (1 Sam 16:18; 17:37; 18:12, 28-29; 2 Sam 5:10) and gave him success in everything that he set out to do. God also gave David favor among the people (1 Sam 18:16) so that the people wanted David to become king and even confessed that it was just a matter of time before he took his rightful place on the throne (2 Sam 5:2). Throughout the history of David's rise, a number of important elements about David are highlighted:

1. David was selected by God to replace Saul: God dispatched Samuel to anoint David as the king designate after Saul had been rejected by God (1 Sam 16). When Samuel came to the house of Jesse in Bethlehem of Judah, seven of Jesse's sons had to pass before the prophet before David was selected. God reminded Samuel, "Do not consider his appearance or his height," the "outward appearance" of the candidates, because God "looks at the heart" (v 7). The concern about not placing emphasis on the appearance or the height of the individual set David apart from Saul, who was known for being handsome and tall (9:1-2). The text indicates the strength of David's leadership would be his obedience to God, not in his physical attributes.

2. David was a young man characterized by courage and faith: On David's path to the throne, he demonstrated that he was an individual who had great faith and courage. Nowhere is this exemplified more than in the Goliath narrative (1 Sam 17). While Saul and his men cowered in fear in the face of the Philistine warrior, David volunteered to confront Goliath who had defied the armies of God. Saul agreed to let David challenge Goliath, and David went out to meet the warrior with a sling, a few stones, and "in the name of the LORD of hosts, the God of the armies of Israel" (v 45 NRSV). David's defeat of Goliath demonstrated his great trust in Yahweh who had saved him "from the paw of the lion and from the paw of the bear" (v 37 NRSV).

3. David was popular among the people: On David's path to the throne, God gave David favor in the eyes of the people of Israel. David became so popular among the Israelites that when it came time for David to become king the people had already anticipated it would happen (2 Sam 5:2). David proved himself to be a great leader in battle and God gave him success against Israel's nemesis, the Philistines. As a result, the women sang his praises (1 Sam 18:6-7) and the people of Israel and Judah loved him (v 16). In an ironic twist, the text notes that Saul's own children "loved" David even though their father was suspicious of him and tried to annihilate him on different occasions. The love that Saul's children displayed to David is evident in a number of important ways. First, Saul's son Jonathan in a very telling move handed David the symbols of royal power: his robe, armor, sword, along with his bow and belt. Jonathan's gesture signaled that he knew David would be the next king of Israel (v 4), which was particularly significant in light of the fact that Jonathan was the rightful heir to Saul's kingdom. Jonathan willingly stepped aside and relinquished his rights as an heir so that David could take his place as the next king of Israel. Second, Saul's children demonstrated their love for David by putting their lives at risk to save him. Jonathan interceded for David at Saul's court and signaled to him that it was not safe for David to return to his family (1 Sam 19:1-7; 20:1-42). Michal, Saul's daughter, married David and saved his life by helping him escape by outwitting her father's servants (19:8-17). The efforts of Jonathan and Michal in coming to David's defense stand in sharp contrast with those of their father who was bent on killing him.

4. David acted nobly and righteously toward Saul: Throughout the story of David's rise, Saul's obsession with killing David is repeatedly contrasted with David's merciful and respectful treatment of Saul. On two occasions David was presented with the opportunity to take revenge on Saul for the suffering the king had caused him. In both situations (1 Sam 24; 26), David refused to kill Saul, who represented the "Lord's anointed." David's magnanimity toward Saul in the face of persistent provocation presents David as being more virtuous and righteous than Saul. Saul's words to David, "You are more righteous than I; for you have repaid me good, whereas I have repaid you evil" (24:17 NRSV), serve to underscore David's character and present him as a more favorable option for kingship than Saul. David's kind treatment of Saul even caused the king to proclaim, "You will surely be king and . . . the kingdom of Israel will be established in your hands" (v 20).

5. David the successful politician: The history of David's rise presents David as a shrewd and successful politician. David slowly and methodically strengthened his political reputation among the people, which allowed him to build a power base that eventually came to rival Saul's kingdom. The first phase of David's political rise began during his flight in the wilderness in which a group of 400 men looked to him as a leader (22:2). David also became a vassal of the Philistine king Achish during this period and was given the city of Ziklag to rule (ch 27). While at Ziklag, he and his men made raids on various peoples and presented the captured booty to the families and clans that would eventually comprise the tribe of Judah (30:26-30). David's political career continued to grow as the families and clans in the south anointed David as king of Judah (2 Sam 2:1-4). David ruled over the tribe of Judah from Hebron where he remained for seven and a half years. The last phase of David's political ascension occurred after the death of Saul's son Ish-Bosheth

(4:5-7). When Ish-Bosheth was murdered, the last remaining barrier to Saul's throne had been removed and the northern tribes endorsed David as their king (5:2-5). David ruled as king over Israel for thirty three and a half years and he was able to establish a dynasty that continued in existence for over 400 years.

As the new king over Israel, David and his men captured the city of Jebus (Jerusalem), which became known as "the City of David" (v 7). David also retrieved the ark of the covenant and brought it to the newly established capital of the united monarchy (ch 6). This was a deft move by David because he hailed from the territory of Judah and was not from the northern tribes that Saul once ruled. Since the ark represented a significant religious symbol to the people of the north, it was an ingenious way for David to make himself favorable to the people once loyal to Saul. In addition, David enjoyed military success against the nations around him and was able to extend Israel's influence far beyond the borders of Israel proper so that David was able to carve out a respectable empire (8:1-14).

Scholars who have studied the history of David's rise have noted that it displays the characteristics of an "apology" and functions as a "defense" of David (McCarter 1980a, 489-506; Weiser 1966, 325-54). A careful reading of the material related to David's rise indicates several disturbing features about the manner in which David came to the throne. Information from the text could suggest that David was not just a passive player in the drama that unfolded between Saul and himself but that he had an active role in gaining the monarchy. First, David associated with rough men who represented the outcasts of society and functioned like mercenaries. David relied on their help during his flight from Saul, and they assisted David when he made brutal raids on various groups in the southern portion of Israel (1 Sam 27:8-11). These men also provided "protection" to the people in the territorial tribe of Judah while expecting repayment in return (25:1-17).

Second, David understood the importance of making the right personal connections with people who could help him advance his political career. This was especially true of the women David married. David married Michal, Saul's daughter, and thus became the son-in-law to the king and a member of the royal family. David also married Ahinoam (v 43), who, ironically, is also listed as Saul's wife (14:50). Some scholars have argued that David took Saul's wife for himself on his path to the throne (Levenson and Halpern 1980, 507-18). If true, then David was able to strengthen his political position through such action. David also married Abigail, the widow of Nabal (25:42). Nabal was a wealthy man who had tremendous influence among the clans and families in the southern portion of Judah. Through his marriage to Abigail, David acquired Nabal's wealth and solidified his status among the tribes who would ultimately coronate him as king of Judah. David also had a wife named Maacah, who was the daughter of King Talmai of Geshur (2 Sam 3:3). The territory of Geshur lay outside the land of Israel on the northeastern border. Through

Maacah, David was able to solidify a political ally that was located right on the edge of Saul's kingdom. Thus it appears that David benefited handsomely by the women he married.

Third, David profited greatly from the deaths of people associated with the house of Saul. Gradually, the "competitors" for Saul's throne were eliminated so that David's path to the throne became wide open. Saul and Jonathan died while fighting the Philistines (1 Sam 31); Saul's general, Abner, died while negotiating the transfer of the northern tribes to David's side (2 Sam 3:27); Ish-Bosheth, Saul's remaining son, was assassinated by two renegades (4:7); and the Gibeonites killed off the remaining male members of Saul's family (21:7-9). In each of these cases the person(s) responsible for the murder had connections to David in one form or another. The Amalekite who claimed to have killed Saul came to David with Saul's crown and armlet in hand (1:10-11); David's general, Joab, murdered Abner after he agreed to help bring the northern tribes to David's side (3:27); Recab and Baanah returned to David at Hebron bringing Ish-Bosheth's head in hand after they assassinated him (4:8); and David personally gave the Gibeonites permission to annihilate Saul's descendants, which in the long run assured that none of Saul's offspring would be able to challenge him (21:6, 9).

The essential purpose of the history of David's rise, scholars contend, was intended to address these issues and demonstrate that David was not an outsider who carefully and cruelly plotted his way to the throne but became the king of Israel through legitimate means. First, even though David hailed from the territory of Judah, and thus an unknown figure to Saul and the northern tribes, he was not an interloper because he became a member of Saul's family and thus had some legal claim to the throne. Throughout the narrative complex Saul called David "my son" (1 Sam 24:16; 26:17, 25) and he became the "son-in-law" to the king (18:18, 21-23, 26-27). Moreover, Jonathan, the king's son and rightful heir, essentially bequeathed rights to the throne to David (v 4) and acknowledged that David would be king one day (23:17). Moreover, Saul even made the claim that David would ascend to the throne, thus "legitimating" David in the eyes of the audience (24:20).

Second, the history of David's rise also attempts to distance David from the murders of key people associated with Saul. On almost every occasion when the person(s) responsible for the murder approached David, he proclaimed his innocence, denounced those who had committed the act (2 Sam 1:14-16; 3:28; 4:10-12), and then had them executed. Moreover, in the case of the deaths of Jonathan and Saul, the text locates David far away from Mount Gilboa (the place where Saul and his sons were killed), thus proving that David could not have been involved with their deaths. Thus, David is "cleared" of wrongdoing even though others have brought charges against him (16:7-8).

Apology of Hattusilis

This late thirteenth-century B.C. Hittite text represents one of the earliest examples of a political apology in the ancient world. The text seeks to justify the political ascendancy of Hattusilis by claiming that he came to the throne through legitimate means. Within the apology certain themes are emphasized:

1. A genealogy that indicated he came from a royal line: either by birth or through marriage.
2. References to the failure and disgrace of previous kings, thus highlighting the need for a new leader.
3. The new king enjoyed divine sponsorship and was shown to be more pious than the previous ruler.
4. The new king was a merciful ruler, especially to those that opposed him previously.
5. A line of succession was established in order to avoid conflict at the death of the king.

Old Testament scholars have long noted the close parallels between David's rise (1 Sam 16—2 Sam 5) and Hittite apologetic literature. Like the account of Hattusilis, the story of David's rise was intended to justify David's claim to the throne and defend his character from various criticisms and allegations (Hoffner 1975, 49-62).

e. *The Succession Narrative*

Rost also identified a second important part of the life of David, which he titled the Succession Narrative. Unlike the story of David's rise, the Succession Narrative is much less idealistic and presents a David who was prone to moral failures, was a disappointment as a father, and one who was beset by all manner of familial and political dysfunction. Rost labeled the material in 2 Sam 9—20, 1 Kgs 1—2 the Succession Narrative because it focuses on the central question, "Which one of David's sons will succeed David as king of Israel?" Throughout the narrative complex various "contenders" for the throne appeared and different factions vied for control of the kingdom. Since David's wife Michal failed to produce an heir for the king (2 Sam 6:23), the successor to David derived from one of his other wives. Thus, a contentious and bloody struggle among David's children ensued. Absalom murdered his stepbrother Amnon for the rape of Tamar. Absalom later fomented a revolt against David and established himself as king for a short period until he was eliminated by Joab (2 Sam 14—19). David's son Adonijah, who had backing from influential people such as Joab, proclaimed himself king at the end of David's life (1 Kgs 1). Adonijah's attempt to gain the throne was thwarted by a faction that successfully persuaded David to make Solomon king (chs 1—2). Solomon's throne was only solidified after he successfully removed the people who had opposed him earlier (ch 2). Thus, by the end of the Succession Narrative, Solomon emerged as David's heir but not without substantial conflict and bloodshed.

The bitter events that led up to Solomon's coronation are set within a theological framework. The reason why David experienced contention among his family and suffered political setbacks stemmed from his affair with Bathsheba and the murder of Uriah, Bathsheba's husband (2 Sam 11). The prophet Nathan condemned David's behavior through the use of a parable, and David sealed his own fate by condemning the rich man of the story who stole the poor man's sheep: "As the LORD lives, the man who has done this deserves to die; he will restore the lamb fourfold, because he did this thing" (12:5 NRSV). In pronouncing this verdict, David unwittingly implicated himself for the murder and brought down a legal sentence on his head. An examination of the events that follow David's tryst reveal that David's words were prophetic in that he did pay fourfold for his transgressions: the first son born to Bathsheba died, Amnon was killed by Absalom, Absalom perished in the revolt against David, and, finally, Adonijah died at Solomon's bequest. The events that transpired in David's life and in his family were also the fulfillment of Nathan's oracle against David: "Now therefore the sword shall never depart from your house, for you have despised me, and have taken the wife of Uriah the Hittite to be your wife" (2 Sam 12:10 NRSV). In the Succession Narrative, then, an important lesson is conveyed to the audience: even David, God's anointed, could not flaunt or disregard God's law without being subject to divine correction. David paid a tremendous price both personally and politically for his transgressions.

In examining David's life in Samuel, then, it becomes apparent that the Deuteronomistic editor(s) have divided his life under two distinct headings: "David under the Blessing" and "David under the Curse" (Carlson 1964).

f. The Appendices

The last four chapters of the books of Samuel (21:1—24:25) are comprised of an assortment of materials. These materials include: a narrative about the expiation of Saul's guilt (21:1-14), two lists of heroes and their deeds (21:15-22; 23:8-39), two songs of thanksgiving (22:1-51; 23:1-7), and a narrative about the expiation of David's guilt (24:1-25). Although they may appear to be arranged in a haphazard fashion, scholars realize that these chapters are carefully organized in a chiastic structure pattern (see Behind the Text on 2 Sam 21:1—24:25). This structure highlights important themes, such as the abuse of royal power and the omnipotence and mercy of God.

D. Theological Themes

Throughout the books of Samuel a couple of prominent theological themes and ideas are stressed:

I. Leadership

Throughout the DtrH and the books of Samuel specifically, faithful leadership is an important theological concern that is continuously highlighted. The books of Samuel concentrate on the leadership of three main individuals: Samuel, Saul, and David. In Samuel, and throughout the DtrH, the health and well-being of Israel's community is directly dependent upon the quality of its leaders. The success of a leader is not judged on external factors that humans would use to evaluate a leader's effectiveness: political success, military victory, physical appearance, age, human resources, or financial status. In the books of Samuel, as in the whole of the DtrH, the true measure of a leader's effectiveness is based on one criterion: his faithfulness and obedience to God. Throughout Samuel and the DtrH, God caused the Israelites to flourish and prosper when their leaders feared God, but the community suffered when they disregarded God's instruction. In Samuel, as in the whole of the DtrH, political and military success came as a result of the leader's faithful observance of God's instruction, but defeat and instability occurred when the leader waned in his commitment to God.

Within Samuel various types of leadership are stressed:

a. The Monarchy

The books of Samuel are set within a time of an important transition in Israel's history. The period of the judges closes and the monarchy emerges. The people's request for a king was tantamount to apostasy, and thus the origins of kingship receive a negative theological evaluation. Prior to the time of Samuel God had functioned as Israel's de facto king, but the establishment of human kingship represented Israel's rejection of God's leadership over the community. God, nevertheless, permitted the Israelites to have a king even though the desire for a king was displeasing to God. Israel's king was chosen by God and anointed through the agency of the prophets. Moreover, God subjected the king and the people to certain stipulations, namely: "If both you and the king who reigns over you will follow the LORD your God, it will be well" (1 Sam 12:14*b* NRSV). The text is clear that the people and their leader remained under God's authority and both were exhorted to remain faithful to him. Israel's destiny was intimately tied to the leadership of the king and the prospects of a blessed future were predicated on the king's obedience. As the story of Israel plays out in Samuel and Kings, the narrative shows that it was the failure of Israel's leaders that ultimately led to the decimation of the northern kingdom in 721 B.C. and the southern kingdom in 586 B.C. Thus, the history implicates both the people of Israel, who demanded a king in the first place (1 Sam 8; 12), and Israel's leaders for the exile.

b. The Failure of Saulide Leadership

Although God selected Saul to be Israel's first king (1 Sam 9:1—10:16) the text of Samuel consistently reminds the reading audience that his tenure as king amounted to a great disaster. Theologically speaking, Saul's kingship is characterized by a series of poignant ironies. On the one hand, Saul appears to possess the physical tools and qualities that most people would think make a great leader: he was tall and nice looking, he came from an affluent family, and he proved to be a capable military leader at times. On the other hand, however, the text strongly implies that looks can be deceiving. Throughout the narratives in Samuel, Saul shows that he lacked faith when the community faced opposition, he offended God (and Samuel) by making sacrifices he was not authorized to make, and he failed to follow through on God's directive to destroy the Amalekites. Moreover, Saul never fulfilled the purposes for which God originally selected him, in that he never defeated the Philistines. The sad portrait of Saul's failed monarchy was the result of his own actions and misdeeds. In the end, Saul's monarchy was "rejected" and it ended in a bitter irony: he died at the hands of Israel's enemies and his body was strung up in a mocking fashion (ch 31). Moreover, the prospects and hopes for a successive Saulide line were forever jeopardized because of Saul's actions (13:8-15).

c. The Success of Davidic Leadership

God's rejection of Saul prepared the way for the arrival of God's preferred king: David. Throughout 1 Sam 16—2 Sam 8, especially, God's blessing on David and the success he enjoyed both personally and politically stand in sharp contrast to Saul's doomed kingship. Unlike Saul, David is not known for his physical characteristics but for his devotion to God. Whereas Saul lacked faith in God at critical points in the narrative, David's life was punctuated by moments where he depended upon God for support and strength: while fighting Goliath, for example, and when Saul pursued him in the wilderness. David's righteousness also superseded that of Saul's, and the narrative makes it clear that the prospects of David's leadership were preferable to Saul's or someone from his lineage. Throughout the narrative, the text also makes the point that David was able to accomplish what Saul could not.

God's favor toward David is especially evident in the special covenant God established with David and his household. In the covenant text of 2 Sam 7, God essentially promised David that his line would never come to an end and that his kingdom would be secured forever. This promise, which was severely threatened at the end of the monarchical period and in the exile, provided hope to the Judean community during the postexilic period. God's promise to David was ultimately fulfilled in Jesus, who descended from the house of David and through whom God was able to establish his eternal kingdom.

d. The Rise of the Prophets

The emergence of the prophets coincided with the development of monarchy in Israel's society. Whereas the king presided over the political and military affairs of the kingdom, the prophets served as the religious and moral voice of the community. The prophets functioned as God's spokespersons, and they held the religious leaders, the king, and the people accountable to God. Throughout Samuel, prophets have an important role in Israel's society. The prophet Samuel, for example, called the people to obedient living (1 Sam 7:3-4), functioned as the king designate who anointed Saul and David at God's behest, and delivered words of instruction or judgment when the king (13:8-16; 15:17-23) or the religious leaders did not listen to God's voice (3:1-18). Moreover, Samuel also provided prophetic announcements that declared God's intentions regarding the destiny of Saul's future (28:15-19), Saul's dynasty (15:3-8), and David's monarchy (v 28).

Throughout Samuel, the text notes various prophets who had interactions with David. Outside of Samuel, the prophets Gad and Nathan were the main channels by which God communicated to him. Through the word of the prophet, God established his covenant relationship with the house of David (2 Sam 7), but God also issued strong warnings and messages of judgment as well. The prophet Gad, for example, commanded David to return to the land of Judah (1 Sam 22:5), the prophet Nathan rebuked David after his affair with Bathsheba and the murder of Uriah (2 Sam 12:7-15), and the prophet Gad announced the coming of a plague after David took the census (2 Sam 24:10-14). To David's credit, each time that Gad and Nathan confronted him about his sin, David humbled himself in contrition before God. As God's spokespersons, then, the prophets had the authority to keep the king in check and were a visible reminder that the king remained under God's authority.

2. Reversal of Fortune

Reversal of fortune "as an index of divine sovereignty" is another motif that permeates the books of Samuel (Youngblood 1992, 561). Throughout the stories of Hannah/Samuel, Eli and his sons, and Saul and David, the text demonstrates that God has the ability to exalt the humble and humble the arrogant/haughty. (See the Song of Hannah in 1 Sam 2:6-8.) As a result of God's working in the affairs of humanity, a formerly barren woman (1:5-6) was able to give birth to one of the greatest prophets/priests/judges in Israel's history (2:19-20); pain and humiliation were turned into joy (1:18); a future without children changed drastically with the birth of six (2:21). Men of privilege (vv 12-16), chosen to serve as priests for the community, died in shame (4:11-12). Two lowly and unsuspecting individuals, one searching for donkeys (9:3-4), the other tending sheep (16:11), became the first two kings of Israel (10:1; 16:13). God's anointed and exalted leaders were abased (15:11, 28; 2 Sam 12:9-10). God's ability to change the circumstances of individuals in the books of Samuel was not disconnected from human response to the divine, however. The fate of individuals was affected by their piety and obedience to the divine will as well as by their pride and unfaithfulness to God.

3. Reward-Punishment Theology

The books of Samuel clearly explicate Deuteronomistic reward-punishment theology. Basically, the Deuteronomistic editor(s) supported the idea that God would bless those who were obedient and bring punishment on those who disobeyed. This theological view of life was borne out of their understanding of the Mosaic covenant. The Mosaic covenant follows the patterns and format of ancient Near Eastern treaties, which included a list of stipulations that the vassal was required to keep in order to receive blessings from the suzerain and the threat of severe punishment for disobedience. The Mosaic covenant, which was conditional in nature, conceived of Israel's relationship to God in similar ways: blessings for obedience (Deut 7:12-24; 28:1-14; Lev 26:1-13) and curses for disobedience (Deut 28:15-68; Lev 26:14-46).

Throughout Samuel, and the DtrH, the reward-punishment schema operated at the individual level and at the level of the community. God brought judgment on those who broke God's command, such as Eli and his sons for their perverse behavior at the sanctuary at Shiloh (1 Sam 2:27-35), Saul for disobeying God's command (13:8-15), and David for his involvement with the Bathsheba and Uriah fiasco (2 Sam 12:7-14). The Israelites also suffered defeat and humiliation at the hands of the Philistines because of the lack of obedience and their misuse of the ark (1 Sam 4:1-22). Samuel also warned the Israelites that they would experience pain and suffering by requesting a king to lead them (8:10-18).

God also blessed those who demonstrated piety and faith in God. God blessed Hannah with a son in spite of her barren condition (1:11-19), God honored Samuel among the people of Israel for his faithful service (3:1-21), God gave David favor among the people and Saul's family (18:1-14), God established a special covenant with David and his family (2 Sam 7), and Israel gained victory over their enemies as David remained true to God (5:17-25; 8:1-14).

The Deuteronomistic editor(s) constructed the rest of the DtrH around this reward-punishment schema. It provided a theological rationale for why God's favor and mercy were extended to those who were obedient and explained why catastrophes like those of 721 B.C. and 586 B.C. occurred. Over time, however, other biblical writers began to challenge this Deuteronomistic way of perceiving and interpreting reality as certain psalms (44:9-22; 73:4-12) and the book of Job (21:1-34; 31:1-40) attest.

COMMENTARY

THE BOOK OF FIRST SAMUEL

I. THE PREMONARCHICAL PERIOD IN ISRAEL: SAMUEL AND THE ARK NARRATIVES (1:1—7:17)

A. The Birth of Samuel (1:1-28; 2:11)

BEHIND THE TEXT

The initial unit of 1 Samuel opens with the narrative account of Samuel's birth (1:1-28), includes Hannah's song of praise and thanksgiving (2:1-10), and concludes with the brief notice that Samuel **served Yahweh in the presence of Eli** (v 11*b*). The syntactical, literary, and thematic cues within the text indicate the opening scenes of ch 1 naturally conjoin 1 and 2 Samuel with the book of Judges; yet, they also suggest that an important shift within the plotline of Israel's narrative is taking place. On the one hand, 1 Samuel directly follows Judges in the Hebrew Bible, thus linking this book with the latter in terms of canonical arrangement. More substantial evidence indicates a stronger connection to Judges, however. The setting of 1:1—2:11 is situated at the sanctuary in Shiloh, the identical location where the men of Benjamin seized wives for themselves at the end of Judges (21:15-24). In addition, the adjectival phrase **there was a certain man** (1 Sam 1:1*a*) shows a close literary affinity with the introduction to Manoah, Samson's father (Judg 13:2), as well as the stories of Micah (Judg 17:1) and the Levite (Judg 19:1*b*). This canonical relationship is enhanced by the fact that the story of Elkanah and his family takes place in **the hill country of Ephraim** (1 Sam 1:1*a*), the same tribal territory that is mentioned in Judg 17. As a result of this evidence, the reading audience is left to deduce that the opening events of 1 Samuel follow naturally from the time of Judges.

Other grammatical and syntactical considerations, however, indicate that the story line is also moving in a new direction. The Hebrew syntax of 1:1a (*and* there was a certain man) indicates the beginning of a new scene within the overall narrative structure. Moreover, the formal introduction of a new set of characters in ch 1 (i.e., Elkanah, Hannah, Eli) signals the opening of a distinct narrative sequence. The emergence of Samuel, in particular, shifts the setting of the story from the time of the judges to the period of the monarchy. Samuel is essential for the development of Saul's kingship (esp. in chs 8—12), and he is responsible for the establishment of David's monarchy as well (1 Sam 16—2 Sam 24). Since Samuel is the man to whom Israel owes its monarchy, he becomes a pivotal figure during this transitional phase in Israel's history.

Even though the birth of Samuel functions as the climax of the first chapter (1 Sam 1:19-20), the information regarding Hannah's barrenness (v 2), Peninnah's cruel treatment of Hannah (vv 6-7), and Hannah's prayer and vow (vv 10-11) develops the palpable tension leading up to Samuel's initial appearance in the story (v 20). In addition to the two wives and the boy Samuel, this unit introduces the reader to four men who are critical to the story line: Elkanah, Hophni, Phinehas, and Eli. While Elkanah basically disappears from the story line after the birth of Samuel, Eli and his sons play more prominent roles throughout chs 1—3 in that they served as the main priests at the Shiloh sanctuary. As the main priests at Shiloh they also functioned as the primary caretakers of the ark of the covenant. The text also indicates that they largely contributed to the overall religious and moral decay of the priesthood at this time.

The story of Samuel in chs 1—3 is intimately tied to the sanctuary at Shiloh. Along with Shechem (Josh 24) and Gilgal (Josh 5), Shiloh served as one of the main religious centers in Israel's past. According to the OT, both the tent of meeting and the ark of the covenant resided there in premonarchical times (Josh 18:1-10; 19:51; 21:2; 22:9; Judg 20:26-28). Shiloh lay about nineteen miles north of Jerusalem, in the hill country of Ephraim. Recent archaeological excavation points to the remnants of a cultic site there with extensive architectural features that can be placed in the first half of the eleventh century B.C. (Halpern 1992, 1214). This dating would place it roughly at the time of Eli and Samuel (ca. 1050 B.C.). The Philistines, in all likelihood, later destroyed the sanctuary, an event that Jeremiah alludes to in his book (26:6, 9).

Elkanah made yearly pilgrimages to Shiloh in order to present offerings and sacrifices before Yahweh. It is possible that these pilgrimages were connected to the autumn festival known as the Festival of Booths or Succoth (Deut 16:13-15), but the text never directly says so. The text also notes that his wives, Hannah and Peninnah, and his children regularly accompanied him to the sacred site. While outlawed in modern western society, bigamy was not an unusual practice in the ancient Near East. In ancient cultures, if a man's primary wife was not able to provide a son, and thus ensure the preservation of the family line and a direct heir to the family estate, he would take a second wife in order to produce a male descendant. Although allowed by Mosaic tradition (Deut 21:15), polygamous arrangements often presented a political, economic, and social threat to the barren wife (Schneider 2004, 46-61). These marital arrangements also had the power to enflame sharp tensions within the family unit. This appears to be no less true in the case of Elkanah's household. The bitter rivalry that developed between Hannah and Peninnah became particularly hard on the former. The pain and frustration over Hannah's situation eventually drove her to pray for a son, resulting in a vow to dedicate him as a Nazirite to Yahweh. Yahweh eventually answered the prayer of Hannah, who later fulfilled her part of the vow by returning the boy to Yahweh. Thus, one of the main purposes of this opening unit is to provide an explanation as to how Samuel became associated with the Shiloh sanctuary and later displaced Eli and his sons as the main priest there.

IN THE TEXT

I. Prologue (1:1-3)

■ I The prologue commences by introducing Samuel's family tree. Elkanah, Samuel's father, is described as a man from **Haramathaim Zophim.** In Hebrew, this phrase literally means "the Double Heights (of) Zophim." Since this location is not mentioned anywhere else in the OT, many modern translations try to emend the text in order to make sense of this reading. Some have translated the text to read "Ramathaim of the Zuphites" (JPS). Another, and more attractive, way to translate this phrase is "[a man from] Ramathaim, a Zuphite" (NIV, NRSV) or "one of the Zuphites from Ramathaim" (Tsumura 2007, 107). The latter two options preserve Elkanah's Zuphite lineage (referenced in v 1*b*) and place him at Ramathaim, which is the plural form of Ramah. Ramah is designated as Elkanah's hometown in 1:19 and 2:11, and it has been associated with the ancient city of Rentis, which is located about sixteen miles east of Tel Aviv (also called Arimathea in the NT). The plural form of Ramah (Ramathaim, which can also be read "two hills") is utilized here because there were probably two hills associated with the site: one in the city and the other utilized as a "high place" (9:25).

Elkanah is further identified as the **son of Jeroham, the son of Elihu, son of Tohu, the son of Zuph, an Ephraimite** (v 1). The name **Elkanah** literally means "God acquired (a son?)," and the inclusion of the patronymic formula after his name raises a couple of important issues. First, the inclusion of the rather long registry of names may indicate Elkanah was a man of some means (Gordon 1986, 72). Not only does the long pedigree indicate he came from a well-to-do family, but the fact that he could support two wives lends credence to this notion as well. It is ironic, however, that the men listed in his lineage are not well known and they do not play a prominent role in the OT. In spite of this, the patronymic formula is the typical literary devise used by biblical writers to formally introduce important figures such as prophets, priests, and/or kings. The fact that the text includes Elkanah's family tree as a prelude to Samuel's arrival is a subtle clue that Samuel would be special; maybe even anticipating his future role as a prophet and priest (Mauchline 1971, 42). Second, Elkanah's ancestor Zuph, who is only identified as an Ephraimite, did not descend from a prophetic or priestly family. This issue presented peculiar difficulties for later editors and interpreters of the story of Samuel. Since the text indicates Samuel performed prophetic and priestly functions at Shiloh, later traditions "compensated" for Samuel's nonexistent priestly heritage. First Chronicles 6:16-28, 33-38, in particular, addressed this issue by modifying Samuel's history line by listing Zuph as a descendant of Levi. This important genealogical shift thereby ascribed to Samuel Levitical (priestly) bloodlines. Moreover, the Chronicler placed Elkanah and Samuel among the Kohathite clan, whose major responsibility was to care for the ark of the covenant (Num 3:31). It is understandable why the Chronicler located Samuel among this clan, considering that he did have some affiliation with the ark (1 Sam 3:3).

■ **2-3** Verses 2 and 3*a* provide further information about Elkanah. Whereas v 1 refers to his ancestral history, v 2 provides information about his wives. In v 2*a* **Hannah** is listed first, thus indicating her personal importance to Elkanah and her status as the primary wife. The name **Hannah** may mean "charming" and thus would explain why she was favored by Elkanah (Klein 1983, 6). **Peninnah** is listed second, probably emphasizing her role as the secondary wife. The order of their names is inverted, however, in the second part of the verse. In v 2*b* Peninnah is mentioned first with the added notice that **Peninnah had children** while ***Hannah did not have children.*** The text positions Hannah after Peninnah in the second half of the verse to remind the audience of the latter's barren condition, which is crucial to the development of the story line (Alter 1999, 3). The name **Peninnah** may mean something like "prolific," thus it is a fitting appellation in light of the fact that she was able to produce multiple children for Elkanah (Klein 1983, 6). Hannah's name is also suggestive in light of her special circumstances, because it is etymologically similar to the Hebrew word for favor (*ḥēn*). Provided that she could not have children at the beginning of the narrative, Hannah's name later takes on new significance as Yahweh showed favor to her by not only providing Samuel but several other children as well (2:21).

The text also notes that Elkanah traveled to Shiloh ***on a yearly basis to worship and to offer sacrifices to the Lord of Hosts*** (1:3*a*). The grammatical construction of v 3*a* (*miyyāmîm yāmîm* = "from year to year"), coupled with the two infinitives (***to worship and to offer***), is noteworthy, because it indicates ongoing action or consistent activity. The reference to Elkanah's regular pilgrimage to Shiloh suggests that he was a pious man who feared Yahweh. Verse 3*b* closes out the subunit by noting that when Elkanah went to the sanctuary

Hophni and Phinehas, the two sons of Eli, were *there.* The fact that the text does not read "Eli and his sons" points to the notion that the worshiper expected to encounter Hophni and Phinehas at the sacred site but not Eli (Frolov 2002, 140). This would indicate that Eli remained in the background while his sons took the lead role in officiating at the site. The reference to Eli's sons in this verse also prepares the reader for the next chapter, in which they will be the subject of the editor/narrator's focus.

2. Elkanah's Family at Shiloh (1:4-8)

■ **4-7a** This section recounts what generally took place when Elkanah's family visited the shrine at Shiloh. The unit opens at v 4a with the phrase ***and it would happen on the day Elkanah sacrificed*** and proceeds in vv 4b-7a to provide a parenthetical note describing Elkanah's habitual actions at the time of sacrifice. These verses recount that he would give to ***Peninnah and her sons and daughters a portion*** of the sacrificial animal. However, to Hannah he would give her ***one portion faceward.*** The meaning of the latter phrase has perplexed scholars for generations. The Hebrew word that is employed is a dual form (*'apāyim*) and literally means "faces." Some have translated it as **a double portion** (Hertzberg 1964, 24; NIV, NRSV), a "worthy portion" (KJV), or "in her face," as in frustration over Hannah's inability to provide children for Elkanah (Frolov 2002, 143). In light of the following phrase, which states that Elkanah **loved** Hannah (JPS, "Hannah was his favorite"), we may probably take it that Elkanah presented the portion to Hannah in such a manner, such as giving her a larger portion than was merited, or in a very personal or caring manner (thus "to her face"), so that it honored her (a "portion of honor," Caquot and de Robert 1994, 33) above Peninnah. Second, the text recounts that **her rival *wife would provoke her sorely*** in order to irritate her (v 6). Peninnah's harsh treatment of Hannah is captured more accurately by the Hebrew. Not only did she show hostility toward Hannah (thus **her rival**), but she did it purposely in order to "cause thunder" or to "agitate" her. In English, this phrase could even be rendered to "browbeat" or to "bully" her (Mauchline 1971, 46). The LXX does not contain a statement about the "rival wife" and how she provoked Hannah in v 6. Instead Hannah's pain is caused by the Lord who prevented her from having children. Verse 6 in the LXX reads: "For the Lord gave her no child in her affliction, and according to the despondency of her affliction; and she was dispirited on this account, that the Lord shut up her womb as to not give her a child." In the LXX, Hannah's despondency is caused by her barrenness, not Peninnah's provocation.

The embittered rivalry that the Hebrew text captures so poignantly existed because Peninnah was jealous that Hannah remained the favored wife of Elkanah, even though Peninnah produced children for him. The rivalry between Elkanah's wives similarly recalls the contentious encounters between Sarah and Hagar (Gen 16:4-6) and Leah and Rachel (Gen 30:1-3). The echoing of these traditions from the patriarchal history has an important bearing on the interpretation of this story. In biblical history, children born to a previously barren woman generally indicated something unique or special about the status of that child (i.e., Isaac, Jacob, Joseph). Since Hannah's child was conceived with the assistance of God, the reader is left to anticipate that Samuel would serve an important role in Israel's society. The following chapters (esp. 1 Sam 3—7) indicate that this is indeed the case. Verse 7*a* ends the parenthetical statement by noting that this scenario ***would happen year after year as long as she would go up to the house of the Lord.*** Thus, not only was Hannah's barrenness a source of pain and humiliation, but the repeated ridicule that she had to endure no doubt caused her unspeakable grief and heartache.

■ **7*b*-8** Verse 7*b* connects with v 4*a* by noting that in response to this situation Hannah ***would cry and not eat*** during the mealtime, thus underscoring her intense grief. On one occasion Elkanah responded to Hannah's plight by asking, ***Why are you crying and why don't you eat, and why is your heart fallen? Am I not better to you than ten sons?*** Elkanah in v 8 basically "hammered" Hannah with four short staccato questions to try and assuage Hannah's feelings (Fokkelman 1993, 31). Elkanah's response, though well-intentioned, essentially misunderstood Hannah's personal situation and clumsily overlooked the root of her problem. Although Elkanah tried, he was not able to provide the healing words that would have brought lasting comfort to her. In the ancient world, a woman's social status, financial security, and fulfillment in life were found in bearing sons (Alter 1999, 4). Elkanah's love and attention, no matter how important, would never be able to meet these specific needs in Hannah's life.

Taking these verses together, then, one realizes that Hannah's plight was an extremely frustrating and unimaginably difficult one; she was barren, her rival wife repeatedly and purposely antagonized her on account of her barrenness, and her husband was rather oblivious to her own needs and the source of her frustration, pain, and sadness.

3. Hannah's Vow to Yahweh (1:9-11)

■ **9-11** These verses recount Hannah's response to her difficult circumstances. On one specific occasion Hannah went into the sanctuary to pray and present her grief before the Lord. Since Yahweh had closed her womb, only Yahweh, the giver of life, could open it (Evans 2003, 16). While there, the text notes that ***Eli was sitting on the seat next to the doorposts of the temple of Yahweh*** (v 9). Even though Eli would not greet the people when they came to sacrifice, he did serve in some capacity (limited?) at the shrine. Most likely he was confined to the inner portion of the sanctuary where people like Hannah came to pray. The text in v 9 makes a reference to the ***doorposts of the temple,*** which may indicate that the Shiloh sanctuary was a more permanent structure and not just a tent shrine like the tabernacle from the wilderness traditions (Klein 1983, 8; see Ps 78:60, which may indicate otherwise). While in the sanctuary Hannah *prayed to the Lord, weeping bitterly.* The description of Hannah's crying is significant. The syntax includes the use of the infinitive absolute (*bākōh tibkeh*) in describing Hannah's emotional response. The grammar intends to convey severe crying (i.e., she "really cried") or heavy weeping on Hannah's part. Thus, the reader is given a glimpse into the intense grief she experienced.

Hannah's intense prayer in vv 10-11 also included a vow. She prayed: *If you will truly look upon the affliction of your maidservant and remember me and not forget your maidservant and give to your maidservant seed of men, I will give him to Yahweh all the days of his life and a razor will not come upon his head.* Two important issues are related to Hannah's prayer. First, Hannah's request, that Yahweh "look upon" her affliction and "remember" her, distinctly echoes the plight and the outcry of the Israelites when they were in Egyptian bondage (Exod 2:23-24; 6:5). The narrator thus carefully draws a comparison between Hannah's suffering and the painful memories of Israel's ancestors in Egypt.

Second, Hannah's vow is significant because it is not given in the usual quid pro quo fashion (i.e., if you do X, then I will do Y). Hannah basically said, If you give X, then I will give Y. Hannah's vow therefore indicates that Samuel would not only be a gift from God, but her son would be a gift given back to God (Hamilton 2004, 215). It is presumed that Samuel would be a Nazirite, since she promised that *his hair would not be cut* (Num 6:5; Judg 13:5; 16:17). The LXX and 4QSam[a] further add the notice that he would "not drink wine" either. In examining this language, it becomes apparent that the narrator makes a connection with the book of Judges, particularly the story of Samson. Unlike Samson, who failed as a Nazirite and broke his vows at every turn, Samuel would be an exemplary Nazirite demonstrating great faithfulness to God as both prophet and priest. This "rearview" reflection on the story of Samson thus intimates that a new chapter and brighter future will emerge among Israel's religious leadership with the advent of Samuel.

Nazirite

The term "Nazirite" derives from the Hebrew word (*nāzar*) meaning to "consecrate" or "set apart." Nazirites displayed their devotion to God through distinctive behaviors such as observing prohibitions against cutting the hair, drinking wine or other fermented beverages, and touching the dead. Nazirites were either called by God or dedicated by their parents at an early age. In addition to Samson (Judg 13—16) and Samuel, men and women could vow to become temporary Nazirites for a designated period of time. The book of Numbers provides specific legislation pertaining to the terms and obligations of the Nazirite vow (6:1-21).

4. Eli and Hannah at the Sanctuary (1:12-18)

■ **12-18** This section of text records the rather lengthy interchange between Hannah and the priest Eli at the Shiloh sanctuary. While Hannah prayed, Eli carefully observed Hannah's behavior and body language. The Hebrew grammar in v 12 centers on and underscores the earnestness with which Hannah prayed: Hannah *continued to pray before Yahweh.* The meaning of the verb (*hirbetâ*) in this phrase can be translated "to be great or many." Thus, Hannah "multiplied" her prayers or she prayed "without ceasing."

Eli, who could not hear her speak and noticed only that her lips were moving, **considered her to be a drunken woman** and commanded that **she remove the wine from herself** (vv 13-14). Hannah quickly responded to Eli's gruff response and misguided accusation by stating that she was not a drunken woman given over to **wine** and **strong drink** (thus covering the gamut of intoxicating beverages), but rather, in her grief, **poured out her soul before Yahweh** (v 15).

The irony in this exchange cannot be overlooked. First, the ineffectiveness of Eli as a priest is apparent. As a priest, he should have been in tune to a supplicant with a heavy heart. Instead, he was unable to interpret effectively Hannah's actions and falsely accused her of wrongdoing. This is just one sign that points to the hapless condition of the religious leadership and the overall state of affairs at the Shiloh sanctuary.

Second, in Hannah's response to Eli, the text uses a verb that is usually used for pouring out a liquid as a description for her prayer (*šāpak*). The same term is a technical term that can be used in conjunction with a sacrifice or offering that is poured out (Deut 12:27) or as a sign of deep contrition (Amos 5:8; 9:6) and sorrow (Lam 2:19).

Thus, Hannah was not imbibing wine or strong drink but was pouring out her soul—the type of offering and outpouring that came from a distressed heart or troubled spirit. While Elkanah's sacrifices and offerings were of the traditional type, Hannah's sacrifice and offering included a type of lament. Moreover, Eli mistakenly accused the future mother of a Nazirite (who would be required to stay away from wine and intoxicants, see Num 6:3) of being drunk herself! The irony is rich, to say the least.

When Eli realized this grave mistake he quickly proceeded to pronounce the following blessing upon Hannah: **May the God of Israel give to you your request that you have asked from him** (v 17b). The construction of this phrase in Hebrew may also be taken as a promise that God would indeed act on her behalf: **The God of Israel will give to you what you have asked from him.**

It is also significant to note here that between vv 16-28 (including 2:20), words associated with the verb "to ask" (*šā'al*) occur no less than nine times. This can be seen from the following outline (Hamilton 2004, 215):

> Verse 17: Then Eli answered . . . "the God of Israel grant your *asking* that you have *asked* of him."

Verse 20: "She named him Samuel, for she said, 'I have *asked* him of Yahweh.'"

Verse 27: "And Yahweh has granted me my *asking* that I *asked* of him."

Verse 28: "Therefore I have caused him to be *asked* for by Yahweh. All the days of his life he is the *asked*-for one."

2:20: "Then Eli . . . would say, 'May Yahweh repay you with children by this woman for the *asking* that she *asked* of Yahweh."

The constant reference to Hannah's "asking" or her "request" has caused some scholars to see oblique references to King Saul, and thus conclude this opening narrative originally pertained to his birth (Stolz 1981, 16). Although Saul's name derives from the passive form of the same verb (*šāûl*), there is no substantial evidence outside of this narrative to maintain this position. In Hebrew, the narrator/writer is using a grammatical construction called alliterative etymology, where both words begin and end with the same consonants. The narrator/writer of this text deliberately utilizes similar words to create a sharp dichotomy between Samuel, for whom Hannah asked, and Saul, for whom the people will ask in chs 8 and 12. The foreshadowing is even more patent: barren Hannah asked for the child she did not have; later, barren Israel would ask for the king she did not have (Polzin 1989, 24-25).

Immediately after Eli pronounced this blessing/promise on Hannah, the text notes that she **ate and went her way and her face was not fallen again** (v 18). The blessing/promise that Hannah received appears to have revived her spirits. Not only did she partake of the food she once rejected, but the phrase **her face was not fallen again** employs an interesting wordplay. The term for **her face** (*pāneyhā*) sounds very similar to the name Peninnah, thus a pun on her rival's name intimating that she would no longer be an issue or concern to Hannah.

5. Samuel Is Presented to Yahweh (1:19-28; 2:11)

■ **19-28** The text moves quickly from Hannah's prayer and Eli's blessing/promise to the birth of Samuel; the answer to Hannah's prayer. When the couple returned from Shiloh the text immediately notes that "Elkanah knew his wife Hannah, and [**Yahweh**] remembered her" (v 19*b* JPS, NRSV). The term "to know" (*yādaʿ*) is used in the OT as a sexual euphemism (Gen 4:1). However, whereas Elkanah knew Hannah, as in a brief sexual encounter, Yahweh actually remembered her. That Yahweh "remembered" Hannah is a direct referent to her supplication in v 11, thus demonstrating that Yahweh "observed" Hannah's suffering and never "forgot" her request. The allusion once again to the Exodus tradition, where Yahweh "saw" Israel's affliction, "heard" the outcry of the people, and "remembered" the covenant he made with their ancestors cannot be ignored. The similarities of these two traditions remind the reading audience that God deeply cares for those who are vulnerable and experience suffering.

When Hannah's son was born she gave him the name **Samuel** because, *from Yahweh I asked him* (v 20). The name **Samuel** (*šemû'ēl*), however, is not etymologically related to the verb "to ask." Although a number of scholars have tried to explain the meaning of his name, Samuel can probably best be read as "God heard" (i.e., Hannah's prayer). Hannah cared for Samuel and weaned him (probably around age three or four; see 2 Macc 7:27) before she returned him to Yahweh. Once the boy was old enough Hannah came to the sanctuary at Shiloh and presented materials for two sacrifices. The first consisted of "three bulls, one ephah of flour, and a jar of wine" (1 Sam 1:24 JPS). Based on the information from the LXX, 4QSam^a, and the Peshitta, it may be better to read this as "a three-year-old bull and bread." These elements were probably meant for a votive offering in light of the vow she made earlier (Num 15:8-10).

The second offering was much more valuable and precious: the boy Samuel himself. Hannah **brought** (v 24a, b) Samuel to the sanctuary and offered him to Yahweh by relinquishing him to the care of Eli. Although two different verbs are utilized in v 24 to refer to Hannah's "bringing" Samuel (*vātā'ălēhû* and *vātbi'ēhû*), they are both causative verbs, thus underscoring her role in delivering the boy to God. In presenting Samuel to Eli, she had indeed fulfilled her part of the vow (v 28). Samuel, in essence, became a "living sacrifice" to the Lord as a result of Hannah's gesture.

The text never indicates how leaving Samuel at Shiloh affected her personally, but one can only imagine the heavy emotional price she paid by leaving her only child with Eli. The text notes that she would visit Samuel once a year (2:19); it is difficult to believe, however, that this would have allowed Hannah enough time to develop an intimate relationship with her son. The type of sacrifice and faithfulness demonstrated on Hannah's part rivals that of Abraham who also showed a willingness to sacrifice his only child (Gen 21).

■ **2:11** When the initial unit closes, the text reminds the reading audience that Samuel remained at Shiloh where he **served Yahweh before Eli the priest.** The verb in 2:11b is a participle (*mĕšārēt*), thus denoting that Samuel continuously and faithfully served Yahweh under Eli at the sanctuary. True to the vow and intentions of his mother, Samuel became a living sacrifice in the service of God. This statement not only informs the reader of the moral integrity and religious devotion of the lad, but it also demonstrates how the prayer and dedication of a pious woman produced one of Israel's greatest leaders.

FROM THE TEXT

1. One of the things that we learn in examining the life of Hannah is that life is not always fair. God does not always spare us from unfortunate circumstances or situations. There are times, or seasons, in life in which we may experience hardships or face opposition that brings us pain or heartache. Along the journey we may even encounter people that aggravate our pain (as

in the case of Peninnah) or come across those who try to help but are oblivious to our situation and personal needs (as in the case of Elkanah).

During those times in life we learn a couple of important lessons through the story of Hannah. First, God is keenly attentive to those who are suffering. The OT consistently witnesses to the fact that God is on the side of the humble, hurting, weak, and oppressed. Like the Israelites in Egyptian bondage, God sees the pain of his children and hears the cries of those who are suffering. God is also at work in the midst of those situations to bring about his plan, even when we may not always be aware of God's intentions. Like Hannah, God remembers those who call on his name in times of distress and can even bring something wonderful out of our misfortune. As is witnessed in Hannah's song of praise and thanksgiving (see commentary on 2:1-10), God exalts the lowly and brings honor to the weak. Samuel represented one of God's greatest leaders in Israel's history, yet, like the children of Sarah and Rebekah, he emerged as a blessing in a time of uncertainty.

Second, Hannah's own actions are instructive. In a time when she had few choices or options, Hannah did not lose faith in God and brought her complaint to him in prayer and tears. The text indicates that Hannah had to endure her suffering for a period of time, yet she brought her request before God, the One who could truly help her. It was out of her great anguish that she called upon God, and God looked upon her situation. God not only interceded for Hannah by providing a child but gave her several more children as well.

2. Hannah's faith and piety also emerge in the text. In asking God for a child, Hannah did not present her request as a bargain tactic in order to blackmail God: if you do this, I will do this. Hannah was not presumptuous in that manner but realized that if God provided a son, the son would be returned as a gift/offering back to God. There are times when people will make deals with God in order to ensure their request is granted. Such an attitude indicates that the supplicants are not truly concerned about seeking God's will but are more concerned about attaining or acquiring what is desired. Moreover, they mask their true intentions in pious language. Hannah proved that her heart and prayer were genuine in that when Samuel was given to Hannah, she returned him to the sanctuary as a living thank offering to God.

3. We also learn an important lesson about the connection between worship and service. Samuel was a gift to God, and his life was characterized by continued service to God. Even when Samuel was a young lad the text notes in 2:11 that he served God in the presence of Eli. Another way of understanding this text is to say that Samuel served God by serving Eli. Many times our understanding of worship is too narrow, thinking that worship only takes place in a sanctuary or church. The example of Samuel reminds us that worship is also connected to fulfilling our family and work roles in daily life. This understanding of worship not only applies to adults but children and young people as well. Oftentimes our children have the mind-set that they cannot

do anything significant for God until they get older. However, it is important for them to understand that they worship God by obeying and helping their parents, by striving to do well in their schoolwork, and by treating siblings and friends with respect and kindness. Thus, worship is connected to the things they do on a daily basis. The same is true for adults. Adults also worship God by fulfilling their roles as spouses, parents, employees, and neighbors to the best of their abilities. Oftentimes people feel that their lives are just ordinary and that they are not doing important work for the kingdom of God. They may believe that by not serving God in a foreign country as a missionary or in a full-time ministry role in a church, their lives have little relevance or impact on the world. The text reminds us that we honor and worship God when we faithfully and wholeheartedly fulfill the roles in which we find ourselves, no matter how ordinary or mundane they may seem. Remember, **Whatever you do in word or deed, do it all in the name (and for the glory) of the Lord** (Col 3:17).

B. Hannah's Song of Thanksgiving (2:1-10)

BEHIND THE TEXT

Scholars would agree that Hannah's song of thanksgiving must have derived from a different literary setting before it was ascribed to Hannah and inserted here. First Samuel speaks of Hannah having six children (Samuel plus five others [2:21]) but the poem speaks of a barren woman who has seven children (v 5). The tenor of the poem is national, speaking of male enemies and military metaphors (v 4).

The prayer for the king (v 10) does not fit the story of Hannah since Samuel never served as a king and even spoke out against the institution of kingship. Also, v 11 joins 1:28 without difficulty, thus indicating that the song had been inserted into the text by the editor/redactor(s) of the books of Samuel. Scholars have noted the similarities of language and style to Ps 113 and other hymns of praise in the Psalter (Birch 1998, 980). Others have even commented on the similarities of this psalm with 2 Sam 22 and Ps 18 (Carlson 1964, 45-46). Even though this poem of thanksgiving may have been originally situated in a different literary and cultic setting, it is, nevertheless, appropriate to the context of the story of Hannah, because it centers on the theme of God's ability to intercede in human affairs and bring about a reversal of fortune. This message clearly resonated in the life of Hannah, who suffered from the pain of barrenness yet experienced the joy of motherhood as well. The words of this psalm of thanksgiving praise the God of Israel who is able to work miracles in the lives of the lowly and exalt the humble to a position of greatness.

IN THE TEXT

■ **1-3** The opening phrase identifies the song initially as Hannah's prayer: **Hannah prayed and said.** As Hannah's private prayer, it is intensely personal and therefore conveys a first person perspective, especially in v 1. Phrases such as "my heart exults" (NRSV), **my horn is *raised,*** "my mouth derides my enemies," "I rejoice in my victory" (NRSV) convey the personal quality of this song. The supplicant in this song can rejoice based on the incomparability of God. There is ***no one as holy as Yahweh, no one besides Yahweh, and no rock like our God*** (v 2). The terms used here to describe God center on God's holy character and strength, the basis for God's greatness. As a result of God's sovereignty and purity, a warning is given those who are arrogant and proud since God is a God of knowledge who weighs human actions. Inherent within these verses is the idea that no one has the right to boast or be arrogant since God pays attention to human circumstances, judges them, and sets them in balance when necessary. Even though the song never identifies Peninnah per se, her taunting and ridicule of Hannah come to mind in these verses (see 1:6).

■ **4-8** These verses logically flow from the previous statements about God's ability to change the fortunes of the mighty and the lowly. They provide a specific catalogue of reversals brought about by God's own power. Verse 4*a* centers on the powerful who have been brought low ("the bows of the mighty are broken" [JPS, NRSV]) and then (v 4*b*) shifts to the weak who have been made strong ("the feeble gird on strength" [NRSV]). Verse 5*a* continues this series of comparisons by referring to those **who were full** and then ***hired themselves for bread,*** and "those who were hungry are fat with spoil" (NRSV). Verse 5*b* reverses the order by referring to the weak first and then the mighty. In this instance the woman **who was barren has borne seven** and "she who has many children is forlorn" (NRSV). Verses 4-5 especially echo God's intervention in the life of Hannah who was barren but later given several children.

Verses 6-8 recall that it is God who is the power behind these reversals of fortune. The focus shifts from the hope of those in need of God's help to a doxology of praise to God (Birch 1998, 981). Unlike v 1, which highlights the role of the supplicant, vv 6-8 magnify the power and activity of God. These verses confirm that it is God who "kills and brings to life; he brings down to Sheol and raises up. . . . makes poor and makes rich; . . . brings low [and] exalts. . . . raises up the poor . . . ; lifts the needy . . . , to make them sit with princes and inherit a seat of honor" (NRSV). The writer can state this theological belief because "the pillars of the earth are **[*Yahweh's*]**, and on them he has set the world" (v 8*b* NRSV). In essence, the voice in this psalm underscores the notion of God as Creator, the One who has established the earth and set it in place. Since God demonstrated both the ability and the might to accomplish this amazing feat at creation, the writer is reassured that God also has the power to intervene in a time of need.

■ **9-10** The last two verses of this song flow out of the preceding section. The God who is able to change the fortunes of the powerful and the weak (v 9) is also the God who distinguishes between the faithful and the wicked and judges **the ends of the earth** (v 10). God "will guard the feet of his faithful" while "the wicked shall be cut off in darkness" (v 9 NRSV). The poem underscores the notion that it is not by one's own power or might that a person prevails, but it is God's power that transforms the social realities in which one lives. Thus, the faithful are those who put their faith in God's power and allow him to work in their personal situations.

Because of this certitude, the writer of this song can confidently proclaim that God will shatter his enemies and give victory to his people. In the context of this psalm the writer in v 10 specifically identifies **his king** as the one who will receive this power, who is also called **his anointed**. Interestingly, the poem that begins as Hannah's personal prayer ends with a statement about Israel's king. The poem essentially anticipates the eventual arrival of a king, and Hannah's son would play an integral role in anointing Israel's first king and establishing the political office of the monarchy in Israel's society.

FROM THE TEXT

1. Hannah's song is instructive to modern believers at various levels. First, Hannah's song is a reaction of thanksgiving and praise in light of the miraculous way God worked on her behalf. Hannah was mindful to thank God both in her actions (by presenting Samuel as an offering to God) and in her words of celebratory song. As a recipient of God's grace, Hannah did not forget to show her gratitude in her excitement over Samuel's birth, but she remembered the One to whom she owed so much. Hannah's reaction is very different from the Israelites who wandered in the desert for many years. The generation who witnessed God's miraculous power and experienced liberation from Egyptian bondage forgot what God had done for them during the intervening years between the exodus and settlement. As a result, that generation became known as ingrates and complainers who forfeited the blessings of the promised land because of their ingratitude (Ps 78). In the NT, Luke reminds the reading audience of the ten lepers who were made whole, but only one returned to worship and thank Jesus for the healing he provided (17:11-19). The Bible reinforces the notion that gratitude is a noble quality that should be evident within the life of every believer. Through gratitude, we proclaim our thankfulness to God for the way he has worked in our situations, and we acknowledge that we had to depend upon him for his help and strength. Gratitude should also be extended at a human level. It is important that we show our appreciation to friends, neighbors, family members, coworkers, members of the community of faith, and even strangers for the help, thoughtfulness, and care they displayed toward us. In doing so, we demonstrate that we did

not take their acts of kindness for granted and we affirm the significant impact they made on us.

2. The melody of Hannah is echoed in the song of Mary in the NT (Luke 1:46-55; see also commentary on 1 Sam 2:26). As both of these songs attest, God was able to work in seemingly impossible circumstances to bring about the birth of a special son. In the cases of Hannah and Mary, the child born to these mothers would have a profound role in transforming the religious situations into which they arrived. Samuel became the faithful prophet/priest/judge of the people of Israel through whom God purified the corrupted sanctuary at Shiloh. Jesus, who embodied the very being of God, humbly entered the world to purify the human race of sin and disobedience. It is significant that God did not select the most notable women to mother these significant sons, but the lowly and barren; the kind of women most people would overlook as insignificant. In the examples of Hannah and Mary, we are powerfully reminded that in terms of salvation history, God often works in paradoxes. God does not always seek out the most powerful, wealthy, or popular individuals to effect his salvific purposes in the world. Rather, he often works in and through unlikely circumstances and the unsuspecting individuals to bring his purposes to fruition.

3. In the song of Hannah we are reminded that life is subject to change and God is able to reverse the fortunes of both the feeble and the strong. As the life of Hannah illustrates, God can exalt the lowly as well as bring healing and happiness to the one experiencing pain. God can also humble the arrogant and lay low the powerful. The song of Hannah is instructive on this point, "For the Lord is a God of knowledge, and by him actions are weighed" (2:3 NRSV). God is acutely aware of the actions of humans on earth, and he dispenses his justice and mercy where appropriate. As part his plan, God has also endowed people, institutions, and nations to be agents of his justice and mercy in the world. God is at work through a variety of means to provide aid and comfort for the weak, the sorrowful, the hungry, the destitute, and the vulnerable. God also works through various organizations and institutions to make sure that those who commit injustice and exploit the pain and suffering of others are punished. In light of this, it is our calling and obligation as Christ's representatives to be instruments by which God enacts change in the lives of people and society.

C. Eli and His Sons (2:12—3:1a)

BEHIND THE TEXT

This unit centers on the activity of Eli and his sons at the Shiloh sanctuary. It is clear that the primary function of this text is to draw a sharp contrast or distinction between Eli's corrupt sons and the faithful prophet/priest Samuel. Indeed, the entire unit draws attention to this fact by referring to the sons of Eli as ***worthless sons*** (v 12a) at the very beginning of this section. The

Hebrew phrase used to describe the sons (*běnê běliyāʾal*) is very similar to the statement reiterated by Hannah in 1:16*a*, in which she implored Eli not to take her for a **worthless woman** (*bat běliyāʾal*). The wordplay on these texts is intentional and thus the writer/narrator is deliberate in creating a sharp dichotomy between the posterity of the two families. Hannah's son, Samuel, would be good and Eli's sons, Hophni and Phinehas, were wicked.

The deceitfulness of the priesthood is painfully evident in the actions of Hophni and Phinehas and those who officiated over the religious ceremonies with them at Shiloh. Not only did Eli's sons pervert and manipulate the sacrificial process for their own gain (vv 13-17), but they also engaged in sexual activity within the sanctuary's precincts (vv 22-26). The notice about the sons' sexual activity is troubling for a couple of reasons. First, the syntax employed in v 22 (the verb *šākav* + *ʾet*) is similar to other places in the OT that refer to rape (Gen 34:2, 7; 2 Sam 13:14) or other forms of sexual abuse.

Second, the type of sensual activity that took place at the sacred site also smacks of Canaanite fertility practices. It becomes apparent in this section that the Canaanization of Israel's society, beginning with the period of the judges, had even permeated the most sacred spheres of life. The narrator, at the same time, strategically alludes to Samuel's piety among these uncomplimentary reports about Eli's sons (vv 18, 21*b*; 3:1), so that the reader is consistently reminded of Samuel's goodness and faithfulness to Yahweh and the abject failure and despicability of the Eliade priesthood. The favorable allusions to Samuel, however, remind the reader that a change in the religious status quo is imminent. These intermittent reports function to provide an alternative to the picture of doom surrounding the house of Eli. Thus, Samuel, in a sense, is legitimated in the eyes of the narrator while Eli's household is soundly rejected.

The scandals and sexual impropriety of the priesthood at Shiloh were met with a harsh word of denunciation from an anonymous **man of God** (vv 27-36). The unnamed prophet delivered a scathing judgment on Eli's household, which climaxed with the announcement that Eli's family line would come to an abrupt end. From a literary and narrative standpoint, the inclusion of this section is designed to prepare the reader for the eventual downfall of Eli's priestly line. It not only provides a theological justification for the eradication of the Eliade priesthood but also prepares the way for Samuel to emerge as Israel's main prophet/priest in Israelite society.

IN THE TEXT

I. Eli's Sons in Action (2:12-26)

■ **12-21** In addition to being called worthless, the text notes that Eli's sons **did not know Yahweh** (v 12). The Hebrew term used here (*yādaʿ*) can denote intimate knowledge of an individual or even God. It is evident from their actions that Hophni and Phinehas neither knew Yahweh nor revered him.

Verses 13-17 give clear evidence of this by providing a summary statement regarding their inappropriate activity at the shrine. This section starts with a notice detailing the acceptable and/or customary **manner of the priests** (v 13) who officiated at the site. According to priestly code of conduct, when the worshipper came to the sanctuary the meat that was offered would be boiled first and then the attendant of the priests would take a **three-pronged fork** and stick it in the **pot** or the **jar** or the **caldron** in which the meat was being prepared. At that point, whatever the fork brought up would be regarded as the priest's portion to consume. This routine was considered acceptable, because it emphasized the role of the divine in determining which portion would fall to the priests ("all that the fork brought up" (v 14 NRSV), and it ensured that the fatty or premiere portions of the meat would be consumed as an offering to Yahweh first.

Eli's sons severely breached the sacred elements of this protocol, however. At Shiloh the attendant, who is unnamed in the text yet operated on behalf of Hophni and Phinehas, literally threatened the worshippers to hand over the meat. If the worshipper refused to give the meat to the attendant, he would take the meat from the worshippers' hands by force. The purloining of the sacrificial meat thus took place before the fatty and premiere portions of the animal could be completely cooked. Moreover, the priests picked the best portions of the animal for themselves to be **roasted** and not boiled. Thus, the sacrificial animal became the priests' personal meal instead of a sacrifice reserved for Yahweh.

This behavior was not only contemptible in the eyes of the people, but it disregarded acceptable practices according to priestly law (Lev 7:23-25, 31; 17:6). These actions also pointed to the fundamental avarice of the priests as they showed contempt for Yahweh's offering. It is not surprising then that the narrator points out that the actions of these young men constituted a **very great sin before the Lord** (v 17). In essence, they treated Yahweh and **Yahweh's offering with contempt.**

The scandalous actions of the priesthood are immediately juxtaposed with a favorable report about young Samuel in vv 18-21. Whereas Eli's sons despised the Lord's sacrifice, Samuel, who himself represented a living sacrifice, **ministered** faithfully before Yahweh (v 18a). The verb in v 18a, as in 2:11b, is a participle (*mĕšārēt*), which indicates ongoing or uninterrupted service to the Lord. According to the text, Samuel ministered by wearing a linen ephod along with the robe his mother brought him (v 19). The ephod represented an important part of priestly apparel. It was probably a short skirt or apron bound around the waist (Mauchline 1971, 52). Although Samuel was not the main priest at Shiloh and we do not hear of any priestly functions he carried out at this point in the narrative, his role as a priest is anticipated by the ephod he wore. Samuel would serve a priestly role later, especially as it related to his responsibility in offering sacrifices (7:9).

The favorable impression of Samuel is solidified further with the closing statement in v 21*b*, which states, **the young boy Samuel grew up in the presence of Yahweh.** The text reinforces the dichotomy between Samuel and Eli's sons through the use of a wordplay in this statement. The verb used to describe Samuel's "growing up" and maturation (*gādal*) before God (vv 21, 26) is similar to the adjective used to identify the sins of Eli's sons in v 17 (*gedōlâ*). Thus, it becomes evident that while Eli's sons moved further away from God, Samuel continued to remain close/faithful to Yahweh, even growing up in his presence. Here the reader is reminded once again of Samuel's piety in the face of ongoing priestly decadence.

■ **22-26** The favorable statement about Samuel in v 21 is immediately followed by this section that highlights the malfeasance of Eli's sons. According to the text, Hophni and Phinehas were **laying with the women who were standing at the opening of the tent of meeting** (v 22). Eli heard about his sons' actions from the reports of **all the people of Israel,** and he later condemned their escapades as evil deeds. He warned them that sins against another person could be mediated, but if they sinned against God, no other higher authority could intercede for them (Klein 1983, 26). The reference to the women who served at the site appears to recall Exod 38:8, which also alludes to women who performed menial duties at a sacred site (the tent of meeting). As mentioned above (see Behind the Text), the language and syntax used to describe the actions of Hophni and Phinehas in relationship to the women speaks to the illegitimate nature of these encounters.

The grammar of v 22 leaves open the possibility of a couple different interpretive options. First, the language may indicate that Eli's sons forced themselves upon the women, such as in the case of molestation or rape. If this is what is meant, then it underscores the wickedness of the sons and their penchant to abuse their power and position. In this case, the women would be seen as victims not only of their lustful intentions but of their "ecclesiastical" authority as well. Second, it is also possible that the noted sexual activity was associated with fertility practices and thus the women functioned more like cult prostitutes. If this meaning is intended, then it would provide evidence that the religious complexion at Shiloh took on a Canaanite appearance. Such activity is similar to that which is reported to have taken place at the time of Abijah (1 Kgs 15:12) or Josiah when cult (male) prostitutes were associated with times of worship (2 Kgs 23:7).

Although Eli chastised his own sons, the fact remained that he was old ("ninety-eight years" [4:15]), his health was failing, and it was quite apparent his sons had little regard for his authority or his warnings. It is significant that the verbs that refer to the actions of the sons in 2:12-26 are stative in aspect, which means that they denote the sons of Eli repeatedly committed these violations. Thus, their actions at the shrine did not represent one-time occurrences but established or routine behavior. Eli's denunciation of Hophni and

Phinehas therefore held little chance of reforming his sons. In light of their habitual and brazen acts, it was no surprise that even the people of Israel knew what Eli's sons were doing. This state of affairs represented a sad commentary about Eli's household as well as the religious climate at Shiloh.

In the midst of this gloomy report about the religious conditions at the time of Eli and his sons, however, the writer/narrator includes another positive statement about Samuel: **he grew in stature and in favor with Yahweh and men** (2:26). While Eli's sons were losing favor with God and the people, Samuel was gaining the support of both. The note about Samuel's piety also sounds very similar to the statement Luke made regarding Jesus when he was a young boy: "And Jesus grew in wisdom and in stature, and in favor with God and men" (2:52). Evidence for the connection between Samuel and Jesus is further strengthened after careful consideration of the details surrounding their births. In both cases, a devout Jewish woman conceived a (special) son through divine intervention (1 Sam 1:19; Luke 1:26-37). Moreover, both women sang a song of praise and thanksgiving extoling the God of Israel who is able to exalt those that are humble and humble those who are exalted (1 Sam 2:1-10; Luke 1:46-55). Such evidence indicates that one of Luke's underlying theological purposes was to emphasize Jesus' role as a prophet of God (Ehrman 2008, 132). That Luke found in Samuel a model by which to compare Jesus says something important about the status of Samuel and how he was perceived in the ancient Jewish community.

2. Condemnation of the House of Eli (2:27-36; 3:1a)

■ **27-36** On the heels of the previous two sections a **man of God** came to Eli personally. The term **man of God** is one that is essentially synonymous with "prophet" (2 Kgs 1:9). Many scholars are in agreement that this announcement is either the work of the Deuteronomistic editor(s) or it could even be a post-Deuteronomistic insertion into the text. There are a couple of reasons for this opinion. First, the anonymous man of God is often understood to be the mouthpiece of the Deuteronomistic Historian (Gordon 1986, 84). Second, the prophet's message speaks of events that were fulfilled considerably later in Israel's history, particularly at the time of the Davidic monarchy. The contents of his address specifically anticipate the establishment of the Zadokite priesthood during the united monarchy (see below).

The message of the man of God is couched in typical prophetic speech form. The address proper begins in v 27 with the standard message formula, **thus says Yahweh,** and continues by recalling God's action in selecting Eli's ancestral **household** to be priests who would **go up to my altar, to burn incense, and to wear the ephod** (v 28). According to this prophet, God had selected one household to perform these priestly functions from the exodus/wilderness period. Ironically, the text never records the occasion when God selected Eli's ancestors for this task. Most likely, the household alluded to in v 28 either refers to the Levites (Deut 33:8-11) or to the Aaronite priesthood (Lev 8:12, 30). How Eli's family became associated with the prophet's statement remains unclear.

The man of God continued his address by levying specific charges against Eli and his sons: (1) they looked with a "greedy" (NRSV) eye at the Lord's sacrifices and offerings, and (2) Eli honored his sons more than God by taking the choicest parts of the offerings from the people of Israel. Unlike vv 12-17, which only indicted Hophni and Phinehas for participating in sacrificial abuse, v 29 extends the indictment so that Eli is included with his sons. After the man of God specified the charges against Eli and his sons (vv 27-29), he then pronounced a judgment oracle (vv 30-36) that detailed the punishment for their sin. In terms of their punishment, the man of God emphasized two things: first, Eli's household would be cut off (i.e., destroyed) with only one member of his family allowed to survive; and second, God would establish "a faithful priest" and "build him a sure house" (v 35 NRSV). This priest would replace Eli's household, and, according to the man of God, would do that which is in accordance with God's heart and God's soul. He would also **walk before the Lord's anointed for all times.**

It is tempting at first to believe that Samuel fulfilled the words of the prophet, especially in v 35. Samuel is called a "faithful" (*ne'ĕmān*) prophet in 3:20, which is similar to the term used in v 35 for the **faithful** (*ne'ĕmān*) priest and the "sure" (*ne'ĕmān*) house that was promised. Moreover, Samuel also played a crucial role in anointing Israel's first kings: Saul (9:16; 10:1) and David (16:13). As enticing as it may seem, the distinction between the "priest" (2:35) and the "prophet" (3:20) cannot be overlooked. In addition, the judgment oracle of the man of God came to fruition at two distinct periods in Israel's history: first in Eli's lifetime and then in the days of David and Solomon. The decimation of Eli's house occurred when Hophni, Phinehas, and Eli died when the ark was captured in battle (4:17-18) and again when Saul massacred the priests of Nob (1 Sam 22:11-23). The one priest who survived the massacre, Abiathar, became one of David's main priests. Solomon, however, expelled Abiathar to the town of Anathoth (1 Kgs 2:26-27), which allowed the Zadokite priesthood to become the dominant priestly family in Jerusalem. Thus, at the time of Solomon, the Zadokite line replaced the line of priests descending from the house of Eli. The former became the faithful house who ministered before the king in Jerusalem, and the descendants of Zadok served as the main priests at the Jerusalem temple until the destruction of the city in 586 B.C.

■ **3:1a** As in the previous sections, an unfavorable report about Eli's household is followed by a positive statement regarding Samuel: **and the young man Samuel served Yahweh in the presence of Eli.** The verb, as in 2:11 and 18, is a participle thus denoting Samuel's continuous, faithful service to Yahweh at the sanctuary.

The constant comparison/contrast with Eli's sons and Samuel helps to organize and bind this unit together from a literary standpoint. By structuring the material in this manner, the unit contains an element of symmetry so that the three negative statements about Eli's sons are counterbalanced by three positive remarks concerning Samuel.

1*a*. Eli's Sons: manipulated the sacrificial process (2:12-17)

1*b*. Samuel: grew in the presence of Yahweh (2:21*b*)

2*a*. Eli's sons: had sex with/raped the women at the shrine (2:22-25)

2*b*. Samuel: grew in favor with God and men (2:26)

3*a*. Eli's sons: would die by the sword (2:27-36)

3*b*. Samuel: ministered before Yahweh in the presence of Eli (3:1*a*)

An examination of the text indicates that as this textual unit comes to a close, the reader or audience anticipates the coming prophetic/priestly role of Samuel at the sanctuary. Samuel, who has been consistently faithful to God and Eli, would also be the faithful prophet/priest of the people of Israel.

FROM THE TEXT

In this unit we see an important message about the direct relationship between the quality of religious leadership and the effectiveness of the ministry of religious institutions. Throughout chs 1—3, the text indicates that the religious leadership at Shiloh left much to be desired. The descriptions of Eli as a father and priest indicate he was ineffective, and his sons did not honor God. Yet, these were the people who were serving as God's ministers to the people. The story of Eli and his sons powerfully reminds us that just because a person works in ministry, it does not ensure that the individual walks closely with God or is sensitive to the people who come to worship. Even though Eli, for example, served as the priest at Shiloh he still could not perceive the actions of a hurting individual who was praying before God.

In the story of Eli and his sons, even the laity appeared to be more pious than the leadership. When quality leadership is lacking in a community of faith, the people "in the pews" can spot the deficiency. Moreover, if godly leadership is lacking, there can be much activity that takes place at a sacred site, yet God's presence is absent. In the case of Shiloh, all kinds of religious activity was going on; however, the "word of [God] was rare" there (3:1*b*). In religious parlance, that is the same as saying the church was dead. However, when a genuine and pious leader such as Samuel arrived on the scene, the conditions at the sanctuary changed dramatically. The word of God, which was rare under Eli, appeared again to Samuel and to the people. Moreover, the people knew that Samuel was a true prophet who led them into the proper worship of God. Thus we learn that when God's people are in the right places of leadership, the community of faith has the potential to come alive and flourish.

D. Samuel's Dream Theophany (3:1b—4:1a)

BEHIND THE TEXT

This unit is often titled "Samuel's calling" by various commentators (Ackroyd 1971, 41; Tsumura 2007, 171-72). However, the tradition regarding Samuel in this text does not fit the standard criteria of a typical call narrative. For instance, there is no formal commissioning of Samuel for service, and it lacks an expression of unworthiness common to others called to a specific task (i.e., Moses [Exod 3—4], Jeremiah [1], Isaiah [6]). One commentator has suggested, however, that this text has less to do with calling Samuel as a prophet than with inaugurating him as a prophet through whom Yahweh mediated his word (Birch 1998, 992). It is probably more appropriate to label the experience Samuel had at Shiloh as a "dream theophany" (Gnuse 1978, 379-90). The dream Samuel experienced basically legitimized him as the only source of God's word at Shiloh. It was through Samuel that God would direct his message to the house of Eli and the Israelite people.

Although the contents of the theophany in 1 Sam 3:11-14 presuppose the message of the man of God from the previous chapter (2:27-36) and they reaffirm Yahweh's commitment to stand by that word (3:12-13), God's message to Samuel never mentions anything about a survivor among Eli's household nor does it include information about the prophet who would replace Eli. It does, however, reiterate that Eli's house would come to an abrupt end. Samuel was chosen by God to inform Eli of the word that was revealed to him. In this transitional period, however, Samuel had not learned how to distinguish the voice of God. Ironically, Samuel needed Eli's help in both recognizing God's voice and learning how to respond to it. Thus, Samuel learned to communicate with God from the person he would eventually replace. Significantly, it would be through Samuel, and not Eli, that the word of Yahweh would return to the people of Israel (3:1b).

IN THE TEXT

I. The Religious Situation at Shiloh (3:1b-3)

■ **1b-3** The previous unit ended with the note that Samuel served God before Eli (3:1a). This section opens with the profound statement: *And the word of Yahweh was rare in those days and visions had not gone out* (v 1b). As before, the narrator makes a clear contrast between the faithful servant, Samuel, and the deteriorating priesthood and religious conditions at Shiloh. The notion that Yahweh's word had not been communicated or that visions had not been seen indicates that although all the accoutrements of worship (i.e., priests, sacrifices, sanctuary) existed at Shiloh, the visible expression of God's presence remained distant and infrequent. God's word was **rare** or "precious" at this time, thus insinuating that God had not been communicating to or through the religious personnel at the sanctuary.

Adding to this unfavorable report on the religious situation at Shiloh is the physical description of Eli himself: **his eyes were failing and he was unable to see** (v 2). The notice about Eli's failing health also functions as a critique of his ineffectiveness as a priest. The report about Eli's diminishing sight in v 2 functions like a metaphor indicating his inability to perceive God's word, because he lived in darkness (Alter 1999, 16). The reference to Eli's sight is especially pertinent in the context of Samuel's "dream theophany," which took place at nighttime. Eli could not see in the darkness even though the lamp of God was still burning (Exod 27:20-21). Likewise, he could not "see" or "recognize" at first that God was talking to Samuel during the night. Eli only perceived that God was communicating with Samuel after the lad repeatedly interrupted the tired priest.

The location where Eli and Samuel slept at the time of the theophany is also symbolic. Eli was in his own room and separated from the ark. Samuel was **lying down in the temple . . . , where the ark of God was** (v 3). Based on this description, Samuel must have slept in the inner sanctuary where the ark resided. It is noteworthy that Samuel, the prophet/priest designate, remained near the presence of God, which was symbolized by the ark of the covenant. Eli, the soon to be deposed priest, slept at a distance from it. The imagery is fitting considering that Yahweh's presence no longer abided with Eli as it was with Samuel. This is also the first, albeit brief, reference to the ark in Samuel. Outside of v 3 and the Ark Narrative (chs 4—6), the ark does not play a significant role throughout the remainder of 1 Samuel. Although the text makes a point to link Samuel with the ark in v 3, he never appears with it again. The writer/narrator probably made a point to include the ark in this chapter because it had important implications for Samuel's dream theophany.

2. Yahweh's Word to Samuel (3:4-9)

■ **4-9** The dream theophany in vv 4-9 is built around Yahweh's repeated calling out to Samuel. Verse 4 notes that **Yahweh called to Samuel** and Samuel responded by running to Eli with the reply, **Here am I, for you called for me** (v 5). Although Samuel did not recognize God's voice and mistakenly went to Eli instead, his response (**here am I**) is telling, because it indicated the spirit of a willing servant. The phrase **here am I** is typical of a servant responding to God's invitation to service or testing in the OT (Gen 22:1; Isa 6:8).

Eli's response to Samuel, however, **I did not call you, return and lay down** (v 5), is made up of two commands and thereby suggests Eli was somewhat perturbed that Samuel had awoken him from his slumber. Like an obedient servant, though, Samuel **returned and lay down.** Yahweh called to Samuel a second time in v 6, but on this occasion Samuel arose and **walked** to Eli instead. Samuel may have feared a harsh response from the old priest or maybe he was unsure or insecure about what was transpiring. As on the first occasion, Samuel responded with the phrase **here am I, for you called me** (v 6). This time Eli called Samuel **my son,** a term of endearment (or puzzlement?), possibly to calm or reassure Samuel. However, the commands Eli reiterated to Samuel earlier remained the same, **return and lie down.** Yahweh called a third time and Samuel returned to Eli with the typical servant response. On this occasion, though, Eli finally perceived (v 8) that it was Yahweh who called Samuel. The text provides the explanation for Samuel's ignorance: **Samuel did not yet know Yahweh** (v 7*a*), **for his** word . . . **had not yet been revealed to him** (v 7*b*). These statements indicate that the writer/narrator was sympathetic to Samuel's naïveté and thus "overlooked" his lack of understanding in this matter. Eli, on the other hand, did not have an excuse. The fact that it took him three times to realize that it was God who was speaking to Samuel insinuated that it had been a long time since he had heard the voice of God (v 1*b*). When Eli finally recognized his error, he instructed Samuel to say the following words when heard the voice again: **speak** . . . **for your servant is listening** (v 9). It took time, but Eli finally provided the information that would put Samuel in the proper position to hear God's message.

3. Yahweh's Message to Samuel (3:10-21; 4:1*a*)

■ **10-18** When God called again (v 10) Samuel responded in the manner that Eli had instructed. Eli's instructions proved to be correct, because when Samuel recited the words Eli provided (v 9) Yahweh began to speak directly to Samuel. Yahweh specifically conveyed a message about Eli's family. Yahweh reaffirmed that what had been spoken in reference to Eli's household earlier (2:27-36) would come to pass in full, **from beginning to end** (3:12). Unlike the message from the man of God in 2:27-36, Yahweh indicted Eli specifically and made him personally responsible for the failure of his household to fulfill its priestly responsibilities. God stated (3:13) that Eli knew that his sons **blasphemed** him yet he did not **rebuke them.** For his failure to reprove Hophni and Phinehas, Eli's household would be punished forever. The fatalism of this message is captured by the notice that no sacrifice or offering would be able to expiate their sin. Their fate had been sealed, and Eli's warnings to his sons earlier (2:25) became prophetic.

Upon the conclusion of God's message, Samuel was afraid to report to Eli what he heard, thus he "lay there until morning" (3:15 JPS). Eli, however, wanted to know what God had told Samuel and basically threatened him ("may God do so to you and more" [NRSV]) if he withheld the information. Samuel obediently reported to him everything God had said; he *did not hide anything from him.* When Samuel relayed to Eli what God had spoken, Eli responded with the words: *Yahweh will do what is good in his eyes* (v 18). What else could Eli say in response to Samuel's message? Yahweh had spoken and the old priest resigned himself to the fact that God's word would be accomplished, even if it meant the destruction of his household. Eli's response to Samuel's message is significant, however, because he essentially acknowledged Samuel's status as a prophet. Samuel was no longer a prophet in training, for God had now directly spoken to him.

This chapter marks an important milestone in the life and development of Samuel. Not only had Samuel encountered God in a dream theophany, but God also assigned Samuel his first task (test?) as a newly appointed prophet. By all accounts Samuel passed his first test successfully. First, he did not distort or alter the message he received from God. He carefully and accurately mediated God's word to Eli. Second, he faithfully delivered the judgment oracle to Eli, the one who would be on the receiving end of that word. Samuel did not run from this responsibility, even though it meant he had to confront the man who reared him. This could not have been an easy task, since Eli was like a father figure to him. Third, Samuel also obeyed Eli and his orders by revealing to him everything God had spoken. Thus, Samuel proved his faithfulness on two fronts: one, by listening to and conveying God's message to Eli, and two, by continuing to respect and obey Eli.

■ **3:19—4:1a** This unit closes out with another favorable statement regarding Samuel: **Yahweh was with him . . . All Israel knew, from Dan to Beersheba, that Samuel was a true prophet to Yahweh** (vv 19-20). Here again, Samuel, the faithful prophet/priest, is compared/contrasted with Eli's sons. Whereas all the people of Israel knew the wicked actions of Hophni and Phinehas (2:22), all of Israel, **from Dan to Beersheba** (i.e., the entire country), knew that Samuel was a true prophet of Yahweh (3:20). The evidence of Samuel's faithful devotion to God is also witnessed in the changed conditions at Shiloh: **Yahweh continued to appear at Shiloh for Yahweh revealed himself to Samuel at Shiloh by the word** (v 21). With Samuel as the religious leader at the sanctuary, God's word returned to the people. The syntax implies that as long as Samuel remained the main prophet/priest, God continued (*vayōseph*) to make himself known there. This marks a dramatic change from what the religious conditions were like when Eli and his sons ran things at Shiloh. The text implies that with Samuel at the helm, the sanctuary at Shiloh was in good hands.

FROM THE TEXT

The narrative about Samuel in this section highlights the essential qualities of a godly leader. Not only did Samuel enjoy an intimate relationship with God by which he could hear and discern his voice, but he also faithfully delivered the message that God conveyed to him. Samuel carried out the task for which he was assigned, even though it was a difficult one for him personally. It was not an easy task to tell the man who was his mentor, and a father figure to him, that God was going to bring destruction on his family. It had to be especially painful for Samuel to bring this hard message to the man who reared him since he was little. Yet, Samuel obeyed the voice of God and Eli by relaying God's word to him.

Samuel's example helps us realize that a godly leader stays true to the mission that God has assigned. The prophet Jeremiah, for example, had to preach an unpopular message to the people of Judah during the waning days of the kingdom. Even though he faced persecution and severe resistance, and he experienced personal heartache and frustration as a result, he nevertheless fulfilled God's call as a prophet to the people of Judah. We are reminded that as a leader whether in the church or in industry, there will be occasions when the desire to be popular and well-liked will tempt us to avoid confrontation or stand firm in the face of antagonism. Being a leader means that an individual has to make hard choices, confront wrongdoing, choose a course of action with which not everyone agrees, face ridicule or slander, experience loneliness or abandonment, encounter moments of doubt or insecurity, convey a hard word, and even be misunderstood. It is in times like these that our commitment to the position in which God placed us or the cause God has entrusted us with can be sorely tested. The good and faithful leader, however, seeks above all to please God and gain his approval by staying true to the mission, rather than striving for convenience and the approval of others.

E. The Capture of the Ark of the Covenant (4:1b—7:1)

BEHIND THE TEXT

First Samuel 4:1b—7:1 is entirely devoted to the subject of the ark of the covenant. Chapter 4 recounts the story of how the Philistines captured the ark in battle and brought it back to their home territory. Chapter 5 records the plight of the Philistines as the ark resided among their community. Chapter 6 covers the ark's return to Israelite territory.

According to the canonical arrangement of the text, this unit directly follows 4:1a and ends at 7:1. This arrangement, however, raises interesting and important questions about the compositional history of this material. After the statement in 4:1a (NRSV), "And the word of Samuel came to all Israel," Samuel, who figured so prominently in chs 1—3, essentially disappears from the narrative and does not return until 7:3 with the phrase, "then Samuel said to all the house of Israel" (NRSV). The glaring absence of Samuel between these two reference points has caused many scholars to conclude that this material constituted an independent tradition that was later joined with the Samuel traditions during the book's editorial process (Miller and Roberts 1977).

Because there are so many references to the ark in this unit (thirty-seven in the NRSV) it has become common in scholarly circles to refer to this material as the Ark Narrative. The ark traditions, which are primarily located in chs

4—6, also appear in 2 Sam 6. Scholars have placed the composition of this tradition at the time of David and Solomon in order to legitimize the Davidic monarchy (see also Introduction and Behind the Text for 2 Sam 6:1-23).

While many scholars have posited that the Ark Narrative originally existed as an independent tradition, a number of other commentators have tried to see the unity of these texts based upon its literary and contextual relationship within the overall structure of 1 Sam 1—8. Hamilton, for example, questions whether the absence of Samuel in the ark traditions has more theological significance than compositional significance. He notes, "The absence and silence of Samuel point to Israel's neglect of prophetic ministry at this critical time in their history, what with both the priesthood corrupting and the Philistines threatening to make themselves permanent rulers of Palestine" (2004, 224). He adds that when the Israelites are pressed by the Philistines, they send for the ark but not for Samuel.

In a similar manner, Willis has also shown that chs 1—7 have a natural flow to them (1) one, Yahweh prepares a man to lead Israel through a crisis (1 Sam 1:1-4*a*); (2) the crisis is described with the Philistines in detail (1 Sam 4:1*b*—7:1); and (3) the successful manner in which that man guides Israel through the crisis (1 Sam 7:2-17) (1971, 298).

An examination of the final form of the text (what scholars refer to as synchronic analysis) also indicates that the ark traditions connect well with the Samuel traditions on a thematic basis. In chs 2—3 Yahweh pronounced through the man of God and Samuel's theophany that Eli's sons would die and that his priestly house would come to an end. The Ark Narratives fulfill this function in that they provide the information as to how Hophni and Phinehas, along with Eli, met their ultimate destruction. It is only after the Ark Narrative that Samuel emerges as the primary religious figure in Israelite society and the one who will anoint the first king. Thus, the ark traditions do serve as a fitting link between chs 1—3 and 7 ff.

I. The Setting of the Ark's Capture (4:1*b*-4)

■ **1*b*-4** The text moves abruptly after 4:1*a* to report that the Israelites had gathered to meet the Philistines in battle (v 1*b*). Although no official reason is cited for the cause of this conflict, historical and archaeological research suggests that the Philistines presented a growing political and military threat to the Israelites, beginning in the thirteenth century B.C. and continuing into the period of the judges (Mazar 1992, 308-28; see esp. Judg 13—16). In preparing to fight the battle, the Israelite armies encamped at a place named **Ebenezer,** which is literally translated "the stone of help." This site lay about two miles east of **Aphek,** where the Philistines had situated their troops. Both of these sites lay at the southern end of Plain of Sharon, to the west of the hill country of Ephraim. Aphek had strategic value because it guarded an important trade route from the coastal plain into the hill country.

As the battle between the Philistines and Israelites ensued, the Israelite army suffered a terrible setback. The text records that **four thousand** Israelites had been struck down in battle. When the defeated armies returned to the camp at Ebenezer the elders of the community inquired about the defeat (v 3 NRSV): "Why has [Yahweh] put us to rout today before the Philistines?" Ironically, even though the Israelites camped at a place titled "stone of help," Yahweh provided little assistance in their battle against the Philistines. The elders' question in light of this defeat is also significant, for it presupposed Yahweh's active involvement in the humiliation of Israel's troops. Although no answer to their question is provided in these verses, the clear implication from this rhetorical question is that the reason Israel lost was due to the ark's absence on the battlefield (Klein 1983, 41).

The obvious solution to this problem therefore could be found in retrieving the ark and bringing it into battle with them. The elders prescribed this very course of action: ***let us take the ark of the covenant of the Lord from Shiloh and let it come into our midst, then it will save us from our enemies*** (v 3). The request to fetch the ark in order to bring military success, however, reveals something of the people's attitude toward it: it was seen as a guarantee of survival and victory. In essence, the ark was no more than a good luck charm or a talisman and, as a result, the Israelites turned what God intended to be a symbol into an idol (Hamilton 2004, 224). The grammar of v 3*b* (lit., ***it will save us***) shows that the Israelites had placed their trust in the object rather than in God.

2. The Capture of the Ark (4:5-11)

■ **5-11** When the ark was brought into the camp, the Israelites responded with a great shout or war cry, which was typical of holy war contests (Josh 6:5; Judg 7:20; 1 Sam 17:20, 52; 2 Chr 20:21-22). This shout was so loud the text notes (with hyperbole) that "the earth resounded" (v 5 NRSV). The latter term (*hûm*) connotes "excitement." It can be used as a personal reference (1 Kgs 1:45; Ruth 1:19) or to the land of Israel (i.e., "the land was agog with excitement," Mauchline 1971, 70). The picture of the earth brought into a state of commotion is used in Psalms, for example to express awe created by God's advent (97:3-5; Ackroyd 1971, 49).

As a result of the Israelites' loud roar, the Philistines realized that the ark of God had come into the camp. The presence of the ark also struck fear into the hearts of the Philistines, because they realized that God was in Israel's midst. The Philistines were apprehensive because they had heard of the reports about how God had struck the Egyptians with plagues and pestilence (Exod 7—12). When the Philistines made reference to the Egypt traditions, they talked about God in the plural: ***who can save us from the power of these mighty gods, these gods who smote the Egyptians with every kind of plague*** (v 8).

Two important questions arise in response to the Philistines' statement. One, how did the Philistines come to hear about the plague traditions in Egypt? Was the report of God's dealings with the Egyptians and Israel's enemies in the wilderness common knowledge among people living in that region of the world? It is possible that God's reputation had preceded him in much the same way that Rahab knew of God's great power when the spies entered Canaan (Josh 2:10). Second, why did the Philistines refer to Israel's God as "gods"? The Philistines mistakenly took the Israelites as polytheists. Had the Israelites' example of worshipping Canaanite fertility deities in the land of Canaan led them to this conclusion? Or, was God's demonstration of power in Egypt so terrorizing that it appeared many deities fought on behalf of the Israelites? Although the text raises interesting questions at these points, answers are not forthcoming.

The Philistines' initial response to the arrival of the ark was one of defeatism: ***Woe is us.*** Their reaction indicated they believed they were in peril. Even though the Philistines exhibited fear at the prospects of facing the Israelites and their god(s), the command to ***strengthen themselves*** (v 9) and fight like men was given. The Philistines braced themselves for battle because they did not want to become servants to **the Hebrews.**

The Philistines' use of the term **Hebrews** is the first instance where this occurs in Samuel. The term is generally a pejorative one. Many scholars take it to refer to an outlaw class of people called *apiru* known throughout ancient Egypt and Canaan. They were understood to be a nomadic people who lived near cities who sometimes tried to take hold of lands. They were outcasts who formed social groups of people who had abandoned urban life, including, but not exclusive to: slaves, debtors, fugitives from lawsuits, the generally disaffected and mercenary military retainers (Mendenhall 1973; Tsumura 2007, 193).

The Philistines' fear of serving the Hebrews trumped their fear of the God they worshipped. Thus, the command to go to battle was followed and the Philistines again struck "a very great slaughter" (NRSV) upon the Israelites, killing **thirty thousand** men on this occasion and sending the others ***to their tents*** (v 10). Although the ark accompanied the Israelites into battle, the slaughter turned out to be worse in the second round of battle. Not only did the Philistines defeat the Israelites, but they captured the ark and killed Hophni and Phinehas, the sons of Eli, in the process (v 11). Yahweh's word regarding Eli's sons had been fulfilled in the battle with the Philistines, but Yahweh's honor and reputation had also suffered a great setback with the ark's capture.

3. Report of the Capture of the Ark (4:12-18)

■ **12-17** In the aftermath of the battle, a messenger from the tribe of Benjamin with torn cloths and dirt on his head came to Shiloh in order to report the results of the battle. Although some scholars have identified the messenger with Saul (who was also a Benjamite), no conclusive evidence supports this notion. Eli anxiously sat on his chair by the road into the city, because he worried (lit., "his heart trembled" [NRSV], *ḥārēd*) over the status of the ark of the covenant (v 13). It is interesting that Eli was more concerned about the ark than the welfare of his owns sons. Maybe his sons were already dead to him personally.

Because Eli was old, he could not see the messenger come into the city. Eli could hear, however, the great cry of the people when they learned that the ark had been lost in battle. Losing the ark was a terrible blow, and the word that is used here to describe the outcry of the people in v 13 (*zāʿaq*) is a typical response for those experiencing severe agony or oppression. This language is particularly reminiscent from the time of the judges (Judg 3:9, 15; 4:3; 6:7; 10:10) and the period of Egyptian bondage when Israel suffered mistreatment at the hands of foreigners (Exod 3:7). When Eli heard the commotion, he inquired about the cause of the outcry. The messenger told him about Israel's defeat, the death of his sons, and the capture of the ark. When Eli heard about the capture of the ark, not of his sons' death, he fell backward from his chair, broke his neck, and died. The word of God against Eli and his sons had come to fruition with the defeat of Israel's armies and the capture of the ark.

One has to wonder, however, if Yahweh had a greater purpose in mind than Israel's military success or the protection of his own reputation. Was God more concerned about cleansing the priesthood and preparing the way for Samuel to become the main priest at Shiloh than Israel's security? Although this question is not answered yet, as the narrative continues forward the answer appears to be in the affirmative.

■ **18** With the death of Eli, the narrator makes two last comments about the priest: he was **old and heavy** and **he judged Israel for 40 years.** In the final remarks of this unit, we cannot overlook the fact that the writer/narrator takes one last jab at Eli before he passes on. The word used to describe Eli's weight or heaviness (*kābēd*) is also related to the word that is translated "honor" or "glory." The use of this word directly recalls the indictment of the man of God in 2:29 who accused Eli of "honoring" his sons more than God by taking the choicest part of the sacrifice. The writer/narrator thus links Eli's weight with his own misdeeds, indicating he got fat on the portions of the offerings that were reserved for Yahweh (2:29). It is unclear why the writer/narrator of this text incorporates Eli into the succession of judges who ruled Israel between Joshua and Saul (Judg 10:2-3; 12:7, 9, 11, 14; 16:31; 1 Sam 7:6). Eli primarily functioned as a priest, and it is quite obvious from the text that he did not "rescue" the Israelites from Philistine aggression. It may be that the writer/narrator included the time element to support the chronological framework that he used to organize and structure Israel's history (Noth 1991, 39-40).

4. The Report of a Child's Birth (4:19-22)

■ **19-22** In the wake of Eli's death, ch 4 ends with the birth report of Eli's grandson. The shocking news of the ark's capture and the report of her husband and father-in-law's deaths sent the pregnant wife of Phinehas into labor. The woman, who is only known as Eli's daughter-in-law and Phinehas's wife, crouched while giving birth to the child, a scene reminiscent of the Israelite women giving birth on stools in Egypt (Exod 1:16). In the midst of her agony, a son was born, but when she was given the news of his birth she remained silent. The only words she could utter when naming the boy was **Ichabod** (v 21), which in Hebrew is translated "where is the glory?" This birth account is similar to the birth of Ben-Oni, later named Benjamin, whose name signified Rebekah's struggle during childbirth (Gen 35:17-18). The boy's name is appropriate, for it symbolized the fact that the glory of Yahweh disappeared from Israel when the Philistines had taken the ark in battle (1 Sam 4:22). God's glory did not depart from Israel when Eli or his sons had died. The loss of the ark also implied the (temporary) defeat of Yahweh at the hands of the Philistines.

5. The Ark Is Taken into Captivity by the Philistines (5:1-12)

■ **1-5** After the defeat of the Israelite armies, the Philistines transported the ark to their home territory. The Philistines first brought the ark to the ancient city of **Ashdod** and set it in their temple next to the image of their chief god, **Dagon** (v 2). Dagon was an ancient fertility deity attested at the cities of Ebla, Mari, and Ugarit. In Ugaritic literature Dagon was known as the father of Baal, and his name is linked linguistically to Northwest Semitic words for grain, cloud, or rain. In addition to Ashdod, the Philistines had built a temple for Dagon at Gaza (Judg 16:23) while other Israelite towns appear to have had affiliations with this god as well (Josh 15:41; 19:27).

In placing the ark next to the image of Dagon, the Philistines appear to have made a couple of important statements: one, they honored Yahweh for abandoning his people; two, they acknowledged the power and superiority of their own god (Miller and Roberts 1977). However, when the Ashdodites returned to the temple in the morning, they realized that Dagon lay prostrate before the ark. The symbolism of this image is significant. In lying prostrate before the ark, Dagon, in essence, honored Yahweh, the God of Israel, and recognized the superiority of Yahweh's power over his own. The language employed in v 4a (**Dagon had fallen with his face to the ground before the ark of Yahweh**) intimates subservience before a superior presence. In essence, Dagon's prostration before the ark amounted to an act of worship.

The Philistines returned the image to its former place, apparently thinking that the idol had somehow mistakenly fallen. Their great surprise came, however, on the following morning when they returned to the temple and saw that the idol lay prostrate on its face before the ark a second time. In addition, Dagon's head and the palms of his two hands had been cut off and were lying on the threshold of the temple (v 4). The only thing that remained intact was the "torso" or "stump" of Dagon (based on a reading from the LXX). The fact that this event repeated itself on two occasions indicated this was no mere accident. Instead, the ark, which represented the presence of Yahweh, contained a divine power superior to the Philistine god Dagon. The scene of Dagon lying prostrate before Yahweh without his head and hands continued to be remembered in tradition as an etiology. That is to say, it provided a rationale as to why the priests of Dagon and or anyone else entering the temple would not step on the threshold (v 5).

■ **6-12** The hand of Yahweh was also heavy upon the people of Ashdod and it devastated them. According to v 6, Yahweh struck Ashdod and its environs with **tumors.** The word for "tumors" in Hebrew (*baʾepōlîm*) is difficult to translate. Some scholars have taken it to refer to swelling of the lymph glands, especially in the armpit or groin, which was characteristic of the bubonic plague. Others have taken this word to mean boils or abscesses at the anus. The Masoretic scribes responsible for the Hebrew text have retained a reading that can also be translated as "hemorrhoids." However we define the calamity the Philistines experienced, it was terribly unpleasant and humiliating (although if they were hemorrhoids, it would have been humorous to an Israelite audience), and the men of the city were afraid at the terrifying display of Yahweh's power. The men of the city also said that the ark of God could not stay with them. Assembling the other Philistine lords together, they inquired what they should do with the ark.

The leaders of **Gath,** another important Philistine city, suggested that the ark be brought to their city (v 8). However, when the ark was transported to Gath, Yahweh's hand was heavy on the people there, and the citizens of Gath were afflicted with the same plague/tumors. The ark was then sent to the Philistine city of **Ekron,** and when it was brought to the city the Ekronites (v 10) cried out saying, **Why did you bring the ark of the God of Israel to me in order to kill me and my people?** The response of the people of Ekron indicates that they did not request the sacred object, for they were aware of its devastating power. As a result, the Philistine leaders were gathered with the instruction to send the ark back to its original place, because it had caused a deathly panic among the people. Like the other Philistine cities where God's hand was heavy on the people, the citizens of Ekron were stricken with the plague/tumors. The text notes that the cry (*šavʿat*) of the city even reached heavenward (v 12).

It becomes clear in reading this chapter that Yahweh smote the Philistines and their cities on three specific occasions. As a result, the Philistines, not the Israelites, cried out because they were under the control of a foreign power. This scenario represents a dramatic reversal from the cycle of oppression in Judges, for example, where the Israelites cried out to God because they had been defeated by their enemies. The Philistines may have captured the ark, but they did not capture Yahweh. Yahweh demonstrated his dominance over the Philistine god Dagon, in much the same way that Yahweh showed his superiority over the Egyptian gods/goddesses of Egypt in the plague narratives of Exodus (chs 7—12). Yahweh's ability to humble the Philistines (as well as Israel's other enemies) would also be an important reason to critique the people's request for a king later. God's ability to deliver Israel repeatedly from her enemies in the past made the people's demand for a king that much more objectionable (12:1-19).

6. The Philistines Prepare to Move the Ark (6:1-9)

■ **1** Not sure what to do with the Israelites' cult object, the ark basically sat in a field, away from any population centers for **seven months.** The number seven is significant, because it implies that the suffering of the Philistines had reached the maximum limit (Tsumura 2007, 213).

■ **2** During this time, the Philistines gathered their **priests** and **diviners** for solutions as to how they should **send it back to its place.** The reference to **its place** is unclear. Does it refer to Israel in general or to the Shiloh sanctuary specifically? Since the ark eventually returned to Beth Shemesh (vv 11 ff.), the former may be insinuated.

■ **3** The Philistine priests and diviners provided a solution in that they warned the people not to send it back empty. Rather, they instructed the Philistines to return the ark in a manner that recognized their own guilt in capturing it in the first place. Thus, the return of the ark in this case would function as a type of reparation offering. The Philistines believed that by sending the ark home they would be healed and receive forgiveness for their actions. The term for **return** (*shûv*) in vv 3-4, 8, and 17 is in the causative stem in Hebrew where it is also used in conjunction with the word for guilt offering (*'āshām*). Because of the syntactical construction, the text could be read as "return, restore, or to make restitution" (as in Num 5:7-8; 18:9). The grammar indicates, therefore, that the Philistines were intent on making restitution for taking the ark from the Israelites.

■ **4-6** The reparation offering itself consisted of *five golden tumors* as well as *five golden mice* (v 4). The number five is significant because there were five Philistine lords who ruled over the five major Philistines cities (also known as the Pentapolis). The golden tumors, representing the plague, were intended to rid the land of contamination, and the five mice represented the carriers of the plague that hounded the people. This gesture would be understood as giving **glory** to the God of Israel (v 5) and the priests warned them not to **harden** their hearts and refuse to recognize Yahweh as the Egyptians had done in the past (v 6). In vv 5-6 a pun is employed to emphasize this instruction by indicating that forgiveness would come about by giving "glory" (*kābōd*) to

God and not "hardening" (*tekabdō*) their hearts. This language directly recalls the stubbornness of Pharaoh's heart when he refused to let the Israelites leave Egypt (Exod 7:3, 13; 8:15, 32). As a result of his obstinacy, the Egyptians endured terrible consequences by the hand of God. The same fate awaited the Philistines if they followed his example.

Verses 5-6 also tie in with the statements in 5:6 where Yahweh's hand was "heavy" (*vatikbad*), and 5:11 where the hand of God was "very heavy" (*kabdâ mĕʾōd*). The heaviness of God's hand on the Philistines brought them to the place where they were ready in 6:5 to give "glory" (*kābōd*) to God.

■ **7-9** These verses supplement the Philistines' question (v 2) about how they should send the ark back to Israel. In addition to the golden tumors and mice, the officials commanded the people to **get a new cart** and "two milch cows" (JPS, NRSV) that had not borne a yoke (v 7). The fact that both the cart and cows had not been put to secular use indicated that they qualified for the ritual task. According to the instructions given, the milch cows would pull the cart that contained the ark, and the golden items would be placed in a separate box or bag next to the ark. The Philistines took great pains not to offend Yahweh. The Philistines then sent the ark off and "let it go its way" (v 8 NRSV).

The purpose of this ritual, which was based on divination, was to determine if the plagues had come by the hand of Yahweh or if they had happened by coincidence. In the minds of the leaders, if the cows took the ark straight to the territory of Israel (i.e., Beth Shemesh), then the Philistines would know that Yahweh had brought the plagues upon their people and their land. The Philistines ensured the accuracy of this test by making the trial more severe in that they used animals not accustomed to pulling a cart. In addition, they sent the calves of the milch cows away from them so as not to distract them (v 7). All of these careful preparations ensured that the divination they engaged in would accurately determine the source of the plagues.

7. The Ark Returns to Beth Shemesh (6:10—7:1)

■ **10-18** The Philistines did as they were commanded. They connected the two milch cows to the cart, placed the ark and the box/bag of items next to it, and sent it on its way. According to the text, the animals went straight on one road in the direction of Beth Shemesh, not turning **to the right or to the left** (v 12). This phrase is significant in the DtrH because it implies total obedience to the will of Yahweh (Josh 1:7; 23:6). Thus, even the milch cows appeared to be under the control of Yahweh's hand.

The Philistines followed behind the cart up to the border of the city of Beth Shemesh in order to see what would happen to it. Understandably the Philistines were happy to see that the ark arrived at the city, thereby revealing the source of the plague. The Philistines were also relieved to know that the plague would not visit their cities again. As the cart approached the city, the citizens of Beth Shemesh were harvesting wheat when they looked up and saw the ark approaching (v 13). Traditionally, the time of wheat harvest occurred during the months of May and June, and the timing of the event would ensure that a great number of people would witness its arrival.

The citizens of Beth Shemesh **rejoiced** when they saw the ark, similar to a homecoming celebration (v 13). The ark finally came to rest in a field called **Joshua** (v 14). In an ironic twist, the ark that had been in a Philistine field for seven months arrived home and came to rest in an Israelite field. The return of the ark to this particular field was suggestive for a couple of reasons. First, here is another Joshua who is connected with someone or something arriving in the land of Canaan after an extended absence (Josh 6—12). Second, the ark's journey from Philistine lands back to Israel signified the completeness of its return. The ark's return indicated that the presence of Yahweh resided in Israel again, thus reversing the remarks of Eli's daughter-in-law when it had been taken into Philistine custody (1 Sam 4:21).

Rejoicing at the arrival of the ark, the citizens of Beth Shemesh utilized a giant rock from the field as an impromptu altar. On this rock, the citizens cut up the wood of the cart and offered the cows as a burnt offering (*'olâ*) to Yahweh (v 15). Interestingly, the Philistines sent the cows, the ark, and the golden tumors and mice as a restitution/reparation offering. In the land of Israel, however, the people of Beth Shemesh turned it into a burnt offering. The sacrifice most likely amounted to a thanksgiving offering commemorating the return to the land both of the ark and Yahweh's presence. The Levites are briefly mentioned in v 15*a* as participating in this sacrifice, but this verse interrupts the narrative flow between v 14 and v 15*b*. A critical reading suggests that the notice about the Levites is a later insertion into the text. This is understandable considering that officiating sacrifices became the major or sole responsibility of the priesthood in subsequent history.

■ **6:19—7:1** Even though the people of Beth Shemesh celebrated the arrival of the ark, the Hebrew text recounts that **some of the men . . . looked into the ark** and Yahweh struck **seventy men, fifty thousand men** (v 19). The language here is confusing with regard to the number of people killed. The reason why the number 50,000 is included remains unexplained. The NRSV, for example, simply retains "seventy men." This represents a better reading in light of the fact that 50,000 appears to be an unrealistically high number. In addition, the LXX version states that the **sons of Jeconiah** (instead of **some of the men** in the MT) were killed because they did not rejoice with the people of Beth Shemesh at the ark's arrival. This is a reading that is retained in some modern translations (NRSV), while others stick to the Hebrew text (NIV; JPS). Thus, according to the Hebrew text, some of the men were killed because they moved too close to the ark, while in the LXX the sons of Jeconiah were killed because they did not rejoice when it returned. In either case, Yahweh's punitive action toward these individuals prompted the people of Beth Shemesh to request that the people of **Kiriath Jearim** take the ark from them (v 21). Kiriath Jearim was located near Beth Shemesh (Josh 15:9 ff.) in Canaanite territory. The city appeared to have some associations with the worship of Baal since it was also known as Baalah (Josh 15:9), Kiriath Baal (v 60), and Baalah of Judah (2 Sam 6:2). This fact makes the request of the people of Beth Shemesh to transport it there more curious. This is where the ark would remain located, however, until David returned the ark to Jerusalem (2 Sam 6).

FROM THE TEXT

1. One of the lessons we learn in studying the Ark Narrative relates to the interaction between human events and God's providence. Even though the Israelites may not have understood how the capture of the ark of the covenant would have benefited them, God, nevertheless, was accomplishing something very important in Israel's midst. God's providence stands behind this text so that all the events that transpire come under his control. It was through the capture of the ark of the covenant that God was able to fulfill the word against Eli and his sons, thereby purifying the religious culture from the corrupt influence of the priesthood. These turns of events ultimately opened the door for Samuel to become God's faithful prophet/priest to his people.

To the Israelites, however, it may have appeared that God was actively working against them as he remained silent while Israel was defeated by the Philistines and their greatest religious symbol was carried off into captivity. In the process, God may have appeared not only detached to the Israelites but even impotent against the gods of the Philistines.

This, in turn, raises an interesting theological question about the nature of God: does God ever allow his character or reputation to be humiliated for a greater theological purpose? If one reviews the content of Israel's story and the life of Jesus, the answer is yes. In the Babylonian exile, the greatest catastrophe of Israel's past, the same questions were being raised by the faith community. Reading the Psalm literature, for example, we see that complaints went out that God was negligent, or asleep, and that God had been mocked by the Babylonian armies and foreign gods. However, through the exile, God was purifying the community of faith, atoning for the sins of Israel's community, and preparing a community to be restored for a new and more intimate type of relationship.

When Jesus was hanging on the cross and suffering the ignomy of persecution, humiliation, and abandonment, God may have also appeared to have been defeated. Nevertheless, it was through the humiliation of the cross that God was preparing the way for the world to receive salvation through the atoning work of Christ. Thus, God has allowed himself to be humiliated when there is a greater salvific purpose at stake.

2. The Ark Narrative also testified to the greatness of God. As the ark traveled throughout Philistine country, God's power was on display in every territory where the ark appeared. God demonstrated his power and authority

by humiliating Dagon, the Philistine god, and by striking the Philistine people with plagues. As a result of these events, even the Philistines came to recognize and respect the awesome power of Israel's God. This is also reminiscent of the Exodus traditions, in which God's power was on full display for the Egyptians and the Israelites to see. Not only did the exodus traditions serve as a foundational belief for Israel's covenant tradition, but even the Egyptians recognized God's awesome hand in these events. The Ark Narrative teaches us that when God is at work in our world and performing great deeds in society and culture, he is also revealing his character in a manner that even those who do not know God, or who even oppose God, can learn something about his nature and come to revere him. Ultimately, God is working in the events of human history even though we may not always detect it, and he is glorified in the events that transpire under his providential care.

3. The ark traditions also speak to Israel's attitude toward God. The Ark Narrative suggests that the Israelites had come to take God's presence for granted or treated the ark as a talisman. In essence, the Israelites believed that God was at their disposal and anytime they needed help or a victory all they had to do was carry the ark into battle with them. The Israelites basically treated the ark like a good luck charm, ensuring that God would bless them in their endeavors. When the Israelites were defeated by the Philistines, they falsely believed that the defeat came about because they did not bring the ark into battle. Through Israel's defeat, God showed the people of Israel that God was in charge of history and that he would not be manipulated by this kind of thinking.

This attitude can creep into the minds of modern believers as well. Often we take God for granted when things are going well in our lives, and only seek God's presence in a time of catastrophe or when we seek a blessing. This attitude indicates that our relationship with God is not based on love or reverence for God but one that is utilitarian in nature. We want God when it is convenient for us. In this way we distort and pervert the proper order or nature of the relationship between ourselves and God. Instead of being in the role of a servant before God, in essence we want God to serve our purposes. For many folks, therefore, their faith is self-serving and ultimately narcissistic in nature. This type of relationship is not based on genuine love or respect, but only on selfish ambition.

F. Samuel as Judge (7:2-17)

BEHIND THE TEXT

First Samuel 7:2 directly follows the end of the ark tradition at 7:1. In 7:2-17, Samuel reappears as the central figure in Israel's story. With Eli and his sons killed off, Samuel stands as the undisputed religious leader of the community. As mentioned in the previous section, Samuel may have been absent from the ark traditions because they were already a self-contained unit when they were incorporated into the DtrH. However, a synchronic reading of the text may also raise some other questions regarding Samuel's absence. For example, did the people not believe that Samuel was a military leader and thus not capable of leading them into battle? Did they not envision him as the primary religious leader as long as Eli and his sons were alive and therefore did not invite him to accompany the ark? It is also appropriate to ask, did the Philistines defeat the Israelites because Samuel was not leading them into battle? These questions are interesting and may provide alternate clues as to why Samuel is not present in 4:1a—7:1.

The reality is, however, we do not have enough information to answer these questions with any sense of authority. In 7:2-17, it does become clear that Samuel comes across as a legitimate leader the people look to after their failure in the battle with the Philistines and the people of Beth Shemesh had been struck down with plagues. In 6:20 the people of Beth Shemesh asked this important question: **who can stand before this holy God?** That question, in essence, is answered in ch 7: Samuel is worthy to stand before Yahweh. Samuel not only appears as Yahweh's unqualified leader among the people but also comes across as an effective mediator of Yahweh's covenant and leader of holy war (v 8).

IN THE TEXT

1. Samuel Presides over Israel's Repentance (7:2-4)

■ **2-4** This section opens with the statement (v 2), *it was many days that the ark was housed at Kiriath-jearim, and they multiplied, even twenty years.* The number of years that are reported here are hard to correlate with the 480 years given for the time of the Exodus until Solomon began building the temple (1 Kgs 6:1). Klein notes that according to this scheme 45 years passed between the Exodus and conquest, 253 years are allotted for the oppression and "saviors" of premonarchical Israel, 136 for the minor judges, and 46 years for the kings up to the fourth year of Solomon (1983, 65). The statement in v 1 most likely refers to the time that elapsed from the ark's return from Philistia until the battle that is reported in 7:7-11 (Caird 1953, 914). The twenty years therefore must indicate a period of time the Philistines continued to oppress the Israelites.

The theme of foreign oppression is very characteristic of the cycle found in the DtrH: sin-oppression-cry to Yahweh-deliverance (Klein 1983, 66). In this context, however, Israel did not cry out as in times past, but v 2*b* notes that they **mourned after Yahweh.** The language here is difficult to translate and some interpreters have taken this to mean "yearned after the LORD" (JPS) or "lamented after the LORD" (NRSV). Did this mean that they mourned after Yahweh because the ark was in Kiriath Jearim and they thought Yahweh was dead (Eslinger 1985, 230)? Did they mourn because they suffered under Philistine oppression? Or, did it imply that the Israelites demonstrated a sense of contrition and a desire to be reconciled with Yahweh? The surrounding context seems to indicate that the people demonstrated a sense of remorse for their actions—a desire to repent.

Samuel's exhortation to the people in the following verse would also point in this direction. In v 3, Samuel uses a phrase that occurs frequently throughout the DtrH as a precondition of restoration: ***if you will return to Yahweh with all your heart.*** The phrase "to return to Yahweh with all of one's heart" is a central tenet of the kerygma of the DtrH (2 Kgs 23:25) and it is found in prophets such as Jeremiah (3:10; 24:7; 29:13). Samuel's call to repentance contained specific requirements: the Israelites were to "remove the ***foreign*** gods and the Ashtaroth from your midst and direct your heart to the LORD and serve Him alone" (v 3 JPS). The import of Samuel's message called for the exclusive worship of Yahweh as an essential part of repentance. This message figured prominently throughout history (Josh 24:23; Judg 10:16) and implied a return to complete obedience and faithfulness to Yahweh. The name Ashtaroth is the plural of Ashtart, a Canaanite goddess of love and war who was closely associated with Baal. Her name is usually vocalized in the OT so that it sounds like the word for "shame" (*bosheth*) in Hebrew (i.e., Ish-Bosheth).

Samuel's message was also conditional in nature; if the Israelites returned to Yahweh, then Yahweh would deliver the Israelites ***from the hand of the Philistines*** (1 Sam 7:3). Here repentance and military victory went hand in hand. Samuel's word of instruction implied that the reason Israel had been defeated by the Philistines and continued to be tormented by them, was that they were not completely devoted to Yahweh. Even transporting the ark to battle would not guarantee victory as long as they were disobedient. The events of 4:1-10 highlighted this important lesson. Samuel emphasized that it was Israel's relationship with God that mattered most.

When the people heard these words they "removed the Baalim and Ashtaroth and they served ***Yahweh*** alone" (v 4 NRSV). Baal, like Ashtaroth, is in the plural form here. Baal was the main fertility deity in Canaanite religion. Often depicted with a lightning bolt in his hand, Baal was responsible for making it rain and bringing fertility to the land. A significant source of temptation for the Israelites, the people would often turn to the Canaanite gods/goddesses to ensure fertility for their crops, flocks, and family.

2. The Assembly at Mizpah and Philistine Defeat (7:5-14)

■ **5-6** Samuel directed the people to assemble at the town of **Mizpah** (v 5). This is a location where other important religious ceremonies had taken place previously (Judg 20:1, 3; 21:1, 5, 8), and it would be the place where the people would select Saul as king (1 Sam 10:17). Shiloh is not mentioned as the rallying point because it may have already been destroyed by the Philistines. Although Mizpah can be translated as "the lookout," the actual identification of the town remains a mystery. It is generally identified with Tell en-Nasbeh some eight miles north of Jerusalem in the tribal territory of Benjamin (Gordon 1986, 106). Others have suggested that Mizpah should be identified with Nebi Samwil, which is located five miles northwest of Jerusalem (Klein 1983, 66). More important than its exact location, however, Mizpah became associated as the place of repentance where Samuel interceded on behalf of the people.

Part of the ceremony that took place at Mizpah included a water ritual in which the people **poured water on the ground and fasted** (v 6). The OT does not record another water ritual such as this, but some have suggested that it could correlate with the autumn Festival of Booths. This interpretation remains speculative. Both water pouring and fasting appear to indicate sorrow and repentance, however. The Israelites' act of contrition was also followed by a confession in which they acknowledged they had sinned before Yahweh (**we have sinned against Yahweh**). Like the book of Judges, Israel's confession served as a prelude to deliverance. Here, Samuel's act of intercession is also interpreted as one of his roles as a judge in Israel (v 6).

■ **7-11** Israel's return to Yahweh had implications for the political situation, especially in regard to holy war. As before, the Philistine lords marched out to meet the Israelites for battle when they heard the Israelites had gathered at Mizpah. On this occasion, the people implored Samuel to intercede for them and ***cry out to the Lord our God to save us from the hands of the Philistines*** (v 8). In this context, the familiar expression "cry out" is utilized. Like the book of Judges, Yahweh's deliverance was preceded by Israel's cry to God. Although Samuel is called a judge here, his role resembled that of a mediator of holy war. It was Yahweh who would fight Israel's enemies, and the victory would be God's alone.

Samuel also offered a lamb as a whole burnt offering, which indicated that no part was reserved for consumption by the worshippers. Samuel then **cried out** to the Lord on **behalf** of the people (v 9). Unlike ch 4 where Yahweh remained silent in the battle against the Philistines, Samuel's supplication brought about an immediate response (v 9*b*). The text notes that the Lord thundered (*rāyam*) against the Philistines. Thunder served as a weapon of holy war (1 Sam 2:10; 2 Sam 22:14) as well as other elements of nature, such as lightning (2 Sam 22:15; Pss 18:14; 77:18-19), hail (Josh 10:11, 14), darkness (Josh 24:7), the celestial bodies (Judg 5:20), or even disease (1 Sam 5:6).

The text indicates that the proper conditions had been met for success on this occasion, which had been missing previously. According to the text, Yahweh "thundered with a mighty voice . . . and threw [the Philistines] into confusion; and they were routed" by the Israelites (v 10 NRSV). Even though the Israelites were able to defeat their enemy, it was really Yahweh who fought for them. The Israelite men were able to put the Philistines to the chase and they struck them down at Beth Car. The precise geographical location of Beth

Car is not known, even though some have suggested that it is related to Beth Horon the lower, about eight miles west of Mizpah (Klein 1983, 68).

■ **12-14** The defeat of the Philistines provided an occasion to erect a memorial commemorating Yahweh's victory. In v 12, Samuel took a stone and set it up between Mizpah and **Shen.** The exact whereabouts of Shen is uncertain, but the etiology of setting up the stone provides the theological point. The name of the stone is Ebenezer, which translated means "stone of help." While other people such as Jacob set up a pillar to mark the spot of Yahweh's theophany, the use of stone here reflects the editor(s) attempt to avoid the polemic against pillars in the DtrH (Deut 16:22; Josh 24:26-27). The stone symbolized and commemorated the assistance Yahweh provided the Israelites in defeating the Philistines on this occasion.

The text notes in v 13 that the Philistines were **subdued** and **the hand of the LORD was against the Philistines *all the days of Samuel.*** The hand of Yahweh had been against the Philistines when the ark was situated in Philistine territory, now Yahweh's power over the Philistines was mediated through Samuel. Moreover, the Israelites recovered land that the Philistines had taken previously, and they came to peace with the Amorites (i.e., the Canaanites of the land). It is important to note that the defeat of Israel's enemies and the restoration of land came as a result of religious obedience, not military might. This is a theme that permeates the narrative of the battle at Jericho (Josh 6) in which the Israelites' faith and obedience resulted in a military success and the appropriation of land. Moreover, the Israelites experienced military victory when Samuel presided over the assembly, not a king. Samuel was not a military hero per se but was a faithful prophet/priest/judge of God who led the people in repentance and sacrifice. It was Samuel who cried out on behalf of the people and as a result Yahweh responded with a resounding victory. This chapter, therefore, endorses Samuel (along with prophets in general) as the legitimate leader of the people.

3. Samuel as Judge (7:15-17)

■ **15-17** This chapter closes with a brief notice about Samuel's ministry in vv 15-17. According to these verses, Samuel served as a judge who made a circuitous route from **Bethel, Gilgal,** and **Mizpah.** All of these cities represented important religious centers in Israel, and they were located in the relatively small area of central Palestine. In addition to prophet and priest, Samuel's responsibilities included activities usually associated with judges; namely, civil and various administrative duties, including the administration of justice. When Samuel finished his circuit, the text notes he would return home to his town at Ramah.

FROM THE TEXT

The story of Samuel that emerges after the Ark Narrative reminds us that godly leadership is necessary in order to lead people to repentance and genuine relationship with God. In the case of Samuel, it was only after he uncompromisingly confronted the people with their sin that they turned their hearts back to God. As a result, Israel was renewed as a people and God fought against Israel's enemies. Not only did God defeat the Philistines, but the land that Israel had lost previously was restored to them as well. Throughout the OT, repentance and obedience always preceded restoration. God can only restore individuals and the community of faith spiritually if sin, both hidden and covert, is confessed.

Repentance is also accompanied by hearing an authentic word from God by a leader or individual who is willing to confront wrongdoing. God, throughout Israel's history, consistently prepared and introduced faithful spokespersons to confront the people's disobedience in order to elicit confession. In the story of Samuel, we see that the prayer of Hannah resulted in the emergence of God's faithful prophet/priest who called Israel to put away the foreign gods and prayed on behalf of the people. Today, God continues to raise up faithful leaders who call upon the people of God to walk in obedience. The question becomes, Will the people follow?

II. THE EMERGENCE OF THE MONARCHY IN ISRAEL: SAUL, ISRAEL'S FIRST KING (8:1—15:35)

A. Israel Asks for a King (8:1-22)

BEHIND THE TEXT

The events following the Ark Narrative in chs 4—6 and the assembly in ch 7 prepare the reader for the next phase of 1 Samuel: the establishment of the monarchy in Israel's society. Scholars generally view chs 8—12 as a literary unit that centers on the rise of Saul's monarchy in particular. Within this unit, chs 8 and 12 are central to the overall structure and story line in Samuel and the DtrH in that they recall the people's request or their asking for a king. Chapters 9—11 thus present Saul to the audience as the one "who was asked for" by the people.

The people's request for a king in both chs 8 and 12 stands in sharp contrast to Hannah's request for a son in ch 1. Hannah's asking was taken as pious supplication, the people's request for a king, however, was deemed apostasy. In asking for a king, the Israelites not only rejected Samuel, but, more significantly, they rejected Yahweh as king over the community. At the end of this unit (ch 12) the people came to realize that their request amounted to sin (vv 17-19).

This understanding of the origins of kingship thus casts the idea of monarchy in the DtrH in a questionable light. God, however, eventually allowed the institution of kingship, but the king would have to be subservient to God's instruction as it was mediated through prophetic voices (12:14-15). The development of kingship, no doubt, had tremendous religious and political implications for Israel's society. In this manner, chs 8 ff. are similar to the schema in the book of Judges in that the demand for a king started the rebellion cycle all over again. The cycle that begins in ch 8 continues into the book of Kings and ultimately ends with the destruction of Jerusalem (2 Kgs 25:1-21).

With regards to the manner in which Saul is presented in chs 8—12, critical scholars have noted that alternating portraits emerge. In examining this material, it becomes clear that two distinct portraits of kingship and Saul appear: one is positive and the other is negative. The following outline distinguishes between three negative portraits of monarchy and two positive portraits:

Negative: 8:1-22 (Request for a king)
Positive: 9:1—10:16 (Saul's anointing by Samuel)
Negative: 10:17-27 (Saul the reluctant monarch)
Positive: 11:1-15 (Saul saves the Israelites)
Negative: 12:1-25 (Samuel's denunciation of kingship)

Scholars have noted that the mixed portraits of Saul may say something about the disparity over how people perceived the institution of monarchy within Israel's society. In essence, some liked it and thought it was a positive thing, while others did not like it and considered it a form of apostasy. In looking at the outline above, the overall evaluation of the monarchy, and Saul, is unimpressive. Two positive portraits of Saul are enveloped by three negative ones. Even though Saul may have had some positive qualities and characteristics, overall his monarchy was deemed to be a failure. The failure of Saul's kingship also served to highlight the glories of David's reign and kingdom.

IN THE TEXT

I. The Setting (8:1-3)

■ **1-3** The syntax of 8:1a indicates that a new literary section is beginning. The words ***and it was when Samuel was old*** suggests that an unspecified amount of time has passed since the close of ch 7. The text does mention that Samuel ***set his sons as judges over Israel.*** We do not know by what authority Samuel took this action. Eli's sons had taken over for their father, now Samuel's sons, Joel and Abijah, are established as their father's heirs. Even though the names Joel ("Yahweh is God") and Abijah ("My father is Yahweh") have special significance, they do not fare any better than the sons of Eli. Samuel's sons did not ***walk in his ways and they were bent on gain, they took bribes and perverted justice*** (v 3). The comparison between Eli and his sons and Samuel and his sons may raise eyebrows about hereditary succession according to the text. Samuel was an exemplary priest/prophet of Yahweh; however, that did not ensure that his sons would also follow their father's example. We may also wonder whether or not these notices in some way implicated Eli and Samuel as fathers. The same phenomena would prove true during the period of the monarchy; good kings produced evil sons and vice versa (1 Kgs 15:1-15; 2 Kgs 21:19-26).

2. The Request for a King (8:4-22)

■ **4-10** As in the case of Eli's sons, the people knew the reputations of Joel and Abijah. The elders of Israel came to Samuel's hometown in Ramah to meet with him there. When the elders conferred with Samuel they reminded him that first, Samuel was old, and second, Joel and Abijah did not walk in his ways. As a result, the people wanted a king like the other nations to lead them (v 5). A couple of points are noteworthy here about the elders' statement to Samuel. First, the phrase **such as all the other nations** may have a negative connotation that suggested that the people would also behave like other nations. Samuel may not have been opposed to kingship; he was perhaps against the people's desire to be like the nations surrounding them. Second, in the ancient world, a king was supposed to be a guarantor of justice and righteousness in society. The fact that Samuel's sons perverted justice, and thus could not establish righteousness within the community, may indicate the reason why the people requested a king instead. Whatever the reason for the request, Samuel was ***dismayed*** that they would ask for a king. The verb in v 6a (rā'a') indicates something bad or evil about the request. Thus the translation should probably read ***this thing was bad/evil in the eyes of Samuel.***

When Samuel heard the elders' request, it brought him much displeasure and consternation. Like his mother before him, he presented his complaint directly to Yahweh during a time of duress (v 6). Although Samuel took it personally, Yahweh urged Samuel to see this as an illustration of their rejection of Yahweh. In rejecting Samuel, they rejected the God who appointed Samuel to lead God's people. Yahweh, therefore, told Samuel to **hear the voice of the people for all that they said to you because they have not rejected you, but me from being king over them** (v 7). Yahweh noted that the people, in essence, rejected him and not Samuel, which is a theme that appears in other parts of the DtrH (1 Sam 10:9; 12:12). Gideon, for example, had also warned that asking for a king was tantamount to a rejection of Yahweh's leadership (Judg 8:22-23). The term for rejecting (mā'as) is a technical term for sin (2 Kgs 17:5), thus linking their request with disobedience. Like the period of the judges before this, the people's rejection of Yahweh is tied to putting their confidence in someone or something other than Yahweh. In this respect, the cycle that began in Judges (sin-punishment-cry for help-restoration) continues anew in 1 Sam 8.

■ **11-18** Throughout vv 11-18, Samuel explained what the people could expect from their king. Sometimes called the "law" or "manner" of the king, these verses provide an idea of what life would be like for the Israelites. According to Samuel the people could expect the following from their king:

Verse 11: The king **will <u>take</u> your sons**
Verse 13: The king **will <u>take</u> your daughters**
Verse 14: The king **will <u>take</u> . . . your fields and vineyards and olive groves**
Verse 15: The king **will <u>take</u> a tenth of your [seed crops and vineyards]**
Verse 16: The king **will <u>take</u> your [male and female slaves], your cattle and donkeys**
Verse 17: The king **will <u>take</u> a tenth of your flocks**

An observation of the repeated verbs in vv 11-17 reveals that the king would basically **take** (*lāqaḥ*) from the people, either in the form of service to the king or in the form of taxation, with a portion of their crops and animals set aside for the king and his administration. In essence, kingship would be an invasive institution and it would constitute a heavy burden upon the people.

Samuel also informed them in v 18 that the people would **cry out** to Yahweh because of the king they had requested. The language here again resembles painful times from Israel's past. The people cried out under Egyptian mistreatment, and they also cried out when they were threatened by their foes in the time of the judges. Thus, the biblical text depicts the institution of monarchy in the same light. It would be a heavy, taxing experience to live under the control of the king. These words would come to fruition during the days of Solomon, in particular, whose oppressive policies would be the source of angst among the northern tribes and serve as the catalyst for the schism of the kingdom of David (1 Kgs 12:1-16).

■ **19-22** In spite of Samuel's warnings, the people ***would not listen to Samuel*** (v 19) and still demanded a king. In v 20 the people claimed that they essentially needed a king to lead them in battle. This is a different rationale than was provided earlier (vv 4-5). The people sought military protection and political safety even if it meant that that they would become slaves/vassals to their king. The people's request is curious in light of the fact that God had humiliated the Philistines previously in the Ark Narratives (4:1a—7:1) and when Samuel presided over the assembly at Mizpah (7:10-11). Nevertheless, God allowed them to appoint a king, the very institution that would ultimately lead to their downfall.

FROM THE TEXT

In the course of this section the people of Israel eventually asked for a king. God had provided Samuel to be the religious and judicial leader of Israel's society, but the people wanted something more. It is interesting to see the dichotomy between the request that Hannah made in the first part of Samuel and the request of the people in ch 8. In the first case, the prayer/request of a faithful and pious woman produced a godly son who brought God's blessing to the people, but the request of a stubborn and ungrateful people resulted in the development of kingship. Samuel warned the people what it would be like to live under the rule of the king, but the people refused to listen to him.

When God allowed the people to have a king he told Samuel that they were not rejecting Samuel, but God himself. The king that the people asked for, however, would have serious consequences for the people and the future of Israel. The very thing that they asked for would cause them to cry out, just like they did under Egyptian bondage and foreign oppressors from the time of the judges. Ultimately, it would be the monarchy that would be held responsible for the downfall of the kingdom. This narrative reminds us that sometimes individuals or communities of faith want their own way instead of seeking God's will on a particular matter or issue.

Whether out of impatience, anxiety, or jealousy we can want something so badly that we do not consider the warning signs or take into account the consequences of what we are demanding. There are times in life we may ask God for something and God will allow us to have what we desire. However, the thing we ask for may, in the long run, become the very thing that becomes a source of pain or heartache to us. God can use those occasions, however, to wake us up and lead us back to him in repentance. They also serve to teach us and remind us that we can avoid distressing, sometimes catastrophic, outcomes by simply listening to God's voice and seeking God's will in the first place.

B. Saul Chosen as King (9:1—10:27)

BEHIND THE TEXT

Chapters 9—10 serve as the core within the larger unit that extends from chs 8 to 12. Whereas chs 8 and 12 center on the request for a king and function as the unit's framework, chs 9—10 focus on the selection of Saul as Israel's king. Scholars have noted that chs 9—10 are comprised of separate accounts pertaining to Saul's selection. In 9:1—10:16 God selected Saul to deliver the Israelites from Philistine oppression (9:16) and was later anointed by Samuel in a private meeting (10:1). This tradition is favorable to Saul in that he is portrayed like one of the judges from the previous era. In the second account, Saul was chosen among the populace (vv 17-27) through divine means (vv 20-22). Hints of Saul's troubled monarchy are carefully introduced in the narrative, however. The fact that he is singled out from the community through the casting of lots (vv 20-21) raises concerns about him personally and his impending monarchy (see below), and he comes across as a reluctant leader (v 22) as well. In addition to the narratives in ch 10, a third report associates the establishment of Saul's monarchy with the covenant renewal ceremony at Gilgal (11:14-15). These observations indicate that multiple traditions about the inception of Saul's kingship existed originally, and they give witness to the complicated transmission history of the books of Samuel as a whole. The Deuteronomistic editor(s) later adopted and arranged these diverse materials to give them their present shape.

IN THE TEXT

1. Saul's Introduction (9:1-2)

■ **1-2** The introduction to Saul begins with an account of his family lineage. There are a total of six generations listed in v 1, seven if we count Saul. The text opens with the notice that, *there was a man from Benjamin and his name was Kish, son of Abiel, son of Zeror, son of Bechorath, son of Aphiah, son of a Benjaminite, a man of valor.*

A number of important observations stand out about Saul's family tree. First, the men on the list hailed from the tribe of Benjamin, a detail that the writer of this text makes a point to mention twice. This by default made Saul a Benjamite who came from the city of Gibeah. Gibeah, in Benjamin, was the location where the rape and dismemberment of the Levite's concubine took place in Judges (ch 19). One has to wonder if anyone from Saul's family (i.e., father or grandfather) participated in that horrible crime. Chronologically speaking, the lineage goes back several generations, which meant that Saul had family members alive when the rape was committed. At the very least, Saul had family members involved in the bloody civil war that followed the crime since only 600 men survived the battle.

Second, Saul's father, Kish, is called "a man of wealth" (NRSV). The term used to describe his father (*gibōr ḥāyil*) can also be translated as *a man of valor* or "a warrior." This translation is very fitting if Kish was involved in the civil war in Judg 20.

Third, we do not have any information about Saul's mother. Although nothing is reported about her in the text, Judg 20 indicates that the 600 male survivors from the tribe of Benjamin procured their wives from the city of Jabesh Gilead or seized them among the women at Shiloh. If Saul's mother was one of the women seized from Jabesh Gilead, then it not only ties Saul back to the terrible scenes of Judg 19—20 but also explains why Saul came to the rescue of the people of that city when they were threatened by the Ammonites (1 Sam 11).

The events of Judg 19—20 thus stand as the backdrop to the introduction to Saul's family in 1 Sam 9:1. Even though Saul has not officially emerged in the textual tradition yet, he does arrive with this information already hanging over him like a cloud. The rhetorical impact that this has on how Saul is presented to the readers and the effect that it has on how they perceive him cannot be overlooked or underestimated.

Saul is presented to the reader for the first time in v 2. The text recounts, ***and to him there was a son, whose name was Saul.*** The name Saul (šā'ūl) is the passive form of the verb "to ask" (šā'al). Thus his name is more properly translated as "the asked-for one." This name is appropriate considering the Israelites "requested" or "asked" for a king earlier. The people's wish was granted in the form of the son of Kish. The text also includes a statement about his physical qualities, ***there was none among the children of Israel more handsome than he, and he was taller from his shoulder up than any of the people.*** It is interesting that the text would first draw attention to his appearance and his height, not his reverence for Yahweh. This is also the case when he was selected to be king among the people (10:23).

Warning flags about Saul are again raised. First, the remarks about Saul's physical attributes are reminiscent of Absalom, who was also known for his nice features (2 Sam 14:25-26). Outward characteristics, however, do not ensure a successful leader; in fact, they may foreshadow just the opposite. Absalom's reign ended in humility and disgrace, the same would hold true for Saul. The point is being made: looks can be deceiving. Even though Saul possessed all the outward (superficial?) characteristics that people look for in a leader (i.e., affluent family, tall, and handsome), a leader's devotion to God was the true measure of his success.

Second, when the text refers to Saul's height, it employs a word (gābōah) that sounds almost identical to Saul's hometown (gib'â). In doing so, the writer of the text will not let the reading audience forget about the horrible events of Judg 19—20. The cloud of that ignoble and despicable affair continues to haunt Saul even though he was not there.

2. Saul Chosen and Anointed (9:3—10:16)

■ **3-10** The story in which Saul is formally introduced is a rather curious one. The text notes that ***the donkeys/asses which belonged to Kish, the father of Saul, had gone astray*** (v 3). Here we have another portent that may indicate something suspicious about Saul's pending monarchy. Although donkeys could be seen as animals of nobility, in the OT God's greatest leaders were shepherds before they took on a prominent leadership role (i.e., Moses and David). The fact that Saul was out looking for his father's donkeys is a harbinger that he and his monarchy would be a disappointment.

Saul and his father's servant traversed all throughout the territory of Ephraim and Benjamin to find the animals. Their efforts met with little success. When they came to the land of Zuph, Saul was ready to turn back. The servant persisted that they should press on to find **a man of God** who could help them in the matter of their lost donkeys (v 6). It is peculiar that even though Samuel was known as a true prophet throughout the land of Israel (from Dan to Beersheba), Saul did not seem to be aware of who he was. In vv 6 and 8, Samuel is called a/the **man of God,** which was synonymous for prophet.

The two men eventually came to the land of **Zuph**. Zuph was located in the territory of Ephraim, near the city of Ramah, which is also mentioned in conjunction with Samuel's lineage (1:1). Although the city like the prophet is unnamed in v 8, the later context insinuates that the city was Ramah, home of the prophet Samuel. When the young men considered this option, Saul raised concerns that they did not have anything to give the prophet. As a means to support themselves, prophets often received money when people came for advice/help. Prophets had to be careful, however, not to tell people what they wanted to hear just to make money. Saul did not have any money with him. Although his father was a rich man, Saul was penniless. Ironically, the servant, not the son, had money with him and volunteered to pay a quarter shekel of silver to the prophet. In biblical times this would have amounted to about .403 ounces, not much by any standard. Saul agreed to the servant's proposition and they went to the town where the man of God lived.

Verse 9 concludes this section with an interesting statement that should be taken as a parenthetical insertion. It provides clarification about the relationship between prophets (*nābî*) and seers (*rō'eh*) in Israel. This notice indicates that the terms were basically synonymous, with both groups fulfilling similar roles in Israelite society.

■ **11-16** When Saul and the servant reached the unidentified city, they acquired the whereabouts of Samuel from the women who came out to draw water. Water holes served as convenient places to meet people and find out important information (Gen 24:15-20; 29:2-12; Exod 2:15-19). The text recounts, however, that before Saul came to Samuel, God had already prepared Samuel for Saul's arrival. In the context of God's message to Samuel (1 Sam 9:16), God revealed to Samuel that he would anoint Saul as a **leader** (*nāgîd*) of the people. The term used here is different from the one that is used for king (*melek*) in the OT. The term "king" at times could be viewed negatively, because it became associated with a political position or institution that could abuse its power and privilege. Such theological overtones were not associated with the term *nāgîd*. God also said that the designated leader would free God's people from Philistine oppression. In this manner, Saul appeared like one of the judges from the previous era (Judg 3:9, 15; 4:3; 6:6; 10:12-14; 1 Sam 12:8, 10).

■ **17-26** When Saul and the servant met Samuel, the prophet reassured Saul that he was the man for whom they were looking. After inviting him to his home, Samuel told Saul the lost donkeys he was seeking had been found. In addition, Samuel informed Saul of his pending leadership role. When Saul heard Samuel's words, he responded as one who was unworthy for the position, much like Gideon did when he was called to his task (Judg 6:15): he was from the smallest tribe of Israel and from a humble family (1 Sam 9:21). Samuel, however, did not reply to Saul's response; instead he brought Saul and the servant to the hall where the meal was being served.

The meal may have represented an anticipatory coronation banquet in light of God's word to Samuel about Saul earlier. Saul was to sit as the **head of the guests who were invited** (v 22). In a similar fashion, two of David's sons, Absalom and Adonijah, held banquet sacrifices with guests when they sought to succeed David (2 Sam 15:10-12; 1 Kgs 1:9-10). Although the meal may have been a preliminary to Saul's coronation, Samuel did not reveal any information about Saul's pending anointing at this time.

■ **9:27—10:8** When Saul arose in the morning, Samuel sent the servant on ahead so he could convey the message God had spoken to him in private. Samuel began by taking out a flask of oil and poured some on his head. Samuel also kissed Saul and reported to him saying, **Has not *Yahweh* anointed you *ruler* over his inheritance?** (1 Sam 10:1). Samuel also reiterated the word that he received previously regarding Saul (9:6); Saul would save the Israelites from the hands of Israel's enemies.

In order to reassure Saul of this message, Samuel provided three signs to verify that this word was from God. First, two men by the tomb of Rachel would find the donkeys. Second, Saul would encounter three men by the oak of Tabor in which they would give Saul bread. Third, when Saul traveled to a place called Gibeah of God (lit., ***the hill of God***), he would encounter a band of prophets coming from the shrine who would be in a state of prophetic frenzy. Not only would he encounter this band of prophets, but the spirit of God would possess Saul and he would be transformed into a different person.

■ **9-16** In verses 9-13 the word that Samuel proclaimed regarding the band of prophets was fulfilled, thus confirming that Saul was God's choice as the leader of the Israelites. The spirit of God possessed Saul, and he began to prophesy like the other prophets. Saul's behavior prompted one of the men to ask, **Is Saul also . . . among the prophets?** (v 11). This proverbial saying, at its heart, questioned whether Saul would be a king like David and Solomon later, or whether he would be a charismatic judge-prophet such as Samuel and the judges before him. The spirit rushed upon Gideon (Judg 6:34), Jephthah (11:29), and Samson (14:6, 19; 15:14) when God selected them, and the spirit also came upon David at the time of his anointing (1 Sam 16:13). Paradoxically, the spirit of God that seized Saul in such a mighty way would also depart from him later in an instant (16:14, 23) and be replaced with an evil spirit (16:15-16, 23; 18:10; 19:9).

The Call Narrative

Scholars have noted that Saul's calling shares a number of similarities to those of Moses, Gideon, and a number of the classical prophets. Call narratives included the following elements (Birch 1971, 55-68):

1. A divine confrontation took place. This confrontation was initiated by God or could be mediated through a prophet (1 Sam 9:15).

2. The introductory word in which the specific basis or ground for the commission (vv 16-17).
3. The objection raised by the one being called (v 21).
4. The commission that was revealed through the word of God and accompanied by an anointing (10:1).
5. The commission was accompanied by a sign that served to reaffirm God's selection of the individual (vv 1, 5-7*a*).
6. The reassurance that God was with the individual who was called (v 7*b*).

When Saul returned home, he was questioned by his uncle about his whereabouts, not his father. It is puzzling that the uncle is unnamed here. It has been proposed that his uncle is Ner, the father of Abner, but this remains speculative (Alter 1999, 57). Although Saul divulged information about the donkeys, he did not say anything about the matter of kingship. Saul's silence on the subject, however, prepares the readers of the text for the public selection ceremony in 10:17-27.

3. The People Select Saul (10:17-27)

■ **17-27** The events of 9:1—10:16 lay behind the scene in 10:17-27. Although Samuel anointed Saul for kingship previously, the people had not played a role in the selection process. The previous section, in many respects, portrayed the selection of Saul in a rather positive light. God initiated the process by telling Samuel to anoint him, and God selected Saul to defeat Israel's enemies (9:16; 10:1). In this unit, however, the text takes a more dim view of kingship in that it is seen as a rejection/rebellion against God.

This unit opens with the notice that Samuel *assembled the people before the Lord at Mizpah* (v 17). Mizpah was the place where the people asked Samuel for a king initially, and it was at Mizpah that the king would be selected from among the people. At the beginning of the assembly Samuel prefaced the selection process by conveying a prophetic word from Yahweh. Samuel's speech to the assembly in v 18 begins with the familiar messenger formula, *Thus says the Lord: I brought Israel up from Egypt, and I rescued you from the hand of the Egyptians and all the kingdoms that were oppressing you.* Samuel's recapitulation of Yahweh's gracious deeds on behalf of Israel would generally be placed in the historical prologue of the covenant in the ancient Near Eastern treaty tradition. Israel's redemption from Egypt served as the basis for the Mosaic covenant (Exod 20:1). In this context, however, it became the means by which to juxtapose Israel's request for a king with God's leadership over the community. Israel's request for a king did not serve as an entrance into a covenant with Yahweh but demonstrated how the Israelites rebuffed Yahweh's gracious leadership in the past for the human leader they desired.

The text reiterates this point in v 19 when it notes: *You, today, have rejected your God who saved you from all your calamities and your distresses when you said you will set a king over us.* God had saved the Israelites before, why did they need a king now? The term for rejection (*mā'as*) is used here as it was in 1 Sam 8:7. Israel had rejected God by asking for a king; later, however, God would reject the king they requested (16:1).

Samuel then gathered the tribes together to determine from which tribe the leader would emerge (10:20). The process to determine the selection of the king also raises interesting questions and suspicions about Saul since it conjured up images from a disastrous time in Israel's past; namely, the selection of Achan as the culprit who broke the rules of holy war (Josh 7). The following elements of Josh 7 and 1 Sam 10:17-27 are highlighted:

1. The order of the selection process (moving from tribe-clan-family-individual) is nearly identical in both contexts (Josh 7:16-18; 1 Sam 10:20-21).

2. The language used to describe the person being chosen by lot (*vayilākēd*) is identical in both accounts (Josh 7:14, 17; 1 Sam 10:20-21).

3. Both Achan and Saul would be accused of holding back the spoils of battle that were to be devoted to destruction (Josh 7:11, 20-21; 1 Sam 15:13-15, 20-21).

The rhetorical impact of the parallels between Saul and Achan on the reading/listening audience cannot be overlooked. Serious questions are raised about Saul and his impending monarchy in light of the fact that instances of casting lots in the OT are located in contexts of illicit action (see also Jonah 1:7).

The perceptive reader/listener of this tradition would have recognized the similarities with the Achan fiasco and sensed that there was something curious or even amiss about Saul being singled out from the community in this fashion. Moreover, Saul has been associated with two of the most troubling memories from Israel's history up to this point in the story: the rape of the Levite's concubine (Judg 19—20) and the Achan tragedy (Josh 7). The echoing of these dark episodes at Saul's introduction in 1 Sam 9—10 signals that he is essentially doomed from the start and that his kingship will be another failed chapter in Israel's story.

When Saul was selected by lot to be king, the people looked for Saul but he could not be found. The people inquired of God as to his whereabouts, and God said he was hidden among the **baggage** (10:22). Saul's hiding insinuates that he was bashful and reluctant to step into this new role (**he has hidden himself**), a response similar to his initial reaction to Samuel's words earlier (9:21). Saul may have been plagued by a sense of inferiority or insecurity. Incidentally, the man who possessed fine physical qualities lacked internal courage. Later Jewish interpretation tried to compensate for Saul's inadequacies by noting that he slipped off for some quiet prayer and Bible study (Gordon 1986, 121). Saul's struggle with insecurity will reappear when he finds himself in a stressful and difficult situation with the Philistines (13:8-12).

Samuel then presented Saul to the people and instructed them to look upon the one whom **Yahweh has chosen** (10:24). When the people observed Saul (and his physical appearance [v 23]), they shouted, **Long live the king!** The people's request for a king had been granted.

Not everyone was satisfied with the selection of Saul (v 27). There were some ***worthless fellows*** (*běnê běliya'al*) who doubted Saul's ability to save the Israelites. Such disbelief in the leader's ability to be successful also plagued Moses (Exod 14:11 ff.). These individuals **despised him** and would not bring him the tribute due to the newly appointed king. These men are not identified, but Gibeah, to which Saul returned (1 Sam 10:26), was home to the "worthless fellows" (*běnê běliya'al*) or the "perverse lot" responsible for the rape of the Levite's concubine (Judg 19:22).

FROM THE TEXT

In this section, God selected Saul to be king over the people of Israel. Saul, as his name suggests, was the answer to Israel's prayer. When the text introduces Saul, the text immediately draws attention to his physical characteristics and qualifications. The text insinuates that outward appearances equate with effective leadership. In modern society, when people consider choosing a leader, they often primarily take into consideration the physical qualities of the individual. Modern social research has even confirmed this fact. The people of Israel were no exception in that they also paid attention to Saul's outward appearance as a criterion for leadership.

The story of Saul, however, reminds us powerfully that in the kingdom of God it is not the most beautiful, tallest, or strongest people that make the most effective servants of God. One can look to the life of Mother Teresa to understand this point. Mother Teresa was not necessarily tall or the most physically attractive person. However, to the people of Calcutta, India, for whom she humbly cared so many years, she was a giant and a beautiful individual. We see this irony all the time throughout Scripture. God always uses the weak, the small, the humble, the poor, and the most unlikely candidates in order to fulfill God's mission on earth. What matters most is the condition of one's heart. Those that respond to God's call and follow in simple trust and obedience often do the greatest things in advancing the kingdom. God is able to use these folks because they are not able to take pride in or depend on their natural abilities alone, but they depend on God for their strength and guidance. When God uses the unlikely person to advance the concerns of the kingdom of God, however, it is God who ultimately receives the glory and honor for the results that take place.

C. Saul Defeats the Ammonites (11:1-15)

BEHIND THE TEXT

Both 9:1—10:16 and ch 11 are similar in that they portray Saul in a more positive light. In ch 11, the text highlights Saul's military capabilities and his aptitude for leading the Israelites in battle. In this chapter, the citizens of Jabesh Gilead were threatened by a Transjordanian people known as the Ammonites, and in the midst of their oppression they cried out to God to rescue them. In a manner similar to the book of Judges, the spirit of God rushed upon Saul and he defeated the Ammonite threat.

In calling the troops to battle, Saul took two oxen and cut them into pieces and sent them throughout the various parts of Israel—an eerie similarity to the rape and dismemberment of the Levite's concubine in Judg 19. Whereas 1 Sam 9:1—10:16 indicate that Saul was chosen to defeat the Philistines, Saul instead overcame a people from the Transjordan region. Saul may have been concerned about the people of Jabesh Gilead because his mother originated from this area. Although he defeated the Ammonite forces, other texts in the Saulide traditions indicate that he still did not defeat Israel's greatest nemesis, the Philistines.

IN THE TEXT

1. Saul Versus the Ammonites (11:1-13)

■ 1-13 After Saul had been chosen as king among the people, the text describes a situation in which Saul exhibited his military prowess. The Ammonite king Nahash besieged the Transjordan city of **Jabesh Gilead** (v 1). The MT does not provide a reason why Nahash attacked the city. However, other textual traditions such as the DSS text of 4QSam^a and Josephus (*Ant.* 6.5.1) provide information that sets the context for the events in vv 1-4. According to reconstructions based on these other textual traditions, Nahash oppressed the Gadites and Reubenites and he gouged out the right eye of all the Israelites who lived across the Jordan. Seven thousand men, however, escaped from the Ammonites and fled to the city of Jabesh Gilead. This is where the Hebrew text opens at v 1.

Based on this reconstruction, the reader understands why Nahash wanted to attack the city, since prisoners from previous battles had fled to the city and were holed up there. The men of Jabesh Gilead stated that they wanted to **make a treaty** with Nahash (v 2). Nahash responded by saying that he would agree on the condition that the **right eye of every one** of them were gouged out. The act of gouging out the eyes is known to have been practiced by the Assyrians and Babylonians (2 Kgs 25:7). It was a political gesture designed to bring disgrace upon the Israelites. The following verses indicate (1 Sam 11:5-

11), however, that it would be a man from Benjamin (lit., "son of the right") who would save their right eyes. The people of Jabesh requested a seven-day respite so that they could find a savior figure to deliver them (v 3). Since Nahash allowed the respite, he must have been confident that no such individual could be found. When messengers reached Gibeah, the hometown of Saul, they delivered a report to the people of Gibeah regarding their situation. The people of Gibeah wept over this news (v 4). Considering the close relations between Gibeah and Jabesh Gilead (Judg 20:12-14), the people's reaction is not surprising.

When Saul approached the city after driving the cattle from the field, he inquired as to why the people were crying (1 Sam 11:5). When he heard the report about the situation at Jabesh Gilead, **the spirit of God rushed upon Saul . . . and his anger burned greatly** (v 6). As mentioned before, the notice about the spirit rushing on Saul recalls the period of the judges when God raised up charismatic leaders to confront an enemy. Saul's anger over the plight of the people of Jabesh Gilead also mirrors Samson's when the spirit of God led him to kill thirty at Ashkelon (Judg 14:19). In response to this news, Saul took a yoke of oxen, cut them into pieces, and sent them throughout all Israel (1 Sam 11:7)—a scene eerily similar to Judg 19:29. Like the Judges narrative, this was done in order to rally the troops at a time of crisis. Terror fell upon the people after Saul threatened those who would not join the battle against the Ammonites.

Saul mustered the forces at a city called Bezek and the men of Jabesh Gilead were given word that they would be saved. Saul divided the troops into three columns and in the morning they struck down the Ammonite forces. One may wonder why Saul would show loyalty to the citizens of Jabesh Gilead and want to protect them. If, as we have raised the issue earlier, his mother was one of the women taken from this area according to Judg 20:12-14, then he may have felt a sense of familial and social responsibility to help them.

2. The Renewal of Kingship at Gilgal (11:14-15)

■ **14-15** After the battle report, the text recalls a tradition when the monarchy was inaugurated at Gilgal. At Gilgal the people declared Saul as king before Yahweh. Sacrifices accompanied Saul's inauguration as a sign of celebration. In observing the traditions regarding Saul, however, the careful reader notices that there are three occurrences when Saul is made king: one, at the time of Samuel's anointing (10:1); two, when he was selected among the community at Mizpah (10:24); and three, at the inauguration of Saul at Gilgal (11:15). These different accounts of Saul's inauguration would indicate that there were separate traditions regarding how Saul became king. During the editorial process these traditions had been brought together by the Deuteronomistic Historian(s).

FROM THE TEXT

This chapter offers one of the positive evaluations of Saul. It is interesting that this takes place in a setting when he successfully helped the Israelites conquer an enemy that physically intimidated and brutalized them. Saul is presented as a savior figure that God appointed to liberate his people from oppression. The text notes that Saul became "angry" (v 6) when he heard about the plight of the citizens of Jabesh Gilead. In so doing, it reminds us that there are occasions when it is acceptable to possess a righteous anger over an unacceptable state of affairs. Such anger prompts us to take action and get involved when certain situations require it. Jesus, for example, became livid when he observed how the merchants defiled the temple and exploited the people who came to worship God.

God permits individuals and/or nations to step up and defend themselves and others from tyranny, oppression, brutality, and exploitation. This not only includes the use of physical force such as self-defense or military engagement, but it also encompasses the many other ways we can fight injustice/oppression. This includes, but is not limited to: changing laws, creating new public policies, engaging in peaceful negotiation, participating in civil disobedience, becoming an advocate for the powerless, providing financial or material assistance, volunteering our time and energy for a charity or missions, utilizing various forms of media to bring public awareness, or finding an organization where one's voice/complaint can be heard. By engaging in activities that oppose the multifarious forms of injustice, racism, exploitation, intimidation, and inequalities we enter into a partnership with God by which we work to transform society and create a world where righteousness and justice can be established.

D. Samuel's Farewell Address (12:1-25)

BEHIND THE TEXT

This represents the last chapter in the unit on the establishment of Saul's kingship. The unit closes out with a final great speech by Samuel. This speech, which is Deuteronomic in its origins and language, closes out the period of the judges and Samuel, and transitions to the period of the early monarchy (Noth 1991, 17-26). In Samuel's final speech to the people, the prophet spoke out against Israel's desire and request for a king. He reiterated that God was a faithful leader in Israel's past. In addition, Samuel defended his character by asserting that he had not robbed the people or taken from them as the king they requested would do. Samuel's displeasure regarding kingship is later counterbalanced by the people's contrition and request for forgiveness. In an ironic way, Samuel does not outright dismiss the possibility of having a king, but it is made clear that Israel's obedience should be directed toward God first. If the Israelites and their king honored God above all, God would remain faithful to them. If they abandoned God, then they would be swept away from the land (v 25). This chapter also closes the book on the figure Samuel, whose name only shows up in a brief reference in 25:1.

IN THE TEXT

1. Samuel's Opening Remarks (12:1-5)

■ 1-5 This text has often been called Samuel's farewell address. Unlike other great leaders from Israel's past (Moses: Deut 33:1-29; 34:5-8; Joshua: Josh 24), Samuel's farewell statement is separated from the notice about his death (25:1). By portraying this text as Samuel's farewell address, the biblical writers place Samuel among the great leaders of Israel's history.

In this first section of the address, Samuel appears very defensive and self-protective in his remarks. Samuel defended his character and cast the request for a king as a negative thing. He noted that the **king will walk before you** (v 2) even though Samuel had walked before the people from his youth.

Moreover, Samuel, in defense of his character, also took parting shots at the institution of kingship. In vv 3-4, especially, Samuel reiterated the word "take" that is so prevalent in 8:11-17. Samuel asked the people, **Whose ox have I taken? Whose donkey have I taken? . . . From whose hand have I *taken* a bribe?** (v 3). These statements stand in sharp contrast to the king who Samuel said would take from the people earlier.

These questions also caused the people to reflect on Samuel's leadership, and they replied, "You have not . . . taken anything from the hand of anyone" (v 4 NRSV). The people's response not only vindicated Samuel as God's leader but also made them completely responsible for rejecting Samuel. In essence, they had no excuses for requesting a king and would only have themselves to blame when they suffered under the king's leadership.

2. Samuel Addresses the People (12:6-25)

■ 6-25 This section opens with a recounting of Israel's history and a defense of Yahweh. Samuel covered the history of Israel up to that period, from Jacob (v 6a) through Moses and Aaron (v 8) down to the present moment when Israel encountered Nahash (v 12). Samuel reiterated throughout this section that whenever the people had been confronted by an enemy, Yahweh consistently responded to Israel's cry for help; even when Israel had not been faithful to Yahweh. Basically, this speech underscored Yahweh's faithfulness to the people, and that when they cried out to God, he came to their rescue and delivered them. Samuel was befuddled, therefore, as to why they cried out for a king at this juncture in their history (v 12).

Samuel also crafted his message rather cleverly, for in his response he did not mention his sons, who were corrupt like Eli's sons. Moreover, he did not mention the fact that Saul, the present king, had just defeated Nahash and delivered the Israelites from his threats. According to Samuel, there was nothing wrong with judgeship from the preceding era, and it should not give way to a monarchy. By exalting the previous generation, which lived under the judges, on a pedestal, Samuel effectively condemned the present generation and their demand for a king.

Samuel's words were confirmed by a thunderstorm that developed in the dry season (vv 17-18). This unnatural weather event (it was early summer when thunderstorms were unexpected) proved that Samuel was not just a rambling old man, but that his words carried the authority of God no less. The people responded to the thunderstorm by asking Samuel to pray on their behalf so that they would not be killed. Moreover, the people admitted (v 19) that their asking for a king amounted to a sin ($h\bar{a}t\bar{a}$'). Samuel recognized that the request for a king was a bad thing, but he admonished them to continue to follow Yahweh and **serve the LORD with all your heart** (v 20). This characteristic Deuteronomistic phrase (7:3; 1 Kgs 8:23; 14:8; 2 Kgs 10:31; Jer 24:7; 29:12) reminded the Israelites that even though having a king did not represent the ideal situation, the next best option was to remain obedient to Yahweh while living under the control of the monarch. Moreover, Samuel reassured the people that he would continue to pray for them, but if they did not *fear Yahweh and serve him faithfully,* then Yahweh would sweep them away in exile (1 Sam 12:25). Later history proved this to be the case for both the northern kingdom of Israel (2 Kgs 17:7-18) and the southern kingdom of Judah (2 Kgs 25:1-21).

FROM THE TEXT

The account of Samuel's farewell speech to the people of Israel reminds us of God's great mercy and his willingness to work on behalf of humanity in spite of its sin and rebellion. Even though the Israelites rejected God by demanding a king, God did not cast them away or disown them. God continued to act redemptively toward his people even though it meant that certain elements of their covenant relationship had to be adjusted. God relented and permitted the Israelites to have a king, but the king and the people were exhorted to put God first and serve him wholeheartedly. The story of God and Israel in 1 Sam 12 is one that is repeated throughout all of Scripture. God has had to continuously overcome the mistakes and failures of humans and their tendency to demand that they have their own way. This was true in the garden with the first couple (Gen 11), in the wilderness period when the Israelites tested God and complained repeatedly (Exod 16—17; Num 10—25), in the settlement period when the Israelites compromised with the Canaanites (Judges—Kings), in the postexilic period as the Israelites struggled to remain faithful to God (Isa 57—58; 64—66), and into the intertestamental period and the time of Christ. The Bible consistently and boldly reiterates that in each generation God has graciously responded to the problem of human sin and provided the spiritual resources to heal the damage it causes. Through Christ's atonement, God's saving and healing grace continues to be at work in the world; reminding us that he will never abandon humans because of sin, but, instead, is always seeking to be reconciled to them and to restore them.

E. Saul's Shortcomings and Downfall (13:1—15:35)

BEHIND THE TEXT

First Samuel 7—12 essentially represents the end of Samuel's judgeship and the beginning of the monarchical period in Israel. Kingship was based ultimately on the rejection of Yahweh's leadership, not Samuel's as he claims, in Israel's community. Yahweh granted Israel a king in response to the people's asking. Saul, whose name means "the asked-for one," appears at first sight to be a good candidate: he is tall and nice-looking, and he comes from an affluent family. Saul also successfully led the Israelites into combat with Israel's enemies, particularly the Ammonites. Moreover, the language surrounding Saul's battle against the Ammonites resembles the period of the judges, when God raised up a deliverer to save Israel from its enemies. Saul also went to battle against the Philistines, Israel's main nemesis, which appears to be the primary reason Yahweh chose Saul in the first place. Thus, the text, on the one hand, portrays Saul in a positive light.

The next three chapters in Samuel are taken together because they are bound by a common theme: Saul's failure as the new monarch. Unlike the previous unit, which portrayed Saul favorably at moments, these chapters all point to one of Saul's various shortcomings and/or bad choices. By the end of this unit, it becomes obvious to the reader that Saul turned out to be a poor choice as king: he presided over offerings that Samuel should have officiated, he made a rash vow/oath that nearly cost Jonathan his life, and he disobeyed God's orders in the battle against the Amalekites. By the end of these three episodes, Yahweh is so disappointed in Saul that he is eventually rejected by Yahweh as king. The level of dissatisfaction with Saul caused Yahweh to claim that he regretted that he made Saul king (15:11). Chapters 13—15 thus serve as an important link between what has taken place in the previous unit and what follows after. Saul's rejection ultimately paved the way for David to emerge as the central character for the remainder of the books of Samuel.

Prior to ch 13, the people confessed to Samuel that their asking for a king amounted to sin; however, Samuel reminded them that kingship would be acceptable if the king and the people stayed faithful to Yahweh. This unit shows that the king did not follow Yahweh with his whole heart and thereby paid a tremendous price for his disobedience.

IN THE TEXT

1. Saul's Introduction (13:1)

■ 1 First Samuel 13:1 uses the standard formula to introduce the reign of a king in the DtrH (see 1 Kgs 14:21; 22:42). This formula usually states the age of the king at the time of accession and the amount of years that he ruled over Israel/Judah. In the case of Saul, however, the Hebrew text is corrupt and unreliable. The text in v 1 literally reads that Saul was *one year old when he became king and he ruled as king over Israel for two years.* Two things are immediately problematic with this formula. The notion that Saul was one year old when he became king cannot be sustained. Although three LXX traditions provide the number **thirty** (the NIV has adopted these numbers), the reality is that we do not know the age of Saul and thirty may be too young for Saul considering he had a son who was old enough to be a warrior (see below). For this reason, the NRSV and JPS have left this portion of the text blank. The idea that Saul ruled for only two years also is an unlikely reading and may have required a number before it. Acts 13:21 uses the round number forty for Saul's reign (the NIV inserts "forty" here as well), and Josephus also ascribed the same length to Saul's reign. The number forty, however, is generally understood as a round number for a generation when more specific numbers are unknown. Although some have argued that the number "two" is accurate and should stand as is, many modern scholars would question this assumption and opt for a different reading (Driver 1966, 96-97).

2. Saul Attacks the Philistines (13:2-7a)

■ 2-7a In this subunit, Saul appears to fulfill the mission for which he was chosen: to fight against the Philistine forces. Immediately after introducing Saul in v 1, the text opens in v 2 with the notice that Saul selected 3,000 men for his army: 2,000 were with him at **Micmash** and the hill country of **Bethel,** and 1,000 were with his son Jonathan at **Gibeah** in Benjamin. The army arrangement not only alludes to Saul's military acumen but also highlights that the hostilities between the Israelites and the Philistines had reached a high level at this point. The battle that begins in ch 13 also continues in various forms through ch 14. At the beginning of this battle, the text highlights that Jonathan initiated combat operations against the Philistines (as he will in ch 14).

The Philistines

The Philistines were among the Sea Peoples who first appeared in the Eastern Mediterranean at the end of the thirteenth century B.C. They were displaced from their homeland in the Aegean during the tumultuous period at the end of the Late Bronze Age. At this time the Egyptian and Hittite Empires were in a state of decline, and the Sea Peoples exploited this power vacuum by invading territories previously under Egyptian and Hittite control. In about 1190 B.C.,

Rameses III clashed with them, defeated them, and settled the invaders in the coastal towns of Gaza, Ashkelon, and Ashdod. Sometime after 1150 B.C., destruction at these sites indicated the Philistines drove out their Egyptian overlords by force. The Philistines then formed a coalition of five towns (Gaza, Ashkelon, Ashdod, Ekron, and Gath) known as the Pentapolis. For the next 150 years (until 1000 B.C.), the Philistine confederation was the most powerful entity in this part of the world. The Philistines clashed with the Israelites during the settlement period (Judg 13—16) and the early monarchy (1 Sam 13—14; 31). David was able to subdue the Philistines and inflict a crushing defeat on them. Although weakened, the Philistines did exist into the period of the divided monarchy, often forming alliances with other countries in their struggles with the territories of Israel and Judah (Amos 1:6-8; 2 Chr 21:16-17).

Verse 3a notes that Jonathan **struck the fortress/garrison of the Philistines which was in Geba.** Two observations stand out with regard to this statement. First, the Hebrew indicates that the Philistines established a military compound/fortress (*něṣib*) in Saul's hometown of Gibeah (**Geba** is a shortened form of Gibeah; see Miller 1975, 145-66). The Philistines extended their presence deep inside Israelite territory. In an ironic twist, the Philistines set up shop in the hometown of Saul, the one whom God chose to drive the Philistines out of Israel. Second, Jonathan, and not Saul, took the fight to the Philistines and he "struck" (*vayyak*) a major blow against the Philistines. In reading these statements the question comes to mind, "Is the text beginning to hint at Saul's weakness as a leader?" Not only do the Philistines camp out in Saul's backyard, but his son leads the charge against them. The details of Israel's war against the Philistines through the rest of ch 13 and into ch 14 provide more evidence that this is the case.

When Saul realized that Jonathan initiated the attack, he blew the **shopher** or trumpet (a usual custom to call the troops to battle) and summoned, **Let the Hebrews hear!** Saul's use of the term **Hebrews** in v 3 is both unusual and problematic, because the Israelites never referred to themselves in this manner. The phrase may be emended based on the LXX to read: "The Hebrews have rebelled." This reading would allude to the Philistines' indignation at Jonathan's attack on their garrison.

Although Jonathan initiated the strike (v 3a) on the Philistines, the text ascribes the action to Saul (v 4a). Since Saul was king, he was given credit for the raid. In light of the fact that the Israelites had gained momentum in the battle, the people were called out to join Saul at Gilgal.

The Philistines responded to these events by amassing an impressive force: 30,000 chariots, 6,000 horsemen, and the foot soldiers were **as numerous as the sand on the seashore** (v 5). The hyperbole of the last statement insinuates that the Israelites were feeling overwhelmed by this powerful display of force. Consequently, the Israelites took cover in **caves**, in **holes,** in **rocks** and

tombs, and ***cisterns*** (v 6). Not only did the people hide, but a number of them fled Saul and crossed the Jordan into the territory of Gad and Gilead (v 7*a*).

3. Saul Makes an Inappropriate Sacrifice (13:7b-15a)

■ **7b-15a** This text is taken as a subunit based upon the fact that it describes one of two scenes (see ch 15) in which Saul was rebuked by Samuel for not obeying God's command. This text also disrupts the flow of the previous section (vv 1-7*a*) and the following units (vv 15*b*-23; 14:1-52). Most likely, this text was inserted by another hand in order to explain the reason why Saul's dynasty never materialized (McCarter 1980b, 228).

This section opens at v 7*b* with the notice that those who joined Saul at Gilgal came to him ***trembling.*** The people's fearful response and their lack of confidence in Saul ultimately led him to make a rash decision (v 9). The setting of this text echoes the holy war traditions in which a sacrifice was required before the Israelites could engage in battle. Samuel instructed Saul to wait seven days for him (10:8), but seven days passed and Samuel still had not arrived. Samuel's absence also discouraged Saul's troops and as a result their morale weakened. Without the presence of Samuel, would Yahweh aid them in the fight against the Philistines?

As the situation continued to deteriorate for Saul and the Israelite troops, Saul began to wonder how to keep his forces from abandoning their position. The text indicates that the people already began to leave Saul (v 8*b*). In response to these difficult circumstances, Saul requested that the ***burnt offering and the peace offering be brought to him*** (v 9). Saul, in essence, took priestly matters into his own hands and presented the offerings himself. The Hebrew text indicates that just as soon as Saul finished offering the sacrifices, Samuel appeared on the scene. The timing of Samuel's appearance may raise some suspicions here. Is it possible that Samuel was laying a trap for the king? Samuel appears to play a "cat and mouse" game with Saul: he is not absolutely late but has waited to the last possible moment to arrive (Alter 1999, 72). If Samuel was testing Saul to see if he would remain obedient, he made it a difficult one considering the pressure Saul was under.

13:2-15*a*

When Samuel met Saul in v 11 he presented him with the accusing question: ***What did you do?*** Here, Samuel uses a prophetic speech form in which questions were asked by the prophet to establish the facts, just like the procedure in a judicial process. Saul reacted rather defensively in his response to Samuel: ***I saw that the people were scattering away from me, and you yourself did not come at the appointed time*** (v 11). Saul tried to pin the blame for his failure on Samuel. Saul even used an emphatic form in reference to Samuel (***you yourself***), thus underscoring Samuel's delay in coming to Gilgal. Moreover, he recounted that because the Philistines were mustering at Micmash he "forced himself, and offered the burnt offering" (v 12 NRSV). This was an action he did not want to take but had to do out of necessity. One can almost sympathize with Saul and his situation and understand why he offered the sacrifices. However, Samuel's harsh response in v 13 brings the reader back to why Saul was in the wrong. Samuel said, **You have acted foolishly and you did not observe the commandment of Yahweh your God who commanded you.** Not only did Saul disobey Yahweh's command according to Samuel, but Samuel also told him that Yahweh would punish him for his actions.

Up to this point in the story of Saul, no information has been provided regarding the duration of Saul's kingdom. Samuel indicated that God had intended to establish an eternal kingdom for Saul (v 13*b*). Because of Saul's disobedience this plan had now been changed and Yahweh would select a leader **after his own heart** (v 14). The failure of Saul's dynasty to materialize because of his disloyalty to Yahweh also mirrors the plight of Jeroboam I, whose dynasty was cut short because of his disobedience (1 Kgs 11:37-38; 14:6-10).

Although never mentioned by name, David is obliquely introduced in the text before he officially appears in the narrative (as he is in 1 Sam 15:28). Although dynastic succession becomes an important theme in the books of Samuel and Kings, the text indicates that Jonathan would not succeed Saul; thus indicating Israel's new leader would arise from another location. The man (David) to follow Saul is designated as the ***prince*** or **leader** of God's people (v 14). With the notice that Saul's house would be cut off, the way was prepared for David to emerge as the leader who would eclipse Saul. As Samuel completed these fatal words to Saul, he arose and left Saul at Gibeon in Benjamin.

4. Saul's Battle with the Philistines Continued (13:15*b*-23)

■ **15*b*-23** The text at this juncture essentially picks up where v 7*a* left off. Saul was left with 600 men who would fight against the Philistine forces (v 15*b*). The number 600 is curious, because it echoes the number of men that fled from the civil war in Judg 20. The connection between the two narratives is difficult to discern; however, it should not be overlooked since a number of other clues in the Saul narratives tie directly back to that horrific scene (see below). The only other piece of information that is included in this battle report relates to Philistine troop movements: the main body broke up into three separate parties to advance on Saul's men (1 Sam 14:17). The tactic Saul used against the Ammonites earlier was being used against him. Although the battle report is truncated here at the end of ch 13, the story line picks up again in ch 14.

Verses 19-22 close out this chapter by informing the readers that Saul and his men were at a military disadvantage against the Philistines. The Philistines were skilled iron/metal workers, but the Israelites were not. Any farming implements or weapons consisting of iron had to be made by the Philistines. The Philistines refused to make weapons for the Hebrews, because they would use them against the Philistines (see commentary on 4:9). The Philistines would sharpen their farm implements and they charged the Israelites a ***pim*** for their services, which amounted to two-thirds of a shekel. This information provides an explanation as to why the men with Saul and Jonathan did not have metal weapons with them, such as swords and spears.

Pim

> The term *pim* (*pîm*) in the OT is a *hapax legomenon*, meaning that it occurs only one time in the biblical text (translated from the Greek, lit., "read once"). The term is non-Hebrew and the weight belongs to a non-Israelite metrology. A number of *pim* weights have been discovered in Israel, but their place in the ancient metrological system is obscure. Some scholars claim it to be a distinctly Philistine measure of weight, which fits the context of I Sam 13:21 (Cook 1988, 1053-54).

5. Jonathan and the Philistines (14:1-23*a*)

■ **1-5** With the basic background of the skirmish between Saul's men and the Philistines established in ch 13, this subunit details in more graphic description the heroic efforts of Jonathan as he initiated the attack against the Philistine forces. In so doing the narrator is careful to distinguish between Saul's inaction against the Philistines and Jonathan's willingness to take the fight to them. As a result, Jonathan comes across in a very favorable light, while Saul is depicted as an abject disappointment.

Verse 1 opens with the standard formula for a narrative unit, **one day.** The time lapse between the events at the end of ch 13 and the beginning of ch 14 is undetermined, but v 1 links up with the battle notice in 13:18.

13:15b—
14:5

Verse 1 recounts the occasion when Jonathan took the initiative to confront the Philistine nemesis. This is evident as Jonathan encouraged his ***armor bearer*** to go over to the Philistine garrison. While Jonathan was poised to fight, Saul remained ***sitting*** **under a pomegranate tree in Migron** (14:2). The Hebrew text highlights Saul's dereliction in that it uses the participle form (*yōšēb*) to describe Saul's sitting. The syntax implies that Saul continued to sit under the tree without (any intention of?) moving. Even though Saul was accompanied by his **six hundred men,** the prophet **Ahijah,** and the **ephod,** Saul never moved against the Philistines. Rather, it was Jonathan who once again (13:3) decided to take action against the foe. Jonathan, moreover, did not announce his intentions but kept the matter hidden from his father. It is possible Jonathan feared his father would not allow him to approach the garrison, or it may be that Jonathan grew tired of waiting for his father to act and was eager to engage them.

Jonathan's path to the Philistine garrison was both a tortuous and dangerous one. In order to reach the garrison, he had to climb down through one rocky crag and up another (vv 4-5). The names of the crags themselves indicate the danger of the mission: **Bozez** means "swampy" and **Seneh** can be translated as "thorny." Although such a move may seem reckless, the rugged terrain provided him the necessary cover to move against the Philistines with stealth.

■ **6-15** Even though Jonathan faced great odds with this maneuver, his actions were motivated by his own faith in Yahweh. Jonathan engaged in holy war and his words and actions indicated his awareness that God's presence was with him. He referred to the Philistines in a derogatory fashion by alluding to them as **uncircumcised** and he placed the battle within the providence of God by stating, *perhaps the Lord will act for us* (v 6). Jonathan was also aware that, with God, numbers did not matter, since **nothing can hinder the Lord from saving, whether by many or by few.** The armor-bearer also stood in league with Jonathan, who responded by saying, *Do according to all that is in your heart, incline/turn for yourself, I am with you according to your heart* (v 7).

Circumcision

The act of removing the foreskin on males was not a rite exclusively practiced by the Israelites. According to Jeremiah, the people of Egypt, Judah, Ammon, and Moab also circumcised young males (9:25-26). The Greek historian Herodotus, writing in the fifth century B.C., contended that circumcision originated with the Egyptians. Archaeological evidence also supports the notion that the Egyptians practiced circumcision as early as the twenty-third century B.C. and Syrian warriors circumcised about 3000 B.C. For the Israelites circumcision played an important role in their religious life. It symbolized God's special covenant with Abraham and his descendants (Gen 17:9-14). The term can also be understood metaphorically in terms of one's wholehearted commitment to God (Deut 10:16; 30:6; Jer 4:4). In the books of Judges (14:3) and Samuel (1 Sam 14:6; 17:36), the Philistines are called uncircumcised as a standard epithet of contempt for them, and as evidence that they were not indigenous to the Semitic world (Gordon 1986, 137).

Jonathan's actions also indicated that he was relying upon the presence of God to direct his path. Not unusual in a time of holy war (Judg 6), Jonathan laid out a scenario by which he would know/discern God's intentions and whether the attack upon the Philistines was supported by God. If the Philistines taunted them (lit., **come up to us**), then he would take this as a sign that God had given the Philistines into their hands (1 Sam 14:10).

When the Philistines responded in the manner mentioned above, Jonathan was assured that God **has given them into our hands.** Not to be missed in this phrase is the pun on Jonathan's name itself, for it literally means "Yahweh has given." In vv 6-8, the text also uses a lengthened form of Jonathan's name (*yĕhōnātān*). The lengthened form of his name also underscored Jonathan's subservience to Yahweh and his role as Yahweh's vessel. Considering the context, Jonathan's name and actions are meaningful.

When Jonathan struck the Philistines, Yahweh gave him success. In this attack, Jonathan and his armor-bearer killed about twenty men, and terror broke out among the camp.

■ **16-23** It was only after one of Saul's watchmen observed the battle go back and forth that Saul finally took action and engaged in battle. Before going to battle, he first of all counted his men and it was determined that Jonathan and his armor-bearer were not present. Saul then called for **the ark of God** to be brought to him (v 18). The Hebrew text is inaccurate or corrupt at this point since the ark of God was located in Kiriath Jearim (according to 1 Sam 6). The LXX employs the word "ephod" here, and this is probably a better reading. The ephod contained the Urim and the Thummim (Exod 28:30), two divine objects that were consulted to determine God's will in a specific matter or situation.

Before the priest could consult the Urim and Thummim, Saul gave the command to **withdraw your hand** (v 19). The sound of the confusion in the Philistine camp may have provided enough evidence that they did not need to consult God any further on the matter. It is also possible to deduce that Saul became impatient with protocol related to holy war, as he did by offering the sacrifices in place of Samuel (1 Sam 13:7b-15). If so, then this would be the second occasion when Saul's impatience got him into trouble.

Yahweh brought military victory to the Israelites that day (14:23a). The Hebrews who had gone over to the Philistine side had returned to Saul and Jonathan, and the men who hid in Ephraim also gave chase to the Philistines. It is important to note, however, that it was Jonathan's faith in Yahweh and daring action that facilitated the victory and nothing that Saul had done.

6. Saul's Rash Oath (14:23b-46)

■ **23b-30** The battle pressed on to Beth Aven and entered into a new stage. As a result of this battle the troops became **hard pressed.** Even though the battle swung in Israel's favor, Saul's men became fatigued and hungry (v 28). In the midst of this situation Saul put the people under a curse/oath (v 24). Saul's oath essentially forbade the soldiers to eat any food before evening. Any individual who violated this ban was subject to death (v 44). Saul's decision was a foolish one since it limited the effectiveness of his troops in fighting the Philistines. The proof of his recklessness is found within the language itself. In Hebrew, the form of the word for making an oath (*vayōʾel*) sounds similar to the verb to "be foolish" (*yāʾal*). The wordplay is hard to miss. Other translations refer to it as "a very rash act" (NRSV), "a great error" (Klein 1983, 130), and a "trespass of ignorance" (LXX). Why Saul took this drastic action remains unclear, but it should be pointed out that yet again, Saul made a tragic blunder during a time of holy war.

When Saul's troops came upon some honey in the field, they did not eat it because they were afraid of Saul's curse (v 26). Jonathan, because of his position on the battlefield, did not hear the oath uttered by his father. Being a practical soldier, however, Jonathan dipped the edge of his staff in the honeycomb because he was hungry. As soon as he took the honey, **his eyes brightened,** meaning that his strength returned and he was revived (v 27). When the soldiers made Jonathan aware that he violated the ban his father placed on the troops, he denounced his father's actions by claiming that Saul "troubled the land" (v 29 NRSV). Like Achan, who brought trouble (*'ākar*) on the Israelite community by stealing the spoils of war (Josh 7:25), so Saul "troubled [*'ākar*] the land" by his actions. The food that had revived Jonathan's spirits would have also renewed the strength of Saul's troops. Jonathan even admitted that if the troops would have been permitted to eat the spoils of battle the blow against the Philistines would have been greater (1 Sam 14:30). Saul's unwise and rash oath, however, inhibited rather than promoted greater success.

■ **31-35** In spite of Jonathan's actions, the battle continued on to **Aijalon**, about twenty miles west of **Micmash** (v 31). Understandably, the troops and the people became extremely weary and famished. The battle continued well into the evening and at nightfall the soldiers took the spoils of war—including sheep, oxen, and calves—and slaughtered them on the ground. The text indicates that the men ***swooped down*** (like vultures) on the plunder, underscoring the severity of their hunger (v 32). Because they were so famished, the men did not give any thought to properly preparing the animals for consumption, thus they ate them with the blood still in them. In the process, the men unwittingly violated an important cultic statute (Lev 19:26; Deut 12:23-27).

Saul realized that his men acted faithlessly and violated priestly injunction. In response, he required that they roll a large stone upon which they could slaughter the animals that were in their hands. Saul then turned the rock into a makeshift altar upon which the animals were slaughtered. Saul's actions here seem hypocritical. Prior to this episode Saul gave little thought to following proper religious protocol (1 Sam 13:7*b*-15; 14:19). In this context, he took careful efforts not to offend Yahweh. The text may be pointing this out to demonstrate Saul's inconsistencies and thus highlighting another character flaw in him.

■ **36-46** At the conclusion of the sacrifice, Saul urged the men to continue to pursue the Philistines until the light of day, leaving no survivors. The troops replied favorably, but the priest among them suggested they consult God on the matter first. When Saul agreed to go along with this plan and inquired of God, he received no answer from the Lord (v 37). The absence of any reply was as good as "no." Saul ascertained that the reason God did not respond favorably to his inquiry was because there was sin in the camp. Saul therefore gathered the officers of the troops to determine the guilty party. Once the guilty party was identified, he would be punished by death, even if it was his son Jonathan.

In order to determine the culprit, a binary division was proposed with Saul and Jonathan on one side and the officers (lit., "corners") on the other. The irony of this scenario is that the troops knew Jonathan had eaten the honey, yet they waited for Saul to come to this conclusion (v 39). The first test included the use of the Urim and the Thummim. When these were consulted Jonathan and Saul were singled out from among the troops. The second phase included casting of lots to identify the guilty party. The method of casting of lots echoes the story of Achan at the battle of Ai (Josh 7:16-18) and the selection of Saul as king (1 Sam 10:19-21). At this point the troops tried to prevent Saul from taking further action. However, Saul did not listen to them, and when the lots were cast Jonathan was found to be the guilty party. Jonathan did not deny taking the honey, and Saul was poised to take the life of his son. Saul's willingness to take the life of Jonathan also conjures up the grizzly story of Jephthah whose oath/vow claimed the life of his daughter (Judg 11:34-40). Jonathan did not meet the same fate, however. The troops reminded Saul that Jonathan's victory was a sign that God was with him, and they redeemed his life.

In 1 Sam 13—14, Saul is presented as an obstacle to success against the Philistines. Saul "sat around" while the Philistines occupied a garrison in his hometown; Jonathan, rather than Saul, initiated two attacks on the Philistine compounds; Saul declared an oath that caused the troops to become famished in a time of battle and prevented Israel from experiencing a greater victory over the Philistines; and he contributed to the troops' violation of religious protocol. Moreover, Saul was willing to kill Jonathan, the very person who was so instrumental to Israel's success against the Philistines. Throughout chs 13—14, Jonathan appears to be the candidate who would fulfill God's word to Samuel (9:16) and would therefore be a fitting heir to Saul's throne. Saul's disobedience in 13:7b-15a, however, prevented Jonathan from succeeding Saul and the long-term establishment of Saul's kingdom.

7. Miscellaneous Reports About Saul's Battles and Household (14:47-52)

■ **47-48** These two verses recount the glorious achievements of Saul's reign. This information most likely derived from a different source, one that was very pro-Saulide in its perspective, since it diverges so dramatically from the other traditions related to Saul's battles. Saul is given credit for military victories over Israel's neighbors: **Moab, the Ammonites, Edom, the kings of Zobah** (which was an Aramean kingdom)**, the Philistines,** and **the Amalekites.** Nowhere else in Samuel is it recorded that Saul fought the kingdoms of Moab or Edom, but ch 11 preserves his battle with the Ammonites. Chapters 13—14, especially, recount Saul's wars with the Philistines, but the text is clear that he never subdued them. Saul's failure to devote the Amalekites to destruction (ch 15) later prompted Yahweh to reject him.

■ **49-51** A registry of Saul's family is provided after the notice that he *secured* his kingdom in v 47. This is not surprising since it hints at a possible dynastic succession once Saul's monarchy had been established. Three of Saul's sons are listed first: **Jonathan, Ishvi, and Malki-Shua**. Of the three sons, only Jonathan has a significant role in the biblical narrative. Ishvi is most likely a variant on the name Ish-Bosheth (2 Sam 2:8) and Esh-Baal (1 Chr 8:33). Malki-Shua is listed as one of the sons who died with Saul at Mount Gilboa (1 Sam 31:2-3) along with Abinadab who is not referenced in 14:49.

In addition to his sons, the text makes reference to Ahinoam, his wife. Nothing is known about her, but David later took an Ahinoam as his wife (and for the possible connection with Saul's wife see the comment on 27:43). Saul's daughter **Michal** married David (18:17-28) and later saved him from Saul (19:11-17). The text also remembers Michal as never producing a potential heir for David (2 Sam 6:23).

Abner was Saul's field commander. He is known as the son of **Ner**. Both Ner and Saul's father, **Kish**, were the sons of **Abiel**. The family registry indicates that Abner was a blood relative of Saul.

■ **52** The chapter closes with the notice that there was **bitter war** between Saul and the Philistines. Therefore, Saul kept his eyes open for a **mighty . . . man** or **warrior** who could be of service to him. Although the text never mentions David by name, he would later serve in Saul's army and fight against the Philistines with great success.

8. A Divine Command (15:1-3)

■ **1-3** The battle with the Philistines in chs 13—14 takes a backseat in ch 15. The Philistines, however, will again occupy Saul's and Israel's attention in the following chapters. In this chapter, the Amalekites become the main opponent of Israel's army.

This subunit opens with Samuel's report to Saul of a divine command. Samuel reminded Saul that Yahweh sent him to anoint Saul as king over Israel. With his credentials established, Samuel then proceeded with the standard prophetic speech form: "now **hear** the words of the LORD. Thus says the LORD of hosts" (vv 1-2a NRSV). A couple of interesting points should be considered in this context. First, the Hebrew verb (šāmaʿ) often means to "hear" or "listen," but the syntax in this phrase (šemaʿ leqôl) indicates that it should be translated more properly as "obey." Moreover, Samuel referred to Yahweh as "the LORD of hosts" (NRSV). The term "hosts" (sebāʾôt) can also be translated as "armies." Considering the following context, which is once again concerned with the theme of holy war, it is a fitting designation for Yahweh.

After the introduction, Samuel conveyed Yahweh's charge to Saul: **now go, and smite Amalek and utterly destroy all that is to him, and do not spare him, and you will kill both man and woman, infant and suckling, ox and sheep, camel and donkey** (v 3). Although the Hebrew reads **Amalek** as a singular and uses a masculine singular suffix throughout this verse, this should be taken as a collective noun and thus refers to the Amalekite people/nation. Samuel commanded Saul to participate in the ban (ḥērem), which required that all the people, animals, and possessions had to be destroyed. The grammar of v 3 even highlights this notion by setting the objects to be destroyed in a lengthy string of direct object chains, beginning with the adults and including the children and the animals. The implication being that nothing was to be spared.

The practice of complete destruction was associated with holy war, in which the battle was viewed as an act of worship and the spoils of the battle were presented as an offering to Yahweh who fought for Israel. Thus, it was considered a religious undertaking. Although proscribed in Deuteronomic law (Deut 13:12-18; 20:1-20), it was a practice that was not consistently kept in the OT during Israel's history. Recent scholarship has even questioned whether the practice was standardized or uniformly applied. Some have also questioned whether this was an ideal kept alive only among the prophets.

Cherem

The term refers to a category or status of things and people that were consecrated irrevocably into God's ownership and unavailable for secular use. The *cherem* or ban appears most often in the context of holy war (Josh 6—8, 10—11), in which captured booty would be offered up to God. The ban extended included material possessions as well as enemy populations (Deut 20:16-17; 1 Sam 15:3). There were occasions when material booty and cattle did not fall under the ban (Deut 2:34-35; 3:6-7; Josh 8:2, 26-27; 11:14). Legislation in Deuteronomy utilized the concept of the ban to include the elimination of foreign religious elements (7:2, 26; 13:16, 17, 19). The prophets also used the term as a threat when God would direct holy war against his people (Isa 43:28; Jer 25:9; Mal 4:6) or in the future against Israel's enemies (Jer 50:21, 26; 51:3; Mic 4:13).

Why would God command Samuel to give Saul this message? First Samuel 15:2*b* indicates that this is God's retributive judgment upon the Amalekites and their actions toward the Israelites as they traveled through their territory when they came out of Egypt. The text recalls the tradition in Exod 17:8-16 when the Amalekites attacked the Israelites as they were living in the wilderness. Under the leadership of Moses and Joshua the Israelites defeated the Amalekites in battle (see Num 14:26-45, which preserves a different account). In return for this defeat, Yahweh also uttered the threat that any remembrance of Amalek would be blotted out under heaven. Even though the summary of Saul's military achievements in 1 Sam 14:48 states that Saul rescued the Israelites from Amalek's hand, his failure to utterly destroy them in this context signaled not only his disappointment as God's anointed but that David would have to confront them and "clean up" Saul's mess during his reign (27:8; 30:1-31; 2 Sam 8:12).

9. The Battle Against Amalek (15:4-9)

■ **4-5** Saul began the battle with the Amalekites by mustering his troops at a place called **Telaim**. Telaim, which is mentioned in Josh 15:24, is listed as one of the cities in Judah. Its location is somewhere in the Negev near Ziph. Ziph is located about twenty-two miles south of Hebron, thus its position in the southern part of Judah is secured. The number of troops that Saul assembled is rather large: **two hundred thousand foot soldiers** from Israel and **ten thousand** from Judah (v 4). These numbers do not correspond with previous statements about Saul's troops or other battle reports. Some scholars have tried to make sense of these numbers by saying that the word for "thousand" should be taken as a military unit rather than a number. According to this view there were 200 military units from Israel and ten from Judah. Some have also argued that the high numbers could be used for rhetorical effect; namely, that Saul had superiority in this conflict and thus there was no excuse for his failure to execute Yahweh's command.

■ **6** Saul approached the city called Amalek, which is mentioned only here in the OT. The wadi in which he waited to ambush the Amalekites is also unidentified. Before the major assault, Saul offered amnesty to the people known as the Kenites. Unlike the Amalekites, the Kenites treated the Israelites with loyalty/kindness on their march from Egypt. The Kenites also settled in Judah near Arad (Judg 1:16), and Jael the Kenitess killed Sisera in Israel's battle with Jabin (4:11-22). David later dealt kindly with the Kenites as well (1 Sam 27:10; 30:29).

■ **7-9** Saul struck the Amalekites (1 Sam 15:7) and chased them from Havilah to Shur on the way to Egypt. The geographical indicators are again confusing. The narrator may have been influenced by Gen 25:18, which considered Havilah to Shur as the extent of Israelite territory. The text notes that Saul caught **Agag,** the king of Amalek, alive, but he devoted to destruction all of the people with the sword (1 Sam 15:8). Moreover, the text notes that Saul and his men spared Agag, the best of the flocks, the first and the second born, the vineyards, and all the good things they were not willing to put under the ban (v 9). The Hebrew term that is used in v 9 with regard to Agag (*vayaḥemōl*) not only means "to spare" but also can mean "to have compassion" on someone or something. This is the same language that is used when Pharaoh's daughter had pity on baby Moses (Exod 2:5-6). Only the things that were worthless, however, were placed under the ban (1 Sam 15:9). Thus, Saul spared the good booty but gave God the undesirable portions. Echoes of Eli's sons taking the best portions for themselves find their way into this scene (2:12-14).

10. Samuel Confronts Saul (15:10-35)

■ **10-21** Saul's failure to devote everything to destruction prompted a response from Yahweh through Samuel. In v 10 Yahweh's word comes to Samuel with this statement: *I am sorry that I made Saul king.* The word for *sorry* here (*nihameti*) is significant, because it is the same word that is used in Gen 6:6 in regard to the creation of the human race. Although it can be translated as "repent," in this context it connotes the idea of "regret" or "disappointment." Unlike Yahweh's disappointment in Saul, Samuel responded in anger over Saul's disobedience. Some have argued that Samuel was angry over God's disappointment in Saul, and the prophet's attempt to intervene on Saul's behalf, but the text here remains unclear.

When Samuel went the next day to deliver the word to Saul, Samuel was told that Saul actually went to Carmel to erect a monument to himself. It was customary for a king in ancient times to erect a pillar in order to commemorate a great victory (see 2 Sam 8:3, where David also established a victory monument). Saul's self-congratulatory act is rather astounding in light of Samuel's accusations in the following verses. Samuel eventually met Saul at Gilgal, the same place where Saul's kingship was confirmed (1 Sam 11:14-15) and where Samuel first confronted Saul (13:7b-15a). When Samuel approached Saul, the king greeted the prophet warmly, reassuring Samuel that he had fulfilled the command of Yahweh. In spite of Saul's declaration, Samuel's response uncovered Saul's deceit: **What is the bleating of the sheep in my ears, and the lowing of the cattle I am hearing?** (v 14). The biblical writer/narrator has included an important wordplay here. Samuel includes the words that were previously used to refer to obedience (*šamaʿ lĕqôl*) in 15:1. The word for "bleating" (*qôl*) plus the word for "hearing" (*šōmēʾā*) thus serve to point to Saul's disobedience rather than his faithfulness to Yahweh. Moreover, the verb for "hearing" (*šōmēʿa*) is a participle that indicates that as long as Samuel continued to hear the sound of the sheep/cattle, Saul was really disobeying God.

Saul's response to Samuel is equally interesting, because he basically thrust the blame on the army while attempting to exonerate himself. Saul used the third person plural when he said, **They have brought them from the Amalekites which the people have spared from the best of the sheep and the cattle in order to sacrifice to the Lord your God** (v 15). By phrasing his language in this manner, Saul disassociated himself from the act of disobedience. In the second part of that verse he then stated: **but the rest we devoted to destruction.** In this statement Saul included himself when making reference to the things that were devoted for destruction, thus trying to highlight his obedience.

■ **22-23** When Samuel heard Saul's remarks, he immediately went to the crux of the matter; the issue of listening/obedience. The Hebrew word (*šamaʿ*) is repeated in Samuel's famous statement: **Does the Lord take delight in offerings and sacrifices as much as in obeying** [*šāmʿā beqôl*] **the Lord? Behold, obeying** [*šāmaʿ*] **is better than sacrifice and attending the fat of rams** (v 22). In this well-known phrase, in which Samuel underscored the essential component of faithful leadership, the writer/narrator of the text has utilized a syntactical form that is reminiscent of the previous section. Here the form šāmʿā beqôl is used, which is idiomatic for obedience. In the first instance the infinitive form is used, and in the second case the participle form is utilized. This is significant because both verbal forms indicate ongoing, continuous, or uninterrupted action. This literary formation thus highlights the quintessential point of this text: continuous obedience to the voice of God is better than any sacrifice that humans could offer. Samuel announced that rebellion (*merî*) against God is tantamount to other great sins: including divination, wickedness, and idolatry.

As a result of Saul's indiscretions, God had a final word for the king through Samuel: God would **reject** him as king over God's people (v 23). The irony of this last phrase cannot be missed, because in asking for a king the people rejected God (8:7), God now rejected the king that they requested. In both cases the same form of the Hebrew word for rejection (*māʾas*) is used, thus tying these two scenes together.

■ **24-31** When Saul heard the fateful words of Samuel he could only respond in contrition. Saul recognized not only that he transgressed the word of Yahweh and Samuel but also that he feared the people and obeyed their voice instead. Sadly, Saul obeyed the people rather than God. However, the words of contrition did not change the outcome; Yahweh's rejection meant that the kingdom would be handed over to another. The polemic against Saul most likely came from those close to David. Even though David's name is never mentioned in this context, it served the interests of those wanting to exalt the Davidic monarchy. Here David is referred to as Saul's **neighbor** who is better than the king (v 28). In a scene fitting the time of Ahijah and Jeroboam (1 Kgs 11:30-33), Saul grabbed Samuel's garment and tore it in half. The event held great symbolism and provided the platform for Samuel's message for Saul: ***The Lord has torn the kingdom away from you*** (v 28).

■ **32-35** The chapter closes in a significant way. Agag, the Amalekite king who had been spared by Saul, was brought before Samuel the prophet. Unlike Saul, who was required by God to annihilate Agag, the prophet hewed down the Amalekite king in short order (v 32). Samuel's action resonated; it was the prophet who obeyed Yahweh rather than the king. With the slaying of Agag completed, Samuel and Saul departed from each other for the last time. Saul went home, and Samuel would soon anoint the next king over Israel.

FROM THE TEXT

1. The chapters on Saul's kingship teach us a number of important lessons. One of the things we learn in examining the life of Saul is that Saul had the opportunity to either be a good and faithful servant of God or he could become a real disappointment. The choice was his. In looking at the narratives on Saul, we realize that God appointed him for an important task (to defeat Israel's enemies) and Saul possessed the potential to accomplish these tasks. The text bears out that in some instances Saul partially fulfilled the respon-

sibilities for which he was chosen. However, the overall theme of Saul's life is that he did not live up to his potential. The text makes it clear that it was not God's fault or even Samuel's, but it was clearly Saul's own choices and actions that contributed to his disappointing record. This reminds us that as individuals we can either choose to fulfill our potential in God, or through our own choices and actions we can miss out on the opportunities that God has planned for us.

2. In looking at the issue of leadership as it relates to Saul, we see that Saul failed as God's leader for a number of important reasons:

a. In ch 13 Saul overstepped his bounds as king by offering sacrifices that Samuel should have offered. Not only did Saul overextend his authority by breaching the role of a prophet, but an examination of this text reveals another important reason why Saul committed this foolish act. The text notes that when the Philistines had gathered for battle and Samuel was delayed in making the sacrifice, the people started to get nervous. As the people's courage and morale began to fade, the people began to desert Saul. Saul, however, allowed the concern over people's perceptions of him and a situation that was quickly deteriorating to dictate how he would respond in turn.

As a leader, Saul was more afraid of what people might think of him than what God had commanded him through Samuel. Thus, Saul made a bad choice out of insecurity and pressure rather than trusting God and waiting for Samuel. This reminds us that in a leadership position, we cannot always worry about whether or not people may like us. The greatest leaders in life often have to make difficult, and even unpopular, decisions for the greater good. The measure of a great leader is that he or she has the maturity, fortitude, and faith in God to make tough decisions, no matter whether they please the people all the time. Great leaders maintain their faith and composure even during chaotic times. It is not difficult to make a hurried or rushed decision when a situation seems to be deteriorating. However, during those times the chances increase of making a hasty decision that could have detrimental effects down the road. Saul allowed a crumbling situation to pressure him into rushing a course of action that was later denounced as foolish by Samuel himself.

b. Saul also made another blunder as a leader of God's people. In a time of battle, Saul made a rash decision that anyone who would eat before sundown would be devoted to destruction. Saul's quick decision, however, was an impractical one that did not take into consideration the well-being of the men under his authority. As a result, the troops under Saul's command became faint and had to slow down their attack because they were tired and hungry. Moreover, the decision Saul made nearly cost his own son his life, if it had not been for the men who interceded on Jonathan's behalf. This narrative on Saul's life reminds us that if we make decisions without fully considering how they will impact the individuals underneath our care, then we act unwisely and put our people at a disadvantage. Godly and successful leadership tries to anticipate whether our decisions will have long-term negative consequences or put people in a position to succeed.

c. The last issue we see regarding Saul is his lack of obedience in ch 15. In this chapter God gave Saul a specific command, to devote the Amalekites to destruction. Saul did not follow through with the command and only gave a portion of the spoils as an offering to God. When Samuel confronted Saul, he reminds us of the true element of godly leadership: obedience. In this chapter Samuel reminded Saul that obedience is the greatest gift that one can offer God, and it is the one that God is most impressed with. Samuel echoes the sentiments of the great prophets of the OT that God is not impressed with our worship or our offerings if our heart is not right with God. Living a godly and pious life outside the sanctuary must accompany worship if our faith is going to be authentic. Anything less than that is not good enough. Saul realized this in his own life, and as a result, he forfeited the opportunity to have a ruling dynasty in Israel. God selected another to be king because Saul could not be counted upon to carry out God's wishes.

III. DAVID'S RISE TO KINGSHIP (1 SAMUEL 16:1—2 SAMUEL 8:18)

A. David's Anointing and David at Saul's Court (16:1-23)

BEHIND THE TEXT

This chapter is treated independently based on the merits of literary/grammatical analysis and for its thematic concerns. Chapter 16 formally introduces David in the text. Prior to this juncture in 1 Samuel, hidden polemics and oblique references only hinted at David's anticipated arrival. Chapter 16, however, represents the first time David actually emerges as the main figure in the books of Samuel. Like Saul, David's path to the throne begins with an anointing scene. Chapter 16 comes on the heels of the ignoble statement about Saul in 15:35*b*: ***and the Lord was sorry that he made Saul king over Israel.*** With this statement in place, the scene is set for David's ascent to kingship and control of the kingdom. This chapter basically serves as a preface for the remaining narratives pertaining to David's life.

The narratives regarding David's ascension to the throne in 1 Sam 16—2 Sam 5 are referred to in scholarly circles as "The History of David's Rise" (see "The History of David's Rise" in the Introduction). This block of material demonstrates how David rose from a simple shepherd boy to the king over all the tribes of Israel. In the story of David's rise to kingship, David comes across in a very favorable light. The reader gets the overall impression in this section that God's hand is on David and gives him success in everything that he does. David is portrayed as an up-and-comer in Saul's court (1 Sam 16), a man of faith and courage (ch 17), a popular figure among the people of Israel and Saul's own family (chs 18—20), a noble man who is generous toward Saul (chs 24; 26), and a successful politician who turned Israel into a respectable nation state (2 Sam 3—5).

This portrait, however, stands in opposition to the picture that emerges of David in 2 Sam 9—1 Kgs 2 (see "The Succession Narrative" in the Introduction). Chapter 16 begins David's journey to the throne, first with his anointing by Samuel and then with his introduction to Saul's court.

IN THE TEXT

1. Samuel Instructed to Anoint David (16:1-5)

The story of David that begins in ch 16 falls into two main sections. The first (vv 1-13) refers to David as God's choice as king. The second (vv 14-28) identifies David as Saul's choice. By arranging the material in this fashion, the writer/narrator of this chapter intended to emphasize the priority of God's initiative in selecting David over against Saul's. It also highlights the differences that led to the kingship of Saul and David in the first place: the people asked for and selected Saul; God sought after and chose David.

■ 1-5 God's initiative in selecting David is witnessed in Yahweh's speech to Samuel in v 1. Although Samuel may have mourned the rejection of Saul, Yahweh was already looking ahead to the future. Yahweh rejected Saul (as the people rejected Yahweh earlier by asking for a king [8:7]) and he instructed Samuel to fill his horn with oil and travel to the house of Jesse in Bethlehem. Unlike ch 15, which highlighted the word "hear" and/or "obey" (šāmʿa), the key word in ch 16 is "see" (rāʾâ). Yahweh told Samuel that he had "seen" (i.e., provided, chosen) a king from the sons of Jesse. Whereas the rejection of Saul was based on his "not listening to" or "obeying" Yahweh, David was now recognized as an exercise in right "seeing" (Birch 1998, 1097).

Samuel was afraid that traveling to Bethlehem to anoint Saul's successor could be taken as a sign of treason. In light of this Samuel thought **Saul will kill me** (v 2) for traveling to Bethlehem. God instructed Samuel to take a heifer with him so that Samuel could say that he was making a sacrifice to Yahweh in case anyone asked Samuel why he was in Bethlehem. Yahweh's word may seem duplicitous at first thought, but the sacrifice would serve as the pretext by which Samuel could meet Jesse and his family. The sacrifice would have been offered after the anointing ceremony took place.

Samuel obeyed Yahweh's command and traveled to Bethlehem. The elders of the city **trembled** with fear because they did not know Samuel's intentions (v 4). Moreover, they believed Samuel's visit provided a pretext by which Saul could exact revenge on them for treason. Their question to Samuel, **Do you come in peace?** indicated their desire to discern the reason for Samuel's visit (v 4). When Samuel told them he came to sacrifice, he commanded them to "purify" (JPS) or "sanctify" (NRSV) themselves, which was customary preparation for a sacred event (v 5). Whereas the elders made their own sacred preparations, Samuel personally sanctified Jesse and his sons for the sacrifice.

2. David Is Anointed (16:6-13)

■ **6-13** When Samuel traveled to Jesse's house to anoint Israel's next leader, Jesse's sons were brought before him. When Samuel **saw** (*wāyāreʾ*) the oldest son, **Eliab,** he presumed immediately that this was the Lord's choice. Yahweh, however, rebuked Samuel rather abruptly, reminding him not to look at his **height** or his **appearance** (in Hebrew these statements are negative commands). Yahweh's word to Samuel in v 7 makes a sharp dichotomy between Saul and David, since these were the same words used to describe Saul earlier (9:2; 10:23). Considering that these were the same physical qualities that Saul possessed, we may take it that Samuel, like the people of Israel, based the qualifications of leadership on whether an individual could pass a simple eye test (16:6).

Yahweh told Samuel, however, that he rejected (*mĕʾastîhû*) Eliab, just like Yahweh had rejected Saul (v 1) (and similarly to the people who rejected Yahweh when they requested a king [8:7]). Yahweh's rationale was simple: Yahweh does not see (*yireʾeh*) as humans do; they are apt to look at outward appearances (as in the case of Saul), but the Lord looks at one's **heart** (v 7). The "heart" in the OT refers to the will and character of a person. This statement thus lays out one of the primary criteria for successful leadership according to biblical teaching: the effectiveness of a leader/king is associated with his obedience to Yahweh.

When Yahweh rejected Eliab, the other sons were brought before Jesse. Two of these sons are named, **Abinadab** and **Shammah,** but the other four are not mentioned (vv 9-10). Like Eliab, Yahweh rejected these candidates and Samuel had to ask Jesse if he had any other sons. Jesse replied that his youngest son was **tending the sheep.** The image of David as a shepherd is a significant one. In the OT, God's greatest leaders tended the flock before they became the leader of Israel's community (i.e., Moses and David). That David is a shepherd quietly foreshadows and anticipates his role as one of Israel's greatest kings. The text also draws attention to his role as a shepherd at critical points in David's story (16:19; 17:15, 34-36). The term for shepherding is also significant in that it is etymologically similar to the word for "see" (*rōʿeh*). Thus, the narrator creatively reinforces the idea of seeing in this chapter with David's occupation as a shepherd. It is also significant that David is the eighth and youngest son of Jesse. To most people this would make David unfit for kingship. This fact only underscores, however, that Yahweh does not see as humans do and chooses people most would ordinarily overlook.

When David officially appears in this text, he does so passively in that he is brought before Samuel. This fact insinuates that David did not campaign for this task nor was he actively seeking the office of king. When David was brought before Samuel, the text notes that David was **ruddy,** he "had beautiful eyes" (NRSV), and he was ***nice looking*** (v 12). Although the text reiterates that appearance did not matter to God, the text seems to delight in the notion that God's choice could also be nice looking. When David appeared before the prophet, Yahweh told Samuel immediately to anoint him since **he is the one.** Although he may not have been Samuel's first choice, David was God's first choice. Samuel then anointed David in a manner similar to Saul. Like Saul, "the spirit of the LORD came mightily upon David from that day forward" (v 13 NRSV). Unlike Saul, from whom the spirit "departed" (v 14), the text indicates that the presence of God would be with David continuously (v 13 NRSV, "from that day forward").

3. David Is Introduced to Saul's Court (16:14-23)

■ **14-23** The operative word in the second section of ch 16 is the Hebrew term "breath" or **spirit** (*rûah*). The "spirit" of Yahweh that descended upon David **departed from Saul** (v 14a). In place of Yahweh's spirit, the text notes that Yahweh sent an **evil**/bad spirit to terrify Saul. The idea that Yahweh would send an evil spirit to torment Saul may be a difficult or unusual one to a modern reader. However, it must be kept in mind that seldom does the biblical story attribute secondary causation to a particular phenomenon. In the ancient Hebrew mindset, all things (both good and bad) ultimately emanated from God. However, this does not absolve Saul from responsibility for his own behavior, and it was his disobedience that caused a rift in his relationship with Yahweh.

At the same time, the evil spirit may also be understood as a sickness or malady. In the case of Saul, this may even relate to his emotional and psychological problems. Saul is portrayed in the text as being unstable emotionally and often battles bouts of insecurity, depression, rage, and paranoia. In modern language, Saul's **evil spirit** may be equated with his psychological and emotional dysfunctions. The evil spirit that tormented Saul nevertheless provided the occasion by which David became associated with Saul's court. David's presence in Saul's court was intended to be a remedy for a troubled spirit.

Saul's servants suggested that a musician skilled with the lyre could bring relief to him (vv 15-16). Even Saul's servants were certain that music would help sooth his soul. It is no surprise that Saul even commanded his servants to "provide for me someone who can play well" (v 17 NRSV). One of the servants responded by saying that "I have seen a son of Jesse the Bethlehemite who is skillful in playing" (v 18 NRSV). The notice about David's musical talents is noted elsewhere in Samuel and throughout David's story (2 Sam 23:1). David is depicted as the composer of psalms and patron of music (6:5), and in various superscriptions he is cited as the composer of over eighty psalms. The Dead Sea Scrolls from Qumran claim that David composed 3,600 psalms and 450 songs. Rabbinical tradition states that David wrote the entire book of Psalms (*B. Bat.* 14-15).

David was also described by the servant as being "a man of valor, a warrior, prudent in speech, and a man of good presence" (v 18 NRSV). Although important qualities to possess in their own right, the servant more importantly testified that *Yahweh is with him.* The notice about Yahweh's presence is a major theological theme in the stories related to David's rise to power (16:13; 18:14, 28; 2 Sam 5:10). In developing this theme, the text carefully highlights Yahweh's presence as the source of David's success.

Saul acted on the servant's suggestion and summoned David personally (1 Sam 16:19), uttering his name for the first time. The text is also careful to show that David entered Saul's court passively. That is, David simply came to Saul's court at the request of the king. This is an important point to consider as opponents of David may have accused him of taking an active role in replacing Saul's household (see Introduction). When David arrived at Saul's court he "took the lyre and played it" (v 23 NRSV). Whenever the evil spirit terrified Saul David's music would bring the king relief. Saul became enamored with David, and the text notes that he "loved him greatly" (v 21 NRSV). Saul's fondness for David was also shared by his children (18:1, 20) and the people of Israel (18:16). As a result of God's favor upon him, David was beloved by everyone. Saul was so impressed with him that he even made him one of his armor-bearers (16:21).

FROM THE TEXT

The story of David in ch 16 reminds us that God does not look at human beings or their potential in the kingdom of God based on outward appearances or status. This is a fallacy that was proven true in the story of Saul. The text reminds us that whereas humans look on **the outward appearance,** God **looks at the heart** (v 7). It would be the heart of David that made him a faithful servant of God, and it was his confidence in God that allowed him to accomplish extraordinary things. God does not discriminate based on our physical characteristics or age, but God looks at our obedience and willingness to serve him as the greatest qualities one can possess. Although David may have been disqualified by the criteria of others, God selected David and was able to bring blessing to the people of Israel through him. Likewise, God is able to use the talents, abilities, and energies of individuals that others may overlook to build the kingdom of God.

B. David and Goliath (17:1-58)

BEHIND THE TEXT

The story of David and Goliath is one of the most famous episodes among the Davidic traditions. Even people who have little or no religious background are familiar with it. Modern scholars have posited that ch 17 represents a classic case of epic storytelling. It is rich in explicit detail, it contains extensive use of vivid dialogue, and there is strong characterization and interaction among characters (Alter 1999, 150-51).

This chapter also represents the third occasion when David is introduced to the reader. David first emerges in 16:1-13 with the anointing by Samuel, in vv 14-24 as the court musician to Saul, and here in ch 17 as the military champion of Israel. Interestingly, however, this tradition shows no awareness of the material in ch 16. In ch 17, Saul has to ask about David's identity, for example, and the tradition about a champion warrior named Goliath is told in 2 Sam 21:19 as well (see also 23:24). In 2 Sam 21:19, a man named Elhanan of Bethlehem killed Goliath the Gittite (another name for someone from Gath) whose "shaft of [the] spear was like a weaver's beam" (NRSV); a similar detail used to describe the armor of David's opponent in 1 Sam 17:7. Scholars have used this evidence to suggest that the story of David and Goliath was created by those in Davidic circles based on the exploits of Elhanan. Other pieces of information would indicate that this chapter has been carefully crafted in order to portray David in ideal terms and to give support to the Davidic monarchy.

First Samuel 17 also presents significant textual problems that suggest the narrative has a complicated transmission history. The tradition preserved in the Old Greek text (LXX) is much shorter than the one found in the Hebrew text (MT), the manuscript traditions on which modern translations are based. Moreover, in the LXX, particularly LXX^B, vv 12-31, 41, 48*b*, 50, and 55-58 are missing (as well as 18:1-6*a*, 10-11, 12*b*, 17-19, 21*b*, 29*b*-30). This evidence indicates that two versions of David's encounter with Goliath existed: an earlier version reflected in the LXX and a later, expanded account found in the MT (Tov 1985, 97-130). By all accounts, the shorter text appears to be the more original while the MT and the other LXX renditions are expansions of the earlier story. While it is possible to posit that LXX and MT are combinations of two completely independent sources, the fact that they do not represent a complete or coherent account on their own mitigates against this view. Nevertheless, in ch 17 David comes across as a young man of great faith and courage. In both textual traditions, David fights against the Philistine champion and wins. This would not be the first time that David had success over Israel's main nemesis—a mission that was originally intended for Saul.

IN THE TEXT

1. The Introduction of Goliath (17:1-11)

■ **1-11** These verses basically set the stage for the battle between David and Goliath. In vv 1-3 the text notes that the Philistines were back to fight the Israelites. While Saul was anointed and commissioned to face this threat (9:16; 10:1), chs 13—14, along with this one, intimate that the Philistine threat was never satisfactorily addressed. The text continues to note that both armies camped along opposite ridges with a valley running between them. The armies were stationed in the southwest portion of Judah near the Philistine border and the cities of Ekron and Gath specifically.

In the midst of the geographical setting, Goliath is first introduced in the text (v 4). The name Goliath is Philistine in origin and he is called a **champion** (lit., *a man between the two*) from the city of **Gath**. As the text introduces Goliath, however, the reader notices that the writer/narrator of this text focuses immediately on Goliath's physical qualities and appearance. In terms of his height, the Hebrew text lists Goliath as "six cubits and a span" (JPS). This information runs contrary to the LXX tradition, which reads "four cubits and a span." If we take the Hebrew text as it is, Goliath measured 9 feet and 9 inches tall. These dimensions would indicate that Goliath was taller than any human remains uncovered by archaeologists to date. If the LXX tradition is preferred, then Goliath stood 6 feet 9 inches tall. In light of textual and archaeological evidence, the LXX represents the more accurate reading. However, even according to ancient standards Goliath's height remains very impressive.

The description of Goliath's armor progressively moves from head to toe; from top to bottom. The writer/narrator of this text was especially enamored with Goliath's equipment because three verses are devoted to its description (vv 5-7). According to the text, his head was covered by "a helmet of bronze" (NRSV), his chest was protected by "a coat of mail [which weighed] five thousand shekels of bronze. He had greaves of bronze on his legs and a javelin of bronze slung between his shoulders . . . and his spear's head weighed six hundred shekels" (vv 5-7 NRSV). In addition to his impressive display of armor, Goliath also had a **shield bearer** who went out before him. All in all, Goliath is portrayed as an impregnable fortress. The writer/narrator drew careful attention to his armor in order to emphasize the sizable challenge that lay ahead of David as well as the armaments in which Goliath put his faith. Unlike Goliath, David's victory came about as a result of Yahweh's help, not because of his trust in weaponry.

The Philistine champion not only stood in front of the Israelite army wearing this impressive military equipment but also presented a personal challenge to them. Goliath, in a bombastic manner, invited the Israelites to **choose a man** who would come out to fight him (v 8). If Israel's man could defeat Goliath the Philistines would become Israel's servants. If Goliath defeated the Israelite champion, then Israel would serve the Philistines. Contests between individual soldiers who represented larger armies were not uncommon in ancient times, as texts from Egypt, Greece, and Persia attest (Ackroyd 1971, 138; Mauchline 1971, 132; Gordon 1986, 155). In spite of the challenge, Israel's troops remained "dismayed and greatly afraid" (v 11 NRSV).

2. David and the Flock (17:12-30)

■ **12-30** While the text describes Goliath in impressive detail in vv 4-11, the writer/narrator creatively shifts his focus to David in vv 12-30. As previously mentioned, this entire section is missing in LXX^B and the story picks back up at v 31. The MT text, however, introduces David in a way that greatly contrasts him with the pompous Goliath. David arrives in a humble fashion and without fanfare. He is simply described as *the youngest son* of Jesse (a detail already recorded in ch 16) and as a *shepherd* of his father's flocks (17:14-15). Unlike ch 16, however, the text notes that three of his older brothers had already joined the ranks of Saul's army and that David shuttled back and forth between Jesse's flocks and the battlefront in order to carry supplies and messages (17:15, 17-18).

Goliath's challenge went unheeded for **forty days**, thus underscoring both Saul's and Israel's inaction (v 16). In light of this, David was sent by his father to the battlefront with **grain** and **bread** for his brothers, as well as *cheese* as a gift for their commander (vv 17-18). Like Joseph (Gen 37:14), David was dispatched to inquire how his brothers as well as Israel's troops were fairing. When David arrived at Saul's camp the armies had taken their sides opposite the valley with shouts of war ringing in the air. As David heard these rumblings, he dumped his baggage and found his brothers to determine what was transpiring on the front lines (1 Sam 17:22). As David arrived at the forefront, Goliath made another challenge to Israel's army. The response of Israel's troops was one of **fear** and *retreat* (v 24), and the men *spoke in awe of him.* Even though Saul's warriors interpreted Goliath's arrogant challenge as an affront to Israel, none stepped forward (v 25). The promise of freedom and the hand of Saul's daughter could not entice anyone to confront the Philistine warrior.

David, who had heard Goliath's taunts, viewed Goliath's bullying and bantering as a blatant attack on Israel's army and Israel's God (v 26). Although David interpreted Goliath's actions theologically, **Eliab** was bothered by David's inquiry regarding royal rewards (v 28). He also accused David of abandoning his responsibilities at home by venturing to the front lines. The dialogue between David and his older brother in vv 28-29 sharpens the contrast between David, his brother, and the Israelite army in general. David was ready to stand up and fight for Israel and defend the reputation of Israel's God, while the other men, including his brother, were not.

3. David and Saul (17:31-40)

■**31-40** In this subunit, David's courage is contrasted sharply with the cowardice of Saul and the Israelite army. David took up the challenge to confront Goliath while the Israelite army cowered in fear. David was brought before Saul and delivered this message to the king: *Do not let anyone's heart fall on account of him* (v 32). David volunteered to fight the champion, but as Saul heard the suggestion he reminded David that he was just a *young man* and Goliath had been a warrior since his youth. David's confidence, however, was borne out of his previous experiences as a shepherd. When David watched over the flock he had to kill both lions and bears. David used these experiences to remind Saul that it was Yahweh who gave David victory over these predators and, as a result, Yahweh would also **deliver** David from this Philistine (v

37). David's experience was not unlike others in the OT, in which God often used the events of the past to prepare an individual for a new task (i.e., Moses).

When Saul heard David's response, he put his armor on David in preparation for battle. The irony of David, the future king, putting on the armor of Saul, the present king, cannot be overlooked. It would only be a matter of time before David replaced Saul. Moreover, the text seems to be critiquing Saul again in that he was derelict in leading the troops into battle and rescuing the Israelites from the Philistines. This was the original task for which God selected Saul (9:16), now David was coming to his aid. Throughout the rest of Samuel, it becomes apparent that David will be the one to fulfill God's word to Samuel in 9:16, as he enjoyed success against the Philistines on multiple occasions.

The distinction between David and Saul is also attested in the way both figures viewed the battle. Up to this point, David couched his view of the battle in theological terms in that he perceived Goliath's threats as defiance against God's army and by recalling Yahweh's protection as he shepherded the flocks. Saul, however, viewed the battle in purely human terms, a young boy versus a champion warrior. Thus it comes as no surprise that Saul thought that battle armor would protect David. David tried on Saul's armor but was not able to walk while wearing the cumbersome gear (17:39). David removed the equipment and took the simple weapons that he was accustomed to using while tending the flock: a staff, some stones, and a sling. The text insinuates that David's trust was in Yahweh, because he would not be able to overpower Goliath with superior armor and weaponry.

4. The Battle with Goliath (17:41-54)

■ **41-54** When Goliath came out to meet David, his armor-bearer walked in front of him. As Goliath looked over David, he also underestimated him since he was just a ***youth, ruddy and nice looking*** (v 42). Goliath **despised** David because he thought the Israelites were making sport of him by sending out a lad to fight with a sling and stones. His question, **Am I a dog, that you come at me with sticks?** (v 43), is evidence of the offense he took at such a notion. In addition, Goliath cursed David by **his gods** (v 43). While Goliath invoked his gods, David came to the Philistine in the power of the God of Israel (v 45).

David took umbrage to Goliath's words and retaliated by saying that Goliath trusted in sword and spear, but David came "in the name of the LORD of hosts" (v 45 NRSV). **Name,** in the minds of the Hebrews, embodied the power of the person who bore that appellation. Thus the name of Yahweh represented God's omnipotence and reputation as a warrior. Confident in the name/reputation of God, David proclaimed that Yahweh would give him victory and Goliath's head would be given to **the birds of the air** and the wild animals **of the earth** (v 46). According to David, the battle would not be won through swords and spears but through Yahweh who would give Goliath into the hands of the Israelites.

Unlike the dialogue that immediately precedes this scene, the actual battle report is told in brief detail (vv 48-49). For the narrator, the essence of the battle was not the physical description of combat but the theological dialogue that took place between David and Goliath. In terse detail, the text notes that David took a **stone, . . . slung it,** and it **sank** into Goliath's head (v 49). David also removed Goliath's sword and cut off the head of his opponent, just as he predicted. The defeat of Goliath served as a testimony that God had provided the victory for David and the Israelites. Consequently, when the Philistines saw their champion was dead, they fled. The Israelites chased them back to **Gath** and **Ekron** with injured Philistines falling along the way.

The Sling as a Weapon

David's use of the sling and stones to kill Goliath (1 Sam 17:40-50) illustrates the effectiveness of this primitive projectile in combat. Stones could be used as shock weapons, such as hitting an enemy on the head, but when launched from a sling they became a lethal projectile. In the hands of a skilled warrior, slings were known to be deadly accurate (Judg 20:16).

This section ends in v 54 with the curious statement that David took Goliath's head to **Jerusalem.** This is a clue from the text that the tradition regarding David and Goliath was committed to writing after the Davidic monarchy was firmly established in the capital city. Jerusalem would not fall into Israelite hands until David was king over all Israel (2 Sam 5).

5. Saul Meets David a Second Time (17:55-58)

■ **55-58** This section, once again, provides evidence that the narrative of David and Goliath was developed at a later time. These verses indicate no awareness of the tradition in 16:14-23, nor do they presuppose any prior consultation with Saul about going to battle in vv 31-40. In vv 55-58, Saul attempted to gain knowledge of David by inquiring about the identity of his father. David, however, was brought before Saul only after he killed Goliath; clearly a different account from the one in 16:14-23. Moreover, when David met Saul he was still holding the head of the Philistine, which had already been taken to Jerusalem in v 54. In this section, then, David is introduced to Saul after the battle and is identified only as the ***son of Jesse the Bethlehemite.***

FROM THE TEXT

1. We learn from the story of David that God can use our past experiences to prepare us for future tasks. In the life of David, God was able to use his talent in music and his shepherding skills for a greater purpose later in his life. David not only had to recall these skills when a new situation demanded, but they were invaluable for fulfilling a greater purpose. David's skill in music played an instrumental role in bringing healing to Saul's troubled spirit, and

David's skill as a shepherd was invaluable to him when he confronted Goliath. In both cases, other people benefited from these experiences. God often uses our situations, experiences, or previous education to prepare us for new roles that will be a blessing to others. It is imperative that as individuals we are seeking ways to increase our horizons through education, new experiences, new challenges, and training. We never know when God may put those skills to use in order to advance the kingdom of God.

2. The story of David also serves as a lesson about the relationship between faith and action. In ch 17, David was willing to confront Goliath while the other soldiers of Saul were afraid to engage in battle. In examining this story we come to understand that David had such great faith in God because he could recall moments in his life when God had helped him before. When David was a shepherd, he recalled the moments when God saved him from the lions and the bears, and he had faith that God would help him against Goliath. God's activity in David's life in the past served as a foundation for greater faith in the future. Because David remembered that God had saved him before, he had the confidence that God would help him again. Forgetting what God has done for us in the past becomes a barrier to stronger faith tomorrow.

In the OT, the children of Israel experienced the power of God in the Exodus event. Yet, when they were in the wilderness and faced with many challenges, they lost faith in the God who redeemed them from slavery. The Psalmist reminds us that one reason the people lost faith in God is that they forgot what God had done for them (78:11). The Israelites forgot what God had done for them in the past and, as a result, they became ungrateful and rebellious. Instead of experiencing the blessings found in the promised land, they forfeited all those good things because of their distrust and ingratitude. As believers, it is important that we are always mindful of things God has done for us in our past. When we stop and reflect on the many ways God has answered prayer, worked on our behalf, and supported us through difficult situations, it will give us confidence for new situations that require (greater) trust in God.

3. The life of David also reminds us that when we walk with God all things are possible. Even when we are in situations in which our resources seem small in comparison to the task or challenges we are facing, the text reminds us that God can take the little things we possess to accomplish great things. David confronted Goliath with a sling and some stones, yet with God's help it was enough to get the job done. The story of David and Goliath reminds us that victory does not come through human might, but through the power of God. In this way the story of David aligns with many others where God took something small and accomplished great deeds with it. The only precondition for success is that we remain willing to allow God to use whatever we have to offer him for his purposes and glory.

C. David and Saul's Household (18:1—20:42)

BEHIND THE TEXT

Chapters 18—20 represent another stage in the larger story of David's rise to kingship. David has already been introduced to the reading audience as a shepherd (16:1-13), as a musician in Saul's court (vv 14-23), and as slayer of giants (17:1-55). These three chapters, however, concentrate on David's emerging relationship with various people: Saul, Saul's family, and the wider Israelite populace. Moreover, they will also highlight David's success as one of Saul's army commanders. David's success, however, causes Saul to become increasingly jealous and suspicious of him. Saul's skepticism toward David grows to such an evil pitch that he tries to eliminate him on various occasions using a range of tactics to accomplish this task (18:11, 25; 19:10-11, 20; 20:33).

Throughout these chapters, however, an ironic turn of events begins to develop. While Saul becomes increasingly distrustful and jealous of David, Saul's children and the wider Israelite populace come to respect and love him (18:1, 3, 16, 20, 22, 28). The theme of the people's love for David is so prominent that it helps to bind this material together in chs 18—20 on a literary and thematic basis. The people's love for David also represents one of the major themes and theological functions in David's rise: God gives David favor in the eyes of the people to such an extent that even Saul's children come to adore him. This paradox is developed to the point that Saul's children were willing to disobey their father and lay down their own lives in order to protect David. The contrast between Saul's jealousy and desire to eliminate David on the one hand and the love of Jonathan and Michal on the other is both astounding and powerful. The tension that develops between the various characters (David vs. Saul, Saul vs. Jonathan and Michal, the people vs. Saul) keeps the reader riveted to the drama that unfolds.

While David enjoyed success among the people and on the battlefield, Saul's personal life continued to unravel. David's life followed an upward trajectory while Saul's life went downhill. Saul was paranoid of David, and Saul's obsession with killing David was one of the factors that led to his downfall. The careful reader of the account of David and Saul will have to ask if Saul, at some level, was justified in his skepticism of David.

As one carefully studies David's life, it becomes clear that David's path was paved by important events that helped to catapult him to the throne: he enjoyed important "social" and "political" connections that would benefit him later in his life, he married significant women that furthered his political career, and a number of candidates to Saul's throne die at the hands of people associated with David.

In a very telling text (20:31), Saul angrily rebuked Jonathan's alliance with David by reminding him that, *as long as the son of Jesse is alive on the earth, you and your kingdom will not be established.* Did Saul know something about David that the reader does not? Did he sense that David had ambitions that exceeded being a commander in Saul's army? Did Saul have a right to "keep on eye" on David? As the story of David's rise plays out, the reader may understand Saul's sentiments about David and even come to sympathize with his situation.

Saul's misgivings about David were clear, and his attempt to annihilate him caused David to flee permanently from Saul's household (20:42). Even though Saul and David met on various occasions throughout the rest of 1 Samuel, David never participated in Saul's court again. In the following narratives (chs 21—30) the chasm between the king and the eventual king widened as David's path to the throne materialized outside of Saul's court in the rugged wilderness region.

IN THE TEXT

1. David, Favorable with Jonathan and Saul (18:1-9)

■ **1-5** The unit opens with the phrase *and it happened after he spoke to Saul* (v 1). The reader is to assume that this statement refers to David's conversation with Saul in 17:58. It remains unclear, however, since v 1 simply says "he." Many modern translations insert David here as the subject (NRSV, JPS, NIV) to avoid confusion. The text also interjects an important statement about Saul's son, Jonathan: *the life of Jonathan was bound up with the life of David, and Jonathan loved him as his own soul.*

The statement regarding Jonathan's relationship to David is significant for a couple of reasons. First, this is the first time the reader is clued into Jonathan's affection for David. Was Jonathan aware of David before this? David had, after all, served in Saul's court (16:14-23), so why do we only hear of their relationship now? Second, the language regarding Jonathan's respect for David is significant in light of the rest of the story of David. Jonathan's life was *bound up* (*niqšĕrâ*) with David, implying inseparable devotion to him (see Gen 44:30-31). Jonathan also **loved** [*vayeʾĕhābēû*] **him as himself.** The term for "love" is often used in the formation of treaties in the ancient world and therefore carries with it political overtones (Ackroyd 1975, 213-14). The term thus indicates Jonathan's political loyalty to David in addition to his personal affection for him. Jonathan's loyal devotion benefited David in that he helped save David's life on different occasions, and it helped to open the door to David's political success (see below).

Saul, like Jonathan, highly regarded David, so much so that *Saul took him on that day* and did not let him return to his father's house (v 2). The text engages in an interesting wordplay here. Instead of reading **did not let him,** the text could literally be read *did not give him;* the verb (*nĕtānû*) derives from the same word (*nātan*) that forms the basis for Jonathan's name. Thus, by "not giving" David back to his father, Saul "adopted" David as a second son into his household.

Not only was Jonathan's life bound up with David, but the text playfully ties Jonathan and David through a literary device as well (see below). Jonathan **cut a covenant with David** and Jonathan **stripped off the robe which was upon him and gave it to David, and his armor, his sword, his bow and belt.** The description of Jonathan's actions in v 4 is very significant. First, the items Jonathan bequeathed to David symbolized the accoutrements of royal power. In essence, Jonathan symbolically gave up his position as the legitimate heir to Saul's kingdom for the sake of David. This action accords well with the overall theme and trajectory of David's rise to kingship in that God gave David such favor in the eyes of the people that even Saul's son willingly abdicated his rightful place for the eventual king. Not only does this prepare the way for David's rise to power, but it also attempts to demonstrate that David did not seek the position nor did he coerce it from a member of Saul's household.

Second, the verb "give" (*nātan*) is utilized once again. It was used in reference to Saul and David before, now Jonathan "gives" something to David. David not only gained entrance into Saul's family when Saul refused to give him back to his father but also became a potential heir to Saul's throne when Jonathan gave his royal regalia to him. From a reader's standpoint, one cannot overlook the close connection between David and Saul's family/throne vis-à-vis the person and name of Jonathan.

18:1-9   In addition to Saul's family, David prospered in Saul's service. In a short notice at the end of this section (v 5), the text indicates that David had success **over all that Saul had set him.** Saul even made David a commander in the army, which was **good in the eyes of all the people and all the servants of Saul.**

■ **6-9** These verses provide a glimpse into David's military achievements. The notice in v 6*a* is somewhat problematic. It states, **and it happened when they came when David returned from smiting the Philistine.** Some have argued that there are two originally separate clauses present in this statement: **when they came** and **when David returned from.** The first phrase may have been introduced in order to "smooth" over the interpolation of 17:55—18:5 (McCarter 1980b, 310). If this is the case, then the reference to **when David returned** originally followed 17:54. This appears to be a plausible reading since **the Philistine** is singular, most likely referring back to the Goliath narrative. Thus, 17:55—18:5 was inserted into the larger David-Goliath pericope.

David's success against Goliath also set Saul up for great disappointment. Even though David struck down the Philistine **the women came out from all the cities of Israel to greet King Saul** with singing and dancing on their return (v 6). The text indicates that Saul expected to receive adoration and accolades for the military victory, even if it came through the actions of another. Was Saul guilty of trying to gain credit for David's success? The answer appears to be in the affirmative. The women did oblige Saul and pay homage to him as they sang, "Saul has killed his thousands" (v 7b NRSV). The women, however, did not forget that David's accomplishments far outpaced those of the king when they sang the second verse of this poetic statement: "and David his ten thousands" (v 7c NRSV). The famous phrase sung by the women indicated that people perceived David as the more effective leader in battle. This, of course, made Saul **very angry** because he understood that by magnifying the accomplishments of David the people acknowledged David's success over his own (v 8). Saul also reasoned that if this was evident to the people he governed, it would only be a matter of time before David replaced Saul and acquired his kingdom. All of this made Saul suspicious of David, as the text notes he was **eyeing David from that day onward** (v 9). The verb here (ʿōvēn) is a participle that indicates that Saul continuously watched David with suspicion and envy. The following chapters (esp. 21—26) bear this out as Saul not only kept on eye on David but sought to eliminate him as a political threat.

It is also important to notice that others have had success against the Philistines (God, Samuel, Jonathan, and David), but never Saul. Again, the text implies that Saul failed to live up to the mission for which God originally selected him (9:16). Even the people realized that it was David, and not Saul, who led the troops to victory.

2. Saul Tries to Kill David (18:10-16)

■ **10-11** The notice at the end of the first subunit regarding Saul's suspicions (envy?) of David becomes the basis for Saul's actions in vv 10-16. This section records two separate occasions when Saul tried to kill David. The first attempt is found in vv 10-11. In v 10, the text notes that "an evil spirit from God rushed upon Saul, and he raved [about in] his house" (NRSV). This represents the third occasion when the spirit of God "rushed [ṣālaḥ] upon Saul." The first two produced more positive results in that Saul became like one of the prophets (10:6) and then rallied the Israelites against the Ammonites (11:6). On this occasion an **evil spirit** descended upon him. The notice about the evil spirit is very similar to the reference in 16:14, in which an evil spirit tormented the king. In addition, 18:10-11 is basically a duplicate of the information provided in 19:9-10. Interestingly, the LXX does not contain 18:10-11 in its manuscript tradition. Therefore, it appears that these verses have been added here in anticipation of 19:9-10. Moreover, this information may provide a more authentic description of how David came to be in Saul's court; that is, through playing music for the king. This data would indicate, therefore, that elements of ch 17 (see Behind the Text) have been elaborated and inserted by writers/editors sympathetic to David and incorporated as part of the overall story of David's rise.

The spirit that came upon Saul vexed him, and the language that is used to describe Saul's behavior (vayitnabēʾ = **he raved about**) indicates he became extremely agitated. This verb is generally used to refer to prophetic activity, especially when a prophet would engage in ecstatic types of behavior (Num 11:25-27; 1 Sam 10:5-6, 10, 13). It was while Saul was in this excitable condition that he threw a spear at David. The text is clear that Saul threw the spear with the intent of killing David: "he thought, I will pin David [against] the wall" (v 11 NRSV). Saul's determination to kill David is underscored by the fact that David had to elude him *two times.*

■ **12-16** Unable to kill him on his previous attempts (vv 10-11), Saul *feared David because Yahweh was with him* (v 12). Saul tried another tactic in order to get rid of him. He "removed him from his presence" by making him "a commander of a thousand" (v 13 NRSV). The verb *removed* (*vaysirēhû*) is a causative that indicates Saul actively sought to get David out of his sight. Saul's plan included making David a military commander, thus removing him through "promotion" (Fokkelman 1986, 222). David was given charge of a large contingent of men and essentially was assigned the role of leading the troops in battle (*he would go out and come before all the people*). Since David was such a visible (vulnerable) target in a military campaign, Saul intended for David to die in battle. Ironically, David would employ a similar tactic when he sought to have Uriah killed (2 Sam 11). Saul's plan backfired, however, and it only provided David the opportunity to experience more success in Saul's service. Because the Lord was with him, "David was successful in all his undertakings" (v 14 JPS), a theme that resonates throughout the story of David's rise (see Introduction). When Saul saw David's success, he was "in awe of him" (v 15 NRSV). Whereas Saul feared David (v 12) and "stood in awe of him" (v 15 NRSV), the people **loved David** (v 16).

3. David and Michal (18:17-29)

■ **17-19** Saul devised another strategy in which to try and eliminate David. Understanding the political fallout of killing David himself, Saul hoped that the Philistines would do him in. Saul's machinations were tied to his oldest daughter named **Merab**. The text does not say much about her, she is only mentioned as a prize that David received for his commitment to continue fighting the Philistines. David, however, in an act of humility, questioned the move and wondered how a humble servant such as himself could **become the king's son-in-law** (v 18). Even though David did not take Merab as his wife, the pathway into Saul's family did not remain closed.

■ **20-29** Although Saul's attempt to marry off Merab ended in failure, Saul had a younger daughter named **Michal**. She is another child of Saul who "loved David" (v 20 NRSV). Thus, not only did Jonathan love David, the people of Israel and Judah love David, but Saul's youngest daughter loved him too. It is also significant that the text never says that David loved them, only that they loved David. Saul perceived Michal's love for David as an opportunity to get rid of him; she could **be a snare to him** (v 21). Saul ensured that his plan would succeed in that he commanded his servants to encourage David to marry his daughter. The goal was to convince David that this was something that the king wanted. Thus the message, "The king is delighted with you, and all his servants love you," was intended to soften David and sweeten the deal (v 22 NRSV). When the servants delivered the message to David, he once again mentioned his humble background: *Is it a small thing in your eyes to become the son-in-law of the king?*

The invitation to marry Michal, however, was tied to a mission and thus the privilege of marrying the king's daughter would be earned. The price Saul demanded was a high one: **a hundred Philistine foreskins** (v 25). The Philistines were known in the biblical text as being an uncircumcised people (see 14:6; 17:36), thus underscoring their status as foreigners and people who were not members of the covenant with God. David would have to kill the Philistines before he could fulfill Saul's requirement. The mission was so dangerous that even Saul reckoned that David would **fall** in the attempt (v 25).

The wedding gift was acceptable to David and he, along with his men, struck down the Philistines and he brought the foreskins to the king *in full*. After fulfilling his part of the obligation, Saul fulfilled his part and *gave him Michal, his daughter, for a wife* (v 27). With this move, David became the son-in-law to the king. This had tremendous political significance because David became an official member of Saul's family, thus placing him in a position to become an heir to Saul's throne legitimately.

Saul continued to *fear David* because he understood the **Lord was with him** (on this phrase see 16:18). At this stage of the relationship between David and Saul, the text introduces the idea that Saul *became an enemy* to David all his days (v 29). The verb (*'ōyēb*) is a participle, thus indicating that Saul's hostility toward David went uninterrupted.

4. Closing Statement (18:30)

■ **30** The chapter closes in a way similar to the way it opened, with a statement about David's success against the Philistines. Even though the Philistines (lit., "the commanders of the Philistines" [NRSV]) came out against Israel, David had more success against them than all the servants of Saul. Moreover, David's **name** became *highly esteemed.*

5. Jonathan Intercedes for David (19:1-7)

■ **1-3** Not only did Saul's children love David, but this chapter provides evidence that they even protected him against their father's plan to annihilate him. The first instance where one of Saul's children protected David occurs in vv 1-7. In this context Jonathan attempted to save David by communicating Saul's intentions to him. Saul made his feelings of ill will toward David known by reporting to *Jonathan and all his servants* of his plan **to kill David** (v 1). Being aware of his father's intentions, Jonathan *reported to David* that his father sought to kill him and exhorted him to hide "in a secret place" (v

2 NRSV). While David hid, Jonathan would attempt to ascertain information from Saul and report it back to David. Saul's antipathy toward David stood in sharp contrast to Jonathan's feelings toward him, since Jonathan **took delight in David.** Jonathan's love for David was evident in the way that he worked on David's behalf.

■ **4-7** Jonathan's plan included putting in a good word for David. Jonathan **spoke well of David to . . . his father** and exhorted him not to "sin against his servant" (v 4 NRSV). The use of the term "sin" (*ḥata'*) is usually reserved for the religious realm to refer to sin against God. It can be employed in human relationships when one has missed the goal of right conduct toward another person. In light of this, Jonathan reminded Saul that Yahweh brought a great victory to Israel when David killed the Philistine (Goliath?). As in the case of Jonathan (14:44), Saul was poised to kill the person who brought success against Israel's foes.

Jonathan also exhorted Saul not to sin against **an innocent man** by killing David without cause (19:5). The repetitive use of the word for sin (*ḥātā*) and the description of David as **innocent** (*nāqî*) plays a significant role in the story of David's rise. The text throughout 1 Sam 16—2 Sam 5 continuously reminds the reading audience that David did not have malicious or evil intentions against Saul or his household. In fact, any actions toward David on the part of Saul would be construed as an unprovoked and unwarranted attack on David.

Saul responded to Jonathan's impassioned plea by reassuring him that **David would not die** (v 6). Even though Saul gave this oath to Jonathan (**as Yahweh lives, he will not die**), it did not prevent him later from hunting him down with the intention of eliminating David. Once Saul gave his word, Jonathan "brought David [back] to Saul" (JPS). The language that is utilized in v 7 (*vayābē'*) indicates that Jonathan ushered or escorted David into Saul's presence.

6. Michal Saves David from Saul (19:8-17)

■ **8-10** These verses once again make reference to David's success against the Philistine forces in which he **struck a great blow against them** (v 8). However, David's success also provided the impetus for Saul's dissatisfaction and jealousy of David. Whereas David was gaining against Israel's foe, Yahweh continued to fight against Saul. As in 18:10-11, an evil spirit from Yahweh rushed upon Saul while David played music in his presence. Verses 9-10 of ch 19 are basically identical to 18:10-11; Saul held a spear, he desired to pin David to the wall, and David escaped. As mentioned in the commentary on 18:10-11, 19:9-10 may have been original with 18:10-11 inserted into the narrative at a later time. In this context, the attempt on David's life provided the context for Michal's heroic actions in 19:11-17.

■ **11-17** In this section Michal looked out for David and helped save his life. Prior to these verses, the text underscored Jonathan's role in preserving David's life. In this context Saul's daughter came to David's aid. As the narrative progresses, it becomes obvious that Saul became more forceful and deliberate in his attempt to kill David. In v 11, Saul sent messengers directly to David's house in order **to kill him in the morning.** Michal interceded for David and warned him of impending trouble. Her urgent request, *If you do not flee for your life tonight, you will be killed tomorrow,* demonstrates Michal's love and concern for David. Michal not only urged David to flee but also saved David by her actions: she *lowered David through the window* (v 12). The verb used to describe Michal's actions is a causative (*vatōred*), which indicates that she took the initiative in assisting David out the window. Here, we encounter another woman who heroically assisted an individual's escape by lowering him out a window (Josh 2:15). Like Rahab's house, Michal's may have been built into the city wall so that it was possible David could flee without passing by the city gate.

With Michal's help David was able to *flee and escape* the harm that awaited him (1 Sam 19:12). Michal also covered for David after he left. Michal took the household god (*hatrāpîm*), covered it with goats' hair, and then placed it in David's bed. When the messengers arrived at David's house in order "to take David," Michal simply said, "He is sick" (v 14 NRSV). The ruse did not satisfy Saul's men, and they ordered that David should be presented to Saul in bed so that he could kill him. It was only when the men went to fetch David that they uncovered the idol with the crop of goats' hair and became aware of Michal's scheme. Feeling betrayed by his daughter, Saul inquired, **Why did you deceive me?** Michal, in order to save her own life, indicated that David would injure her if she did not let him leave.

Household Gods

The exact appearance and function of household gods (*tĕrāpîm*) are unknown. The OT, however, affirms that Rachel stole Laban's idols (Gen 31:19) when departing Aram, and Michal placed an "image" in David's bed to mislead Saul's soldiers (1 Sam 19:13, 16). Household gods varied in size; they could be small enough to place under a saddle (Gen 31:34), or they could be life-sized (as in the case of Michal). Some texts (Zech 10:2) associate household gods with divination (Ezek 21:21), and they were often used in conjunction with the ephod (Judg 17:5; 18:14, 17-20; Hos 3:4), which was also used in divinatory functions. Although they may be associated with the "gods" that adjudicated household law (Exod 21:6; 22:8 ff.), their use was condemned elsewhere (1 Sam 15:23), as in Josiah's attempt to eradicate them (2 Kgs 23:24) indicates (McCarter 1988, 793).

7. David Flees to Ramah (19:18-24)

■ **18-24** In this last section of ch 19, David took shelter with the prophet Samuel as he **fled** from Saul's men. David escaped to the city of **Ramah.** Since this city was located in the territory of Benjamin it should not be confused with Samuel's hometown in Ephraim. David and Samuel eventually ended up in **Naioth,** which translated means "encampments," and thus may refer to the camps where groups of prophets lived (v 18).

David hoped to find safety in the company of Samuel, but Saul demonstrated that he would go to any lengths to destroy his rival. Saul, as he did to Michal, sent his messengers to take David, yet when they arrived and saw the **prophets prophesying, the Spirit of God came upon** them and they too started prophesying. The Hebrew term used to describe the prophets' actions (*vayitnab'û*) is often associated with frenetic and ecstatic type behavior. The prophetic frenzy that came upon Saul's men parallels Saul's behavior after Samuel anointed him (10:10-12).

Unabated in his attempts to get David, Saul sent more messengers even though he knew what happened to the first group. When the same thing happened to them, he sent a third contingent, which produced the same results. Saul finally went to Ramah himself, and when he approached the city of Naioth where David and Samuel were located, the spirit of God came upon him and he came under the spell of a prophetic frenzy. Unlike the messengers before him, the effects of the spirit on Saul appeared more dramatic since he "stripped off his clothes, and . . . lay naked all that day and all that night" before Samuel (19:24). The prophetic spell that Saul fell under resembled his previous actions (10:9-13).

Since Saul seemed prone to these types of prophetic outbursts, people openly questioned, **Is Saul . . . among the prophets?** Although the text never associates Saul as having a prophetic lineage, he nevertheless engaged in prophetic activity on at least two occasions.

8. Jonathan and David Again (20:1-42)

■ **1-11** David escaped Saul's advances at Naioth and returned to Jonathan. David's exasperation and frustration with Saul's relentless pursuit of him is evidenced in his question to Jonathan in v 1, *What is my guilt and what is my sin before your father that he is seeking my life?* The verb for *seeking* here (*mĕbaqēš*) is a participle that connotes the unyielding pressure that Saul had been applying toward capturing David. Jonathan responded with a note of incredulity to David's accusation since he believed Saul would tell him everything **great or small** he proposed to do. Saul, however, knew of Jonathan's affection for David, and therefore tried to conceal information about his attempts to eradicate David from him. David even understood this to be the case (v 3), since it would *grieve* Jonathan to know of Saul's plan.

Even though Jonathan did not have all the information, he nevertheless exhibited his loyalty to David by stating, "Whatever you say, I will do for you" (v 4 NRSV). The two proposed a test to determine Saul's true intentions toward David. The time was close for the Festival of the New Moon. This was an occasion celebrated with special offerings (Num 28:11-15) and could last for three days or more. David purposely dismissed himself from the festival and hid for three days. If the king inquired of David's whereabouts, Jonathan would cover for him by stating that he went home to Bethlehem for a yearly sacrifice. If the king answered favorably in regard to David's absence, then Jonathan knew that all was well. If Saul became angry, then he knew that Saul meant him harm. In addition, David also appealed to the covenant that the two developed and requested that Jonathan treat him with covenant loyalty. The depth of this covenant relationship is found in David's request that Jonathan should kill him if he was guilty (v 8) and Jonathan's willingness to tell David of any evil Saul devised against him.

New Moon Festival

Since the Israelite calendar was lunar, it is not surprising that the first day of each lunar month, like the Sabbath, was set apart to worship God. The Festival of the New Moon and the Sabbath are often mentioned together in the OT (Isa 1:13; 66:23; Ezek 45:17; 46:1), with the new moon of the seventh month carrying special significance (Lev 23:24 ff.; Num 29:1-6; 2 Chr 5:3; Ezra 3:6; Neh 8:2). As a prominent festival, there was no mourning or fasting on this day, and it was a day of rest from ordinary work (Amos 8:5). The new moon could be a chosen time to hold an annual family sacrifice (1 Sam 20:5 ff.), as well as a feast reserved for family and royal court (1 Sam 20:5, 18, 24-27, 34). The offerings proscribed for the new moon were greater in quality and quantity than those required for the Sabbath (Num 28:9 ff.). This day was considered an opportune time for peace offerings to God (Num 10:10) and a time when God was thought to be especially near. As such it was a good time to seek God's special guidance, particularly through the prophet (2 Kgs 4:23) (Hartley 1988, 527-28).

■ **12-17** The plan that was proposed appeared acceptable to both parties. Jonathan reassured David that if Saul was pleasantly disposed to him, he would let David know this; if, however, Saul meant David harm, Jonathan would not only inform David of his actions but also send him away in peace/safety. Jonathan also reiterated his desire that **the LORD be with you,** a theme that has reverberated throughout the story of David's rise up to this point (see comment on 1 Sam 16:18). Jonathan, however, also asked something in return. Jonathan anticipated David's future monarchy, because he made sure that David extended covenant loyalty (*ḥesed*) to him if he remained alive (v 14). If Jonathan died, he requested that David show eternal kindness to his household (i.e., his family). Jonathan even made David reiterate the stipulations of this covenant a second time (v 17). The covenant that David made with Jonathan and his posterity became important during David's monarchy, because David fulfilled his part of the covenant by providing for Jonathan's son, Mephibosheth (2 Sam 9).

■ **18-23** The festival of the new moon provided the occasion to test the plan. David did not attend the festal meal and thus his seat was "vacant" (v 18 JPS). Jonathan instructed David to take refuge **the day after tomorrow** where he hid *the other time* (v 19). These two phrases are a little difficult to read in the Hebrew. The first literally reads "the third time," which probably indicates two days after the day that Jonathan and David agreed to the plan; thus "the third day."

The second phrase reads "on the day of the incident," which recalls the events of 19:1-7, where David hid and Jonathan spoke to his father on David's behalf. David was to stay close to the *Ezel stone.* Although this location is not mentioned anywhere else in the OT, it represented a natural place where David could keep himself hidden. Here, he could take shelter until Jonathan discerned Saul's intentions toward David.

Jonathan would shoot three arrows to make David aware of impending danger or safety. Even though arrows could be used in certain divinatory practices (Ezek 21:21), Jonathan's arrows would not be randomly shot into the air. If the arrows fell **on this side of you** (i.e., before the rock), David was safe; if the arrows *went beyond* David, however, David was to leave because **the LORD has sent you away** (1 Sam 20:22). The verb here could also be rendered *has set you free* (i.e., Yahweh has liberated you from danger). Jonathan's employment of a *lad* may have provided a witness who could assure Saul that Jonathan did not meet David while out shooting.

■ **24-34** As David hid in the field, Jonathan went back to his father. At the time of the meal *Saul took his usual place* and **Abner sat next to Saul**. The text says that "Jonathan stood" (NRSV), which may indicate his humble status among the king and the king's general (v 25). The text could be emended, however, to read that he sat **opposite** his father.

David also had a place at this table, but his seat was "vacant" (JPS). Since David was the son-in-law to the king and a member of his family, it is not surprising that David would have been expected to attend the feast. Saul, however, did not give any thought to David's absence thinking **he is unclean** and therefore unfit to partake of this religious ceremony (v 26). Any cultic infringement (see Lev 11—15) would disqualify an individual from participating in a sacred event until he was purified first. Contact with a dead body, for instance, would have made an individual unclean. Since David was one of Saul's warriors, it would not have been unusual for him to have become contaminated as the result of battle.

When David did not show up the second day, Saul began to wonder about David's absence. Saul's description of David as **the son of Jesse** may be an indication of Saul's contempt for David. Jonathan tried to cover for David by stating that he had asked for permission to leave in order to celebrate a sacrifice among his kinsmen. A family could select a particular new moon as the day for an annual family sacrifice. However, Jonathan may have tipped his hand to Saul when he provided David's excuse for being absent: *let me escape to see my kinsmen* (v 29). The word that is used here (*malāṭ*) suggests someone who is running away from or fleeing trouble.

Saul quickly saw through Jonathan's defense of David, and he became angry "against Jonathan" (v 30 NRSV). Saul perceived that he was covering for David and took that as a sign of disloyalty to him. To Saul it was obvious that Jonathan **sided with** David (v 30). The word that is used here (*bōḥēr*) indicates a deliberate, willful choice to ally himself with David. In response, Saul also called Jonathan a **son of a perverse and rebellious woman.** The LXX reads "woman of the street" in place of **perverse,** thus insinuating that he was the "son of a lawless trollop" (Mauchline 1971, 148). Saul's harsh response is strengthened when he invoked *the shame of your mother's nakedness. Nakedness* here is a euphemism for *genitals.* The phrase indicated that her genitals were shamed after having given birth to Jonathan.

Saul realized that as long as David remained alive, Jonathan's kingship (and thus Saul's dynasty) was threatened. This was a realization that Jonathan had already come to terms with, however (18:1-4; 20:14 ff.). For Saul, the only real way to ensure that his dynasty would remain intact was to eliminate David. Even though Jonathan questioned Saul's right and legitimacy to kill David (**Why should he *die?* What has he done?**), he realized any efforts to persuade his father would fail, evidenced by the spear his father threw at him (v 33). Ironically, whereas Saul became enraged with Jonathan in v 30, Jonathan became angry in v 34 over his grief toward David and because his father humiliated him.

■ **35-42** With Saul's intentions confirmed, Jonathan went out **in the morning** (v 35) to apprise David of the situation. As Jonathan shot the arrows beyond David it conveyed the message that David was not safe in Saul's court. Sending the lad back to town, Jonathan met with David, who *fell to the ground and bowed three times before* Jonathan, indicating his love and reverence for the king's son (v 41). Both men **kissed each other and wept,** knowing that their paths would not likely cross again (see 23:16-18, however).

FROM THE TEXT

One of the prominent theological themes presented to us in this section is found in the statement, **Yahweh was with him.** This statement has already been applied to David in earlier contexts (16:18; 17:37) but is highlighted repeatedly throughout these chapters (18:12, 14, 28; 20:13). The text reminds us that as God's children we do not walk alone, but God's presence abides with us continuously in all situations. This is true not only when life is going particularly well for us but also in those situations in which we face opposition and uncertainty. In these chapters we are reminded that God does not fail us or abandon us, especially in times of need. The text highlights the fact that God is dependable even though people and life are not always so.

In the case of David, God's presence helped him gain favor in the eyes of Saul's family and the people of Israel, protected David when Saul attempted to take his life on different occasions, and gave him success on the battlefield.

God's presence not only gave David the strength to endure these hardships but also the knowledge that God was working in David's circumstances to bring about a greater good. In this section David married Michal, the daughter of Saul, which made him the son-in-law to Saul and a potential heir to the throne. Moreover, Jonathan loved David to the extent that he willingly abdicated his right to the throne so that David could take his place instead. David's success as military commander also made David popular with the people of Israel, the people he would rule over one day. Thus, even in these trying times, God was already "preparing" David's path to the throne. Although David may not have envisioned all that God had planned for him, the pieces of that plan were being placed together one step at a time.

This reminds us that our task as God's children is to rest in God's care and providence. We may not always perceive or understand how the circumstances in which we find ourselves are preparing us for a future purpose. Our task is to remain patient and obedient while God is actively at work in our situation. Oftentimes, we do not fully realize how God has been leading us in our personal affairs until after God has guided us through them and we have had the opportunity to reflect and meditate on our experiences. It is then that we come to understand and appreciate the manner in which God faithfully directed our steps while the various elements of our situation came into place.

D. David's Flight from Saul (21:1—23:29)

BEHIND THE TEXT

These chapters recount the initial events in David's life as he fled from Saul in the wilderness. In 21:1, Jonathan and David parted ways, thus representing David's official "split" from Saul's household. While David hid in the wilderness he came in contact with people who would not only protect him from Saul but also be instrumental in helping David on his path to kingship. In ch 21, David acquired assistance from the priest Ahimelech as he fled from Saul (vv 1-9). David also came in contact with the Philistine king Achish, whom David would later serve as a Philistine vassal (vv 10-15). In ch 22, David became the leader of **four hundred men** (v 2) who would form the backbone of David's fighting force while he remained in the wilderness. David also sought help from the **king of Moab,** who provided him and his family refuge while Saul pursued David (vv 3-5).

In the midst of these narratives the account of Saul's execution of the priests of Nob is included between the report about David's flight to Moab and David's rescue of the city of Keilah (22:6-19). This material not only explains how the Eliade priesthood at Nob was wiped out, and thus fulfilled the prophecy of the man of God in 2:27-36, but it also serves to link David with the lone surviving priest, Abiathar (22:20-23). Abiathar proved invaluable to David as he served as David's priest and helped discern God's will in David's battle with the Philistines (23:1-14). Abiathar continued to function as David's primary priest throughout the wilderness period, and he served David when he was selected as king of Judah and later Israel.

The material in this section has been arranged in a kind of "back and forth" manner, alternating between information about David's travels and Saul's pursuit of David. By organizing the narratives in this fashion, the text highlights the frenetic pace at which these events occur. At the same time, the composite nature of these traditions becomes apparent. The larger narrative about the priesthood at Nob (21:1-10; 22:6-19) is interrupted by the notice of David's flight to Gath (21:10-15), and the reports about his stay at Adullam (22:1-2) and his flight to Moab (22:3-4). Moreover, the relationship between David's interactions with Achish in 21:10-15 and David's service to Achish in 27:1-12 remains unclear. Although David had already been introduced to Achish in ch 21, the narrative in ch 27 does not seem to have any recollection of it. Is this a sign that we have multiple independent traditions about David's association with Achish?

Chapter 23 presents its own issues. David was located in the wilderness of Ziph at Horesh according to 23:15 and in the hill country of Hakilah (v 19). This geographical notice appears to link more directly with the material in 26:1 ff., in which the Ziphites know of David's whereabouts and report it to Saul. This analysis indicates that part of the narrative apparently has been interrupted by chs 24 and 25. In addition, in 23:1-5 David inquired of Yahweh about going to battle against the Philistines. It is assumed that David inquired of God with the help of the priest Abiathar since he joined David in 22:20-23. Yet, Abiathar is never directly mentioned in these verses. Abiathar is mentioned in 23:6, which states that **he fled to David at Keilah.** What is the nature of the relationship between 22:20-23 and 23:6 at this point? It appears that we have multiple traditions about how Abiathar came into David's service. Thus we have evidence that the material in these chapters is composite in nature and that the editors/narrators of David's life had various sources at their disposal from which to work. These sources were combined not only for literary effect but for ideological and theological reasons as well.

IN THE TEXT

1. David Escapes to Nob (21:1-9)

■ **1-6** The opening statement, *and he arose and he went,* of v 1 not only separates this unit from the previous one on linguistic grounds but also represents the formal and final separation between David and the house of Saul. After this juncture in the text, David never served in Saul's court again. David's flight from Saul took him to the city of **Nob,** which lay close to the northern side of Jerusalem. Nob was known as a city of priests (22:19), and thus it represented a place of cultic importance. David was met by the main priest,

Ahimelech, as he arrived there. Ahimelech's name is interesting because it can literally be translated "my brother is king." Ahimelech, however, was known as the "son of Ahitub" (v 20) and as the grandson of Eli, thus his brother was never a king. Is his name somehow associated with Yahweh (i.e., Yahweh is king)? The simple answer is, we do not know. It is significant to note, however, that as Eli's grandson, Ahimelech represented the surviving remnant of the Eliad household. Thus, his presence in this context recalls the words of the man of God in 2:27-36.

The text notes that Ahimelech **trembled** as he came out to greet David and he noticed that he was alone (21:1). Since David was the son-in-law to the king, a military hero, and an important leader within Saul's army, Ahimelech probably assumed that David had a military detachment with him. No text before this provides any information as to why Ahimelech would have feared the king, but the later narrative gives evidence of Saul's harsh treatment of the prophets there (22:18). David came to Ahimelech claiming that **the king charged** him **with a . . . matter** that no one else knew about and that he was supposed to meet up with a contingent of young men there. David used this excuse as a pretext to find nourishment from his journey. Ahimelech was the brother of Ahijah, who had joined Saul as his spiritual adviser (14:3; 22:9). Because of his ties to Saul, David may have been unsure whether he could trust Ahimelech and therefore had to disguise his intentions.

The urgency of David's request is evidenced in the language of his demand: **Give me five loaves of bread,** *and whatever else can be found* (21:3). Ahimelech could not give David common bread since he only had "holy bread" (v 4 NRSV; also called **the bread of the Presence**) on hand. The bread referenced here was "set out before Yahweh," in his presence in the holy place of the sanctuary at each Sabbath. According to Lev 24:5-9 the "showbread," as it is also known, consisted of twelve loaves of bread set out in two rows on a table "before Yahweh." Each loaf represented one of the tribes of Israel. Because of its sacred nature, the bread could only be eaten by the priests (Lev 24:9).

Ahimelech made an exception, however, and offered David the special bread only if *the young men had safeguarded themselves from women* (1 Sam 21:4). David assured Ahimelech that the vessels of the young men were holy and therefore they were worthy to partake of the bread. David's response indicates that even war was considered a holy undertaking, and any warrior participating in holy battle had to be ritually clean. Being clean probably meant that the soldiers had to abstain from sexual intercourse before a battle (Exod 19:15), and the reference to the men's *vessels* may be a euphemism for their genitals. Jesus would later invoke the tradition about David eating the sacred bread to stress human need over strict Sabbath observance (Matt 12:3-4; Mark 2:25-26; Luke 6:3-4).

■ **7-9** Even as David ran from Saul, **one of Saul's servants, . . . Doeg the Edomite,** was already at Nob (1 Sam 21:7). Doeg is called an Edomite, which represented the territory south and east of Israel proper. Biblical tradition holds that the Edomites descended from Esau (Gen 25:24-34; 36:1-43), and they enjoyed kinship and cultural ties with the Israelites. According to Deut 23:7, Edomites could enter the "assembly of Yahweh" and there may have been hints of religious ties between Israel and Edom as well (Gordon 1986, 170). Saul may have brought Doeg into his service after fighting battles with the Edomites (1 Sam 14:47).

Doeg is also described as **the leader of the shepherds,** implying that he oversaw Saul's flocks. The phrase that is used here to describe Doeg (*'abîr hārō'îm*), however, can also mean "mighty leader" or "powerful leader." It is doubtful that the text meant to refer to shepherds here, and it may be better to translate it as "chief of Saul's guard" based on the information in 22:17. If we take this second reading as the more appropriate one, it signified that he fulfilled a more violent role, such as a mercenary, in Saul's employ. Considering his role as the executioner of the priests of Nob later in the narrative (22:18-19), this title appears fitting. He may have been detained at the sacred site because he was unclean himself.

In addition to food, David also asked Ahimelech for weapons, claiming that "the king's business required haste" (v 8 NRSV). Up to this point, David's story lacked credibility. He claimed to be on a secret mission, yet he did not have any provisions or weapons on him. Ahimelech did not suspect any foul play from David, and he even offered him **the sword of Goliath, which was wrapped in a cloth behind the ephod** (v 9).

The reference to Goliath's sword here raises the question of how it came into the possession of the priests at Nob. The text notes that David carried Goliath's head (presumably; the text just reads "the head of the Philistine") to Jerusalem along with the notice "but he put his armor in his tent" (17:54 NRSV). The notice in 17:54 is a Jerusalemite tradition and thus anachronistic (see comment on 17:54); therefore, the text could be emended so that the shrine did not refer to David's tent but to Yahweh's tent-sanctuary, presumably at Nob. Only over the course of time did this tradition become associated with the shrine at Jerusalem (Ackroyd 1971, 146). It is also possible that two different versions about the fate of Goliath's sword existed in chs 17 and 21 as well (Klein 1983, 214). The sword appears to have had little practical use for the priests since it was wrapped in a cloth and placed behind the ephod. This would indicate that the sword was just being stored there and not venerated as an important trophy of war.

Although of little use to the priests, David saw the value in it and took it before he left Nob. The text never records what happened to it afterward.

2. David Flees to Gath (21:10-15)

■ **10-15** David once again *got up and fled* from before Saul (v 10). The text indicates that David continued his flight from Saul even though Saul or his men do not arrive at Nob until 22:6. As a result, some scholars have argued that these verses may be a later interpolation in anticipation of David's service to Achish (27:1). Even though these verses may interrupt the flow of the Nob episode, they nevertheless continue the theme of David's flight from Saul. As David continued to travel southward, the text notes that he **came to Achish, the king of Gath** (21:10). Achish was a Philistine king who ruled over Goliath's hometown. Why David would take refuge in the city of the man he reportedly defeated remains unclear. Although kings welcomed exceptional warriors as mercenaries, this explanation does not solve all the problems inherent in the text. This notice thus provides further evidence of the complicated transmission history of the larger David-Goliath tradition as well as those that center on David and Achish.

It should be noted that it was Saul's relentless pursuit of David that drove him into the company of Israel's most menacing foe. Thus, in the story of David's rise, not only did Saul's pursuit of David land David in the presence of the Philistines, but David utilized his position as a Philistine vassal to further his own political ambitions (see esp. chs 27—30). Thus, Saul hurt himself on two fronts.

David's reputation and heroics preceded him, as Achish's servants had heard of David's exploits (21:11). Thinking that Achish and his men would see David as a threat and remove him, he **disguised his judgment and acted like a madman in their hands** (v 13). David was once again in a position where he had to think extemporaneously. Perceiving no alternative or way out of this situation, David feigned his own insanity in order to calm the Philistines and reassure them that he was harmless to them. David played the part convincingly; "he scratched marks on the doors of the gate and let his **spittle** run down his beard" (JPS). David's act even fooled Achish, who wondered why his men brought David to his house. In this text and others, we see that David was a very cunning man, he could think quickly on his feet and he was very resourceful. These qualities served him well as he solidified his rising political status and when he became king over Israel.

3. David at Adullam (22:1-5)

■ **1-2** The flight from Saul continued for David. David traveled from Gath in Philistine territory to the **cave of Adullam** (v 1). Adullam was in the western foothills of Judah (Josh 12:15; 15:35; Mic 1:15), about twelve miles northeast of Gath and roughly sixteen miles southwest of Jerusalem. Adullam served as a rallying point where David's **brothers and *all the* household *of his father* went down to him there.** It is unclear whether David's family joined him at the cave in order to give him moral support during this stressful period in his life, or whether they were being threatened by Saul's advances and thus looking out for their own safety as well. Both answers may be valid, and the latter may be especially true in light of 1 Sam 22:3-5.

David also served as a social and political magnet for some very rough and undesirable types as well. The text notes that *every man who was in distress, who was in debt, and every man who was bitter of spirit* gathered to David at the cave (v 2). The way the text reads indicates that this may have also been a political movement against Saul's authority. The text uses the reflexive form for the verb (*qābaṭ*), which indicates they **rallied themselves** around David and they looked to him as a **leader** (*sār*). The term for **leader** (*sār*) is often used in political contexts to refer to an individual who wields considerable power or control. Usually a *sār* is someone who is second in command to the top commander or king. That the same word applies to David in relationship to these men indicates he wielded authority over them. This was no small band of individuals either considering that the group numbered around 400 people (v 2). These men represented the core of David's bodyguard who remained faithful to him during his time in the wilderness and when he became king. The number of this core group eventually expanded over time to 600 men (23:13).

■ **3-4** These verses portray David acting as an advocate for his own family. No doubt concerned for their safety and well-being, David traveled across the Dead Sea area to the territory of Moab in order to seek help from the king. Although **Mizpah** is mentioned in other parts of the OT, it is never associated with the region of Moab. Up to this point in the text, David did not have any associations with the territory of Moab. His request to **let my father and mother come and stay with you** is really an entreaty form thus demonstrating David requesting a favor from him (v 3). No doubt, David felt comfortable approaching the king considering that he possessed Moabite blood in his lineage (i.e., Ruth). The favor to let his parents find refuge in Moab was not intended to be permanent, just long enough for David to know **what God will do for me**. The text notes David's active role in the process as *he led them before the king of Moab* (v 4). The verb here (*vayanḥēm*) is a causative, thus emphasizing David's initiative in bringing his family to Moab. David knew that his family members would be protected there, and the text underscores David's concern for their safety. The text indicates that David took shelter in Moab as well, for his parents stayed there as long as David **remained in the fortress.** The text underscores the notion that they did not seek refuge in humble surroundings but in a stronghold.

■ **5** The unit on Adullam and Moab closes out with a notice about the appearance of the prophet Gad. Without any fair warning, the prophet Gad is interjected to the story of David. As a result, this verse may have been interjected at a subsequent moment in the editorial process. The prophet Gad only appears one other time in the story of David (2 Sam 24). On both occasions he delivered words of instruction and exhortation. Gad's appearance here is critical to the story line, however. The prophet commanded David to **not reside in the fortress, leave and go to the land of Judah.** The forceful statement initiates David's return to the territory of Judah where he came to the **forest of Hereth**. Thus the story of David was carried out in the land of Judah, not on foreign soil. The exact location of the forest is not clear, but some have suggested that it was a short distance southeast of Adullam in Judean territory (Mauchline 1971, 155).

4. Saul and the Priests of Nob (22:6-23)

■ **6-8** Beginning with v 6, the story line returns to the city of Nob, which was the focus of 21:1-10. The way the text comes to us in its present form, it appears as though the narrative has been spliced by 21:11-15 and 22:1-5. The manner in which these materials have been arranged, however, implies these events are taking place at a frenetic pace. The text continues to move back and forth between David and Saul as it tracks their movements, thus providing a hurried sense of the unfolding action. David had not stopped fleeing from Saul since the time he left Nob, and Saul continued to press his attack heavily against David.

In the opening verses of this unit, Saul learned of the whereabouts of David and his men. However, when Saul acquired this information, he "was sitting at Gibeah, under the tamarisk tree on the height, with his spear in his hand" (v 6 NRSV). The notice about Saul sitting around is reminiscent of the language of 14:2 when Jonathan pursued the Philistines. Saul again appears in a less than flattering light. While Saul's arch nemesis was gaining success against him, Saul was immobile, doing nothing. The inability to capture David frustrated the king, who essentially accused his men of conspiring against him (v 8). Basically, Saul faulted his men for not informing him of Jonathan's covenant with David, whom he blamed for stirring up David against him "to lie in wait" (NRSV).

■ **9-13** Among Saul's servants, **Doeg the Edomite** came forward with information about David. Doeg relayed to Saul that David came to Ahimelech the priest, who **inquired of the LORD** on behalf of David and **gave him provisions and the sword of Goliath the Philistine** (v 10). Doeg's statement about inquiring of Yahweh is a detail that is not mentioned in 20:1-9, although this is admitted by Ahimelech in 22:15. Ahimelech's inquiring (šā'al) consisted of asking Yahweh for guidance on David's urgent mission. Ahimelech's son, Abiathar, later sought oracles for David through the ephod (23:6, 9; 30:7-8).

Believing that Ahimelech aided his archrival David, Saul called for Ahimelech and his father's household to appear before him. Saul essentially accused Ahimelech of conspiring against him through the assistance he provided David. Saul's suspicion of David also caused him to assume that everyone was plotting against him: his son, his servants, and now Ahimelech the priest.

■ **14-19** Ahimelech quickly responded to Saul's accusation. Instead of defending himself, however, he vouched for David's character and proclaimed his innocence. Like Jonathan, here is another individual defending David's virtue. Ahimelech raised the issue of David's innocence by asking Saul in v 14, "Who among all your servants is so faithful as David?" (NRSV). In addition, he reminded Saul that David was the king's son-in-law and that he was honored in Saul's house. Ahimelech then moved from defending David to defending himself. Ahimelech did not deny that he had inquired of God on his behalf, but he did not know of the developing situation between David and Saul.

Saul was not persuaded by Ahimelech's defense, however. Saul's threat, *Today you will surely die, you and all your father's household,* indicated the seriousness of Saul's intentions (v 16). Saul's jealousy had reached such depths that anyone he considered to have assisted David, rightly or wrongly, would be annihilated, even a priest of Yahweh. When Saul turned to his servants and gave the command to kill the priests, *The servants of the king did not wish to send their hands to fall upon the priests of Yahweh* (v 17). Maybe out of sheer respect of the office or possibly divine retribution for such an act, the servants of Saul deliberately disobeyed his charge. When Saul turned and gave the same command to his servant Doeg, he obliged Saul and he *fell upon the priests and* he killed eighty-five men who wore the linen ephod (v 18). Since Doeg was Edomite and not an Israelite by birth, he was willing to do the task that the other Israelite servants refused. Doeg did not stop with the priests either, since he put the whole town to the sword as well: *men and women, children and infants, oxen, donkeys, and sheep.* The process of razing a town and destroying its inhabitants resembled the notion of *cherem* in holy war. Saul disobeyed the *cherem* in ch 15 against the Amalekites, but against the priesthood he observed it. In a sardonic way, the story of Saul becomes so twisted that the actions that were supposed to be applied to the Amalekites were carried out against Yahweh's priests at Nob.

■ **20-23** A lone individual survived the slaughter at Nob. The son of Ahimelech, **Abiathar,** escaped and fled after David. Abiathar represented the only surviving figure from the Shilonite priesthood (see 2:31-33). When Abiathar reported to David about the massacre, David accepted full responsibility for what happened. Because David was not forthright with Ahimelech and kept information about the erupting conflict with Saul hidden, Ahimelech paid the price for assisting David. David confessed, *I have brought about the death of every person of the house of your father* (v 22). David, as a result, offered Abiathar his patronage and his protection. Abiathar was instrumental in David's rise to kingship, serving as his main priest while he was at Hebron and would later share the priesthood with Zadok when David became king over all Israel.

5. David Saves Keilah (23:1-14)

■ **1-5** Chapter 23 relates an incident that took place while David took flight from Saul in the wilderness region. In this instance the Philistines raided the city of Keilah. The text notes that **they told David** about the Philistine incursion on the city (v 1). It is unclear as to who told David this information, but this possibly could refer to the men who were with him. Keilah lay about four miles south of Adullam in Philistine territory. Thus, it should come as no surprise that David knew of the Philistines' whereabouts. The Philistines were **robbing the threshing floor** of the city. The threshing floor contained the grain that was gathered at the time of the harvest. This presented an opportune time for the Philistines to make a raid on the people there.

Before David responded to these developments, he **inquired of the LORD** as to whether or not he should go up against the Philistines (v 2). The text here engages in a bit of a wordplay and makes a couple of important statements from it. First, the term used for **inquired** (*vayîš'al*) is based off the same verbal root word for Saul (*šāûl*). The text draws a sharp dichotomy between the two figures based off Saul's name. David **inquired** of Yahweh most likely through the mediation of Abiathar (v 2). Although the text never mentions him specifically in vv 1-5, Abiathar was already associated with David prior to the opening of ch 23 (22:22-23). Abiathar only came to David, however, after Saul had the priests of Nob murdered. The irony is that Saul as a result of his own actions unwittingly provided David the priest by which to consult Yahweh. This not only furthered the divide between Saul and David, but it continued to drive the wedge between Yahweh and Saul.

Second, David received a response from Yahweh as a result of his inquiry, **Shall I go up?** in 23:2*a*. The language here is significant because David will ask the same question in response to the Philistines in 2 Sam 5:19*a*. In both cases David receives an answer in the affirmative. In 1 Sam 23:2*b* Yahweh stated, "Go; attack the Philistines and you will save Keilah" (JPS). In 2 Sam 5:19*b* Yahweh stated, "Go up, for I will certainly give the Philistines into your hand" (NRSV). The statements in 1 Sam 23:2 and 2 Sam 5:19 stand in stark contrast to those of Saul who also inquired to determine God's will in fighting the Philistines (1 Sam 14:37 = "Shall I go down after the Philistines?"). Unlike David, however, Saul did not receive word from Yahweh in response to his inquiry. As a result, the two figures could not be portrayed more differently. Saul did not receive word from Yahweh and suffered defeat against the Philistines. David, on the other hand, heard from Yahweh and enjoyed success against them. The implications are clear; David would accomplish what Saul could not. Davidic kingship would be superior to that of Saul's monarchy.

Even though David received God's permission to initiate the attack on the Philistines, David's men responded with hesitation and trepidation. Sensing their reluctance, David inquired a second time and the Lord responded, "Yes, go down to Keilah; for I will give the Philistines into your hand" (v 4 NRSV). Interestingly, David received instructions to "go down" for his inquiry to **go up**. David had tremendous success against the Philistines as he **struck a heavy blow** against them and brought away their livestock after the battle.

■ **6-14** Abiathar came to David at Keilah "with an ephod in his hand" (NRSV). The text actually reads that he **fled** to David, but from where? Is this a continuation of the story in ch 22? If so, how do we explain the fact that Abiathar only joined David after he saved Keilah? It may be possible that a different tradition about Abiathar and David was incorporated into the text during the editorial process. The ephod Abiathar brought with him was generally a priestly garment that covered the priest's robe. However, in this context it appears as though it was also used as an instrument of divination that may have contained the Urim and Thummim (see 14:3; 21:9). When David learned that Saul summoned the people to war and was headed toward Keilah, David said to Abiathar, "Bring the ephod here" (v 10 NRSV). David basically consulted the ephod to learn whether Saul planned to come to Keilah and destroy the city "on my account" (NRSV). The Lord answered David with the affirmative: "He will come down" (v 11 NRSV). In addition, David inquired whether the men of the town would also hand him over to Saul. Again, the Lord answered with the affirmative, "They will surrender you" (v 12 NRSV). Learning of his fate through divine consultation, David and his men left Keilah and "wandered wherever they could go" (v 13 NRSV). Even though Saul gave up his expedition, David took shelter in the "strongholds in the wilderness, in the hill country of . . . Ziph" (v 14 NRSV). The hill country of Ziph was part of the Judean hills that lay several miles to the southeast of Keilah. This is in contrast to the town of Ziph, which was situated on a hilltop about five miles south-southeast of Hebron.

6. David Eludes Saul in the Wilderness (23:15-29)

■ **15-18** David continued to hide out in the wilderness of Ziph at **Horesh**. The word **Horesh** simply means "forests" and thus refers to the type of rugged territory in which David took refuge. While David was at Ziph, Jonathan visited him for the last time (v 16). How did Jonathan know where to find David? How were they able to communicate with each other while David remained separated from Saul's household? The text does not offer any explanations to these questions. It is interesting, however, that Jonathan could find David in the wilderness, but Saul could never catch up to him.

In a touching scene between these old friends, Jonathan came to encourage David and reassure him that Saul would not find him. Moreover, Jonathan affirmed that David would be the next king of Israel and Jonathan would be his right-hand man. Jonathan's affirmation of David and his confession regarding his impending monarchy are important, because it symbolized that he would not be a stumbling block to David (even though he was the rightful heir to the throne), and he would even support David as a subordinate to the future king. This understanding was reinforced as the two **made a covenant** with each other (v 18). How does this covenant relate to the one they made in 18:3 (see also 20:8, which has 18:3 in mind)? Is this a reaffirmation of the earlier agreement or is this a new covenant? Or is this a different version of the story? No decisive answers are forthcoming.

■ **19-24a** This section represents another occasion when David was betrayed by someone associated with Saul. First, Doeg the Edomite gave away David's location as he hid from Saul at Nob. Now the inhabitants of Ziph went to Saul at his hometown of Gibeah and revealed to him the whereabouts of David. Even though David enjoyed the love of Saul's family and many of the population, not everyone sought to assist David on his path to the throne. The Ziphites desired to curry favor with Saul in hopes that he would reward them for their loyalty to him. Not only did the people of Ziph relay David's location to Saul, but they also volunteered to take an active part in apprehending him as well: ***we will deliver him into the king's hands*** (v 20). The verb used here (*hasgîrō*) is a causative, which indicates they would take the initiative in capturing him for the king.

Saul displayed happiness and appreciation to a people who remained loyal to him, and he requested that they go back to Horesh to double-check that David was still there. Saul knew that David was "very cunning" and thus could escape at any time (v 22 NRSV). The word "cunning" (ʿārôm) used here to describe David is interesting. It can refer to shrewdness or cleverness and thus it highlights David's resourcefulness as a target of prey. This is also the word that is used to describe the serpent in the garden (Gen 3:1). While the cunning of the serpent brought pain and suffering to the couple in the garden, David was able to preserve his life through his cleverness. When the Ziphites had secured reliable information regarding David's hiding places, they were to relay that to Saul and he would go with them and capture David.

■ **24b-29** Even though Saul enjoyed the loyalty and help of the Ziphites, David remained one step ahead of those who pursued him. David had moved south into "the wilderness of Maon, in the Arabah" (v 24 NRSV). Maon was on a hilltop about eight miles south of Hebron, and David's camp was in the rift valley on the east side of town. When Saul learned that David had moved into this territory, he pressed the chase there.

FROM THE TEXT

1. One of the things that we are reminded of in this section is that as God's children there are times in life when people will actively oppose us and try to hinder us from reaching our goals or potential. Even though God's presence goes with us and God's favor rests on us, others still have the freedom of choice to resist us and even attempt to persecute us. God had selected David to be the next king of Israel, but this did not stop Saul from tirelessly and relentlessly pursuing him. In spite of this harassment, however, God was continuously working in David's personal circumstances to bring about a greater purpose.

While David ran away from Saul, more pieces of David's path to the throne were being set in place. David came into contact with the priest Abiathar during this time in his life. Abiathar became David's priest and would serve him during David's days in the wilderness and when he became king of Judah and later all Israel. David also came into contact with the 400 men who would form the backbone of his fighting force and would prove invaluable to him on his path to the throne. David would even find help from the king of Moab, who provided his family shelter while Saul hunted David down. God was in all of these circumstances to preserve David's life and prepare him for the next stage of his life.

2. It often takes time for God's plan to develop in our lives. God generally works in seasons and not in seconds. This is a hard lesson for modern audiences to grasp. In a modern culture everything takes place quickly and painlessly. We can fly long distances in a matter of minutes. We enjoy food that the microwave cooked in seconds. We can send emails and other forms of communications in the blink of an eye. We watch our favorite television shows in which situations are resolved in thirty-minute episodes. Modern medicine can begin to cure illnesses in a matter of hours. All of these facets of modern life have conditioned us to think that every issue or problem we encounter can be solved immediately and without discomfort.

3. However, our character development, spiritual maturity, and our emotional/psychological growth take time to progress in ways that are healthy and beneficial to us. We need to exhibit patience, for example, as we "work out" or bear troubling situations at work or home. Developing skills and education that will benefit our lives and give us better opportunities in the future occurs gradually over time and through a painstaking process. Many times in life the most positive and long-lasting changes that take place occur after we have endured a period of arduous testing or unpleasant, even painful, experiences. If we are not careful, we can become impatient during these moments and try to take shortcuts that will ultimately short-circuit or hamper our growth down the road. Trusting God and relying on his grace and provision to help us through these kinds of situations not only draws us closer to him but also gives us the strength to persevere while God's purposes are being accomplished in us.

E. David Encounters Saul in the Wilderness (24:1—26:25)

BEHIND THE TEXT

These chapters form a unit based on literary and thematic considerations. Chapters 24 and 26, in particular, help to "frame" this material with ch 25 occupying the middle section. In this unit, David came in direct contact with Saul on two occasions and each time was presented a convenient opportunity to kill him (chs 24 and 26). David also came in contact with Nabal and his wife, Abigail, while he took refuge from Saul (ch 25). In all three chapters, David faced individuals who wanted him dead or disrespected him: Saul and Nabal. In the matters of Saul and Nabal, the issue of revenge also comes to the forefront. Interestingly, only a woman, Abigail, showed respect for David and argued for his innocence. It is interesting that the two men who had contempt for David faced the prospect of death shortly thereafter. Abigail, on the other hand, continued to live and eventually became David's wife.

Scholars have long noted the similarities between chs 24 and 26 respectively (Koch 1969, 142-43; Klein 1983, 234-35). Some of the parallels include the following:

1. David was in the wilderness fleeing Saul (24:2; 26:1).
2. David had ample opportunity to kill Saul (24:3; 26:7).
3. An individual suggested that these opportunities had been ordained by God (24:4; 26:8).
4. David resisted the impulse to take revenge on Saul (24:6; 26:9-11).
5. David took material proof in order to demonstrate he could have taken Saul's life (24:4; 26:12).
6. Saul recognized David's innocence and moral superiority in the matter (24:17-20; 26:21, 25).

Based on the shared qualities of these narratives, different opinions on the transmission history of chs 24 and 26 abound. First, there is a camp that would argue literary dependence of one chapter on the other. There are those who would maintain that ch 24 is actually the younger of the two traditions and therefore ch 26 represents a modified version of it (Koch 1969, 143-44). Others would argue that ch 26 is the older account and ch 24 depended on the former for its existence (Smith 1929, 229-30; Driver 1966, 204; McCarter 1980b, 409-10). Second, another group of scholars maintain a middle-of-the-road position in that both chapters are simply alternate memories of one event (Klein 1983, 236). Third, others would note the similarities between the two chapters but recognize that there are significant differences that exist between them (Mauchline 1971, 173). As a result, this information would suggest that there were two different occasions when David made contact with Saul in the wilderness (Ackroyd 1971, 202; Keil and Delitzsch 1973, 247). Although no clear consensus has been reached in the scholarly community, there is evidence that ch 24 has the hallmarks of being a reconstructed text (Mellish 2006, 79-80). Thus, if any literary borrowing does exist, it appears that ch 24 would be the younger of the two traditions.

Chapter 25 shares a relationship with 23:24-26 in that both episodes take place in the vicinity of Maon. This tradition may be an early narrative and represent a continuation of 23:14 (Mauchline 1971, 167). If that is the case, then this narrative has been wedged into this context based on the central issue of David's refusal to get revenge on an individual who opposed him. Moreover, David's marriage to Michal is not relevant to ch 26 but is presupposed in 27:3. This information provides good evidence that these chapters are not arranged on a strictly chronological basis.

IN THE TEXT

1. David at En Gedi (24:1-22)

■ **1-7** Up to this point in the text, Saul initiated the pursuit of David in order to eliminate him. Even though David was able to elude him, Saul appeared to have all the advantages. The situation, however, changed as David took refuge in the strongholds of **En Gedi** (v 1). En Gedi lay on the western side of the Dead Sea, and it was an area dotted with cliffs and caves—a perfect setting for someone looking to take refuge from a stalker.

Saul mustered a large contingent of **three thousand chosen men** for the task of hunting down David, and they moved in the direction of "Rocks of the Wild Goats" (v 2 NRSV). Saul's intent to kill David is evident by the sheer size of the force he assembled and by the fact that they were not ordinary Israelite troops, but select men to traverse the wilderness and hunt down David.

The actual location of the "Rocks of the Wild Goats" remains undetermined; however, it is a well-established fact that ibex remain plentiful in this location even in modern times. Therefore, the name of this rocky terrain may have derived from the animals that lived there.

As Saul took a break from his pursuit of David, he went into one of the caves **to cover his feet** (v 3). This terminology is a euphemism in the OT meaning "to evacuate the bowels." In the process of relieving himself, however, he made himself vulnerable to David and his men who were hiding in the cave. Saul's back would have been turned away from David, thereby making him unaware of his susceptibility to David.

While Saul sat exposed, David's men made the statement: **The day which the Lord said to you, behold I am giving your enemy into your hand, and you will do to him that which is good in your eyes** (v 4). The invitation by David's men to kill Saul contains interesting language. Up to this point in the narrative Yahweh had not promised to deliver David's enemies (i.e., Saul) into his hands. Do these words, therefore, derive from another tradition that did not make it into our text? Or, do they simply represent the desires and wishes of David's men "cloaked" as the language of Yahweh? The surrounding context would indicate that the latter is true. Moreover, the reader of the text can sympathize with the words of David's men. Would anyone honestly hold it against David if he plotted revenge on Saul for all the trouble and distress he had caused him?

One of the major ideas that emerges in the story of David's rise, however, is that David did not give into the impulse of revenge but rose above the temptation to get even. In portraying David in this manner, the text presents David as a righteous individual, one who was nobler than his associates and Saul.

David did not kill Saul but only "cut off a corner of Saul's cloak" (v 4 NRSV). Even though David spared Saul, **the heart of David was struck** because of his actions (v 5). The text makes it clear that David never took revenge on Saul and that even a small gesture of retaliation against the king incurred guilt. David's reaction reminds the reading audience that David was incapable of hurting Saul and therefore could not have anything to do with Saul's death. This was a charge that some within Israel levied against David after he became king (2 Sam 16; 20).

■ **8-15** David did not kill Saul, yet he intended to get an explanation as to why the king relentlessly pursued him. After leaving the cave, David called out to Saul, **My lord the king!** (v 8). Showing respect and submission before Saul, he bowed with his face to the ground in obeisance. David's actions toward Saul indicated that he was not in pursuit of Saul's throne, and the king hunted him down for the wrong reasons.

David indicated that Saul had been listening to false rumors that ***David was seeking to do you harm*** (v 9). Yet the opposite was true. David even presented the piece of cloth from Saul's cloak as tangible evidence that he could have killed Saul if he so desired. David reassured Saul that he meant no ***evil and rebellion*** (the term for political revolt) and that he had not sinned against him (v 11). David finally left his case with God who would "judge between me and you" (v 12 NRSV) and who would avenge David upon Saul.

David was also incredulous why Saul would bother with someone of the stature of David as he referred to himself as a **flea** and a **dog** (v 14). The text through David's self-deprecating language takes careful measures to safeguard David's innocence and protect his reputation.

■ **16-22** It was after David finished speaking that Saul asked, "Is this your voice, my son David?" (v 16 NRSV). Saul's response in v 16 does not appear to fit the sequential logic of the previous context. Saul had already met David (v 8); why does he ask this question here? Verse 16 shows no awareness of the previous section, which signals that their conversation in vv 16-22 has been inserted.

These verses do, however, fulfill a very important ideological function. First, Saul called David **my son.** This is the first time in the Davidic tradition that he was called the king's son. One cannot overlook the importance of this terminology, since this implies that David was a part of Saul's family. This served Davidic interests nicely, because David eventually became the king of Israel and took control of Saul's kingdom. David accomplished this as a member of Saul's family, not as an outsider.

Second, Saul admitted that David was more righteous than himself. Saul's own admission helps to clarify that David had not acted maliciously toward the king, for Saul stated to David, "you have repaid me good, whereas I have repaid you evil" (v 17 NRSV). Saul's statement would have had a significant rhetorical effect on the reading audience in that it cleared David of any wrongdoing and thus placed all moral failure on Saul. Thus, David appeared to be nobler than the king.

Third, Saul basically admitted that David would become king and that **the kingdom of Israel** would be established in David's hands (v 20). Saul's words thus prepared the way for David's kingship to develop. Moreover, it could develop in a manner that helped to deflect and squelch any criticisms or misgivings that some may have had regarding the circumstances by which David came to the throne. This would be true among people close to Saul, especially those who came from the tribe of Benjamin. Saul's remarks in vv 16-22 thus provide a type of "apology" that not only anticipated David's rise to kingship but cleared David of any wrongdoing in the process. The importance of Saul's remarks from the standpoint of "political propaganda" cannot be overestimated.

2. David and Nabal (25:1-44)

■ **1** This verse breaks the narrative flow at the end of ch 24. The first portion of the verse (1*a*) provides a statement about the death of Samuel. Although Samuel has been nonexistent in the text since ch 16 at David's anointing, the writer/narrator of the text included his obituary at this point. The death notice prepared the reader for the evocation of Samuel's spirit in 28:3-5, however. The notice also indicated how much Samuel was beloved by the people of Israel. The text utilizes a verb (*vayispĕdû*) that indicates heavy grief or wailing on behalf of the people. The people also buried Samuel in his hometown of Ramah (1:1, 19). The second half of the verse (25:1*b*) notes that David left and went to "the wilderness of Paran" (NRSV). Paran was generally located south of Canaan into the northeastern part of the Sinai Peninsula. The Septuagint reads this as "wilderness of Maon" (23:24; 25:2), which was just south of Hebron and thus not as far removed geographically.

■ **2-8** These verses introduce the reader to a new set of characters with whom David will have interactions. The narrative begins in v 2 with the statement "there was a man" (NRSV), which is similar to the introduction to other characters in the OT text (Judg 13:2; 1 Sam 1:1). The statement is also significant because it signifies a literary break or juncture in the text. The text notes that this man lived in **Maon** whose property was situated in **Carmel,** which lay about eight to ten miles south of Hebron (15:12). Moreover, the man is described as being ***very great*** who had "three thousand sheep and a thousand goats" (25:2 NRSV). Based on the description of his possessions, it might be better to read **very wealthy** or "very rich" (NRSV).

In addition to being rich, his name **Nabal** also says something about his character. Nabal is often translated as "fool, foolish" and thus refers to someone whose behavior violated social norms, etiquette, or law. Considering the way he behaved toward David's men later in the narrative (vv 9-13), the reader can understand how he lived up to his name.

Nabal also had a wife named **Abigail** (v 3). The text highlights her positive qualities: she was "clever" (NRSV) and **beautiful**. This description stands in sharp contrast to the qualities of her husband: he was ***hard*** and ***evil in his practices.*** Moreover, Nabal traced his ancestry back to Caleb, one of the heroes from the wilderness era (Num 13—14). Caleb and his family eventually settled in the vicinity of Hebron after the Israelites entered the land of Canaan (Josh 14:13-15). Thus, Nabal had impressive family ties and wealth, and he enjoyed a measure of prestige in the southern portion of Canaan. These "assets" would prove to be a tremendous boon for David and his political career after he married Abigail (1 Sam 25:42).

The events are set at the time of sheepshearing. This represented an occasion for not only a time of work but of merrymaking and feasting as well (2 Sam 13:23-29). It was during this occasion that David sent **ten young men** to speak with Nabal on behalf of David (1 Sam 25:5). David sent the young men to request food and other victuals from Nabal. David instructed his men to remind Nabal that his shepherds ran into no trouble or missed anything while David's men were with them. David's remarks remind one of the modern-day mafia, in which David's request amounted to a demand for protection money.

In reality, however, this was a way for David and his men to make a living while providing protection to those who lived and worked in the area. It also provided David the opportunity to gain favor with the people in southern Canaan; he would provide a service and they would offer food and other material resources as a form of gratitude. David's request thus seemed an appropriate price for policing the area and providing protection from predators. David even instructed his men to make the request politely by using the language **your servants** and **your son** (v 8).

■ **9-12** David's men made the request as they had been instructed. Instead of receiving the news warmly, Nabal responded angrily and churlishly to their words. Nabal simply responded with the question, "Who is David? Who is the son of Jesse?" (v 10 NRSV). Nabal's inquiry was not an attempt to uncover David's true identity but a statement that indicated David acted presumptuously by asking for the victuals. Nabal, who was offended by David's proposition, viewed David as a political upstart and he took his request as a personal threat. Nabal would not take the meat that he slaughtered or the water (the LXX reads wine) he had and give it to David. Nabal even admitted that he did not know where David originated. As far as he was concerned, he was a political renegade who had broken away from his master. After being rebuffed, the men returned to David.

■ **13-35** When David learned of Nabal's response, his immediate reaction included taking military action against him. David gave the stern command to his men, ***Each man, gird up your sword.*** The text notes that **four hundred men** went up to do battle against Nabal (v 13). The group was likely composed of the men who rallied around him at Adullam (22:2).

As David and his men prepared for war, one of Nabal's young men reported to Abigail what had transpired between her husband and David's men. He noted that when David's messengers came to bless Nabal, he returned the favor by shouting **insults** at them. The young man understood Nabal's actions had serious consequences for everyone associated with Nabal; "evil has been decided against our master and against all his house" (25:17*b* NRSV). Considering Nabal's attitude toward David and his men, the young man appealed to Abigail for help; "now therefore know this and consider what you should do" (v 17*a* NRSV). Since Nabal's stubbornness prevented him from changing his mind, it would be up to Abigail to diffuse the situation.

Abigail sprang into action in order to prevent a deadly confrontation between her husband and David's men. The text notes that she "hurried" and gathered an impressive array of provisions for David and his men; "two hundred loaves, two skins of wine, five sheep ready dressed, five measures of parched grain, one hundred clusters of raisins, and two hundred cakes of figs" (v 18 NRSV). Moreover, she placed the food on donkeys and had everything sent on ahead of her as a kind of peace offering.

Abigail understood that sending the gifts in advance would appease David and smooth things over for her personal meeting with him. The scene is reminiscent of the time when Jacob sent messengers and presents to Esau before the two had their encounter (Gen 32:3-21). Abigail's strategy worked and she was able to approach David and his men safely.

Abigail's meeting with David (1 Sam 25:23-36) contained a number of important elements. First, she came down off her donkey and fell on her face before David as a sign of respect and submission. She promptly asked David that she be allowed to speak to him. The phrase "upon me alone, my lord, be the guilt" was a formulaic way of courteously asking for a hearing with David (v 24 NRSV). Moreover, it indicated that if something harmful should result from their conversation she would be the one to bear guilt for it. Abigail told David that her husband acted according to his name (Nabal = fool) and that "folly is with him" (v 25 NRSV). She should not be held accountable for her husband's misdeeds toward David, since she did not see David's men when they paid a visit to Nabal earlier.

The second part of her conversation (vv 26-31) was confessional in nature. In her remarks she emphasized a number of seminal ideas:

1. Yahweh prevented David from taking vengeance upon Nabal (v 26). As a result, David would not have bloodguilt on his hands for the reckless murder of her husband. Her statements remind the reading audience that Nabal's death would not come about as a result of David's revenge, but Yahweh's retribution on Nabal for the manner in which he treated David, Yahweh's anointed.

2. She asked David to forgive "the trespass of your servant" (v 28 NRSV). Although Abigail argued for her innocence before, here she asked David to

overlook her sin toward David. Her plea to David would ensure that David would not take her life once he took on a position of greater authority.

3. Abigail also spoke in v 30 of David's forthcoming kingship ("when [Yahweh] . . . has appointed you prince over Israel" [NRSV]). Her speech here anticipates 2 Sam 7:16 and God's promise to make David a sure house. As a result, commentators generally ascribe 1 Sam 25:28-30, in particular, to the hand of the Deuteronomistic editor(s). It is also noteworthy that Abigail's speech is the third time that an individual made an allusion to David's impending kinship. First, Jonathan admitted as much by giving David the symbols of royal authority (18:4) and in his words to David in the wilderness (23:17). Second, Saul made the proclamation that David would be king while in En Gedi (24:20). Here, Abigail reiterated the same message.

These statements are important because they prepare the reader for David's eventual ascension to the throne. When David did become king over all Israel, it came as no surprise to the audience because the characters in the story of David's rise had repeatedly stated this would happen. Moreover, it also underscored the idea that the people had no objection to Davidic kingship. In fact, they were quite supportive of the notion.

4. Abigail reminded David, "When [Yahweh] has dealt well with my lord, then remember your servant" (v 31 NRSV). Abigail's closing statements (v 31) anticipated David's political ascendency. When David had reached political prominence, she asked him to remember her and what she had done for him. David would not forget Abigail's generosity toward him, because after Nabal's death he took Abigail as his wife. David's marriage to Abigail would also help him politically since Nabal's wealth and reputation among the clans in the southern part of Israel fell to David.

David responded favorably to Abigail's generous gesture and conversation. David reminded Abigail that because of her actions Nabal and those associated with him had been spared. David received the gifts that she brought to him and told her to **go home in peace** (v 35).

■ **36-38** Abigail came home to find Nabal holding a feast, "like the feast of a king" (v 36 NRSV). Nabal's heart was **senseless within him** because he was extremely inebriated. The text engages in a bit of wordplay here. The term for "senseless" (*nābāl*) is synonymous with the name Nabal. Thus, not only was Nabal foolish in the way that he treated David, but he was also senseless in his personal conduct. Abigail waited until the morning to tell him about her meeting with David. When he heard these words, "his heart died within him" (v 37 NRSV). It is difficult to ascertain what the text means by this phrase, since Nabal died ten days later. The text may indicate he had a "heart attack" or some other cardiac event. In either case, the text makes a point to state that **Yahweh struck Nabal** (v 38). David did not kill him, thus rendering him innocent before man and God.

■ **39-42** David learned of Nabal's death. How he found out the reader is never told. The text takes special effort here to inform the reader that Nabal died before he pursued Abigail. David *proposed marriage* to Abigail but he did it by sending his servants to "retrieve" her; David sent them **to take you for his wife** (v 40). The language here would indicate that Abigail did not have much say or control in this situation. David's actions resemble the circumstances at the time of the Bathsheba affair: David dispatched his servants to the woman in question and they brought her to him (2 Sam 11:3-4).

It is likely that this relationship was based not on romance but on political necessity. David knew that his own personal and political position would be greatly enhanced by marrying her. Abigail responded to David's "proposal" by getting up (along with her handmaidens), mounting a donkey, and following the servants to David. In a laconic, almost antiseptic tone, verse 42*b* simply notes she **became his wife**.

■ **43-44** The chapter closes by making reference to David's other wives. The text notes that David married **Ahinoam of Jezreel** (v 43). Jezreel most likely refers to the small Judahite town near Moan, Ziph, and Carmel (Josh 15:55-56). Ahinoam became the mother of Amnon, his firstborn son (2 Sam 3), who later raped his half-sister Tamar (ch 13). The name Ahinoam is only mentioned one other time before this, and that is as Saul's wife (1 Sam 14:50).

Scholars have speculated that in addition to Michal, David at some point also took Saul's wife as his own (Levenson and Halpern 1980, 507-18). Saul's statement in 20:30 may well refer to this event. If so, then David had connections to Saul's family via not only his daughter but also his former wife. The statement in v 44 that **Saul had given his daughter Michal . . . to Paltiel son of Laish** is also suggestive and may support this theory. Since David lost Michal, Ahinoam would be David's link to Saul's family.

It is not surprising that David would ask for Michal back when he was positioned to become the king over the northern tribes (2 Sam 3:13). The reader gains a sense of the political import of these marriages. David solidified his presence in the south through his marriage to Abigail and his future claims to Saul's kingdom vis-à-vis Ahinoam and Michal.

25:39—
26:8

3. David Spares Saul's Life Again (26:1-25)

■ **1-8** This chapter opens with the notice that the Ziphites once again reported David's whereabouts to Saul. Since the Ziphites are mentioned only here and in ch 23 and the opening verse (23:1) is identical to 26:1, scholars often argue that these two chapters were originally a single narrative and later broken up by the insertion of chs 24 and 25. Chapter 26 represents a similar and alternative version of the one in ch 24 (see Behind the Text above). As a result, these two chapters may have originated from a common source but diverged in details over the process of its transmission history.

The story opens with Saul at his hometown of **Gibeah** when the Ziphites provided information regarding the whereabouts of David. David, on the other hand, ***hid himself*** **on the hill of Hakilah** (v 1). Hakilah was in the wilderness region south of Canaan. Saul traveled to this area taking with him 3,000 choice soldiers. Upon entering this region, Saul and his men made their encampment along the road on Hakilah overlooking a city called **Jeshimon** (see also 23:19). David and his men continued to reside and take shelter in the wilderness region.

David, however, sent ***spies*** to establish Saul's location (v 4). David and his men approached the place where Saul and his men had encamped for the night. One of the men with David, **Ahimelech,** is called a **Hittite** much like Uriah (2 Sam 11). The fact that he is called a Hittite indicates that he was a non-Israelite and that David was prone to utilize foreigners like Ahimelech as mercenaries. The other man with David was ***Abishai the brother of Joab.*** Abishai was the nephew of David (1 Chr 2:13-16), the son of his sister Zeruiah. Abishai would later prove valuable to David in combat, as would also his brother Joab. Joab became David's primary military adviser and general during David's wilderness years as well as when he became king over Israel.

David and Abishai found Saul and his general, **Abner,** asleep in a vulnerable position (1 Sam 26:7). Ironically, a spear, like the one that Saul had used to try and pin David to the wall earlier (18:11), now lay ***pinned in the ground at his head.*** David once again had the opportunity to protect his life as well as exact revenge on Saul. Abishai openly made the suggestion that God had delivered up Saul to them and that he should be the one to strike Saul with the spear stuck in the ground (26:8).

■ **9-13** When David heard Abishai's comments he quickly denounced the plan to destroy Saul. As is typical in the story of David's rise, the text goes to great lengths to show that David did not seek revenge on Saul nor would he have a hand in Saul's death. David's language in v 9, ***who can send his hand against the Lord's anointed and be innocent,*** is reminiscent of his remarks in 24:6. In addition, David used the stock phrase in Hebrew (*ḥālîlâ lî*), ***far be it from me,*** in reference to any idea of injuring Saul.

David's reluctance to hurt Saul was also significant in the story of his rise because David came across as being nobler and more magnanimous than Saul. David had every right to get revenge on Saul, but David again refused to do so. Instead of delivering a blow to Saul, David took his **spear** and the **water jug** that were near his head and crossed over the other side so that David stood at a distance from Saul's encampment. These items would be proof that David had the opportunity to kill Saul but did not. This again is similar to ch 24 in which David produced the corner of Saul's cloak to remind him that he could have taken vengeance upon him but refrained from doing so.

■ **14-25** In these verses David held conversations with two of Israel's most powerful men: Abner and Saul. David first of all rebuked Abner for not doing a better job of protecting the king. David even asked Abner the whereabouts of the king's spear and water jug to prove that he had been negligent in allowing David and his men to enter the camp undetected (vv 14-16). In David's estimation, Abner deserved the death penalty for his lack of care for Saul.

David then turned his attention to Saul (vv 17-25). When Saul recognized David's voice he called him **my son** (v 17). Unlike the occasion in 24:16, Saul used this designation before rather than after David's defense. David responded to Saul's words with the respectful and humble reply, **my lord the king.** David's sincerity did not stop him from inquiring why Saul was pursuing him and what crime he had committed that merited Saul's advances. If God had incited Saul against David, then an appropriate sacrifice could be made to appease God's anger. But if it was the work of men that made Saul envious and jealous of David, then they should be **cursed before Yahweh** (26:19). That is, they should be driven from the covenant community ("the heritage of [Yahweh]" [NRSV]) where other gods were worshipped—the same punishment that threatened David.

Saul accepted the blame for the present circumstances and admitted he had been in the wrong (vv 21-24). He acknowledged that he acted as a **fool** toward David, thus conjuring the image of Nabal in the previous episode (v 21). Saul's confession in these verses is significant, because they implicated him and essentially released David from any guilt or wrongdoing in terms of his interactions with Saul. David also presented Saul's **spear** as evidence that he had no intention of taking the symbol of royal power from the king. Moreover, David noted that because he held Saul's life in high esteem, God would watch over his own life and deliver him from distress.

Saul acknowledged David's sentiments and then pronounced a blessing on him (v 25). In a manner similar to the way an elderly father would bless his son, Saul's words to David anticipated and set the stage for David's future greatness as king over Israel (Gen 27:27-29; 49:8-12, 22-26). When Saul and David departed from one another at the end of this chapter, it was the last occasion when they would personally speak to one another. As the curtain closed on their relationship, the words of Saul reverberate in the mind of the reader as David continues on his path toward kingship.

FROM THE TEXT

One of the things that we learn in studying the life of David is that personal revenge does not accomplish God's redemptive purposes in the world. The desire to "get even" with those who have caused us pain, anguish, or hardship is a symptom of the human condition but not of the pious individual. However, as God's children, these narratives remind us that God is the ultimate judge and he will bring about divine justice in time. Even though David had the opportunity (and some would argue the right) to kill Saul, David understood that Saul was God's anointed and it was not his responsibility to exact revenge on him. In the process, David shows us the proper way to respond to those who might deserve revenge and that it is possible to turn the other cheek with God's help. In this manner, David was more righteous and virtuous than Saul. This does not mean that we cannot defend ourselves in the face of danger nor should we seek to put ourselves in a vulnerable position. The text does convey the notion that we should not actively seek to return evil for evil "but overcome evil with good" (Rom 12:21).

F. David Among the Philistines (27:1—30:31)

BEHIND THE TEXT

These chapters are taken together because they cover the period when David served as a Philistine vassal (esp. chs 27, 29—30). The unit shows an element of symmetry in that David was given Ziklag for becoming the servant of Achish in ch 27, and David avenged the destruction of Ziklag by the Amalekites in ch 30. The episode of Saul visiting the medium of Endor in ch 28 has been carefully inserted into the larger narrative unit. Although this chapter may seem out of place, it does connect with the surrounding context in that Saul's visit anticipates the battle of Mount Gilboa (ch 31) and his death on the battlefield (28:19). Moreover, the Philistines' rejection of David in ch 29 removed David from the scene of battle in which Saul died and placed him in Ziklag.

Chapter 27 opens the unit and comes on the heels of the farewell between David and Saul in 26:25. This chapter is unique in that it represents an alternate version of the events in 21:10 ff. Here, David took shelter with Achish, the king of Gath, yet he had already been introduced to him in ch 21. Moreover, ch 27 gives no indication that Achish knew David previously. As such, it is difficult to determine which chapter may have been the original version and which is a secondary or later edition. It is also possible that two independent traditions regarding the relationship between Achish and David existed. The other prominent issue is also similar to the one in ch 21.

Saul appears to be his own worst enemy in that his life devolved in a downward spiral after God rejected him as king (ch 15). As Saul continued to pursue David he drove him into the protection of Israel's enemies. Moreover, David was able to utilize his status as a vassal to the Philistines to help further his own political ambitions. In ch 27, David was given control of the city of Ziklag. Ziklag's location just outside the Philistine plain gave him ample opportunity to continue to raid the southern fringes of the country, solidify social relations among the clans and tribes of the south, and increase his political standing among the people there. David's connection with the southern clans proved invaluable as he became king over the tribe of Judah and then Israel.

Chapter 28 connects to ch 27 via 28:1-2. These verses not only provide the introduction to Saul's battle with the Philistines in ch 31 but also prepare the context for Saul's visit to the medium in 28:3-25. Saul, who did not receive a word from God because he had been rejected, sought the help of the dead prophet Samuel. Saul's conversation with Samuel centered on the impending battle with the Philistines. Saul sought guidance and direction in determining God's will for him from the prophet. Instead of encouraging words, however, Samuel reminded Saul that he had been rejected by God and that God would give Saul and Israel into the hands of the Philistines. Samuel's words essentially sealed Saul's fate and later proved prophetic as Saul died while fighting the Philistines at Mount Gilboa (ch 31). As in the other chapters on the story of David's rise, this chapter continues to underscore the notion that God had his hand on David's life while Saul's life continued to spiral out of control.

Chapter 29 dovetails with ch 30 in that the Philistines rejected David and prevented him from going to battle against the Israelites in ch 31. As a result, David returned to Ziklag in ch 30. When David returned to Ziklag he learned that the Amalekites had destroyed the city and had taken many of its citizens as prisoners. The Amalekites had been an adversary of David before (27:8), but in this context they destroyed Ziklag in an aggressive attack on the city. David responded to the Amalekites' aggression with an attack of his own against them.

In terms of the story of David's rise, however, this episode serves two important functions. First, David's defeat of the Amalekites represents another enemy that David defeated but Saul was unable or unwilling to vanquish. This portrayal of David fits with the theological/ideological agenda of the people responsible for David's story in that it supports Davidic leadership and demonstrates the notion that where Saul failed David succeeded. Second, the events of ch 30 placed David in Ziklag and in the southern fringes of Canaan. Since David was occupied while fighting the Amalekites, he was far removed from the events surrounding Saul's death. Chapter 30 places David in an area of the country in which it would have been impossible for him to have had a hand in the death of Saul. This information in one sense serves as an apology in that it demonstrated David had an alibi to answer the charges of those who claimed that David had a role in Saul's death.

IN THE TEXT

1. David and Achish (27:1-12)

■ **1-4** According to these verses, David took refuge among the Philistines in order to preserve his own life. Saul had been chasing David primarily into territories where Saul maintained control. Saul was never able to adequately stave off Philistine pressure, and thus, the region surrounding the Philistine Plain provided David a place of refuge.

Achish is called the son of Maoch (v 2). Although the name is Maacah in 1 Kgs 2:39, this may represent an attempt to assimilate the name to a form familiar in the OT. Maoch is a native Philistine name, and similar comparisons have been made with Machas or Macha from Asia Minor (Ackroyd 1971, 205-6).

When David traveled to Gath, he took with him **six hundred men** along with his two wives: **Ahinoam** and **Abigail** (vv 2-3). The first wife, Ahinoam, was from Jezreel. Although the Jezreel Valley was in northern Israel, the Jezreel mentioned here is another location. The OT only mentions one other Ahinoam, and that is Saul's wife. As a result, some have argued that Ahinoam was the former wife of Saul who became associated with David. If Ahinoam was Saul's former wife, then she, in addition to Michal, provided an invaluable connection to Saul's household (see comments on 25:43-44). Abigail was the former wife of Nabal, whom David married after Nabal's death. In marrying Abigail, David not only gained access to Nabal's wealth but also political capital among the Calebites and other southern clans.

■ **5-6** When David came to Achish, he was granted control over the city of Ziklag, which provided a gateway into the Negev (v 6). The exact location of the city remains unknown, but two or three sites have been proposed by archaeologists (Fritz 1993, 58-61, 76). The site of Tell esh-Sheriah, in particular, has been suggested to be ancient Ziklag. The site lay on the eastern edge of the coastal plain. Thus, ancient Ziklag was situated close to Judean territory, probably at the very border of the area controlled by Gath.

Ziklag was also known as crown property since it belonged to **the kings of Judah** (v 6). This statement provides evidence that the tradition about David and Ziklag had been committed to writing after Davidic kingship in Judah had already been established.

■ **7-12** These verses recount the incursions by David and his men into the southern portion of Israel when David occupied the city of Ziklag. David and his men were ruthless as they raided **the Geshurites, the Girzites and the Amalekites** (v 8). The text notes that they left *no one alive, man or woman.* David killed off these folks so that no one could report back to Achish how David had harshly treated them. The text may use hyperbole here because the Amalekites "returned" the favor when they attacked the city of Ziklag (30:1-3). As David raided these territories and took booty for himself, he also tricked Achish, who asked him where he raided. David responded that his raids took place in the territory of southern Judah: **the Negev of Judah, . . . the Negev of the Jerahmeel, . . . the Negev of the Kenites** (v 10). Achish believed that David was making himself odious to the people of Israel, but like a wily fox, David was increasing his own position while fooling the Philistine king.

2. Saul Consults a Medium (28:1-25)

■ **1-2** Although these verses may appear unrelated to the events in vv 3-25, they do anticipate the coming battle between the Philistines and the Israelites. They also raise questions about David's role in the war and whether he would remain true to the Philistines or the Israelites. The Philistine king, Achish, attempted to reaffirm David's allegiance in the time of battle. David had fooled Achish into thinking that he was making himself **odious** to the people of Israel (27:12), yet Achish appeared anxious to make sure that David would not join the Israelites in fighting against the Philistines. His statement in 28:1, *You surely know that you and your men will go out with me in the camp,* was not so much a question as it was a subtle demand. The text employs the infinitive absolute form for the first verb (*yādōʿā tēdāʿ*) and an imperfect with the second (*tēṭēʾ*) so that this can be taken as a form of a command. David attempted to reassure Achish by simply stating, "You surely know what your servant will do" (v 2 JPS). David, however, crafted his response in such a manner that he never specifically stated what he would do.

As readers we are left with the question of how David would respond when the Philistines did battle with the Israelites. Would he assist Israel's enemy in battle or would he return to his allegiance with the people of Israel? David chose his words carefully here so that his intentions were never clarified. Achish, on the other hand, took his statement as a sign that David would fight with the Philistines. Achish even believed David to the extent that he made David his **bodyguard** (v 2). However, not all the Philistines were convinced that he would remain loyal to them in a time of war (29:3-4).

■ **3-4** The impending battle with the Philistines is prefaced by the notice of Samuel's death and his burial in his hometown of Ramah. The notice of Samuel's death is first reported almost verbatim in 25:1. Although this verse may seem superfluous, it serves as an important link to the narrative in the following verses. At the time of battle the Israelites encamped at **Shunem**, a town on the southern slope of the hill of Moreh, opposite Mount Gilboa in the valley of Jezreel (see also 29:1).

■ **5-7** When Saul beheld the Philistine camp, "he was afraid, and his heart trembled greatly" (v 5 NRSV). As has been mentioned before, one of Saul's failures as king was his inability to defeat the Philistines. By ch 25, not only had Saul failed to defeat them, but he was also afraid of them. As Saul had unsuccessfully attempted to do in the past, **he inquired of Yahweh, but the LORD did not answer him** (28:6). The reader notes again the irony of Saul's name (*šāʾūl*) and his asking (*vayišʾal*) Yahweh for direction. Saul utilized every religious instrument available to him in order to receive a word from God: **dreams . . . Urim . . . prophets.** Yet Yahweh remained silent.

God's refusal to respond not only reaffirmed his rejection of Saul but also pointed to the utter isolation Saul experienced toward the end of his reign as the leader of Israel. Since Saul did not receive any word from Yahweh, he gave the command for his servants to find a *female medium* (v 7). Saul's suggestion not only highlighted his complete desperation but also symbolized his separation from God as he attempted to engage in a practice that God had forbidden (v 3; see also Deut 18:10 ff.; Lev 19:31; 20:6, 27). The medium was located at the city called **Endor,** a town in the tribe of Manasseh (Josh 17:11) situated a few miles northeast of the Philistine camp at Shunem.

■ **8-14** Understanding the impropriety of his actions, Saul **disguised himself, putting on other clothes** and went to the medium **at night** so that no one would see him (1 Sam 28:8). As Saul came to the medium he gave two specific commands: divine a spirit for him and bring up for him the soul he requested. The medium, however, believed that Saul was setting **a trap** (v 9) in order to kill the woman since Saul had outlawed "mediums and . . . wizards from the land" (v 3 NRSV). After swearing an oath by Yahweh that no harm would come to her, Saul gave the request for her to divine the spirit of Samuel.

It is not clear how, but when the woman conjured up Samuel's spirit, she immediately recognized Saul through his disguise (v 12). Some have argued that it is necessary to read the name Saul for Samuel here in order to make sense of this text. Is it possible, however, that Samuel may have revealed to the medium that Saul was in her presence, or was she able to deduce that it was Saul based upon his requesting Samuel? The text does not give us a clear answer here.

When Saul asked what she saw, she responded "a divine being" (v 13 NRSV). The word that is used here (*'ĕlōhîm*) often means "God" or "god," but it can also mean a "godlike being." Thus, it should probably be read as **spirit** or "ghost." She also saw that he was wearing **a robe,** which is how Samuel is characterized elsewhere (15:27).

■ **15-19** Samuel appeared to Saul in 28:15 and asked the question, **Why have you disturbed me?** Samuel did not refer here to an emotional disturbance but to the interruption of the rest of the dead (Isa 14:9) and his having to leave Sheol (the underworld) to be involved in earthly affairs again (Job 3:12-19). Saul recounted to him that God no longer communicated with him and he consulted Samuel for guidance. Samuel's only response was one of resignation; if God had rejected Saul, he was also powerless to do anything for him (1 Sam 28:16-18).

The Abode of the Dead

The OT does not contain a well-developed theology of life after death. Individuals who died traveled to the "underworld" of Sheol. Sheol is depicted as a place to which one "goes down" (Num 16:30; Job 7:9; Isa 57:9) and is sometimes referred to as a "pit" (Isa 5:14; 38:18; Ezek 31:16; Pss 30:3; 88:3-4; Prov 1:12). Darkness is a key characteristic of Sheol (Job 17:13; Lam 3:6) and its etymology may be related to necromancy (lit., to "ask, inquire"). Thus, Sheol is the place where one engages in necromancy, a practice that usually took place at night (1 Sam 28:8; Isa 45:18-19; 65:4). The OT does not portray Sheol as a place of punishment or reward, but only as a final destination for both the good (Gen 37:35) and bad (Num 16:30). It is the meeting place of all the dead (Ps 89:48). A more developed understanding of the afterlife developed during the intertestamental period in which the wicked suffered punishment after death while the righteous enjoyed happiness and bliss (Lewis 1992, 101-5).

Instead of guidance, Samuel gave Saul a hard word (v 19). He essentially brought three ominous messages to him. First, God had torn the kingdom from Saul and bequeathed it to another. Second, he reiterated that God had rejected Saul for his failure to obey God's command in the matter of the Amalekites (ch 15). Third, Saul, his son, and the Israelite army would be given into the hands of the Philistine army (ch 31). Instead of receiving a word of encouragement or direction from Samuel, Saul was confronted with the knowledge of his personal downfall and the end of his kingdom.

■ **20-25** The chapter closes with a note about what happened to Saul after Samuel appeared to him and the medium. Saul was ***very afraid*** because of Samuel's words and ***he fell to the ground*** (v 20). Moreover, "there was no strength in him" (NRSV) because he had not eaten, probably because he fasted in preparation for his meeting with Samuel. The medium, seeing that Saul was terrified, offered him "a morsel of bread" (v 22 NRSV) to help him recover his strength. Only after being strongly encouraged by his servants and the woman did Saul get up to eat. As a sign of hospitality, the medium prepared "a fatted calf . . . and . . . unleavened cakes" for him to eat (v 24 NRSV). Ironically, the last person to show kindness and mercy to Saul was not God or Samuel, but a medium who dabbled in necromancy.

3. The Philistines Reject David (29:1-11)

■ **1-3** The chapter opens with the notice that the Philistines **gathered** for battle **at Aphek** (v 1). Aphek was situated in north Ephraim far to the south of Shunem. The fact that the Philistines exerted military pressure that far north demonstrates just how formidable their threat to the Israelites had become. The Israelites encamped at **Jezreel,** a town on the northwestern slope of Mount Gilboa. The Philistines had mustered a sizable army that was moving in units of **hundreds and thousands** (v 2). David and his men stayed to the rear of the Philistines with Achish.

The **commanders of the Philistines** showed skepticism toward David and his men, because they did not believe David would remain loyal to the Philistines as they prepared to fight the Israelites (vv 3-4). The Philistines referred to David and his men as **these Hebrews,** a term that they had used in relation to Israelites previously (4:6, see comment there). Most likely, the Philistines viewed them as mercenaries and vagabonds who could shift their allegiance at any time. Moreover, the Philistines understood that David had previously served Saul in his army. What was to keep David from siding with the Israelites and turning his back on the Philistines in the heat of battle?

Achish tried to assuage their reservations, citing David's loyal service to him: ***since he has been with me . . . I have found nothing in him from the day of his falling away until today*** (v 3). In Achish's response, the term for ***falling away*** suggested David actually "deserted" (NRSV; *nāplō*) Saul when he joined up with the Philistine leader. Moreover, the verb is an infinitive connoting

David's continuous abandonment of Saul. Thus, David's presence with Achish served as proof that he had cut ties with the Israelite king.

■ **4-5** In spite of Achish's impassioned defense of David, the Philistine lords maintained their distrust of him and ordered him to go back to Ziklag. Their doubts about David were founded on the notion that he might join the Israelites and "become an adversary to us" (v 4 NRSV). The term for "adversary" here (*śāṭān*) has a wide range of meanings in the OT and is usually translated as "accuser" or "tester." In light of this context, however, it should probably be taken as "antagonist" or "enemy," thus intimating his active resistance against the Philistines.

In the minds of the Philistine lords, their reservations about David were justified since only at the cost of Philistine heads could David merit the favor of Saul (v 4; 18:27). The Philistine commanders even quoted the phrase the Israelites reserved for David (18:7; 21:11) as justification for their actions. David found himself in an interesting position; Saul did not trust him and wanted him dead, and the Philistines were not convinced that he would remain faithful to them in a battle against the Israelites.

■ **6-11** In light of the Philistines' rejection of David, Achish reiterated his admiration of David and recounted David's faithfulness to the Philistine lord. It is significant that once again in the story of David's rise another individual found David innocent of any wrongdoing. On this occasion, however, it was a non-Israelite who lavished praise on David. Achish noted in 29:6 that *I have not found anything evil in you from the day you came to me until this day.*

A significant question arises here in light of Achish's statement about David: if David was so faithful to Achish, what did that mean in terms of his relationship to the Israelite people at this time? Moreover, how would the people interpret David's loyalty to Achish in light of the fact that the Philistines were Israel's mortal enemies? David could have been perceived as a traitor, and this information could be used against him when he became king over the Israelite people.

The material in these verses attempts to address this issue and diffuse any negative criticisms of David it may have generated. The text does this in a number of important ways. First, David was not allowed to go out to battle against the Israelite people. According to vv 6*b*-7, 9 the Philistine lords did not give David or his men permission to accompany them to war. Thus, the text prevents David from fighting against the people he would one day rule over.

Second, David was commanded to return to Ziklag: ***now, return and go in peace*** (v 7*a*). David did as he was instructed: ***And David rose early in the morning, he and his men went in the morning to return to the land of the Philistines*** (v 11). The notice about David leaving the Philistines and returning to Ziklag also serves an important function in that it placed David and his men far away from the battle at Mount Gilboa—the location where Saul died while fighting the Philistines.

After David's departure, the text notes that **the Philistines went up to Jezreel** (v 11). The text goes to great lengths here to show that David and the Philistines moved in opposite directions; David traveled south and the Philistines headed north. The notice in v 11 convincingly places David far away from Jezreel, which in turn meant that he did not have a hand in Saul's (and Jonathan's) death.

Third, Achish vouched for David's character; especially his loyalty and trustworthiness. Achish especially emphasized this in v 9 when he stated, **I know that you are as *good* in my eyes as an angel of God.** The word for *good* (*tōv*) in this context refers to David's character and performance while in Achish's service. Therefore the word can be translated as "blameless" (NRSV), "acceptable" (JPS), **pleasing.** Even though these words came from the mouth of a Philistine, they do speak well of David and underscore the notion that he was a faithful servant. From a narrative perspective, Achish's affirmation of David's character also served an important theological and public-relations function. If a non-Israelite could not find treachery in David, how much more could the Israelites trust David when he became their king? The irony is that he was not a faithful servant but fooled Achish while in his service (27:10-12).

4. David Avenges the Destruction of Ziklag (30:1-31)

■ **1-4** The chapter opens with the notice that "David and his men came to Ziklag on the third day" (v 1 NRSV). The opening statement dovetails nicely with the ending of ch 29 (esp. vv 10-11), thus the text indicates the events are connected. The notice about the "third day" really needs to be read "after three days."

The "three days" of travel is significant in light of the events taking place in this context. It shows that the distance between Aphek in the north (29:1) and Ziklag in the south could not be traversed quickly. Thanks to archaeological discovery, this proved to be a "very reasonable amount of time" for David and his men to reach Ziklag (Tsumura 2007, 638). Thus, a three-day journey separated David from the Philistines.

Moreover, Mount Gilboa, the scene of Saul's last battle (ch 31), remained another thirty-five to forty miles northeast of Aphek. David was therefore far removed from the Philistines and even further from the scene of Saul's last stand. The implication is clear: David did not assist the Philistines in the battle against the Israelites, nor did he have a hand in Saul's death.

When David and his men arrived at Ziklag, the town ***was burned and the women and children were taken captive*** (v 3). The destruction of the city at the hands of the Amalekites also takes the reader back to the story of Saul. Even though David had treated the Amalekites harshly as the leader of Ziklag (27:8), the reader is reminded that Saul was supposed to defeat and completely annihilate the Amalekites at God's command (15:3). Because of Saul's disobedience with regard to the Amalekites (see also the important Deutero-

29:6—
30:4

nomic injunction set forth in Deut 25:17-19), they were alive to attack the town of Ziklag while David resided there. As a result, the people of David's city and David's family suffered the consequences of Saul's unwillingness to obey God's directive. David found himself once again enduring personal anguish because of Saul's actions.

David and the people with him agonized over the destruction of the city and the capture of their family members (1 Sam 30:4). Their anguish is highlighted in the language of v 4: ***David and the people lifted their voices and cried; they cried until they did not have the strength to cry anymore.***

■ **5-6** David's wives **Ahinoam** and **Abigail** are listed as members of the community who had been taken captive. The Amalekites, no doubt, made a political statement by taking the wives of the leader of the city. Most likely, the Amalekites would have either made David's wives servants or, as spoils of war, used them for sexual favors. It is also possible that the women could have been held as hostages for ransom. The fact that only these two wives are mentioned indicates that this narrative correlates to the earliest stages of David's political career. The text informs the reader that David took more wives as he became leader of Judah and when he ruled as king in Jerusalem (2 Sam 3:2-5; 5:13-14).

David also engendered the anger of the people of Ziklag who basically blamed him for the catastrophe. As a result of their irritation, the survivors ***sought to stone him*** (v 6). The people of Ziklag recognized that because of David's absence the Amalekites found courage to initiate the attack. Thus, the people resented David and held him responsible for the loss of their sons and daughters. In the midst of this chaotic and terrible situation David looked to Yahweh for help; he "strengthened himself in [Yahweh] his God" (v 6 NRSV). The syntax of the last statement is significant, because it intimates that his strength was found in his God, Yahweh; a source that transcended, and thus was not affected nor limited by, the shifting circumstances in which humans often find themselves.

■ **7-10** David advised **Abiathar,** the priest who had been with him since his visit to Nob, to bring the **ephod** in order to determine if he should pursue the Amalekites (v 7). Here, as in 23:6, the ephod functioned as an instrument of divination that David utilized to decipher God's will in a situation. ***Shall I go after this band and overtake them?*** (v 8) is very similar to the language that David used elsewhere when getting ready for battle (1 Sam 23:2; 2 Sam 5:19).

Unlike the occasions when Saul consulted God (1 Sam 14:37; 28:6), David continued to receive a divine response from his inquiry. God responded in the affirmative: "Pursue; for you shall surely overtake them and . . . rescue" (30:8 NRSV). The language here is important because the first verb (*rĕdōf*) is a command, and the other two verbs (*haśśēg taśśîg* and *haṣṣēl taṣṣîl*) are infinitive absolutes. The syntax indicates that God not only commanded David to go to war, thus giving him the "green light" to attack, but unequivocally guaranteed that God would give him success in this undertaking.

In response to God's word, David set out with 600 men (v 9). The numbers indicate that David's band grew from the original 400 (22:2). Information regarding the origins and identity of these men remains elusive. Did David come in contact with them while he was in the wilderness, or did they join David when Achish appointed David to rule over Ziklag? The text never fully answers that question, but it may be that both answers apply.

Even though David had 600 men, only 400 accompanied him into battle. These 400 may represent the original members who supported David early on (22:2). The text notes that David and his men crossed "the Wadi Besor" (30:10 NRSV). This wadi is never mentioned elsewhere in the OT, thus identifying it with confidence is problematic. However, some have associated it with the Wadi Ghazzeh, the prominent wadi southwest of Ziklag (Tell esh-Sheriah) by those who have excavated the site (McCarter 1980b, 435). If this is correct, then it would have been one of the prominent wadi systems that drain the Negev into the Mediterranean Sea.

■ 11-14 As David's raiding party moved forward, they encountered a nameless **Egyptian** who had been associated with the Amalekites (v 11). Since the territory of the Amalekites was not situated far from Egypt, it is no surprise that an Egyptian would find employment as a servant in an Amalekite household.

The Egyptian servant had been traveling for three days and was famished. After giving him food and water, David interrogated the young man (v 13): **To whom do you belong, and where *are you from*?** The young man claimed that his master had left him behind after making raids on **the Negev of the Kerethites** and on **the Negev of Caleb** (v 14). The term **Negev** means "south" in Hebrew, thus they corresponded to two areas in the extreme southern part of the country. The first area took its name after the Kerethites. This ethnic group probably originally came from the area of Crete or Caphtor. The biblical text also identifies Crete or Caphtor as the place of Philistine origin (Jer 47:4; Amos 9:7). Thus the two peoples shared a common heritage, with the Kerethites comprising a subset of the Philistines. David came to rely on the services of the Kerethites (along with the Pelethites) and they formed the backbone of his personal bodyguard (2 Sam 8:18).

The Negev of Caleb was probably a subdistrict of the Kenites (1 Sam 25:3; 27:10), which was located in the region south of Hebron. The young man also confessed that the Amalekites had burned down the city of Ziklag. When David learned of this news he asked the young man to lead him to the raiding party.

■ 15-16 The young man agreed to lead David and his men to the Amalekites on the condition that David would not kill him or hand him over to his master.

The location of the raiding party is never provided; however, when David and his men reached the site, the Amalekites were *laying all over the ground, eating, drinking and dancing* (v 16). The syntax suggests that the Amalekites were really "living it up" because of the spoils they had taken in their raids against Philistine lands and the land of Judah. Moreover, all the verbs are participles, which indicates that they had no intentions of slowing down their celebration.

■ **17-20** David launched an impressive attack on the Amalekites "from twilight until the evening" (v 17 NRSV), levying a heavy blow against them. Beside 400 young men who had escaped David's invasion, the text emphasizes the completeness of David's victory. David was able to recover **everything the Amalekites had taken.** The text even makes a point to note that "David recovered all that the Amalekites had taken; and David rescued his two wives. Nothing was missing, [from the smallest until the biggest,] sons or daughters, spoil or anything that had been taken; David brought back everything" (vv 18-19 NRSV). David had even taken all of the flocks and cattle so that it was said, "This is David's spoil" (v 20 NRSV).

■ **21-25** These verses note that David was generous with spoils he had recovered. David did not overlook the 200 men who did not accompany David on the raid. The "corrupt and worthless" men (v 22 NRSV) among the 400 who were with David on the attack against the Amalekites took umbrage to the notion that those who stayed behind should share in the spoils. David displayed a generous spirit, however, when he indicated that those who *watched the baggage* would receive rewards just as those who participated in the raiding party (v 24). In doing so, David enacted a policy of the distribution of booty that is reminiscent of the legislation found in Deut 20:14.

■ **26-31** David not only shared the spoils of battle with his men but also made a number of friends in Israel's southern region. The text lists a number of the places of the people to whom David gave *presents.* **Bethel** was not a part of Judah, and the Septuagint reads "Beth Zur" here, which was a Calebite town in the Judean hills a few miles north of Hebron (Josh 15:58). The location of **Ramoth Negev** is unknown, but it was also called Baalath Beer (Josh 19:8). **Jattir** was a Levitical city in the Judean hills about twelve miles south-southwest of Hebron (Josh 15:48; 21:14).

Aroer was a city in the Transjordan region, but it may be better to read it as Adadah (Josh 15:22), a town in the Negev about twelve miles southeast of Beersheba (McCarter 1980b, 434, 436). The location of **Siphmoth** is unknown. **Eshtemoa** was a Levitical city in the Judean hills about eight miles south of Hebron (Josh 15:50; 21:14). **Racal** maybe a misspelling of the city Carmel, which lay about seven miles south of Hebron (Josh 15:55). **Hormah** may have been close to Ziklag (1 Sam 27:5-6) and included as one of the cities of Judah (Josh 15:30), even though Simeon laid claim to it (Josh 19:4).

Bor Ashan, also known as Ashan, was a Levitical city in the Judean hills a few miles northwest of Beersheba (Josh 15:42; 19:7; 21:16). **Athach** is paired with Ashan (Josh 15:42; 19:7). **Hebron** was in the Judean hills and served as the principal city in the region and became capital of the tribe of Judah when David was first proclaimed king (2 Sam 2:4).

All of these cities represented locations in the southern portion of Judah where David established a substantial presence. David was able to ingratiate himself with the clans, tribes, and families of this region by sharing the spoils of battle with them. The "politicking" David engaged in and the personal connections he made during this time, however, benefited him handsomely on his path to the throne. The same people that David "won over" also constituted the "people of Judah," the people who would one day select him to be ruler over the tribe of Judah (2 Sam 2:4). The work that David was laying during his wilderness years and as the leader of Ziklag paid off for him handsomely in the long run.

FROM THE TEXT

The story of David in this section also reminds us that as individuals we do have a part in shaping and contributing to our own success or failure in life. Even though God was watching over David, he still took advantage of the opportunities that were presented to him on his path to the throne. David, for example, benefited financially and politically from his marriage to Abigail (1 Sam 25). David inherited Nabal's wealth and solidified his standing among the clans/families in the south by taking Abigail as his wife. David also made a number of friends by providing them with gifts from the raids he made on various groups in the southern territories. The relationships that David formed during this formative period in his life and career benefited him tremendously on his path to the throne. It was these same friends that sought to make David king over Judah after the death of Saul. The groundwork for this decision, however, was being laid while David survived in the wilderness.

The lessons provided here may seem counterintuitive to what some Christians believe about the role they have in shaping their own futures. There are those who wait "passively" for God to work out their situations for them, change their circumstances for the better, or provide "a sign" to direct them. Others may not take action or make a decision at all, because they expect God to do everything for them or because they fear that they will "miss God's will" for their lives. God, however, has endowed humans with reason, free will, desire, and the responsibility in making choices that will help them fulfill their dreams, desires, and goals. We add here the note that some of David's actions were politically motivated to gain influence and power and as such they do not serve as ideal examples for us to follow as we strive for success in our lives. Though we need to take advantage of opportunities that come along our way, we also need to avoid actions that are self-centered, actions that would bring injury to others and hinder their opportunities for growth and success in the world.

Israel's Wisdom literature understood and appreciated the significant role people have in affecting the direction (both short-term and long-term) their lives will take. The wisdom writers often stressed a positive correlation between the decisions and the actions people make and the outcomes (whether positive or negative) that they produce. The writers of Proverbs, for example, encouraged their audience to be industrious, plan ahead for the future, guard one's speech, accept discipline, seek good counsel, and avoid pitfalls such as laziness, drunkenness, hotheadedness, gossip, and taking shortcuts in life. The fruits of making sound choices, they understood, resulted in happiness, long life, riches, pleasantness, and peace.

The theology of Proverbs presumes that prudent choices will reap bountiful rewards and that human beings are capable of making these decisions. In studying the life of David and the book of Proverbs, therefore, we learn that God works in conjunction with humanity to achieve these ends both at the societal and individual level. If we are not careful, we can let great opportunities and blessings pass us by if we never engage or take initiative while we wait for God to act on our behalf.

G. The Death of King Saul and Jonathan (31:1-13)

BEHIND THE TEXT

Chapter 31 represents the end of the book of 1 Samuel in both the Hebrew Bible and the Christian OT. As the last chapter of the book it signals the end of the story of Saul. It recounts Israel's battle with the Philistine troops at Mount Gilboa and the demise of Israel's king. The events of ch 31 presuppose the notices in 28:1-2 and 29:1, but they are interrupted by the events surrounding David at Ziklag in ch 30. The details surrounding Saul's death in ch 31 differ significantly from the account of the Amalekite's version of Saul's end in 2 Sam 1. Do we have separate traditions here or is the Amalekite's story contrived? It is difficult to say, but the Amalekite's willingness to bring David Saul's crown and armlet raise other issues (see Behind the Text for 2 Sam 1:1-7).

The story of Saul's tragic end, however, has been building from the time Yahweh rejected him in ch 15 until this point in the narrative. Saul's suicide on Mount Gilboa not only represents the final act in Yahweh's rejection of the king but also signifies his utter failure on many different levels. In evaluating the magnitude of Saul's failure as king, the following information must be taken into consideration:

1. The request for kingship and the inception of Saul's monarchy. The people's demand for a king is situated immediately after the Ark Narratives (4:1—7:1) and the tradition about Samuel leading the Israelites in holy war (7:7-14). Both accounts clearly demonstrate Yahweh's ability to humble and defeat the Philistines (and their god Dagon) whether that occurred directly by Yahweh's hand or through the mediating presence of Samuel. Since Yahweh was capable of defeating the Philistines and had faithfully saved Israel from her

foes in the past (12:6-12), the request for kingship was deemed both unnecessary and a rejection of Yahweh's leadership. The fact that Saul's monarchy developed within this context not only cast his kingship in a negative light but also raised suspicions about the very institution of kingship within the DtrH.

2. The connection with Gibeah. A number of clues within the Saulide traditions echo back to the horrific rape/dismemberment scene and the brutal civil war at the end of Judges (19—20). Saul's connection to these events is underscored, though subtly at times, in various ways:

- His extensive patrilineal lineage that extended back to the 600 male survivors of the civil war (1 Sam 9:1). This also left open the possibility that one of his family members was involved with rape, considering that Saul's hometown was Gibeah.
- The emphasis on his height. The word to describe Saul's height is tied to Gibeah on a linguistic basis (9:2; 10:23).
- The battle with the Ammonites (11:1-14): the cutting of the oxen as a call to arms (v 7) is similar to the dismembering of the Levite's concubine (Judg 19:29), and the rescue of the people of Jabesh Gilead (1 Sam 11:9) recalls this tradition (most likely his mother's home territory; see Judg 21:12-14).

3. Echoes of the story of Jephthah. In both of the story of Jephthah (Judg 10—11) and Saul (1 Sam 14:24-46), a vow/oath was made at a time of conflict that subsequently had grave consequences for the children of the men who made the vow/oath (Judg 11:35-36; 1 Sam 14:44).

4. The connection with Achan. In addition to Gibeah, clues within the Saulide traditions also harken back to the Achan story of Josh 7.

- The manner in which Saul was selected as king (1 Sam 10:17-24) shares close similarities to the process by which Achan was identified as the perpetrator of a holy war crime (Josh 7:16-20).
- The method that revealed Jonathan as the individual who had violated Saul's oath (1 Sam 14:40-42) also mirrored the selection of Achan.
- Like Achan, Saul spared the spoils of war that should have been devoted to destruction (15:13-23).
- Like Achan (Josh 7:25), Saul had brought trouble to the land for his foolish actions (1 Sam 14:29).
- Achan and his family were burned with fire for his disobedience (Josh 7:15, 25); the bodies of Saul and his sons were burned by the men of Jabesh Gilead (1 Sam 31:12).

5. Saul versus the Philistines. Although chosen by God to defeat the Philistine menace, Saul never was able to eliminate the Philistine threat. Various elements in the Saul narratives indicate he failed his mission on several levels.

- The Philistines had a military installation in Geba/Gibeah, Saul's backyard (13:2).

- Saul failed to wait for Samuel and offered the sacrifices himself (vv 5-15). The prospects of a Saulide dynasty were dashed because of Saul's rash act (vv 13-14).
- Jonathan initiated attacks on the Philistines and their strongholds while Saul seemed reluctant to engage them. Jonathan had success against the Philistines, even defeating the garrison in Geba/Gibeah (v 2). Saul only joined the battle with the Philistines after Jonathan's successful forays into Philistine-held territory.
- Saul was a hindrance and an obstacle in the battle against the Philistines. His rash oath caused his men to become famished and fatigued while fighting the Philistines. Thus, Saul's words prevented the Israelite troops from gaining a greater victory over the Philistines. Moreover, the troops were so hungry because of Saul's oath they defied acceptable religious protocol by eating meat with the blood still in it. Finally, Saul's oath put Jonathan's life in danger because he unwittingly violated the ban. Saul was even willing to kill Jonathan, the one God used to bring Israel victory against the Philistines.
- David confronted Goliath while Saul and his troops failed to engage in battle (17:1-58).

In considering this information, a couple of seminal points emerge. First, throughout 1 Samuel various images and scenes from some of the most horrific and disappointing moments from Israel's past converge and come to bear on the Saulide narratives. The rhetorical and theological force of these allusions creates the sense that Saul would be not only a disappointment as king but also a tragic figure who was doomed to failure from the beginning. That is to say, Saul's monarchy would constitute another sad episode in a series of sad episodes from previous eras.

Second, Saul never fulfilled the mission for which he was initially chosen: to save the Israelites from Philistine oppression. Throughout the Saulide traditions, other people (God, Samuel, Jonathan, David) enjoyed success against them, but never Saul. Saul represents a *satan* of sorts in that he was a blunderer who made various strategic errors that stood in the way of Israel's success in the battle against the Philistines. As a result of his failure to deal adequately with the Philistine threat, David emerged as the candidate who would fulfill God's word to Samuel in 9:16.

The magnitude of Saul's failure against the Philistines is most powerfully illustrated in this chapter. At this point in the narrative, the downward trajectory of Saul's life culminates in the act of suicide. In an ironic twist, Saul had to resort to taking his own life while fighting the people he was supposed to deliver the Israelites from. Thus, the disappointing story of Saul comes to a bitter and lonely conclusion.

IN THE TEXT

■ **1-2** The first unit of this short chapter provides information about the circumstances surrounding Saul's death. The chapter opens with the generic phrase **the Philistines fought against Israel** (v 1). The sequence of events recounting Israel's battle with the Philistines at **Mount Gilboa** in 28:4 ff. has been interrupted by the report of David's capture of Ziklag in ch 29. At the resumption of the narrative, Saul and his men were in a dangerous situation; they were losing the battle, many had fled the battle scene, and a number of the troops had ***fallen slain before the Philistines.***

In the meantime, Saul was about to be captured and his sons had been put to death. The sons that are mentioned in v 2, **Jonathan, Abinadab and Malki-Shua,** are listed in the record of Saul's children in 14:49. An examination of the list in 14:49 reveals that one son, **Ishvi** (which may be a variant spelling of Ish-Bosheth [2 Sam 2:8]), was not present with Saul at Gilboa, while Abinadab has been added. The elimination of Saul's sons at Mount Gilboa, however, also had political implications, as it meant there was less competition among his sons for Saul's throne. Only Ish-Bosheth, the offspring of **Rizpah,** Saul's concubine, and **Merab,** Saul's daughter, remained. The sons of Rizpah were eventually put to death by the Gibeonites (2 Sam 21).

■ **3-6** The battle "pressed hard" (NRSV) against Saul, and he was wounded by the archers who had found him. Realizing that the end was near and unable to fight off an attack, Saul gave final orders as king to his armor-bearer: ***Take your sword and pierce me with it lest these uncircumcised Philistines come and pierce me and deal ruthlessly with me*** (v 4).

On a note of bitter irony, the last command that Saul gave as king included his own death warrant. Saul would have rather died by the spear of his own servant than to fall into the hands of the Philistines. Saul's disdain for his opponent is evident by the use of the phrase ***uncircumcised Philistines,*** language that is similar to the Jonathan and David and Goliath narrative (see comment on 14:6 [and sidebar]; 17:36). Saul's last command went unheeded because the armor-bearer **was terrified** and unwilling to kill his master. With no one left to help him, **Saul took his own sword and fell on it** (v 5).

■ **7** When the Israelites on the other side of the Jordan realized that Saul and the rest of the Israelites fled, they abandoned their towns and escaped. As a result, **the Philistines came and occupied them.** Saul never defeated the Philistines; in fact, they grew stronger under his control, even occupying territory the Israelites had once occupied.

■ **8-13** Even though Saul was not alive for the Philistines to torture, they still humiliated his dead corpse in a number of ways. The Philistines **cut off his head,** and they **stripped off his armor . . . put his armor in the temple of the Ashtoreths and fastened his body to the wall of Beth Shan** (vv 9-10).

The scenario is very reminiscent of the David and Goliath narrative: a head was cut off, the armor was put in a temple/sacred place (21:10 ff.), and the corpse taken to a major city. Only on this occasion, the Israelite king suffered disgrace at the hands of his enemies.

In addition, the Philistines paraded Saul's corpse and armor for the sake of taunting the Israelites and reminding the populace that the Philistines wielded considerable influence in the region. It was a group of men from **Jabesh Gilead** who took Saul's body and those of his sons down from the wall and brought them home and burned them there (31:11-12). No doubt this was done in gratitude for Saul's actions toward them earlier (11:5-13) and possibly because Saul's mother was from this area as well.

FROM THE TEXT

The tragic end to the life of Saul reminds us what happens when sin and disobedience consume an individual. Throughout his career, Saul grew further and further away from God, the outcome of which was a steady increase in the level of his despair, anxiety, loneliness, suspicion, and jealousy. The course of events ultimately led to the horrific ending of his life. Paul reminded his readers (and us) that "the wages of sin is death" (Rom 6:23). Jesus also compared sin to those who walk in darkness (John 3:19-20).

Saul's life serves as a powerful example of the devastating impact sin can have on individuals. We are reminded that when individuals stubbornly refuse to accept God's grace and direction in their lives, they too engage in a difficult and painful process that leads them further away from him. As in the case of Saul's experience, the effects of sin can take on many forms: loneliness, pain, regret, guilt, hopelessness, anger, pride, negativity, and self-centeredness, to name a few. Without genuine repentance, the alienation from God coupled with the inability to overcome the power of sin can cause people to become ensnared in a downward cycle that appears out of control.

Sin's grip on an individual's life can be so strong that it can cause a person to engage in behavior, go places, say and believe things that they never imagined was possible. Instead of bearing the fruits of the Holy Spirit, which are wholesome and good, the individual controlled by sin bears the marks of the flesh (Gal 5:16-21). Like Saul, the results of a life dominated by disobedience and sin lead to unwholesome behavior that produces shame and regret. Thankfully, God's prevenient grace is extended to each of us, and it can both reach and deliver even the most hardened of sinners. Because of God's abundant mercy, his ability and willingness to cleanse sin, and his desire to instill within us the power to overcome sin, our story does not have to replicate Saul's sad ending, but it can be characterized by peace, joy, freedom, and life, both abundant and eternal.

THE BOOK OF SECOND SAMUEL

H. The Second Report of the Death of Saul and David's Lament over the Death of Saul and Jonathan (2 Samuel 1:1-27)

BEHIND THE TEXT

The opening chapter of 2 Samuel is divided into two main sections. The first part (vv 1-16) includes an account of Saul's death at the hands of an Amalekite. The information in this text, as we will see, is different from the account of Saul's death at the end of 1 Samuel (31:1-13). At the end of 1 Samuel, Saul died as a result of falling on his own sword. In 2 Samuel 1 Saul was killed off by an anonymous Amalekite warrior. The tensions/contradictions between these two chapters have caused scholars to offer a wide variety of opinions as to their transmission history. Some have argued that the Amalekite soldier was fabricating the story in order to gain David's gratitude and receive a reward from the future king (Keil and Delitzsch 1967, 286).

Others have noted that there were two traditions regarding the death of Saul that have been brought together in the editorial process, thereby preserving the apparent tensions. Finally, arguments have been put forth that suggest ch 1 is a creative composition from someone close to Davidic circles whose primary goal was to protect David from accusations that he had a hand in the death of Saul (Halpern 2001, 78-80). According to this line of thought, this text functions as an apology that served to defend David against attacks from opponents who saw him as the one who arranged the death of Saul and Jonathan, which then provided him the opportunity to lay claim to the throne of Israel.

The second unit in this chapter (vv 17-27) follows the Amalekite's report of the death of Saul and Jonathan. These verses take the form of David's personal lament in response to the events in vv 1-16. The text is poetic in structure and style, and a number of scholars view it as the composition of David himself, which David ordered to "be taught to the people of Judah" (NRSV) (Payne 1982, 159-60; Birch 1998, 1205). The poem takes the form of a dirge or lament for the dead, often referred to as a kinah (*qînâ*) in Hebrew poetry and literature. It is a song for the dead and often looks back on the accomplishments of those being lamented and remembered. A kinah does not speak ill of the dead, and there is no address or mention of God, which distinguishes it from a distress or lament in the Psalms. This dirge is sometimes referred to as "The Song of the Bow," which derives from the language in v 18 (where it is simply called "Bow").

IN THE TEXT

1. An Amalekite Reports Saul's Death (1:1-16)

■ **1-10** Verse 1 opens the unit with the words, ***and it happened after the death of Saul.*** This is an important phrase and cannot be overlooked, because it parallels that of the other two books that precede this:

Joshua 1:1: "After the death of Moses . . ."
Judges 1:1: "After the death of Joshua . . ."
2 Samuel 1:1: "After the death of Saul . . ."

The phrase "after the death of X" appears at the opening of the three main books in the DtrH, and linguistically it binds the three main periods of Israel's history together: the liberation of Egypt, the conquest of Canaan, and the early period of the Israelite monarchy. In addition to this information, the narrator was quick to note that ***David had returned from smiting the Amalekites*** and that he resided at **Ziklag** (v 2). These two notices are extremely important because they situate David far from the battle that took place at Mount Gilboa (1 Sam 31). Mount Gilboa was located in the northern half of the country while Ziklag was in the southern portion on the fringe of the Philistine plain.

David had already been at Ziklag for **two days** (another subtle but important clue to show that David was innocent in the death of Saul) when an unnamed Amalekite approached David **on the third day** and ***bowed down to him*** (v 2). The symmetry here is significant: David, an Israelite, had just struck down a group of Amalekites earlier (1 Sam 30); in this context an Amalekite struck down Saul, the Israelite king.

Moreover, the Amalekite bowed down to David, which would indicate that David enjoyed a measure of political authority at this point in his life. The term that is used for ***bow down*** (*vayištāḥû*) is often employed when someone is demonstrating obeisance before an acknowledged superior. David had been made a vassal ruler over Ziklag by the Philistine Achish (1 Sam 27), and it would not be long until he reigned over the territory of Judah (2 Sam 2:1-4). Does the Amalekite's gesture indicate he was anticipating or even acclaiming David as the new king over all Israel? Also, the Amalekite in this context clearly knew who David was, but how? Had David already made a name for himself at this point and thus his reputation preceded him? In both cases, the answer appears to be in the affirmative.

The Amalekite also came to David with the conventional signs of mourning: **his clothes were torn and dirt was on his head** (v 2). David, inspecting the Amalekite's disheveled appearance, knew that he was the bearer of bad news and thus proceeded to inquire of his whereabouts: **Where have you come from?** The Amalekite reported that he had just **escaped** from the camp of Israel (v 3). David wanted the latest update on the battle and inquired *how things went* (v 4). The Hebrew indicates that David wanted this information promptly because he followed his question with a direct command: *tell me now!*

The Amalekite gave David two pieces of information in his report: first, the army fled and a number of Israelite troops died; and second, Saul and Jonathan had died as well. It is interesting that when David responded to the Amalekite's report he wanted to clarify as quickly as possible the status of Saul and Jonathan and not the Israelites themselves. David asked in v 5, **How do you know that Saul and his son Jonathan are dead?** David's quick response may raise some questions at this point. Did David inquire about Saul and Jonathan out of concern for them? Or, is it possible that David wanted confirmation regarding the deaths of Saul and Jonathan, knowing that his path to Israelite kingship had become clearer? Maybe this is why David was in such a hurry to verify the information surrounding their death notices. It is also possible that David was suspicious of the Amalekite's story to begin with and thought he was lying. David may have perceived that the Amalekite thought he could gain some reward by delivering him this news.

A couple of items about the Amalekite's story would indicate that his version of the events was fabricated, however. First, certain details of his account do not match the narrative in 1 Sam 31. The Amalekite only mentioned the death of Saul and Jonathan and not the other sons who died with Saul on Mount Gilboa (1 Sam 31:2). Second, the account in 1 Sam 31 mentions that Saul fell on his sword (v 4), but the Amalekite claimed he was **leaning on his spear** (2 Sam 1:6). Third, the Amalekite claimed that he *accidentally happened to come upon Saul* while he was leaning upon his spear. Did one accidentally stumble onto a battlefield, on a mountain no less, while the battle was still raging back and forth? His story sounds dubious at this point.

Moreover, the Amalekite was able to retrieve Saul's **crown** and his "armlet" (NRSV) and bring them to David. This information would indicate that the Amalekite got to Saul's corpse before the Philistines did. Is it possible that he was scavenging on the battlefield after the fighting and only then removed the regalia from Saul's body?

As the Amalekite relayed the events back to David, he claimed he came upon Saul as the king was ready to kill himself. When Saul asked the identity of the young man, he simply answered, **An Amalekite** (v 8). This is the first time in the narrative that the man's identity is made clear, and it highlights a certain irony in the story of Saul in general. Saul had gone to battle against the Amalekites earlier (1 Sam 15); is it possible that this Amalekite sought revenge on Saul for killing the Amalekite population? Here was a perfect opportunity to settle an old account made easier by the fact that Saul requested the young man to kill him.

The events of the Amalekite's story thus represented a dramatic paradox: Saul lost his kingship because he did not kill the Amalekite king (ch 15), but at the battle of Gilboa he asked an Amalekite to kill the Israelite king. According to the Amalekite, Saul instructed him to stand over him and kill him, since a *cramp has seized me and life is still in me* (v 9). The phrase here is difficult to translate and modern translations have handled it in various ways: "convulsions have seized me" (NRSV), "I am in agony" (JPS), or **I am in the throes of death.** Each translation preserves the notion that Saul was suffering terribly before he died. The Amalekite obliged Saul and killed him, figuring that he would not survive after he had already fallen. When the job was completed, the Amalekite stripped Saul of his crown and the armlet on his forearm (v 10); two symbols of royal status and power as attested in a list of jewelry the Assyrian king Sennacherib gave to his son (and successor) Esarhaddon (Walton 2000, 322).

■ **11-16** The Amalekite thought that this act would make him eligible for compensation later on when David became king. However, David and his men did not respond in jubilation and gratitude after the Amalekite presented Saul's jewelry; rather, they reacted with a sense of deep sorrow and loss. The text notes that they *tore their clothes, mourned, wept, and fasted* (v 12). David and his men not only mourned over the death of Saul and Jonathan, but they grieved **for the army of the** LORD **and the house of Israel.**

David's sadness over the loss of Israel's king and troops soon turned to indignation at the Amalekite. David inquired in v 14 if the Amalekite was *not afraid to raise your hand against the Lord's anointed?* The statement that David made popular earlier (1 Sam 24:6; 26:9) was now a question and an accusation against the Amalekite. Instead of receiving rewards for his efforts, the Amalekite's actions essentially signed his own death warrant. David ordered one of his young men to **strike him down** (v 15). This phrase applied to Saul who was accused of striking down the innocent (1 Sam 22:17b-18) and in the Solomon traditions he had his opponents killed (1 Kgs 2:25, 29, 31-32, 34, 46). In this context, the Amalekite was struck down as one guilty of committing regicide.

The unit closes out with a powerful statement, "Your blood be on your head; for your own mouth has testified against you" (v 16 NRSV). This declaration is significant as it relates to the overall designs and concerns of the story of David's rise, because it comes as a confession from the mouth of the Amalekite that he, and not David, killed **Yahweh's anointed.**

2. David's Song of Lament (1:17-27)

■ **17-18** These two verses serve as a heading for the lament proper, which follows in vv 19-27. The text notes that "David intoned this lamentation over Saul and his son Jonathan" (v 17 NRSV). This notice indicates the intensely personal nature of this dirge as it represented his feelings of grief over the loss of these two individuals. David enjoyed a close and deep friendship with Jonathan and, at one time, Saul had been like a father figure to him; thus David's loss was heartfelt. David also "ordered that [the song] be taught to the people of Judah" (v 1 NRSV). The insistence on teaching the people of Judah was likely to have been politically motivated. David was not the king of Israel yet, but if the Judean people were shown to be paying proper respect to Saul's memory, this would increase the likelihood that the northern tribes would transfer their loyalty to David, a Judean (Evans 2003, 142).

The song was **written in the Book of Jashar.** Outside of this text, the book of Jashar is only mentioned one time (Josh 10:13). This book was a collection of ancient poems that formed part of the source material lying behind various OT documents (Mauchline 1971, 199).

■ **19-22** The decimation of the army and Saul represented a disaster for the nation of Israel. The terms **glory** and **the mighty** refer to those who fell in battle, and their loss marked an incalculable loss to the nation (v 19). The defeat of Israel's mighty warriors and her king should not be told in the Philistines cities of **Gath** and **Ashkelon** since the **daughters of the Philistines** would rejoice (in much the same manner that the Israelite women rejoiced over the defeat of the Philistines, see 1 Sam 18:7). The women are also called **daughters of the uncircumcised,** which is reminiscent of language used by Jonathan and David (see comments on 1 Sam 14:6 [and sidebar]; 17:26) and by Saul, who did not want to suffer the indignity of dying by their hands (1 Sam 31:4).

The mourning of the nation was such that even nature should participate in it. The **mountains of Gilboah,** the vicinity of Saul's death, were to receive **neither dew nor rain,** nor should they produce crops as a sign of their sadness and despair over those who had fallen on their heights (v 21). Even though Saul and Jonathan fought valiantly and bravely (v 22), they were not able to repel adequately their Philistine enemies.

■ **23-24** Saul and Jonathan were remembered as being "beloved and lovely" and that in death they had been together (v 23 NRSV). This does not imply that they died together at the same place at the same time but that "they had been united in purpose" (Evans 2003, 143); they gave their lives in the defense of their country. They were **swifter than eagles** and **stronger than lions;** two characteristics that made them valiant warriors (v 23). The **daughters of Israel** were instructed to "weep over Saul" (v 24 NRSV). Saul had brought a measure of security and economic stability to the nation; therefore they enjoyed luxuries such as clothes of "crimson" (NRSV; see Prov 31:21) and **ornaments of gold**.

■ **25-26** This section of the poem begins to focus on Jonathan and David's personal feelings of grief over his fallen **brother** (v 26). David expressed his great love and admiration for Jonathan, whose love "was wonderful, passing the love of women" (NRSV). David does not intend for us to think of his love for Jonathan in terms of a homosexual relationship, but rather he emphasized the great allegiance, unconditional faithfulness, and covenant loyalty Jonathan showed him throughout their friendship. The kind of fidelity that Jonathan exhibited toward David through the changing fortunes of their relationship surpassed even the devotion of a woman to her husband.

■ **27** The dirge closes with a further expression of desperation and grief. It reiterates the statement of v 19: **how the mighty have fallen** as a way of bringing closure to the lament. The song does not say anything of the future, but it simply focuses on the grim realities of the present. David did not cry out to God here, because his thoughts were focused on human relationships and the sincere grief he endured.

FROM THE TEXT

This section portrays a David that expresses deep sorrow over the deaths of Saul and Jonathan. Not only did David and his men engage in the ritual act of mourning (vv 11-12), but David's personal feelings for the former king and his close friend are poignantly recorded in David's lament as well (vv 19-27). The recording of David's reaction to the deaths of these individuals is significant, because it shows David's true feelings for Saul in spite of their rough past. David did not "gloat" over the demise of his enemy, and he did not use this occasion to glory in Saul's downfall. In this context, David again shows his righteous and magnanimous character as it relates to Saul. David did not harbor anger or resentment toward the man who tried to kill him, but instead honored his life and memory as he had in the past (1 Sam 24; 26). Because David treated Saul with respect and dignity when he was alive, he was not plagued by personal regret and disappointment when he died. He did not have to live with guilt and shame over the way he treated Saul, but he could say good-bye to him with a clear conscience.

Through the story of David and Saul we are reminded that life is short and death visits every person. Since we never know when death will take our life or the life of a family member or friend, it is essential that we live on good terms with those with whom we have relationships every day. By consistently treating people with kindness, consideration, patience, and understanding, we will never have to experience deep regret when death separates us. The occasions when people experience remorse upon the death of a family member, a friend, a neighbor, or a coworker because they did not take the opportunity to make amends are too numerous to count. By following Christ's exhortation to "love one another" (John 13:34) and the writer of Hebrews' admonition to *live at peace with all people* (12:14), we can be spared the agony of living a lifetime filled with sorrow and disappointment over a broken relationship.

I. David as Ruler over Judah (2:1—4:12)

BEHIND THE TEXT

These chapters are treated together as a unit based on the developments in David's incremental rise to kingship. This portion of Samuel represents the intermediate period when David reigned as king over Judah and before he became king over all the Israelite tribes. During this period of David's life, tensions continued to flare between the house of David and the house of Saul. David's political affiliation with the Philistines along with his burgeoning career in Judah represented a serious threat to Saul's kingdom.

Within this unit, however, it becomes clear to the reader that as these two ruling families confronted one another, David's house progressively gained strength against the house of Saul, especially Saul's son Ish-Bosheth. Moreover, the tide in the hostilities between both camps turned in David's favor when Saul's former general Abner volunteered to transfer the Israelite tribes over to David's side. At the end of the unit, Ish-Bosheth was assassinated so that the path to Israelite kingship was completely clear for David. This unit, therefore, occupies an important element within the story of David's rise, and it reinforces the notion that Yahweh continued to favor David and give him success over the house of Saul.

IN THE TEXT

1. David Anointed as King over Judah (2:1-7)

■ 1 David's political career advanced in incremental stages according to the text. In this unit, David became king over the tribe Judah before he was selected as the king of Israel. The canonical arrangement of the story of David's rise indicates that David became king over Judah after the death of Saul and Jonathan (*and it happened after thus* [v 1*a*]). At the beginning of ch 2, David prayed for himself and asked Yahweh whether he should "go up into any of the cities of Judah" (NRSV). David's prayer is significant, first of all, because it includes language we have seen in regard to the Samuel and Saul traditions. David asked (*šāal*) just like Hannah asked for a son and the people asked for a king.

The statement about David's asking not only binds this tradition with the Samuel/Saul narratives but also plays on the name of the recently deceased king. The syntax thus attempts to draw a sharp contrast between Saul's monarchy and David's emerging kingship. Moreover, in David's inquiry there is a fourfold reference of the verb to "go up" or "ascend" (*ʿālah*).

V 1: "Shall I *ascend* into any of the cities of Judah?"
V 1: Yahweh said to him, *"Ascend!"*
V 2a: "To which city will I *ascend*?"
V 2: So David *ascended* there (Hamilton 2004, 305 [quoting Polzin]).

The structure of the exchange between David and Yahweh is significant for a number of reasons. First, the use of this verb is especially apropos in the context of the story of David's rise, because David was on his ascent to Israelite kingship. Thus, this represents just one, but a significant, stop on his journey to becoming king. With Yahweh responding to David's request in the affirmative, David's path to the throne was essentially sealed.

Second, the language that is employed in vv 1-2 is reminiscent of other places where David inquired of God for an answer:

David: **Should I attack the Philistines?** (1 Sam 23:2).
God: **Go and attack the Philistines . . . Yes, go down and attack the Philistines** (1 Sam 23:2, 4).
David: **Shall I go up against the Philistines?** (2 Sam 5:19a).
God: **Go up, for I have will certainly give the Philistines into your hand** (2 Sam 5:19c).

These statements also pertain to the tribe of Judah (David's home tribe):

The Israelites: "Who shall go up first for us against the Canaanites?" (Judg 1:1 NRSV).
God: "Judah shall go up" (Judg 1:2 NRSV).
The Israelites: "Which of us shall go up first to battle against the Benjaminites?" (Judg 20:18b NRSV).
God: "Judah shall go up first" (Judg 20:18c NRSV).

In the cases when David and/or David's tribal territory of Judah sought to "go up" or "ascend" into battle against the Philistines or the Canaanites and the Benjamites, Yahweh consistently answered in the affirmative. The same response occurs in vv 1-2, thus intimating a similar message; David would gain the throne and be installed as king.

Third, David inquired as to which city he should ascend. Yahweh answered he should ascend to **Hebron**. The reference to Hebron is particularly important, because in Israel's history Hebron had served as the residence of two important leaders: Abraham (Gen 13; 18) and Caleb (Josh 15:13-19). That David would be paired with these significant figures and the city to which they belonged foreshadows David's greatness as an individual and as a leader. The connection to Abraham is especially pertinent because the text will continue to draw parallels between the two figures at other junctures in the story of David (see below). In so doing, the writer/narrator of these traditions intended to portray David as a second Abraham through whom the promises made to the great patriarch would be fulfilled.

■ **2-4** When Yahweh gave David a positive response, he moved to Hebron with his men and his family. The text also mentions in v 2 that **Ahinoam** and

Abigail, the two wives of David, went with him. The text notes that these two wives were with David when he ruled at Ziklag (see comments on 1 Sam 27:1-4).

David's marriage to Abigail helped him solidify his standing among the clans in Judah, and his marriage to Ahinoam would have given him access to the house of Saul. David had married Saul's daughter, Michal, before this, but Saul gave her to another man later. Michal and David would be reunited when David was preparing to take control of all the tribes of Israel (3:14).

David became the leader over the house of Judah when the men of Judah **anointed** him as king (v 4). In anointing David as king, the people of Judah adhered to Deuteronomistic principles (Deut 17:14-15) so that David's monarchy was legitimated on the basis of God's instruction. This is the first time that David was called **king** (*melek*) and in the context of David's rise it was a stepping-stone to greater personal and political achievements.

■ **5-7** This unit closes in vv 5-7 with a notice about David's communications with the people of Jabesh Gilead. David, not wanting to miss a public relations opportunity, made a shrewd move by sending messengers to the men of Jabesh Gilead and pronounced a blessing on them for their role in burying the body of Saul. The men of Jabesh Gilead had been closely allied with Saul, and David wanted to reward them (lit., do a ***good thing***) for their actions (v 6). In return, David reminded them that Saul was dead, and he insinuated that they should act valorous to him, the legitimate ruler of Judah. David, in essence, was using the occasion of Saul's death to gain a new political ally.

2. Ish-Bosheth Established as King over Israel (2:8-11)

■ **8-11** The text picks up again in these verses with information regarding Saul's house. Even though Saul was dead, the monarchy of Israel (i.e., the northern tribes) still belonged to his family. The notice in v 8 provides information about succession in Saul's house. Since Jonathan, the rightful heir, was dead, the throne passed on to Saul's remaining son, Ish-Bosheth. In reality, however, Abner, Saul's general, possessed both military and political power and therefore he personally arranged the transfer of Saul's kingdom to Ish-Bosheth.

The text highlights this fact by immediately drawing attention to Abner and his role in making Ish-Bosheth king. Abner first of all ***took Ish-bosheth and transferred him to Mahanaim*** (v 8). Mahanaim (lit., "two camps") was located on the east side of the Jordan, presumably making Ish-Bosheth's capital safe from Philistine pressure (and David?). Second, Abner made Ish-Bosheth "king over Gilead, the Ashurites, Jezreel, Ephraim, Benjamin and over all Israel" (v 9 NRSV). The verbs in v 8 are both causatives, which underscores the notion that Abner took the lead role in this process. Even though Ish-Bosheth was king, Abner wielded the real power behind the throne.

Little is known personally about Ish-Bosheth. This is the first time that he formally appears in the text. His original name was Ishbaal (NRSV), meaning "man of baal/Baal." The "baal" portion of his name may have been a general epithet for God, or it may have been associated with the Canaanite deity Baal. However, because of its pagan associations, the editor/narrator of this text simply called him Ish-Bosheth or "man of shame." Chronicles retains the name Ishbaal in Saul's genealogy (1 Chr 8:33; 9:39). Ish-Bosheth's territory basically corresponded to the northern tribes that his father Saul ruled over. The reference to the Ashurites is problematic and may have been intended to refer to the people of Asher.

This section closes out with a notice in 1 Sam 2:10-11 regarding the length of the reign for both Ish-Bosheth and David. This is similar to the synchronistic history in Kings in which the chronology of kingship in both Judah and Israel is provided. Ish-Bosheth reigned as king over the northern territory for a relatively short time, **two years.** David, on the other hand, ruled Judah from Hebron for *seven and a half years.*

3. The Battle at Gibeon (2:12-32)

■ **12-32** The nature of the conflict between the house of David and the house of Saul is evident in the events at Gibeon. The unit opens by noting that "Abner son of Ner and the servants of [Ish-Bosheth] son of Saul, went out from Mahanaim to Gibeon" (v 12 NRSV). No particular explanation is given for this move, but David's friendly overtures to the men of Jabesh Gilead (2:4-7) may have provided a reason for Abner to confront David. Joab, David's commander, and David's men went out to meet them at the pool in Gibeon. Although neither king was present, their main generals oversaw the men.

The text notes that both groups of warriors situated themselves on either side of the pool (v 13). As the two groups positioned themselves there, Abner initiated the conversation by proposing that **the young men** with them "come forward and have a contest" (v 14 NRSV). The young men are referred to here as elite warriors (*hāneʿarîm*), not ordinary troops. The text also uses the term *sāḥaq*, which can mean "to play" or "make sport." The question arises whether this was meant to be an exercise in martial arts or whether something else was intended. The word can also refer to "deadly combat." Since this "contest" included seasoned soldiers, it most likely represented a form of battle on a smaller scale or "war games" (Niditch 1993, 95).

The following verses indicate that this engagement was not intended to be just a sporting contest. The proposal was acceptable to Joab and he uttered the words, **Let them arise** (v 14). Both sides divided up into groups of twelve men apiece. The ensuing contest turned out to be a brutal one in which each man seized the head of the other and thrust his sword into his opponent's side so that both men would fall down. The contest was bloody and the place where it occurred received the name **Helkath Hazzurim** (v 16), which translated means "field of sword-edges." Abner and his men came up short in this duel and they **were defeated** (v 17).

The momentum of the story moves from the defeat of Abner and his men to the pursuit of Abner. The text also focuses on three brothers: **Joab, Abishai and Asahel** (v 18). All of these men are called the **sons of Zeruiah,** David's sister (1 Chr 2:16). It is not surprising that three of David's greatest and most trusted warriors were kin. Of the three, Asahel is singled out since he was the one who pursued Abner after the defeat at Gibeon.

Asahel was not only identified as the brother of Joab, but he is called *fleet of foot, as one of the gazelles* (v 18). Asahel's speed was matched only by his determination to overtake Abner. Asahel singularly followed Abner **turning neither to the right nor to the left** (v 19). Abner, the experienced general, warned him on two occasions to desist from following him and pursue one of the other warriors. On the second occasion, Abner told Asahel to turn away because "how . . . could I show my face to your brother Joab" if he struck his brother down (v 22 NRSV). Asahel refused Abner's invitation, and the experienced general struck Asahel in the stomach with the butt of his spear so that it came out of Asahel's back.

Asahel fell and the spot became a makeshift memorial. Whoever passed by the plot where he fell "stood still" (v 23 NRSV). This was a gesture that paid respects to him and commemorated his memory (v 23). With Asahel dead, the two other brothers, Joab and Abishai, picked up the pursuit.

Joab and Abishai hunted after Abner and they came to a hill called **Ammah** (v 24). This hill lay in the wilderness of Gibeon in Benjamite territory. Understandably, the Benjamites, the people of Saul's home territory, rallied around Abner there *as one band* (v 25). Abner basically called for a truce in the hostilities (v 26) by asking the question, **Should the sword keep devouring forever? Do you not know that the end will be bitter?** Abner's grim prognostication was grounded in reality since Abner's forces had essentially dug in (lit., *they had taken their stand*) on the top of the hill and took a defensive posture (v 25). Joab acknowledged Abner's assessment and adhered to the truce at this time. Joab, however, did not forget what happened to his brother and a personal vendetta remained on his mind (3:27).

After this episode, Abner and his men left the area near Gibeon and traveled back to Mahanaim by going through the way of the **Arabah** (v 29). The Arabah usually means plain or desert, but here it possibly means the west side of the Jordan (Campbell 2005, 38). It is possible that they crossed the Jordan just north of the Dead Sea, just like David did when he fled from Jerusalem (2 Sam 15:28). Joab, on the other hand, returned to David at Hebron and the text reports that *twenty* of David's men had been killed while **three hundred and sixty** of Abner's men (who are called *men of Benjamin*) died in the struggle (2:31). Already, however, the writer/narrator was keeping score: David's men killed more of Ish-Bosheth's men. This connoted a decisive victory for David over Saul's house, a contest that would continue to sway in David's favor.

The chapter closes with a notice about Asahel. The text carefully preserves the memory of Asahel, one of David's elite fighters. Asahel was buried in Bethlehem, the hometown of David (v 32).

4. David at Hebron (3:1-5)

■ 1 The general notice in v 1 picks up the theme and concerns where the last chapter left off. In the military conflict at Gibeon, David's men, under Joab, got the better of Abner and his men. Even though Asahel was killed by Abner, the text reminds the reader that David's men killed more of Abner's men. The momentum gained in that battle continues in v 1, which reports that *there was a long battle between the house of Saul and the house of David* (v 1a). *David grew stronger and the house of Saul grew weaker* (v 1b). The truce that was reached between Abner and Joab did not hold. The verbs in v 1b (*hōlēq* and *hōlqîm*) are participles, which clue the reader into the notion that David continued to get the upper hand in this ongoing conflict while Saul's house progressively weakened.

■ 2-5 On the heels of the notice regarding the houses of David and Saul, vv 2-5 provide a list of David's wives and the children who were born to him in Hebron. Many scholars understand this to be an inserted piece of information, because it breaks the flow of the text between v 1 and v 6b. Including information about a king's family in conjunction with the king's reign is not uncommon. The text even does this for King Saul (1 Sam 14:49). The genealogical list may have been motivated by the fact that the northern tribes were about to pledge their allegiance, with the help of Abner, to David.

The list itself is interesting. There are six sons listed in these verses. Three of the sons, **Amnon, Absalom,** and **Adonijah,** were involved in the tempestuous rivalry for the throne. Amnon, who raped his half-sister Tamar, would be murdered by Absalom. Absalom not only avenged his sister's rape but usurped the throne of David. Adonijah proclaimed himself king toward the end of David's life, only to be replaced by Solomon and killed by royal order.

The women on the list basically include women from Israelite territory: Jezreel, Carmel, and Hebron. However, **Maacah** was from **Geshur,** an Aramean country (2 Sam 3:3). David utilized this relationship for political gain against the house of Saul. It is also noteworthy to point out that the son (Absalom) of Maacah, a Canaanite woman, would be at the center of a murder and rebellion that brought David much personal pain and political instability (chs 13—19).

5. Abner Defects to David (3:6-39)

■ 6-11 The notice in v 1 about David gaining strength is matched by the description about Abner. Verse 6b indicates that *Abner was strengthening him-*

self within the house of Saul. The verb used to describe Abner's position in the house of Saul is the same that refers to David's in 3:1*b*, except that it is a reflexive. The language suggests that Abner was the real power behind Ish-Bosheth's monarchy, and his stature and authority in Saul's household continued to expand. Abner, after all, was the one responsible for transferring Ish-Bosheth to Mahanaim and establishing his monarchy after the death of Saul. Moreover, in the continuing battle between the two houses, Ish-Bosheth may have become more dependent on the general, thus making Abner the nominal king.

The two notices about David and Abner, however, bring them into sharper focus. Abner was set to defect to David, which also set the stage for the final confrontation between Joab and Abner. As proof of his growing stature within the house of Saul, Ish-Bosheth accused Abner of taking Saul's concubine, **Rizpah**, and sleeping with her (v 7). Such an act would have been viewed as a usurpation of power in the ancient world. David's son Absalom demonstrated that he overthrew David by doing the same thing (2 Sam 16:21). Whether or not this took place remains unclear.

Abner took exception to Ish-Bosheth's question and accusation with the angry retort (3:8), ***Am I the head of the dog for Judah?*** The reference to a dog is symbolic in that it regularly figures as a contemptible beast, the antonym of the fierce and regal lion (Alter 1999, 209). Abner had fought for Saul and the house of Saul, and Ish-Bosheth's remarks were tantamount to saying he committed a crime of treason. Ish-Bosheth's ingratitude toward Abner along with his accusing question proved to be the last straw for Abner.

Abner vowed that he would throw his support for David (v 10). Just as he did with Ish-Bosheth, Abner would transfer the northern tribes of Israel to David's side so that David would be king over all the tribes of Israel, **from Dan to Beersheba.** Ish-Bosheth realized that Abner was the one truly in charge and therefore could do nothing about it because "he feared him" (v 11 NRSV).

■ **12-16** With the cleavage between Abner and Ish-Bosheth cemented, Abner sent messengers to David with the intent of seeking an alliance with him. Abner sought to make a covenant with David, and in return, Abner would ensure that the tribes of Israel would follow David. Abner's active role is highlighted in the text in that the Hebrew uses the causative stem so that it could be translated, ***My hand is with you to bring to you all the tribes of Israel*** (v 12). Thus, it would be through Abner's mediation that David would gain control over all the tribes.

Abner most likely performed this act thinking that he would gain special standing with David in return for his help. David agreed with this arrangement with one stipulation: Abner would have to bring Michal with him as part of the transaction (v 13). The request to reunite with Michal was no doubt a political move. David would need a connection with the house of Saul to appear as a legitimate ruler over the northern tribes who were under the control of Ish-

Bosheth. Being associated with a member of Saul's family would make David look less like an outsider, considering he came from the territory of Judah.

■ **17-21** Abner came to the people of Israel with an interesting message. First, the words he spoke to them intimated that the northern tribes were "seeking" Davidic kingship (v 17 NRSV). The verb here is a participle indicating that the people desired this for some time.

Second, he couched his message in a way that reminded the people of Saul's failure to defeat the Philistines. God's words to Samuel regarding Saul in 1 Sam 9:16 were applied to David: he would rescue the Israelites from the Philistines and their enemies (2 Sam 3:18). Even though Saul was selected as king for this task, the Philistines became stronger and more entrenched under Saul's control. Saul even lost his life while fighting the very people he was supposed to be protecting the Israelites from. This task would now fall to David, and he would fulfill God's desire for his people.

The text carefully notes that this message was directed at the Benjamites as well (v 19). As the home territory of Saul, Abner made it clear that a leader from Judah would be king over the northern tribes. Although no response is given from the Benjamites, one has to wonder just how much the people of Benjamin were on board with this decision. We will see later that not all Benjamites appreciated Davidic rule (see chs 16 and 20).

When Abner went to David at Hebron to give him his report, he basically stated that all the tribes, including Benjamin, supported this decision (3:19). The new covenant was celebrated with a feast, and Abner and his twenty men participated in the banquet given by David. Abner's enthusiasm for this new arrangement is seen in v 21*a* with three verbs in the first person: ***I will arise, I will go, and I will assemble all the people to my lord the king.***

Abner's exuberance in transferring the tribes to David makes the reader a little wary of his motives. Did Abner expect something in return (i.e., a promotion, special consideration) for his role in transferring the northern tribes to David? It is also easy to anticipate how Joab, David's faithful general, may have viewed Abner as a potential threat.

■ **22-27** Immediately after Abner left, Joab and his men returned to Hebron with spoils from battle. When it was reported to Joab that Abner had come to David and David sent him away **in peace,** Joab became suspicious of Abner's motives (v 25). Moreover, Joab directly questioned David about letting Abner get away. Joab asserted to David that Abner simply used this occasion as a ruse to ascertain information about David's "comings and goings" (v 25 NRSV). Joab sent messengers to Abner and brought him to the "cistern of Sirah" (v 26 NRSV). The text is careful to note, however, that **David did not know** of Joab's actions.

When Abner returned to Hebron, Joab was able to take vengeance on Abner by stabbing him in the stomach for the death of Asahel (v 27). Joab struck down Abner ***within the gate*** of the city. Hebron was designated as a city of refuge (Josh 20:7), where a person could claim refuge for a blood feud and not be held accountable for the revenge murder. However, Joab's actions could not be excused as an act of blood revenge (Num 35:12; Deut 19:11-13), since Asahel disregarded Abner's warnings in a time of battle (2 Sam 2:21-22). As a result, Joab's slaying of Abner constituted murder (3:30), and thus he forfeited the moral and legal sanctuary the city offered.

■ **28-39** The text notes, however, that when David heard of the news he presented an emotional and emphatic protestation over the death of Abner. David's passionate outburst included three important components. First, David claimed innocence with regard to the death of Abner. David's words, **I and my kingdom are forever innocent before** *Yahweh*, remind the reading audience that David did not have a hand in the death of Saul's general (v 28).

It is important to note that the narrator of the story of David takes great pains to make sure that the reading audience knew of David's innocence. David did not know Joab met with Abner (v 26), and he was not present when these events took place (v 28). Also, David was made aware of the murder of Abner only after it had taken place (v 28). This was the second occasion, however, when someone linked to David was associated with the death of an important figure connected to Saul: the Amalekite who killed Saul and brought the royal symbols to David (1:10), and Joab, who killed Saul's former general (3:27).

No doubt these events raised serious questions and concerns about the manner in which David came to the throne. They even suggested that David, in an indirect way, had a hand in the deaths of these individuals. Thus, David's protestation in v 28 rebuked such notions.

Second, David issued a severe curse upon Joab and the ***house of his father*** (v 29). David not only called for various skin diseases, hunger, and death to plague his family but also stated that his household would not lack one "who holds a spindle" (NRSV). This curious statement carries the derogatory meaning "of an effeminate creature lacking manly qualities" (Mauchline 1971, 211). David's words amounted to a direct assault on the manhood of Joab's family members. It insinuates that the men in Joab's family would be "fit only for woman's work" (JPS), since a spindle was used for weaving cloth.

Third, David and his men engaged in mourning rituals (1:12; 3:31) in which they were ordered to ***rip off clothing***, ***put on sackcloth***, and ***mourn*** over the death of Abner (v 31). In addition, David offered words of lament over the slain victim, claiming that Abner did not deserve to die in the manner that Joab killed him (v 33; "Should Abner die as a fool dies?" [NRSV]). Through such actions, David displayed genuine sorrow and indignation over the murder of Abner.

The text even notes that ***all the people recognized*** David's visible expressions of grief over Abner and ***it was good in their eyes*** (v 36). Moreover, all the people ***knew that the king did not have a part in killing Abner son of Ner*** (v 37). David's reaction to the death of Abner accomplished a personal relations victory: he gained the favor of the people of Israel and at the same time cursed the household of Joab. David's actions demonstrated that he sympathized with the northern hero and that he did not have personal involvement in the death of Abner. By crafting the narratives in this manner, it could be proved that David was innocent of this murder, even though it advanced his political career. Chapter 4 narrates the death of Saul's son, and his death was propitious for David's political fortunes as well.

6. The Death of Ish-Bosheth (4:1-12)

■ 1 Chapter 4 represents the last major obstacle that stood in the way of David gaining the throne. The chapter opens with the notice that ***the son of Saul had heard that Abner died at Hebron*** (v 1). The text does not identify who the son is in this verse, but it should refer to Ish-Bosheth even though the LXX and 4QSamᵃ read "Mephibosheth" here. Since Abner functioned as the nominal king over Saul's territory, it should come as no surprise to the reader that Ish-Bosheth's ***hands fell*** in response to this information. This expression is an idiomatic way of saying that Ish-Bosheth's "courage failed" (NRSV) (i.e., "lost his grip" in English) as the result of Abner's loss. Moreover, all of Israel was ***terrified*** or "dismayed" (NRSV) over the news of Abner's death (v 1).

Although no explanation is provided in the text, one has to ask why the king and the people responded in fear to the news of Abner's death. It is possible to assume that they recognized Abner as the true leader of Israel and thus were dismayed that their "king" had fallen. In light of this, the people may have lacked confidence in Ish-Bosheth's leadership skills considering that he had not done anything up to this point to distinguish himself as a competent ruler. It is also possible to deduce that the people feared David and the prospect of submitting themselves to Davidic rule.

News of Abner's death at Hebron (3:27), David's capital, was no doubt troubling to them. The "house of David" had been at war with the "house of Saul" during this time. Was Abner's death (murder?) a harbinger of things to come for the people of Israel? If David and his men treated Abner in this fashion, how would the people of Israel fare if David became king over Saul's old kingdom? Would he treat them fairly or would he impose harsh rule over them? Moreover, David hailed from Judah and not from the northern tribes. Would he be sympathetic to northern ways of living or unsympathetic to their history and concerns? Whatever the reason, it is essential to note that the people of Israel responded with horror to the news of Abner's death.

■ 2-3 The text inserts a brief bit of information on two individuals who had a tremendous influence on the course of events as they relate to David's path to kingship (see esp. vv 5-12 below). **Recab** and **Baanah** are both referred to as the ***sons of Rimmon, the Beerothite who was of the Benjaminites*** (v 2). Rimmon is mentioned elsewhere in this chapter (vv 5, 9), and he is called a Beerothite. The Beerothites were originally a non-Israelite group that eventually became "naturalized citizens" of the territory of Benjamin (Alter 1999, 217).

The brothers were also ***commanders of raiding parties*** and thus experienced killers (v 2). The text provides this notice in light of their role in assassinating Ish-Bosheth in the following verses. It also fits the recurring pattern of a messenger of foreign origin bringing David news of a disaster (1:1-10).

■ **4** The text, curiously, interjects a brief statement about Jonathan's son (i.e., Saul's grandson), **Mephibosheth.** The writer/narrator of David's rise includes this information in anticipation of Ish-Bosheth's imminent death and the question of an heir within the house of Saul. Even though Mephibosheth (also known as Merib-Baal, 1 Chr 8:34; 9:40) represented the heir apparent, his physical disabilities essentially precluded him from being a legitimate contender for the throne. Mephibosheth was ***crippled of feet*** as a result of an accident in which he **fell** and became ***lame*** at *five years of age.*

The term used for Mephibosheth's inability to walk (*vayîpāsēaḥ*) is etymologically similar to the term that refers to the "Passover" (*pesaḥ*) in Jewish tradition. Ironically, whereas the slaughter of a lamb commemorated a series of events that led to the Israelites' freedom from bondage in the Exodus tradition, in this setting, the crippling of a child's feet is connected with the opportunity for David to take control of Saul's kingdom. As much as the text anticipates David's role as ruler over Israel it also looks forward to Mephibosheth's future relationship with David. When David ruled as king from Jerusalem, he had Mephibosheth stay with him and "eat at [his] table" (2 Sam 9:7-13).

■ **5-8** The text returns the focus to the assassination plot by Baanah and Recab on Ish-Bosheth's life. No explanation is provided as to why they intended to kill Saul's son, especially since they came from Beeroth, which was part of Saul's home territory of Benjamin (although Beeroth was originally one of the cities of the Gibeonites, Josh 9:17). The text indicates that this was a brazen and bold act, as both men came to the house of Ish-Bosheth **in the heat of the day** (v 5). This amounted to the noon hour or shortly after, when Ish-Bosheth "was taking his midday rest" (JPS).

Verses 6-7 recount the assassination plot that Baanah and Recab carried out against Ish-Bosheth. The details of the plot remain somewhat sketchy based on textual confusion within the manuscript traditions. The MT actually has two accounts of the death of Ish-Bosheth:

> v 6: (in which the Hebrew has a difficult construction): Both men entered the house ***as takers of wheat*** and they struck him **in the stomach** and fled . . .
>
> v 7: They came "into the house while he was lying on his couch in his bedchamber; they ***struck*** him, killed him, and beheaded him" (NRSV).

The LXX has alleviated the problem of the double reference to the murder in its rendition of the narrative:

> v 6: *And behold, the porter of the house winnowed wheat, and he slumbered and slept; and the brothers Rechab and Baana went privately into the house.*
>
> v 7: *And Ish-bosheth was sleeping on his bed in his chamber, and they struck him and slayed him and cut off his head.*

A comparison of both textual traditions reveals that v 7 is essentially the same in the MT and LXX. Verse 6 in the MT, however, omits the notice about the porter of the house sleeping, which allowed Recab and Baanah to enter undetected. Thus, the LXX represents the better reading of the two traditions since it records only one murder and the events unfold more logically: in v 6 the men enter the house undetected and in v 7 Ish-Bosheth is murdered.

In addition to murdering Ish-Bosheth, the two men took his head and went the "way of the Arabah all night" (v 7 NRSV); the route that extended from Mahanaim to the valley south of the Sea of Galilee (see 2:29). The men brought the head to David at Hebron, thinking that they had done David a great service. Their words, **Here is the head of Ish-Bosheth son of Saul, your enemy, who *sought* your life,** indicate that Ish-Bosheth was a rival to David, even though the text had not indicated it at this point (4:8). Moreover, the two men ascribed the death of Ish-Bosheth to Yahweh who **has given vengeance this day . . . upon Saul and his descendants.**

■ **9-12** David responded to the men and their words in much the same way that he did to the Amalekite who announced the death of Saul (1:1-10). David even alluded to the Amalekite and the fate he met when he delivered the news of Saul's death to David. As in the case of the Amalekite, David had the men killed plus their hands and feet were cut off and their bodies were hung by the pool at Hebron (4:12). The dismembering of malefactors or prisoners was a common practice in the ancient Near East and it was a tangible way for David to denounce their actions and provide convincing evidence that he did not orchestrate Ish-Bosheth's murder (Alter 1999, 219). Critics of David have countered this by arguing that David arranged the murder of Ish-Bosheth and then covered his tracks by killing the individuals who carried out the attack.

An examination at this point into the death reports of Saul, Abner, and Ish-Bosheth show common features among them: the report of the death itself (1:10; 3:27-28; 4:6-8), the elimination of the person reporting the death by David's men (1:13-15; 4:12), an act of mourning following the death (1:11-12; 3:31-35), and a confession of innocence (1:16; 3:26, 28, 36, 39; 4:8-10). Although the text indicates that David was not involved in the murders of these individuals, the circumstances surrounding each one of their deaths seems to implicate David and/or the men associated with him in one form or another. Even the most pious reader of the text may perceive something curious about the events surrounding the death of these men, which, in turn, raise questions about the manner in which David's political career developed.

In spite of David's anger at the men, he did not show remorse for Ish-Bosheth personally. David became more desensitized to the deaths of individuals associated with Saul as they continued to take place. David exhibited great sorrow over the news of the deaths of Saul and Jonathan, then less distress upon learning of Abner's murder, and finally no sadness over the murder of Ish-Bosheth. The reader has to wonder if David became more immune to the killing that surrounded him. Was remorse gradually replaced by feelings of anticipation as he moved closer to the throne with the death of each of these men? The reader is left to draw his or her own conclusions.

The chapter ends with a notice that the head of Ish-Bosheth was buried in the grave of Abner at Hebron (v 12). By the end of ch 4, four important men associated with the house of Saul had been killed: Saul, Jonathan, Abner, and Ish-Bosheth. With each of these men eliminated, the path to kingship opened wider and wider for David.

FROM THE TEXT

The life and example of David in this unit calls to mind the idea that the temptation to compromise our values in order to get ahead in life is both real and powerful. On two specific occasions (3:27; 4:8), people associated with David murdered individuals affiliated with the house of Saul. In both circumstances the people who "eliminated" Abner and Ish-Bosheth thought they were doing David a great service (3:25; 4:8). They believed that by doing away with these men they were helping David avenge his enemies as well as clear a path that made it easier for him to obtain the throne. David made it certain that he would not conduct himself this way nor did he condone the actions of those who did. David vehemently opposed the notion that he would "get ahead" by cheating or through any other dishonest means. In so doing, we are made aware that in life people will take courses of action that are less than honorable in order to advance their personal situation. Whether that is in business, school, relationships, politics, sports or other competitions, and even in ministry, people succumb to the temptation to "cheat" in order to win. As believers, we are expected to practice honesty in everything we do, both great and small, and to live honorably among all people. Being duplicitous in our daily endeavors not only can bring shame on us but also disgraces the reputation of the God we proclaim to worship.

J. David Becomes King over Israel (5:1-25)

BEHIND THE TEXT

This chapter represents an important development within the overall trajectory of the story of David's rise. First, the northern tribes selected David to be their king, thus bringing Saul's kingdom and Judah under David's control (vv 1-5). Second, David captured the city of Jerusalem (Jebus) and established it as the capital city of the newly formed united monarchy. Jerusalem became known as the "city of David" and the eventual home of Solomon's temple. Third, David fended off an attack by the Philistines who viewed David's newly established kingdom as a threat to their own security and survival (vv 17-25). On the one hand, ch 5 represents the culmination of David's journey from shepherd to king, yet, on the other, it also serves as a fitting prelude to chs 6—8, which record the important events that transpired while David ruled from Jerusalem as king.

IN THE TEXT

I. The Israelite Tribes Make David King (5:1-5)

■ **1-5** After the deaths of Abner and Ish-Bosheth, the door opened for David to become king over all the tribes. The text notes (v 1) that **all the tribes of Israel came to David at Hebron** in order to make him king. The phrase **all the tribes of Israel** refers specifically to the northern tribes that had remained loyal to the house of Saul. When the northern tribes came to David they spoke of David in glowing terms. The tribes basically acknowledged that even though Saul was king over Israel it was really David who **led Israel out and brought Israel back** and it was Yahweh who had taken David to be **shepherd over my people Israel** (v 2). The language here is suggestive in a number of ways. First, when the Israelites talk to David they constantly make reference to David in the second person singular (i.e., "you") in v 2:

It was you who led Israel out and brought it in . . .
Yahweh said to you . . .
It is you who will be shepherd . . .

The constant reference to David in the second person is intended to convey the people's conviction that it was really David all along, not Saul, who led them and it was David whom God had chosen (destined) to be king over them. This language essentially legitimated David as the recognized leader over all Israel.

Second, the people referred to David using shepherd language and imagery. In the OT, the figure of a shepherd was a metaphor that often applied to God's greatest leaders (i.e., Moses). David was a shepherd who was tending his father's flocks at the time God selected him to be king (1 Sam 16:11). The text foreshadows that David would be a great leader along the lines of the great heroes of Israel's past. This stands in sharp contrast to Saul, who was out looking for his father's lost donkeys at the time he met Samuel (9:1 ff.). It is fitting that God called David from his father's flock in order to be the shepherd of God's people.

Third, the people's anticipation of Davidic kingship (2 Sam 5:1-2) is very different from their reaction when the prospects of having David lead them seemed likely after the death of Abner (4:1). One has to wonder if this text has been reshaped by editors sympathetic to David in order to make David more appealing to the northern tribes. This information could also derive from a separate tradition that has been inserted into this context. It is difficult to determine which answer is correct, but tensions in the text are present. Moreover, the Israelites said to David that "we are your bone and flesh" (5:1 NRSV), thus showing solidarity with David. David, however, originated from the territory of Judah and in some sense was an outsider to those from the north. This became evident, for example, in the sentiments of the northern tribes when they decided to break free from Davidic rule (1 Kgs 12:16). The language in 2 Sam 5:1-2 supports Davidic purposes and may not always represent the true sentiments of the people.

In Deuteronomistic fashion the elders of the people came to David and anointed him king over Israel (Deut 17:15). In addition, David **cut a covenant with them** (v 3), thus underscoring his role in establishing an official political relationship with the people. In light of the political bonds established with the northern tribes, the unit closes with a brief statement regarding the length of David's kingship: he reigned seven and a half years at Hebron and thirty-three years over Israel. As is typical in the DtrH, the reign of a king is often provided in the regnal formula that introduces the king (1 Kgs 15:2; 16:29; 2 Kgs 3:1; 13:1; 14:2). Forty is also a nice round number that is similar to the time of the judges (Judg 3:11; 5:31; 8:28; 13:1). This is more formulaic than precise historical reporting.

2. David Captures Jerusalem (5:6-16)

As the recognized king of Israel, David made an important political move by establishing Jerusalem as his capital city. **Jerusalem,** which is also called Jebus, was occupied by a people known as the Jebusites (v 6). The El-Amarna letters indicate that Jebus was an important Canaanite city even as early as the fourteenth century B.C. The fact that it remained in existence until the time of David should come as no surprise. There are a number of important reasons why David made Jerusalem the new capital of the united monarchy. First, with an elevation of 2,460 ft., Jerusalem was a stronghold and thus had great strategic value. At that height it was difficult for opposing armies to mount a successful attack against the city. Second, Jerusalem was strategically situated along a natural north-south land route that connected it with important cities such as Shechem and Hebron. Third, Jerusalem was a "neutral" city politically speaking: it was not an Israelite city and thus the people of Israel and Judah did not have any previous affiliations with it. Fourth, because Jerusalem was an important city-state in the Late Bronze Age period, there was already a bureaucracy composed of talented and knowledgeable political officials in place. David would be able to use the skills of these individuals in setting up and organizing his new kingdom (Mendenhall 1975, 155-70). The text reveals that David did have a bureaucratic team at his disposal, even if it was rather meager by modern standards (2 Sam 8:15-18; 20:23-26). This method of statecrafting was well known in the ancient world, and the fact that David would employ former officials of this important city-state should not be surprising.

El-Amarna Letters

In 1887 a peasant woman unearthed several clay tablets at Tel-Amarna, the capital city of the eighteenth-dynasty pharaoh Akhenaten. In all 382 tablets or portions of tablets were recovered from Tel-Amarna: 350 letters and 32 miscellaneous texts. The letters contained royal correspondence between the Egyptian king and various regional powers: Mitanni (northern Syria), Babylonia, Assyria, and Hatti (in eastern Turkey). The tablets also contained correspondence exchanges with Egypt's vassals in western Asia, including Canaan. Exchanges with vassals revealed that Egypt's structure of its Asian empire was composed of a network of city-states stretching from Byblos, Qadesh, and Amurru in the north to Ashkelon, Lachish, and Jerusalem in the south. Each city-state had its own ruler and surrounding agricultural land. The letters also showed that Egyptian overseers were assigned to monitor developments within the empire and collect tribute from the vassals. The vassals often enlisted the support of Egypt when a neighboring city-state was becoming a threat to Egyptian sovereignty, or when groups of mercenaries known as the Habiru posed a threat to trade and the security of the city-states themselves (Higginbotham 2005, 123-24).

■ **6-7** The text notes that David and **his men marched to Jerusalem** against **the Jebusites,** *those residing in the land* (v 6). When the Jebusites encountered David, they issued a strong warning to him: *You will not come hither because the blind and the lame will turn you away.* This phrase has been a source of contention among scholars for decades, because it is unclear what the Jebusites meant. It is possible, as has been proposed on the basis of Hittite texts, that this language relates to the Hittite custom of swearing in soldiers in front of a blind woman and a lame man to indicate the soldiers' fate (i.e., they would become like the handicapped individuals) if they failed in their duties. The Jebusites may have done something analogous here by displaying the lame and blind on the ramparts with a curse against those who presumed to attack the city (Alter 1999, 222).

■ **8-10** In addition, the description of the manner in which David's men overtook the city is no less difficult to interpret. Traditionally it has been understood that David and his men made an attack on the city by going up the water shaft (*ṣinōr*) that led into the city. Archaeologists uncovered what is called the Warren shaft in 1867. This shaft is an underground tunnel situated next to the Gihon Spring outside the eastern wall of the city. This shaft may have allowed David and his men a critical opening into the city by which they could mount an attack against the citizens of Jebus. More recent scholarship has questioned whether this was feasible at the time of David (Shanks 1999, 30-35). If not, the method of entrance into the city remains a mystery.

David's words in v 8 appear to confirm this battle strategy. David did overtake "the stronghold of Zion" (NRSV) and subsequently renamed **the City of David** (v 9). It was a common practice in the ancient world to rename a city after the person who conquered it. David also built up the city, "from the Millo inward" (NRSV). The "Millo" refers to an earthen work of some kind, perhaps a building platform created by filling a ravine. This section closes with the notice that "David became greater and greater" and "the LORD, the God of hosts, was with him" (v 10 NRSV). The text is careful to attribute David's greatness to the God he worshipped.

■ **11-12** Not only did David take the fortress of Zion and rename it the city of David, but the Phoenician king, Hiram of Tyre (Hiram 1 969-936 B.C.) recognized David's accomplishments and his political standing. Hiram sent messengers to David along with "cedar trees, and carpenters and masons who built David a house" (v 11 NRSV). Hiram wanted to establish good political relations with David considering that he shared a border with David's burgeoning kingdom. Hiram's political relationship with the house of David extended into the reign of Solomon, who looked to Hiram to supply the material resources and skilled craftsmen for the temple project (1 Kgs 5:1-60). The fact that Hiram had political ties with David and Solomon (1 Kgs 5:1-10) indicates that the building of David's palace took place later in his reign.

■ **13-16** In addition to the construction of the royal palace, David's house (i.e., family) continued to grow. The text notes that **David took more concubines** (*pilagšim*) **and wives** (*našim*) from Jerusalem. The syntax of v 13 is significant because it is making an important claim about the women David married. The construction (*min yîrûšālaim*) *from Jerusalem* indicates David took wives who were from Jerusalem; that is, he married Jebusite (Canaanite) women from the city. David no doubt used these marriages to bolster or solidify his own standing within the capital. The text never makes a comment about the foreign women David married, even though they presented a religious threat to the community (Josh 23:12-13; 1 Kgs 11:1-4) and Deuteronomy prohibited intermarriage with Canaanite women (7:3-4).

The text also lists the sons who were born to David in Jerusalem: **Shammua, Shobab, Nathan, Solomon, Ibhar, Elishua, Nepheg, Japhia, Elishama, Eliada and Eliphelet** (vv 14-16). Most of the sons on the list have little consequence in the story of David and the succession for the kingdom. Only Solomon would become involved with the struggle for David's throne. As the Succession Narrative unfolds, however, a deep and contentious division developed between a Hebronite faction that supported Adonijah and a Jerusalemite faction that supported Solomon. Solomon's mother, Bathsheba, is not mentioned by name here, but her presence is implied by the reference to Solomon. Bathsheba only became affiliated with David after he established Jerusalem as the capital city (2 Sam 11), a fact that indicates that the present text is not ordered chronologically. Bathsheba was among the Jerusalemite faction who

David's words in v 8 appear to confirm this battle strategy. David did overtake "the stronghold of Zion" (NRSV) and subsequently renamed **the City of David** (v 9). It was a common practice in the ancient world to rename a city after the person who conquered it. David also built up the city, "from the Millo inward" (NRSV). The "Millo" refers to an earthen work of some kind, perhaps a building platform created by filling a ravine. This section closes with the notice that "David became greater and greater" and "the LORD, the God of hosts, was with him" (v 10 NRSV). The text is careful to attribute David's greatness to the God he worshipped.

■ **11-12** Not only did David take the fortress of Zion and rename it the city of David, but the Phoenician king, Hiram of Tyre (Hiram 1 969-936 B.C.) recognized David's accomplishments and his political standing. Hiram sent messengers to David along with "cedar trees, and carpenters and masons who built David a house" (v 11 NRSV). Hiram wanted to establish good political relations with David considering that he shared a border with David's burgeoning kingdom. Hiram's political relationship with the house of David extended into the reign of Solomon, who looked to Hiram to supply the material resources and skilled craftsmen for the temple project (1 Kgs 5:1-60). The fact that Hiram had political ties with David and Solomon (1 Kgs 5:1-10) indicates that the building of David's palace took place later in his reign.

■ **13-16** In addition to the construction of the royal palace, David's house (i.e., family) continued to grow. The text notes that **David took more concubines** (*pilagšim*) **and wives** (*našîm*) from Jerusalem. The syntax of v 13 is significant because it is making an important claim about the women David married. The construction (*min yîrûšālaim*) *from Jerusalem* indicates David took wives who were from Jerusalem; that is, he married Jebusite (Canaanite) women from the city. David no doubt used these marriages to bolster or solidify his own standing within the capital. The text never makes a comment about the foreign women David married, even though they presented a religious threat to the community (Josh 23:12-13; 1 Kgs 11:1-4) and Deuteronomy prohibited intermarriage with Canaanite women (7:3-4).

The text also lists the sons who were born to David in Jerusalem: **Shammua, Shobab, Nathan, Solomon, Ibhar, Elishua, Nepheg, Japhia, Elishama, Eliada and Eliphelet** (vv 14-16). Most of the sons on the list have little consequence in the story of David and the succession for the kingdom. Only Solomon would become involved with the struggle for David's throne. As the Succession Narrative unfolds, however, a deep and contentious division developed between a Hebronite faction that supported Adonijah and a Jerusalemite faction that supported Solomon. Solomon's mother, Bathsheba, is not mentioned by name here, but her presence is implied by the reference to Solomon. Bathsheba only became affiliated with David after he established Jerusalem as the capital city (2 Sam 11), a fact that indicates that the present text is not ordered chronologically. Bathsheba was among the Jerusalemite faction who an affirmative response from God: **Go up, for I have given them into your hand.** When Yahweh answered David, the text utilizes the infinitive absolute form, which emphatically guaranteed (*I have surely given them into your hand*) that God would deliver the Philistines over to him.

When David set out to fight the Philistines he traveled to a place called **Baal Perazim** (v 20). The name of the place is significant because it was there that *Yahweh has caused my enemy to burst forth like bursting water.* Thus the name is an etiology and testified to the victory that God promised he would give David: "Baal" (lord) and "perazim" (burst forth). Although the word "Baal" is a name for the Canaanite deity, it is also a generic term for "Lord" that can refer to God.

The unit ends with another interesting twist. When the Philistines were defeated, the text notes that they "abandoned their idols . . . and David and his men carried them away" (v 21 NRSV). What did David want with Philistine idols? What did he intend to do with them? Did he destroy them or take them back to Jerusalem? We do not know, and the text's silence here can leave the imagination to wonder. The Chronicler clarifies this statement further by noting that David ordered his men to burn the idols (1 Chr 14:12), which was in accordance with the Torah (Deut 7:5; 12:3). The fact that the Philistines abandoned their idols also intimates that they were powerless to aid them in the fight against David's God.

■ **22-25** The Philistines regrouped and prepared for a second attack. They met in the same valley and David again inquired or asked God for direction. On this second occasion, however, God provided a battle strategy instead of an affirmative "go up." Yahweh instructed David that he should "not go up [but] go around to their rear, and come upon them opposite the balsam trees" (v 23 NRSV). Yahweh also gave the instruction that "when you hear the . . . marching in the tops of the balsam trees, then be [aware that Yahweh] has gone out before you to strike . . . the Philistines" (v 24 NRSV). The phrase "when you hear the . . . marching in the tops of the balsam trees" is somewhat confusing, but it may have been an indication to David that when the wind blew the tops of the trees (possibly referring to the time of day the battle would take place), he would know that Yahweh was leading the attack. The waving of the trees in the wind could also have symbolized the "steps of the Lord" as God accompanied David in battle (Hertzberg 1964, 274). **David did just as Yahweh commanded,** thus emphasizing David's obedience to God's instruction (v 25).

David's obedience resulted in success: he **struck them from Geba to Gezer** (v 25). The note about David's victory over the Philistines is important on a couple of levels. First, after this battle the Philistines did not offer a serious challenge to Israel again. The references to David's wars with the Philistines in 21:15-22 and 23:9-17 may possibly be dated to this time (Gordon 1986, 230). The statement in 8:1 is included in a summary statement about David's regional wars and therefore may have occurred near the time of these battles as well. The banishment of the Philistine menace was one of David's greatest achievements, something that Saul was never able to accomplish (see 1 Sam 9:16). Second, the reader is reminded of Saul's failure in light of the fact that the Philistines were driven from Geba. Geba is another form of the word Gibeah, Saul's hometown (see comment on 1 Sam 13:3). The LXX and 1 Chr 14:16, for example, choose to read "Gibeon" here as well. That David was able to drive out the Philistines from Saul's hometown heightens the divergent destinies of both men.

At this point in the narrative, the reader cannot help but notice the glaring differences between Saul and David. God responded to David when he called for instructions but remained silent when Saul made inquiry. God fought for David and gave him success against the Philistines on multiple occasions, while Saul never defeated the Philistines. David followed God's commands; Saul disobeyed the word of Yahweh. The text keeps making the case that David is superior to Saul in every respect.

FROM THE TEXT

The text continues to highlight God's support for David, evidenced by both his military victories and his acclaim among the people of Israel and King Hiram. David's success not only brought him personal and political renown but also had tremendous implications for the religious health of the nation. Through David's triumphs God was also glorified. David and his men captured Jerusalem (the "fortress of Zion") and made it the capital city of the new empire. Jerusalem, however, was much more than just the capital city; it became known as God's dwelling place. Since God's seat or throne was located in the city, it served as the main religious center for the people of Israel. It was there that the people came to worship God in praise and thanksgiving (Pss 9:11; 102:21), and the location where God addressed the people. From Zion, God blessed his people (Pss 128:5; 134:3) and his instruction went forth (Isa 2:3; Mic 4:2). According to the biblical writers, Zion also possesses an eschatological hope for all peoples. It will be the place where universal peace is established (Pss 46:10-11; 76:4; Isa 2:4; Ezek 39:9-10) and divine instruction is dispensed for all nations (Mic 4:1-4).

In this chapter we learn that when God works in our own personal situations he may have a much greater purpose in mind that we never fully anticipate, comprehend, or appreciate. Through David's conquest of Jerusalem, God established Zion as his holy mountain that would be the source of salvation and instruction for his people, and one day for all nations. Even though David could not have envisioned the spiritual impact that Jerusalem would have throughout the centuries, God's plan was intimately linked to David's choice as king and his personal success. Likewise, we many never realize in those moments when God is fulfilling his purpose in us the long-term ramifications that it will have in furthering God's redemptive plan in the world. God could be at the initial stages of doing something extraordinary or significant for the kingdom as he works in our lives, whose eternal impact we may never fathom or believe or see. Our job, then, is to remain obedient to God's voice and open to his leading, because we never know what God's ultimate intentions and plans are as he moves in our personal situations.

K. David and the Ark of the Covenant (6:1-23)

BEHIND THE TEXT

Chapter 6 resumes the story of the ark found in 1 Sam 4:1—7:1. The large gap that separates these sections in the books of Samuel and the time that lapses between the two episodes raises serious questions about the transmission history of the narrative. Scholars have attempted to address these and other issues surrounding these traditions but have not reached a consensus in their conclusions. Some have argued that the Ark Narrative is actually comprised of two distinct sections (1 Sam 4—6; 2 Sam 6), written at different times, which were then combined together as the books of Samuel took shape. Other scholars have analyzed the Ark Narrative by separating out the verses that contain the use of the term "ark of God" from those that use the phrase "ark of Yahweh." According to this line of reasoning, the Ark Narrative can be broken down into two versions of the story, with each emphasizing different themes (Campbell 2003, 303-4). Campbell has posited that the Ark Narrative represents a unified tradition. He has suggested that the Ark Narrative is a continuous account based on the following construction:

From the day that the ark was lodged at Kiriath-jearim, a long time passed (1 Sam 7:2a). *And David arose and went with all the people who were with him from the citizens of Judah to bring up from there the ark of God* (2 Sam 6:2). (2003, 301)

Through his analysis he has shown that it is possible to bridge the gap between 1 Sam 7 and 2 Sam 6.

From a synchronic perspective, the return of the ark to Jerusalem at the time of David helps divide the story of Israel into two distinct eras: the ark at Shiloh and the ark in Jerusalem. Whereas the first era emphasized Israel under the leadership of prophets/priests such as Samuel, the second symbolizes Israel under the leadership of the king. In addition, the transfer of the ark to Jerusalem made an important theological point: God's presence dwelled with the people in the capital of the land of Israel. The ark would eventually be placed in the temple, which was located next to the king's palace. The king would always be reminded that he was God's son (servant; Ps 2) and that God abided with him as he served God's people.

IN THE TEXT

■ 1 The chapter begins with the statement that "David again gathered all the chosen men of Israel ***together***" (v 1 NRSV). This is a rather curious statement because we do not know when he gathered them the first time. The number of men selected, **thirty thousand,** is also significant, because it correlates to the number of men who died when the Philistines captured the ark (1 Sam 4:10). This data appears to provide some linkage with the ark traditions of 1 Sam 4—6, even though it is tentative. Scholars have also noted some other connections as well (Van der Toorn and Houtman 1994, 222):

1. The reference to "a new cart" (1 Sam 6:7; 2 Sam 6:3)
2. The use of rhetorical questions:
    a. "Who will deliver us?" (1 Sam 4:8).
    b. "Who can stand?" (1 Sam 6:20).
    c. "How can the ark of [Yahweh] . . . ?" (2 Sam 6:9).

These literary details provide some coherence to the disparate elements of the ark traditions, but these details in no way solve all of the historical-literary issues inherent within the text.

■ 2 David and all the people went to **Baalah of Judah** in order to retrieve the ark. First Samuel 7:1, however, reports that the ark resided in the city of Kiriath Jearim and remained under the supervision of Abinadab's son, Eleazar. The discrepancy in the place names is apparent, but **Baalah of Judah** ("men of Judah"?) may be equated with Kiriath Jearim according to Josh 15:9. **Uzzah and Ahio,** the sons of Abinadab, also supervised the transfer of the ark. Uzzah and Ahio are not mentioned in 1 Sam 7:1 either, so their presence in this text is intriguing. Scholars have tried to address this discrepancy in different ways. It is possible that Eleazar already died, which would explain why he is not referenced here. It is also possible that the name Uzzah represents a shorter form of the name Eleazar, thus indicating he was still alive. This is a plausible option considering that the name of his brother, Ahio, can be read as "his brother" in Hebrew. Based on this reconstruction, the text could read ***Eleazar and his brother,*** which goes a long way in clearing up the confusion.

■ 3-9 The ark was put onto a new cart, which was driven by the **sons of Abinadab** (2 Sam 6:3). The reader cannot help but think of the Philistines who also put the ark in a new cart when they sent it back to Israel (1 Sam 6:7). Unlike the Philistines who were anxious to get rid of the ark, in this setting David and the people anticipated and celebrated its transfer to Jerusalem. This is evident in the fact that the transportation of the ark was accompanied with dancing and song (2 Sam 6:5), as when the women would come out to sing and dance after soldiers returned from battle. The return of the ark resembled a great liturgical occasion; "the ark of the Lord, long absent from Israel's life, was coming home" (Campbell 2005, 66).

The procession accompanying the ark stopped, however, when the ark was in danger of falling off the cart. The one son of Abinadab, Uzzah, reached out his hand to grasp the ark because the oxen had shaken the cart. The procession stopped at a **threshing floor** (*gōren*). Threshing floors were generally places where divine/religious activities took place in OT times (Gen 50:10; Judg 6:37; 1 Kgs 22:10; 2 Kgs 6:27; Hos 9:1-2) (Ahlstrom 1961, 113-27). Stopping at this site was thus logical and appropriate to those who were escorting the sacred object.

When Uzzah touched the ark, "the anger of [Yahweh burned] against Uzzah; and God struck him there because he reached out his hand to the ark" (v 7 NRSV). This statement has often left readers of the text frustrated and puzzled. Why did Yahweh strike down an individual who only touched the ark accidentally? Even David became angry at God and renamed the place **Perez Uzzah** ("the bursting out against Uzzah") to memorialize the event. Most scholars look to the parallel passage in 1 Chr 13:1-14 to make sense of this event (Evans 2003, 162). According to Chronicles, Uzzah treated the ark with irreverence and thus was deserving of the severe punishment. The text also notes that ***David feared Yahweh*** after this awesome demonstration of power (2 Sam 6:9). The text never mentions that David feared Yahweh until this incident. Was this a wake-up call for David, who needed to be shown the power of Yahweh? Humbled by this event, David inquired, "How can the ark of [God] come into my care?" (NRSV).

■ **10-11** Instead of taking the ark directly to Jerusalem, David brought the ark to the house of **Obed-Edom the Gittite** (v 11). It is ironic that David took the ark to Obed-Edom's for a couple of reasons. First, his name literally means ***servant of Edom*** even though he did not have an affiliation with the territory to the southeast. Second, he is called a Gittite, which is someone who hailed from the Philistine city of Gath. David had affiliations with Gath previously (1 Sam 27) and this was the home territory of Goliath. David most likely became acquainted with Obed-Edom during the time he served as a Philistine vassal. Third, the Philistines had the ark in their possession but returned it to the Israelites previously. Now an Israelite sought the help of a Philistine to serve as a caretaker of the ark. Did David want a non-Israelite or a "neutral" person, one who had no affiliation with Israelite religion, to watch over this sacred object until he could figure out what to do with it? Unfortunately, the text never answers this question.

Fourth, the text notes that when David brought the ark to Obed-Edom's house Yahweh **blessed *Obed-Edom and his household . . . because of the ark*** (v 11). Previously Yahweh brought painful plagues on the Philistines while the ark was in their custody, including the city of Gath. Now God brought blessing on a Philistine while it was in his care. Why did the ark now bring blessing instead of destruction? It is possible to conclude that blessing Obed-Edom's household was a sign to David he did not have to fear the terrifying power of the ark if it was handled in the proper way. This appears to answer the question he raised in v 9 about his ability to be able to adequately care for the ark.

■ **12-13** Once it was reported to David that the ark brought blessing to Obed-Edom's house, David went and brought up the ark to the city of David with **rejoicing** (v 12). The fear that David experienced before was replaced with a sense of celebration. David's enthusiasm toward the ark is also captured by the verb **brought up** (*vāyaʿāl*) because it is a causative, thus indicating David's active role in transporting the ark to Jerusalem. David's changed attitude toward the ark is also witnessed in the way the ark was carefully transported to Jerusalem. The text notes that the bearers of the ark *took six steps and he [David] sacrificed an ox and a fatling* (v 13).

David's deep respect for the ark and his concern for its proper treatment are evidenced by the sacrifices that accompanied the liturgical march. The sacrifices may have been made in order to progressively sanctify the city of Jerusalem so that when the procession arrived it would be ready to receive the sacred object. The text most likely exaggerates the number of sacrifices offered, considering it would have taken countless oxen and fatlings (i.e., rams, 1 Chr 15:26; 4QSam^a) to accomplish this task. This may have been done in order to underscore David's reverential attitude toward the ark, which was going to be housed in Jerusalem.

■ **14-16** As the ark was being transported to Jerusalem "David danced before [Yahweh] with all his might; David was girded with a linen ephod" (v 14 NRSV). The linen ephod indicates that David fulfilled the roles of both priest and king in the procession, which was not uncommon in the ancient Near Eastern world. The linen ephod was a short garment, so that when David danced and leaped about it was likely that he exposed himself before the people who were accompanying the ark. The notice about the ephod is pertinent to v 16, which remarks that when the ark came into the city **Michal, Saul's daughter, looked out the window** and when she saw that David was **leaping and dancing before Yahweh,** she despised him in her heart.

The Ephod

In some priestly legislation in the OT, the ephod is designated as a high-priestly garment (Exod 39:1-3). It is described as a sleeveless top (or apronlike piece of clothing) fastened onto the body with shoulder straps. The ephod, including the shoulder straps and belt, included finely twisted linen woven with gold thread and blue, purple, and scarlet materials. Two onyx stones were affixed onto the shoulder straps with six of the tribes of Israel engraved on each. Mounted onto the ephod by gold rings was the breastplate made of the same gold, blue, purple, and scarlet materials. The breastplate contained the Urim and Thummim (Exod 28:30; Lev 8:8). Outside of the priestly material, the ephod refers to an unadorned linen loincloth worn by cultic functionaries such as Samuel (1 Sam 2:18), the priests at Nob (1 Sam 22:18), and King David (2 Sam 6:14). A number of passages also indicate that an ephod served as a garment covering an idol or some other religious object located in ritual or cultic settings (Judg 8:27; 17:5; 18:14, 17-18, 20; 1 Sam 14:3; 21:9). The ephod could also be deployed for divinatory functions, especially when David sought an oracle from God (1 Sam 23:9; 30:7).

In v 16 the text makes a couple of important observations about Michal. First, Michal is not called David's wife, she is simply referred to as Saul's daughter. This may indicate that their relationship was an estranged one. Was David's relationship to Michal merely a political one by which he had some tangible connection to Saul's family and the members of the northern tribes? If so, the marriage was simply one of political necessity and not one based on mutual love (1 Sam 18:20, 28 only note that Michal loved David). The text also implies something about the nature of their relationship when it notes that she saw **King David** as she looked out the window (2 Sam 6:16). The text does not mention that she saw her husband, but a political official. The text seems to confirm our suspicions.

Second, the notice that Michal *looked out the window* reminds the audience of the occasion when Michal helped David escape "through a window" as Saul and his men attempted to kill him (1 Sam 19:12). In this context she looked at him from a distance "through a window" with contempt as he approached and entered the city (Alter 1999, 228).

Third, the text notes that Michal despised David **in her heart.** Most likely Michal's feelings were caused by David's leaping and dancing while wearing the ephod. As mentioned before, the small garment did not provide David much coverage, which allowed his private areas to be exposed in front of the people. Michal's retort to David in 2 Sam 6:20 seems to indicate this.

■ **17-19** As the ark was brought to rest in the city, it was placed *in the tent that David set up* (v 17). This tent was a temporary house for the ark until Solomon built the temple and it was housed there (1 Kgs 6—8). David also offered up sacrifices and offerings in addition to presenting **a *cake* of bread** and **a cake of raisins** to the multitude in attendance (2 Sam 6:19).

Some scholars have noted that David's festive behavior (i.e., dancing and leaping) and presentation of food upon the return of the ark to Jerusalem shows parallels with the celebration that the Canaanites held for Baal after his annual return from the dead (Seow 1989). In this context, however, the procession has been modified so that the transportation of the ark to Jerusalem symbolized Yahweh's triumphant return to Israel after years of residing in Kiriath Jearim. The notion that the Israelites patterned Yahweh's homecoming on the Canaanite celebration of Baal should not be troubling us, because the Israelites appropriated the Canaanite imagery and liturgy to celebrate and honor the God they worshiped: Yahweh.

■ **20-22** When David returned to his own house, Michal greeted David with scorn and a bit of angry sarcasm. She confronted him in v 20 with the statement, ***How the king of Israel has honored himself today, who has uncovered himself before the eyes of his servants' maids as a worthless fellow might uncover himself!*** Michal's statement is important on different levels. First, her use of the word **honor** (*nikbād*) and **uncovered** (*niglâ*) is significant because when the ark was first captured by the Philistines it was reported that the "glory/honor" (*kābôd*) of Yahweh had "departed" (*gālâ*). Here she sarcastically accused David of both honoring and uncovering himself upon the ark's arrival. The fact that she used these terms here may be an indication of her derision. Through a play on words she insinuated that David really debased himself and Israel, as when God's glory departed the land when the ark was taken into captivity.

Second, she referred to David in the third person ("the king of Israel"), which reinforced her scorn for David. Michal was angry that David comported himself in the way a scurrilous individual would have and not the king of Israel. Her claim that David exposed himself to the maids is a sexual reference, indicating that David's private areas could be seen by the young women. She may not only have endured political resentment but sexual jealousy as David revealed himself to the lowly slave girls (Alter 1999, 229). Michal's statements against David did not go unanswered, however. David defended his actions before Michal, claiming that though they seemed vulgar to her they were displays of pious self-humiliation before Yahweh (v 22).

■ **23** The chapter ends with the notice that Michal did not have children ***until the day of her death.*** David personally ostracized her and thus did not have sexual relations with her after this episode. Since Michal did not produce any offspring for David, questions emerge over where David's successor would come from. This issue is central to the story of David's life and his family as is recorded in 2 Sam 9—20 and 1 Kgs 1—2.

FROM THE TEXT

The narrative regarding the transportation of the ark to Jerusalem has important theological implications for the reading audience. David's desire to bring the ark to Jerusalem speaks volumes about the nature of his kingship and his relationship to Yahweh. By transporting the ark to Jerusalem, David made a powerful statement regarding his priorities as the leader of God's people and the religious path Israel would follow. The text records the events of ch 6 as one of David's first official acts as the newly established king. Transporting the ark to Jerusalem was not just an afterthought on David's part nor an act of political expediency. David first sought to honor the God who had brought him to this point in his life and to acknowledge God's faithfulness to and sovereignty over Israel (Brueggemann 1990, 248). The ark represented a tangible expression of God's presence, and the act of housing it in Jerusalem stood as a symbol that God would continuously take residence in the heart of the nation and would be honored by its king and people.

David was also at the pinnacle of his personal life and political career when he made this religious overture. It would have been both tempting and easy for David to have forgotten God or taken God for granted when he was enjoying such great success. David's mindfulness of God's presence and help in his life was not predicated upon his personal circumstances or situation. In honoring God during the blessed times of his life, and not just in stressful moments when he needed God's help, he lived up to the exhortations found in Deut 8:11-18:

> Take care that you do not forget the LORD your God, by failing to keep his commandments, his ordinances, and his statutes, which I am commanding you today. When you have eaten your fill and have built fine houses and live in them, and when your herds and flocks have multiplied, and your silver and gold is multiplied, and all that you have is multiplied, then do not exalt yourself, forgetting the LORD your God, who brought you out of the land of Egypt, out of the house of slavery, who led you through the great and terrible wilderness, an arid wasteland with poisonous snakes and scorpions. He made water flow for you from flint rock, and fed you in the wilderness with manna that your ancestors did not know, to humble you and to test you, and in the end to do you good. Do not say to yourself, "My power and the might of my own hand have gotten me this wealth." But remember the LORD your God, for it is he who gives you the power to get wealth. (NRSV)

Although these words are recorded as Moses' instructions to the children of Israel, David embodied the message within them. He did not exalt himself or arrogantly flaunt his newfound power, nor did he fail to recall that it was God who made it possible for him to be king over the people of Israel. David's response was not one of arrogance (i.e., my power has accomplished this) but one of humble dependence and gratitude for all God had done for him.

Through David's actions, we are reminded of the importance of Christ's exhortation to seek first the kingdom of God and his righteousness (Matt 6:33). In all of our personal undertakings we are called to make God the first priority in our lives. By recognizing God first in all that we do, we acknowledge our humble dependence upon God and his sovereignty in our lives, and we recognize that it is God's provision and grace that makes everything possible. It is especially important that we remember God and reaffirm our dependence on him during seasons of blessing and happiness. During those times it becomes easy to become self-reliant, erroneously believing that our own strength and ingenuity has brought us success. The true test of our devotion, dependence, and gratitude to God does not always occur during moments of testing, but also on those occasions when life is good.

L. God Makes a Covenant with David (7:1-29)

BEHIND THE TEXT

Second Samuel 7 represents the climax of the story of David's rise to kingship in that God established a special covenant with David and his household. The Davidic covenant represents a departure from some of the other covenants that are referenced in the OT. The Noahic covenant was universal and pertained to humanity in general (Gen 8—9). The Abrahamic covenant included the promises of land and descendants (Gen 15; 17), and the Mosaic covenant was a conditional covenant that was mediated by Moses on behalf of the Israelite community (Exod 20—23; Deut 12—28). God's covenant with David was unconditional and centered on securing David's dynasty.

The chapter contains two major sections. The first (2 Sam 7:1-17) includes an oracle by the prophet Nathan that refers to the formal establishment of the covenant itself. The second (vv 18-29) includes David's prayer of gratitude and praise to God in response to the promises God made to David and his family. Scholars have long noted that the chapter has a complicated literary history in which older source material has been supplemented with later editorial additions and Deuteronomistic compositions. Although the request to build a temple (v 2) appears at the beginning the chapter, the oldest stratum (vv 1-7, 11*b*, 16, 18-21, 25-29) expresses anti-temple sentiments and is primarily concerned with the building of a lasting or enduring dynasty for the house of David (Von Rad 1962, 310-14; Schniedewind 1999, 29-39). It was only later that editor(s) from the period of Solomon (or later) included the material (esp. vv 12-14) related to construction of the temple (McCarter 1984, 220-23) so that they pointed to the achievements of David's heir. Even though this reconstruction separates the subjects of temple building and the construction of a dynasty into two sections, both, oftentimes, went hand in hand in the ancient world.

IN THE TEXT

1. Nathan's Oracle to David (7:1-17)

■ **1-3** This unit is prefaced in v 1 with the words, ***and it was as the king resided in his house and Yahweh gave him rest from his enemies all around.*** This notice not only indicates that God gave David military success (i.e., rest) but also makes a reference to the king's house in which David was residing. The word for ***house*** (*bayit*) in this context is not a specific reference to David's palace, but it is used figuratively here and throughout the rest of this unit as a term that symbolized David's household. In vv 1-17, the text carefully engages in a wordplay that reinforces what God desired to do for David.

David also showed his concern for building a house for Yahweh. Since the king resided in a palace, the ark also needed a permanent home. Although the ark had resided in the sanctuary at Shiloh in the days of Samuel (1 Sam 3), the sanctuary there proved to be a temporary dwelling place rather than a permanent home. David was ensconced in the capital city and therefore compelled to provide a more permanent structure in which to house the ark. It was a common practice in the ancient Near East that a king would build a temple in a city he conquered as a sign of respect and reverence to the god he worshipped. David was no different. The temple was a symbol of the divine presence, and it assured divine benevolence toward the king and his family (Hamilton 2004, 316). David even received the backing of the prophet Nathan, who said to the king, **Go, do all that is in your heart, for Yahweh is with you** (2 Sam 7:3).

■ **4-9a** David's desire to construct a temple and Nathan's message to David in vv 2-3 stand in sharp contrast to the word Yahweh delivered to David vis-à-vis Nathan in vv 4-17. Through the typical message formula (***thus says Yahweh***) Yahweh delivered a word to Nathan at night that was to be delivered to David (v 5). In the address, Yahweh wanted Nathan to convey a number of important messages to David. First, Yahweh referred to David as **my servant** (v 5). The actual phrase **my servant** is significant because it is only applied to one other individual within the DtrH: Moses (Josh 1:2). Since the text directly ties David with Moses, a comparison of the two leaders is made: Moses presided over the people at Mount Sinai; David ruled over the people of Israel from Jerusalem. Thus, the text anticipates that David would be the leader of God's people on par with someone of the status with Moses.

Second, Yahweh reminded Nathan that he had not lived in a **house** (i.e., temple) from the time that he had brought the Israelites from Egypt until the time of David (2 Sam 7:6). Yahweh had lived in a **tent** and a ***tabernacle*** as the Israelites journeyed through the wilderness and settled in the land of Canaan. More importantly, Yahweh did not desire a **house** nor did he ever ask for one.

Third, Yahweh reiterated that he would build David a house (*bayit*) instead. In doing so, Yahweh emphasized his role in leading David from a shepherd of flocks to the ***leader*** of God's people. The term used here for ***leader*** (*nāgîd*) (sometimes translated as "prince") is distinct from the term for "king" (*melek*). The term *nāgîd* emphasized the custodial role of the leader who presided over "God's people." Whereas a "king" represented a form of centralized control and power that was often abused and misused. The imagery and language of shepherding is also significant here because God's greatest leaders started out as shepherds before they took on leadership roles (see comment on 2 Sam 5:2). This notice "foreshadows" David's greatness as a leader and also connects him with Moses, who was also a shepherd before becoming the leader of God's people.

Yahweh also reminded David that "I have been with you wherever you went" (v 9a NRSV). The phrase "I have been with you" (*vāʾhyeh*) is based off the imperfect tense form of the verb (*hāyah*) in Hebrew. This verb not only connotes existence ("to be") but also relates to the divine name "Yahweh" since it derives from the same verb. This is the same language Yahweh used when speaking to Moses from the burning bush (Exod 3:12 = "I will be with you"). Thus, the text points to another parallel that connects David with the figure Moses.

■ **9b-11** Yahweh also made a couple of important promises to David: he would make David ***a great name*** and ***set aside for my people Israel a place and I will plant them and they will dwell in their own place and be disturbed no more*** (2 Sam 7:9b-10). The promise of a great name and a homeland also connects David with the patriarch Abraham. Like David, God promised to make Abraham's name great (Gen 12:2) and to provide land for his offspring (Gen 15; 17). The connection between these two great figures is significant in that God would fulfill the promises to Abraham through David.

Yahweh also promised to build David a **house** (2 Sam 7:11b). By using the term **house** God did not intend to build David a physical structure, such as a palace, but an enduring dynasty, a family. In the ancient world, it was common to refer to a royal family or dynasty as a house. References to the "house of David" have been unearthed in the archaeological record. The famous Tel Dan inscription contains the only reference to the "the house of David" outside the biblical text (Biran and Naveh 1993, 81-93).

■ **12-14a** In building David's house, God promised to raise up a son after David and establish his kingdom (v 12). The reader here cannot help but see references to Solomon, even though his name is not mentioned specifically. God also proclaimed that Solomon would build Yahweh a house (v 13), a "foreshadowing" of the events found in 1 Kgs 5—8. God not only promised a son but also provided for the permanency for David's house in that David's kingdom would be established **forever** (*ʿad ʿōlām*). The promise of descendants also recalls God's promise to Abraham in which he promised to provide him with offspring as well. Thus, in the Davidic covenant the two most prominent elements of Abrahamic covenant intersect: land and descendants.

Yahweh also spoke of David's descendant in terms of sonship: "I will be a father to him, and he shall be a son to me" (NRSV). The reference to the king as God's son was a common theme throughout the ancient Near East. Although the term is not intended to be taken literally, as though God begot the king, it did imply a special relationship between God and the monarch in that God appointed the king to rule in God's stead (Ps 2:7). The king, in response, was supposed to rule the people with justice and righteousness and preserve the order that God established at creation (Ps 89:1-37).

■ **14b-15** The Davidic covenant was also unconditional in nature. The text notes that even if one of David's sons committed iniquity, God may punish the son, but God would never remove his steadfast love for David's household and never tear David's kingdom away from him. The promise would be tested throughout the history of Davidic rule, and there were occasions when God punished David's descendant, but the territory of Judah and the Davidic line were never taken away (1 Kgs 11:11-13). This unconditional aspect of the covenant was distinct from the Mosaic covenant, which was conditional. In the Mosaic covenant, if the people disobeyed God, they would face severe punishment, including banishment from the land (Deut 28:25-37).

■ **16-17** As a final aspect of the Davidic covenant, God also reassured David that his kingdom would endure forever: ***Your house and your kingdom will be established forever before you, your throne will be established forever.*** This statement moves beyond David's son to refer to all his descendants. The Davidic covenant, however, was sorely tested in the exile, and it caused much questioning and reevaluation about the justice, mercy, and integrity of God during the catastrophe (Ps 89:38-52). New Testament writers, however, found within the promises of 2 Sam 7 a messianic foretelling and fulfillment of this covenant in the life of Jesus. The early church fathers saw references in these verses not only to Christ but to Christ's indestructible kingdom as well (Frank and Oden 2005, 351-52).

2. The Prayer of David (7:18-29)

These verses follow on the heels of the establishment of the Davidic covenant. The placement of this text is logical, because it functions, in essence, as a prayer of praise and thanksgiving in response to what God had done for David. Modern scholars have found in these verses various layers of redactional activity. The verses that include the bulk of the prayer (vv 18-21, 25-29) should be taken together and attributed to the same source according to modern scholars (Campbell and O'Brien 2000, 291; Noth 1991, 89). The middle portion of the prayer (vv 22-24), however, has been attributed to the work of the Deuteronomistic editor(s). The prayer essentially is divided into two sections: praise of Yahweh (vv 18-24) and petition (vv 25-29). Two subunits divide the first section into smaller units.

■ **18-21** In the first part David praised Yahweh for his dealings with David and his household. Verse 18 indicates that David **sat before *Yahweh.*** Presumably David was in the tent (6:17; 7:2) and in front of the ark as he prayed. David emphasized his lowly status in the prayer when he states, **Who am I *and my household,* that you have brought me this far?** David's words of humility resemble the dialogue of Gideon, who reminded God of his humble status when Yahweh selected him as judge (Judg 6). As part of his humble response, David recognized Yahweh's role in leading him to this point in his life. The verb "to bring up" (*hăbîʾōtānî*) is a causative, underscoring Yahweh's role in David's rise to kingship. Thus, it was Yahweh who brought David greatness, not the other way around.

■ **22-24** In the second subunit David again recognized Yahweh's greatness. In this section of the prayer, however, Yahweh's greatness is based on what Yahweh had done for God's people, Israel. Yahweh not only redeemed his people and drove out the nations and their gods before the Israelites but also established the people and they recognized Yahweh as God.

■ **25-29** After David's praise of Yahweh in vv 18-24, the text turns to petition. In this section of the prayer, David essentially asked God to make good on the promises that he had made to David, Yahweh's servant. David asked God to ensure that his throne would be established **before you** (v 26) and to "bless the house of your servant so that it may continue forever before you" (v 29).

FROM THE TEXT

This chapter reminds the reader that God seeks to establish covenantal relationships with creation. God's covenant with David is one of four (Noahic, Abrahamic, Mosaic, Davidic) major covenants that are represented in the OT. In each of these cases, God was the one who reached out to humanity in order to establish these special and binding agreements. In God's covenant with David, God was able to fulfill the promises made to the patriarch Abraham by guaranteeing David a great name (7:9; Gen 12:2), land (2 Sam 7:10; Gen 13:14-15; 15:18-20; 17:8), and offspring (2 Sam 7:12; Gen 15:5; 17:5-6). Not only does this text highlight the glories of David's reign, but it also speaks of the faithfulness and dependability of the God who made these promises to Abraham and David. In a covenant relationship, both parties were obligated to keep their respective obligations. The OT reaffirms throughout its pages that God did not take his covenant obligations lightly but fulfilled the demands of those relationships, even in times of uncertainty and challenge.

The other aspect of the Davidic covenant that is important to note is God's promise to provide David an eternal dynasty (2 Sam 7:12, 16). God's promise to David of an eternal kingdom was severely threatened during the Babylonian exile when the Davidic king was taken into captivity (2 Kgs 24—25). For many Israelites the exile challenged their faith in God and his ability to maintain covenant loyalty as his people were scattered throughout the ancient Near Eastern world. Even in exile, though, signs of hope glimmered on the horizon. The Davidic king, Jehoiachin, was released from prison and allowed to dine at the king's table (2 Kgs 25:27-30), and the Davidic leaders Sheshbazzar (Ezra 1:8) and Zerubbabel (Ezra 2:2) returned to Judea after the exile. Thus God had kept his word, in the minds of the Jews (Hag 2:21-23), as the Davidic line remained intact.

Although the postexilic community did not have a Davidic king to lead them, the promises of the covenant text of 2 Sam 7 continued to provide hope that the Davidic king, the Messiah, would appear again. In the late intertestamental period and the first century of the Christian era, the Jewish community believed that the Messiah would emerge as a political leader and help restore Judea's independence from foreign overlords. In the early Christian community, however, believers found in Jesus the fulfillment of God's promises in the Davidic covenant. Jesus descended from David (Matt 1:1-17), was called the "son of David," and ushered in an everlasting kingdom known as "the kingdom of God." Thus, Jesus, like David, fulfilled the promises God made to Abraham (offspring and land), but in a more perfect way. Those who believe in Christ are now called "the children of Abraham." Moreover, Christians hold on to the hope of inheriting land; not a physical plot here on earth but an eternal home in heaven.

M. David's Wars and Administration (8:1-18)

BEHIND THE TEXT

This chapter represents the final episode related to the glory of David's reign. The theme of this chapter, however, is centered on David's military achievements and conquests. Within vv 1-14, the text presents a summary of the various territories that David brought under his control as king of Israel. The report indicates that David was able to extend his influence, and Israel's, beyond the borders of Israel proper into surrounding territories. The text moves from the regions to the southwest (v 1), the east (v 2), the north (vv 3-11), and to the south (vv 13-14). These military victories appear to "fulfill" the promise that God made to David and Israel (7:10-11). At only two points in the text (8:6b, 14), however, does the narrator/editor draw attention to Yahweh's role in David's victories. Some have even wondered if this chapter critiques David, who became obsessed with empire building.

The second section (vv 15-18) is a short list of David's officials. Scholars are of the opinion that this information derived from archival sources and thus has an "official" quality about it. The placement of this material is understandable in light of vv 1-14 because he required bureaucratic officials to help him govern his growing empire. The list of officials in vv 15-18 is similar to the one found in 20:23-26 albeit with some minor exceptions. The latter bureaucratic registry is from a later period in David's reign, since it shows evidence of expansion.

IN THE TEXT

1. Report of David's Wars (8:1-14)

■ 1 On the list of David's conquests, the Philistines are mentioned first. The text notes that *it was after this David struck the Philistines.* The antecedent for *after this* is unclear. Some scholars argue that this verse probably connects better with the events in 5:17-25 where David fought against and beat back the Philistine forces at Rephaim. This opinion may be correct, but it is impossible to say with certainty. It is also important to note that of the three verbs employed in this verse, David is the subject of all three: **David *struck* and subdued them, and he took.** Not only does the syntax indicate that David enjoyed success against the Philistines, but the second of the three verbs (*vāyaknîʿēm*) is a causative, which emphasizes the active role he played in defeating them. Also, the word for "subdue" indicates that David was essentially able to dominate them. The Philistines are only mentioned a couple of times after David's reign in the DtrH (1 Kgs 4:21; 15:27; 16:15), indicating that he had rendered them ineffective.

The text also notes that he took **Metheg Ammah** from the Philistines. Although the identification of this site is unclear, the term **Metheg** literally means "bridle" and **Ammah** means "elbow or forearm." First Chronicles 18:1 associates the site with the city of Gath and its environs, and the LXX simply reads "the marked off territory." Thus, a satisfactory reading remains elusive.

■ **2** David next ***struck Moab.*** The reason for David's attack on the Moabites remains a mystery, considering he had family ties to the region and the king of Moab appeared to have been amicable toward him before (1 Sam 22). It is possible to deduce that when David's kingdom expanded he saw Moab as a potential threat to Israel's security. David's cruelty against the Moabites is underscored as he ***measured them off with a cord and he made them lie down on the ground; he measured two lengths of cord for those who were killed and one measure for those who were allowed to live.*** David marked off some of the prisoners for execution while the survivors became vassals and were required to pay tribute.

■ **3-8** With the southwestern and eastern borders of Israel secure, the text tracks David's movements northward. Second Samuel 8:3 notes that "David . . . struck down Hadadezer son of Rehob of Zobah" (NRSV). Aram, like Israel, was a growing power at this time. In the tenth century a power vacuum existed throughout the Levant, and these two kingdoms sought to fill it. The text indicates that David got the upper hand in this struggle as ***he captured 1,700 horsemen and 20,000 foot soldiers*** (v 4). David also disabled Hadadezer's chariot forces by hamstringing all but 100 of his horses. Hadadezer also received help from the Arameans of Damascus, but David was able to strike down the ***22,000*** reinforcements (v 5). David installed garrisons near Damascus, the capital of Aram, and the people there became his vassals (v 6). David also took material booty from his conquests, the gold shields from Hadadezer and bronze from two cities of Hadadezer: **Tebah and Berothai** (v 8). The LXX version notes that Solomon made the bronze sea, the pillars, washbasins, and all the vessels for the temple with the bronze that David captured.

■ **9-12** David's reputation continued to grow in the region as his military conquests mounted. The text notes that **Tou king of Hamath . . . sent his son Joram to . . . congratulate him on his victory** (v 10). Hadadezer was King Tou's enemy, and thus he was grateful that David defeated him. As evidence of his gratitude, Tou sent David articles of **silver and gold and bronze** (v 10).

■ **13-14** According to vv 1-12, David defeated or subdued no less than four of Israel's greatest threats. Although the text highlights David's success, the lack of references to God's help outside the brief notices in v 6*b* and v 14*b* is quite telling. The statement in v 13 that ***David made a name for himself*** also underscores David's role in his triumphs. The language implies that David became great through his own striving, which was contrary to what God said to David through Nathan earlier (7:9). The language in 8:13 is also similar to that of the Tower of Babel scene (Gen 11:4) in which the people wanted to "make a name for ourselves." Thus, while on the surface the text is intended to glorify the achievements of David, its undercurrents could be construed as a critique as well.

2. David's Administration (8:15-18)

■ **15-18** The chapter ends with a notice about David's administration. David established an impressive kingdom that required the oversight of skilled officials. The text begins with the reference that David **reigned over all Israel** (v 15). Based on vv 1-14 it would be accurate to say that David's influence expanded beyond the borders of Israel proper. David also "administered justice and equity" (NRSV) to the people, which was one of the main responsibilities of the king. As God's leader, the king was expected to maintain the order and stability that God established at creation (Mellish 2009, 168-76).

In order to maintain a civil society David enlisted the help of various individuals skilled in running a kingdom. David made his nephew (1 Chr 2:16), **Joab,** the general of the army. Joab's reputation as a warrior was well known, as he distinguished himself on the battlefield (2 Sam 3:12; 12:26-27; 1 Chr 11:6). **Jehoshaphat** was the recorder or secretary. His greatest role would have been at the court where he kept David informed, advising him, and communicating the king's commands (Baldwin 1988, 224).

Zadok, the son of Ahitub, and **Ahimelech,** the son of Abiathar, functioned as David's priests. Zadok appears for the first time, and his origins are surrounded in mystery. First Chronicles 6:50-53 includes Ahitub in Zadok's lineage, but the problem is that Ahimelech's grandfather was also called Ahitub (1 Sam 22:20). To solve this problem, scholars have proposed that Zadok was the priest of the Jebusite cult before David's conquest of Jerusalem then made a part of David's administration when he became king (Rowley 1939, 113-14). Abiathar had been with David since escaping Saul (1 Sam 22:20), so it is no surprise that David made Ahimelech priest. Some have argued that the names are erroneously reversed so that Abiathar should be listed as the priest. This is most likely true based on other texts (1 Sam 22:20; 23:6; 30:7) that list Ahimelech as Abiathar's father.

Seraiah, also called Sheva (2 Sam 20:25), was the secretary, a position comparable to that of the Egyptian officer who served as the secretary to the king. **Benaiah,** the son of Jehoiada, was a valiant soldier (2 Sam 23:20-23) who oversaw the **Kerethites and Pelethites.** The Kerethites and Pelethites constituted David's personal bodyguard. They were foreign mercenaries associated with the territory of Crete (Albright 1921, 187-94; Montgomery 1951, 86). They played an important role in the coronation of Solomon at the end of David's life (1 Kgs 1:38). The reference to **David's sons** as ***priests*** indicates the priesthood was not yet hereditary. Chronicles lists them as "chief officials" (1 Chr 18:17).

FROM THE TEXT

Our initial reaction in reading this chapter, especially vv 1-14, may be to say that David was a great leader and a successful warrior. He was able to extend his kingdom into areas beyond the land of Israel, establish vassal relationships with the surrounding countries, and build his reputation among the people of that region. All of the success that David enjoyed appears to have come from the Lord who "gave victory to David wherever he went" (NRSV).

It is significant to note, however, that as David's focus shifts from being king over Israel to becoming an empire builder, there is an increasing tendency to become consumed with personal achievement, the accumulation of power, and a trend toward self-reliance. A careful examination of the verbs in this text reveals that David is the subject of the vast majority of them, thus highlighting David's achievement over God's role in the text (vv 6*b*, 14*b*). Within this context, the statement ***and David made a name for himself*** (v 13) raises concerns that David is trying to become an accomplished man through his own striving, hard work, and initiative.

This phrase is also used to refer to the people who built the tower of Babel: "let us . . . make a name for ourselves" (Gen 11:4). The people in Genesis wanted to achieve greatness and renown through their own imagination and ingenuity. As the text reveals, however, their pride and arrogance preceded their downfall, and God humbled them by confusing their language.

The text appears to be hinting at the same message with regard to David. In the story of David, ch 8 represents the high point of his career and personal achievement. After this text, David's life will move, generally, in a downward trajectory throughout the narrative. The pursuit of power and conquest that is hinted at in this text will be exhibited in the kinds of behavior that led to his moral indiscretions, personal humiliation, and suffering. David's life is a reminder to all of us that "pride goes before destruction" (Prov 16:18).

IV. THE SUCCESSION TO THE THRONE OF DAVID (9:1—20:26)

A. David's Dealings with the House of Saul (9:1-13)

9:1-13

BEHIND THE TEXT

This chapter begins the larger unit that extends through ch 20. Whereas ch 8 functions as a summary of David's conquests and the capstone to the story of David's rise to kingship, ch 9 begins a new section in the life of David. Scholars have generally termed this unit the Succession Narrative, because it focuses on the question of which one of David's sons will succeed him on the throne (see Introduction).

Chapter 9 fills a unique role within the overall structure of the Succession Narrative in that it attempts to answer an important question: "How will David deal with surviving members of Saul's household now that he is Israel's king?" Unlike other chapters in this unit, ch 9 actually portrays David in a positive light in that he shows kindness to Mephibosheth, the son of Jonathan, by inviting him to stay with the king. Critics may argue, however, that this is David's way of "keeping an eye" on the remaining heir from Saul's household.

From a synchronic perspective David's willingness to aid Mephibosheth becomes especially important during the revolt of Absalom in chs 11—20 (16:1-4; 19:24-30), yet from a redactional point of view ch 9 assumes that the events of 2 Sam 21:1 ff. have already taken place. Thus, this material is most likely arranged thematically and not chronologically.

IN THE TEXT

The chapter on Mephibosheth can essentially be broken down into two smaller sections (vv 1-5; vv 6-13). In the first section, David basically inquired about the survivors of the house of Saul while in the second David makes preparations to care for Mephibosheth and his family.

■ **1-5** The first section opens with an inquiry of David in v 1: ***Is there anyone remaining from the house of Saul?*** This question suggests that David did not know if any members from the house of Saul were still alive. A synchronic reading of the text indicates that Saul and the sons who were with him on Mount Gilboa had died (1 Sam 31) and Ish-Bosheth had been murdered (2 Sam 4). However, other members of Saul's household still remained, as 2 Sam 21 indicates. This information provides a reason why redaction scholars posit that ch 9 refers to events that occurred after ch 21.

It is unclear why David wanted to know if any remaining members of the house of Saul survived. One reason may include the notion that he wanted to be aware of any potential claimants to the throne that could emerge while he reigned as king. The text, however, offers another reason: David wanted to show mercy to any surviving members of Saul's family. David personally acknowledged this when he stated, ***I will make kindness to him on account of Jonathan*** (9:1). Even though David did not specify the individual here, Mephibosheth is anticipated. (See note on 4:4, for his name Merib-Baal.) David's graciousness to a member of Saul's house was based on David's covenant with Jonathan, Saul's son. The word for **kindness** (*ḥesed*) indicates the notion of covenant loyalty and thus relates to David's obligation to his friend. David also extended *ḥesed* to his political allies, such as Hanun (10:2).

David summoned a servant of the house of Saul in order to find the answer to his question. The servant, who is called **Ziba,** came to David and addressed him with the respectful reply, **your servant** (9:2). David asked Ziba if there was anyone left in the house of Saul to whom he could show kindness. Ziba mentioned the **son of Jonathan,** but he also made a reference to his disability: ***he is crippled of feet*** (v 3). Ziba may have quickly alluded to Mephibosheth's disability in order to downplay any notions that he would be a political threat to David. Jonathan's son is never named here, and he is only identified as coming from the **house of Makir son of Ammiel** (v 5). **Makir** lived on the east side of the Jordan and later became a valuable supporter of David during Absalom's revolt (17:27). Although the servant speaks very tersely in this context, Ziba's attitude toward David will be very different later (16:1-4; 19:27-30).

Ziba also revealed to David that Jonathan's son was located in **Lo Debar**. This city was located across the Jordan (Josh 13:26) just below the Jabbok near the region Mahanaim, the old capital of Ish-Bosheth (Hertzberg 1964, 300). Mephibosheth was located there because of its proximity to Mahanaim, the political center of Ishbaal's rule. David's kindness to Mephibosheth later benefited him personally and politically. The people of that region did not forget how David treated Mephibosheth and they, in turn, supported David as he took refuge near Mahanaim during Absalom's revolt (see Makir above).

■ **6-13** Mephibosheth came to David and when he arrived in the king's presence he *fell on his face and bowed down before him* (v 6). Mephibosheth's response is one of a man who feared for his life. He may have been terrified that David came to execute a member of Saul's family. Mephibosheth did not realize that David came to extend kindness to Jonathan's son. Instead of bringing retribution on Mephibosheth, David offered to restore to Mephibosheth his family's property (probably in the territory of Gibeah) and extended an invitation to eat at the king's table. Eating at the king's table was a great privilege (1 Kgs 2:7; 18:19; 2 Kgs 25:29), and it symbolized good relations between the two parties. David's kind gesture evinced a very humble and undeserving response from Mephibosheth in 2 Sam 9:8: "What is your servant, that you would look upon a dead dog such as I?" (NRSV). As far as he knew, he had not done anything to deserve this treatment. David was also generous to Ziba, Mephibosheth's servant, and his household. All the land that was given back to Mephibosheth would be used to farm and raise food for Ziba's household.

The unit closes with a notice that Mephibosheth had a son named **Mica** (v 12). Ironically, Jonathan's son and grandson would not be eligible for the throne, yet they lived in the king's house. This created an interesting situation in that the families of two royal households shared the same living space. Mephibosheth, however, did not remain a threat to David, since the text ends with the statement that Mephibosheth was *crippled in both of his feet* (v 13). Any reader of this text would realize that Mephibosheth's handicap precluded him from posturing for the throne. The symbolism is also significant in that the debilitated monarchy of Saul is reflected in his disabled grandson who depended on David's mercy for survival.

FROM THE TEXT

This chapter presents David as a man of integrity and compassion. David remembered his covenant with Jonathan by extending his loyalty to Jonathan's household as he promised (1 Sam 20:15-16). As the new king, David could have sought revenge on any survivors of the house of Saul, considering the manner in which Saul pursued David. David, however, displayed kindness and generosity toward the crippled Mephibosheth by providing for his family (and the family of his servant). David's munificent gesture toward Mephibosheth is even more impressive in light of the fact that his internal convictions pressed him to keep his commitment and not because he was coerced to do so.

In fulfilling his covenant responsibilities, David reminds us of the importance of being people who keep our word. It is often easier for us to make promises to others than it is to keep them. Demonstrating the ability to fulfill our obligations and to keep our promises is a sign of maturity and character. We develop the reputation of being trustworthy and dependable when we remain steadfast in fulfilling our oaths. Possessing this quality not only benefits us in our personal relationships and our careers, but it also bears witness to the presence of Christ in our lives. As believers, it is imperative that our words and actions be consistent so that we are not perceived as "phony" or undependable. By remaining true to our word and fulfilling our commitments to others, we let people know that we value them and that they can rely on us. As a result, we develop a trust bond with them that, in time, can lead to deeper relationship with them and the opportunity to share the message of Christ in a more personal way.

B. David and Hanun (10:1-19)

BEHIND THE TEXT

This chapter is often considered an insertion within the larger story of the Succession Narrative. A careful examination of the surrounding literary context, however, suggests that ch 10 serves to provide the necessary backdrop for the story of David and Bathsheba in chs 11—12. This chapter also connects with ch 9 in that David attempted to show kindness or covenant loyalty to someone who had lost a loved one David knew. Redactional considerations indicate, however, that ch 10 may have originated from a different context and inserted here. The unit opens in v 1, for example, with the phrase ***and it happened after this.*** It is difficult to know what event is being referenced.

This is a vague temporal formula that reflects the achronoligical ordering of the text (Alter 1999, 244). Moreover, the reference to Hadadezer as an opponent of David in v 19 does not correlate with the statements in 8:5-8, in which David defeated Hadadezer and made him his vassal. This information suggests that the events in ch 10 must have occurred earlier than the summary statements in ch 8. The material as it comes to us in the text suggests that David's war against the Ammonites (and the Arameans) did not occur in one sweeping military campaign, but took place in stages over the course of an extended period of time. Scholars have tried to reconstruct David's wars in the Transjordan region along various lines:

1. Two-stage conflict: 2 Sam 10:1—11:1 represents the first battle, with vv 15-19*a* serving as a second phase of the war; 2 Sam 12:26 ff. represents the second and closing stage of the battle (Hertzberg 1964, 305).

2. Three-stage conflict: The first battle occurred outside Rabbah (10:6-14), with the second engagement taking place in northern Gilead (10:15-19); the final stage (8:3-8) in the conflict took place when David defeated Hadadezer's coalition (Mauchline 1971, 247-48; McCarter 1984, 278).

3. Four-stage conflict: David defeated the Ammonite-Aramean coalition first (10:6-14), then dealt a blow to the reinforced alliance (10:15-19); Joab started the assault against Rabbah and the city fell under David (11:1; 12:26); David decisively defeated the coalition forces (8:3-8) (Anderson 1989, 146; Carlson 1964, 150).

The above information indicates that scholarly opinions vary on how best to reconstruct the events in ch 10. Although there is not a consensus, it appears safe to argue that the material in vv 6-19 represents two stages within a larger battle against the Ammonite-Aramean forces. The information in vv 1-5, therefore, provides the conditions that precipitated the war.

IN THE TEXT

■ **1-5** The opening verses provide the rationale for the battle against the Ammonites that ensues in vv 6-19. David expressed his desire to show kindness to Hanun, the new king. The text identifies **Hanun** as the **son of Nahash** *the king of the Ammonites* (v 2). Nahash tormented the people of Jabesh Gilead earlier but was defeated by Saul and the Israelite tribes (1 Sam 11). Interestingly, Nahash functioned as an opponent of Saul but treated David kindly (2 Sam 10:2). The text does not provide a reason for the change in policy, but it may be due to the idea that Nahash's enmity toward Saul might have led him to provide refuge or logistical support to David and his men when Saul hunted them down (Alter 1999, 244).

The son's name is important in this respect, because it derives from the word for grace (*ḥēn*). His name is similar in pointing to the passive participle form of the Hebrew word for grace (*ḥānūn*), thus it may be translated as the ***one shown grace***. This is an appropriate appellation considering David's thoughtful gesture toward the Ammonite king in vv 1-2. David sent a contingent of his servants with gifts in order to honor the king by commemorating the memory of his father. However, when the messengers reached the king, Hanun's counselors questioned the move, wondering if they came to honor Nahash or to search the city in preparation to overthrow it (v 3). As a result, Hanun reacted harshly to David's kind overtures. Instead of responding in appreciation, Hanun took the messengers of David and ***shaved half of the beard of each and cut off half their royal garments up to the buttocks and sent them away*** (v 4).

Hanun's shameful and disrespectful treatment of the messengers was essentially a message directed to David personally: do not think about attacking our city! In the ancient world, cutting off half the beard and half a garment so that the buttocks were exposed (in essence feminizing them; Niditch 1993,

118) would have been interpreted as a humiliating gesture, not only for the messengers themselves but especially for the ruler who dispatched them. The clothing they wore (*mādû*) was not standard or regular dress, but royal garments symbolic of the court of David. Thus, they came to Hanun as official ambassadors of David. When it was reported to David what had happened, he met the messengers who felt **very humiliated** (v 5) by what had happened and instructed them to wait in Jericho ("the city of the Palms") until their beards grew back.

■ **6-7** Understandably, Hanun's actions proved to be detrimental to his relationship with David. The text notes that **the sons of Ammon** "saw that they had become odious to David" as a result of Hanun's insult (v 6 NRSV). Anticipating a severe reaction from David, the Ammonites **hired Arameans** from **Beth Rehob** and **Arameans** from **Zobah** (**20,000 foot soldiers**), the king from **Maacah** (along with **1,000 men**), and the men of **Tob** (**12,000 men**). When David heard of the sizable force being assembled in the territory of Ammon, he sent **Joab** his general and **all the host of the mighty men or warriors** (v 7). The word that is used for David's troops (*hāgibôrîm*) indicates that he dispatched only the best fighters to face the Ammonites and their coalition.

The notice that David **sent Joab and his warriors** signals trouble, because David did not lead the troops in battle, which was one of the major responsibilities of the king. David will send the troops into battle again in 11:1 while he stayed home, a situation that resulted in adultery and murder.

■ **8-14** The text moves immediately to the battle scenario, which is described in vv 8-14. The Ammonites went out to meet Joab and his men **at the gate of the city** while the coalition partners remained **in the open country** (v 8). No specific city is mentioned in v 8 and therefore its identity remains unclear. Rabbah represented the capital city of Ammon, but the reader is not informed if this is the case. Some scholars express doubt as to whether Hanun would have been so unwise as to wait until the Israelite troops reached the capital city before taking decisive action. It is for that reason others have proposed that maybe the city in question is Medbah, an Ammonite city further to the south.

The battle plan of the coalition consisted of dividing the forces into two main lines: the Ammonites were at the city while the Arameans of Zobah and Rehob along with the men of Tob were situated in the field. The strategy in effect surrounded Joab and his troops in that there were forces in front of him and behind him.

Joab, who sensed the need to confront both lines simultaneously, split his forces into two groups. Joab took a select group (*běḥûrêy byiśrāʾēl*) to meet the Arameans, and the remaining troops were placed under the command of **Abishai,** his brother, to battle the Ammonites (vv 9-10). This arrangement allowed Joab flexibility in his strategy so that if Joab was outflanked, Abishai would provide support; and if Abishai was overwhelmed, Joab could come to his aid. As the battle unfolded, Joab approached the Arameans who were in the field and they fled from him (v 13). When the Ammonites saw that the

Arameans had run away, they retreated and took shelter in the city. When Joab realized that he had the enemy shut up in the city, he ceased the attack and returned to Jerusalem (v 14).

■ **15-19** The Arameans who fled previously (v 13) regrouped, and another contingent of Arameans beyond the Euphrates were called to supplement Hadadezer's forces. When it was reported to David that the Arameans had reinforced their troops, he went out to the city of **Helam** to do battle. Like Joab, David had success against the Arameans; they fled before him and David killed **700 charioteers** and **40,000 horsemen**, as well as **Shobach the commander of their army** (v 18).

The defeat of the Aramean coalition proved to be an important battle for David's political career. When David defeated Hadadezer, his vassals switched their allegiance to David (v 19). This battle, therefore, essentially solidified David's power in the region, from Israel and the Transjordan to Syria and Aram in the northeast. Thus David's influence expanded well beyond Israel, all the way to the Euphrates.

FROM THE TEXT

The story of David and the war with the Arameans contains both positive and negative elements. On the one hand, we are reminded that unexpected good can come out of a bad situation. Even though David treated Hanun with respect and kindness, Hanun did not reciprocate. The narrative indicates that Israel had to live among the nations and deal with the conflicts that arise between nations (Birch 1998, 1280). Hanun's hostile actions toward David and his men eventually became the pretext for war. Although war is not necessarily a good thing in and of itself, God was able to fulfill his promise to David in part through these events (2 Sam 7:9), and the nation of Israel was blessed through David's conquest. The incidents of ch 10 thus convey the notion that even in times of adversity and conflict, God can be at work in our circumstances to bring about a hidden blessing. Our job is to not lose faith in those moments, but to stay the course and look for the good in all situations.

There is also a cautionary note in the story of David and Hanun. Within the narrative David begins to exhibit behavior that points to a developing problem. When the Ammonites initially assembled their coalition, David sent Joab and his warriors out to battle while he stayed home (10:7). This is a telling statement in that kings in the ancient world were expected to lead the troops in a time of war. David's failure to do so indicates a lapse in judgment and responsibility on his part. David made the same mistake in 11:1, except in that context his dereliction of duty set the stage for his moral downfall. A careful reading of the text highlights this growing trend in David's life: in ch 8 he fought all his battles, in ch 10 he stayed back at first (v 7) and only later joined in (v 17), in ch 11 he reclined at his home in the palace while his troops were in the field (v 1), and in ch 12 he had to be coaxed to fight by his general (v 28).

Through David's example, we are reminded that bad behaviors and habits do not occur suddenly or in a vacuum. They are usually symptomatic of greater problems that have progressed over time. Unfortunately, people do not realize that they have a problem until their lives have been adversely affected by their actions. Sometimes, these same behaviors can seriously injure us or someone else. We learn, therefore, that it is better to recognize our shortcomings early on and admit that we have a problem before it develops into something more severe. God can give us the strength to confront our weaknesses and provide us the resources to address them. By taking this course of action we can save ourselves and others tremendous heartache and pain in the long run.

C. David and Bathsheba (11:1—12:31)

BEHIND THE TEXT

These two chapters are treated together since they are primarily bound together on thematic grounds. Overall, the notices about the war with the Ammonites frame the story of David and Bathsheba and thus provide the necessary context in which the sordid events of David's adultery take place (11:1; 12:26-31). Most scholars would argue that 11:1 serves as an editorial introduction while 12:26-31 derives from other sources, possibly historical archives. Scholars are at odds, however, on how to understand the transmission history of 11:2—12:25.

Some argue that the material in 11:2—12:24 derives from a prophetic author who was providing a theological/moral corrective to David's actions (McCarter 1984, 290). Others argue that 11:2-27a and 12:15b-25 contain the older narrative with 11:27b—12:15a originating from a prophetic hand (Dietrich 1972, 127-29; Wurthwein 1974, 24; Veijola 1975, 233-34; Schwally 1892, 155-56). Based on this reconstruction, David committed his sin of adultery without remorse and thus leaves the reader with the impression that this was the way kings acted (see for example 1 Sam 8:11-17). The material in 11:27b—12:15a, therefore, calls David's behavior into question, which causes David to repent. The question is far from settled, however, in modern scholarship, but elements of the narrative (see esp. 12:7-12) presuppose later events and may indicate a later date of composition.

These chapters present David as one who was vulnerable to abusing his royal power, which is a different portrait in the chapters leading up to these events. Moreover, the setting for this text does not fit neatly with the other accounts regarding David's ongoing battles with the Ammonites. It may be that the battle with the Ammonites was a continuation of the battle that started in ch 10, with ch 8 a closing summary of the completion of hostilities between David and Ammon. However, the matter is left open for debate.

It is significant, however, that the battle scene with Ammon (11:1; 12:26-31) provides the framework for the David and Bathsheba affair. This account not only critiques David for being negligent in his role as king and commander of the armed forces, but it also indicates that the king was susceptible to the abuse of royal power. Moreover, David's transgressions also connect with the following events in the story of David. Scholars have noted that the life of David is basically divided into two sections: David under blessing and David under curse. After David's tryst with Bathsheba and the murder of Uriah, his life was never the same. David was plagued by both internal family matters and political upheaval. The editors of these texts have thus used chs 11—12 as a demarcating line in the story of David.

IN THE TEXT

I. David's Adultery and Murder (11:1-13)

■ 1 The opening verse essentially sets the scene for the events that follow. The text indicates that it was "the turn of the year" (JPS), which has often been translated as **in the spring.** The text not only indicates the time of year but qualifies it with the statement "when kings go out to battle" (NRSV). The verb here is an infinitive (*ṣē'␣t*), which indicates that going to battle was a customary responsibility of the king. However, David did not go out to battle with his troops. Instead, the text notes that **David sent Joab and his servants and all Israel** to battle. It should be noted that the phraseology here is similar to 10:7 when David sent Joab and the army to fight against the Ammonites. Thus David was derelict in his duties on at least two occasions, and the text is already insinuating something important about David's character.

The text also notes that while his men were off fighting in battle **David resided in Jerusalem.** The verb here is a participle (*yōšēb*), which indicates ongoing or continuous activity. In essence, the language insinuates that David did not plan on leaving Jerusalem but made himself at home in his palace. David's presence in Jerusalem also opened the opportunity for the events that transpired in vv 2-27.

■ 2-3 The sordid affairs of vv 2-27 begin in v 2a with the notice that *it was evening and David arose from his bed and walked about on the roof of the king's house* (v 2). The text underscores David's cushy life at home by making a remark about the nap he took at his palace. Although a siesta on a hot day would occur not long after noon, the text indicates that it was evening before David decided to get up from his slumber. Moreover, the verb for walk about is a reflexive (*vayithālēk*), which indicates David was walking around in a leisurely manner (i.e., he was strolling around on the roof). Everything about this scene screams David's privileged position. He enjoyed the comforts of the palace while his servants were out risking their lives for the king.

Since David was on the roof of the king's house, he had the vantage point of looking down on the houses nearby. Scholars have often noted the symbolism of the king's power and authority captured by this imagery. David **saw a**

woman bathing on the roof while he was walking about, and he noticed her physical beauty (v 2). The notice that David **saw** (*vayar'*) her is significant because it utilizes the same language that Yahweh used to refer to David when Samuel anointed him as king designate: "Yahweh does not see [*yir'eh*] as mortals see [*yir'eh*]; they look upon the outward appearance, but Yahweh looks [*yir'eh*] upon the heart" (1 Sam 16:7). Whereas the statement in 1 Sam 16:7 was intended to imply that David would be faithful to God, in this context it presupposes his moral downfall. The name of the woman is not given, only her physical description is provided: **the woman was very beautiful.** Thus David was not interested in her personally, only in her looks.

David sent and inquired about the woman, and it was reported to him that she was **Bathsheba, the daughter of Eliam and the wife of Uriah the Hittite** (v 3). The description of Bathsheba is significant. She is described as being in relationship to other men, notably her father and her husband. In essence, Bathsheba was not just an object to be conquered or manipulated; she was a valuable human being as both a daughter and a wife. David, however, perceived her and treated her in a manner that objectified her, and thus he disregarded her individual worth. In essence, she was an object to fulfill his needs, not a person to be loved.

■ **4-5** David's custom of dispatching people to do his bidding appears again in v 4: he "sent messengers [***and took***] her, and she came to him, and he lay with her" (NRSV). This series of verbs is significant syntactically because it indicates intentional and rapid action on the part of David; the kind one engages in with a single mind and purpose. Bathsheba is also the subject of one of the verbs ("she came to him"). The inclusion of Bathsheba within the string of verbs could be a sign that she was complicit in the affair (Finlay 2005, 223-26).

The careful reader of the text may wonder what Bathsheba's role was in meeting David: an obedient subject responding to the king's orders or willing participant who had something to gain? The LXX provides a different reading here, so that David is the one who initiates all of the action. It reads, "and [he] took her, and went into her, and he lay with her." Thus in the LXX account Bathsheba played a more passive role. Other sections of the narrative, however, indicate Bathsheba had much to gain both personally and politically from this tryst. It was her son Solomon who succeeded David on the throne, and Solomon reserved a seat for her right next to him when he was installed as king (1 Kgs 2:19).

The text also provides the notice that Bathsheba **had *cleaned* herself from her uncleanness** (v 4). This phrase is important grammatically because readers are left to wonder if this is included to say that she cleaned herself after sex with David, or that she had previously cleaned herself after her menstrual cycle. The distinction is important because if the latter option is correct, then the text is underscoring the notion that the baby belonged to David, not Uriah. However, the LXX translates this verse in a way that indicates she cleaned herself after the sexual encounter. The different textual traditions leave both options in view.

In a very terse way, the text recalls that Bathsheba **conceived** and **sent word** to David, **I am pregnant** (v 5). This short but powerful response initiated a series of responses from David in order to clean up the mess he had created.

■ **6-9** In response to Bathsheba's news, David **sent** to Joab who **sent** Uriah to David (v 6). The constant repetition of this verb indicates that David worked through a series of intermediary channels to do his bidding (the verb **sent** occurs eleven times in this chapter). In the process, however, it symbolizes the large gap between the king and the populace. It diminishes the personal contact between king and subject and it objectifies people in the process.

At David's command, Joab, in turn, **sent** Uriah to David. Throughout this section people came to David, but he never went to them. The same held true for Uriah: David sent for Uriah and he **came to him** (v 7). David only sent for Uriah because he was worried about covering up his sexual misdeed. David even feigned his true intentions with Uriah by inquiring about the welfare of the battle. In addition, he also gave Uriah the command to **go down to your house and wash your feet** (v 8). Unlike Bathsheba who had to "come up" to the king's house, Uriah was ordered to **go down** to his house. The phrase to **wash your feet** is a euphemism that implies Uriah should go home to have sexual relations with his wife.

David even tried to sweeten the deal by **sending a present after him** (v 8). Uriah, however, did not go home but **slept at the opening of the house of the king** (v 9). The verb here (šākab) is the same one that is used when David "lay" with Bathsheba. The contrast between David and Uriah could not be starker; Uriah lay on the ground at the entrance of the king's house, whereas David lay with Uriah's wife in the comforts of his house.

■ **10-13** In spite of his efforts, David was told that Uriah did not go home. **They told David** is a plural verb indicating that David's servants spied on Uriah in order to report back to the king (v 10). When questioned why he did not go home, Uriah responded, **the Ark and Israel and Judah are residing in booths and my lord Joab and the servants of my lord are camping in the field** (v 11). Uriah's response includes the use of two participles: **residing** (yōšbîm) and **camping** (hōnîm). This is significant because it conveys the notion that the ark and the troops remained in the field and thus fulfilled the directives of the king. The position of David's warriors stood in stark contrast to that of the king, who was residing in his palace. Uriah also indicated that the thought of going to his house to eat and drink and to lie with his wife was anathema. Such behavior would break the code of conduct as a soldier and display disloyalty to the troops and his leaders.

Uriah's nobility and loyalty is quite apparent when contrasted with David's scurrilous actions. Uriah's nobility is reinforced by his statement: **as you live and as I live I would never do this thing** (v 11). Uriah's words amounted to an oath that meant if he did what David was asking him to do, both the king's life and his life should be taken. It is a sign of how serious he took his duty as a servant of the king and member of the army.

David could only respond by ordering Uriah to stay with the king that day and the next. The order to stay may indicate that David needed some time to figure how he could manipulate his plan and get Uriah to cover his mistake. David tried one last time to get Uriah to go home by plying him with strong drink (v 13). The verb **made him drunk** (*vāyšakkrēhû*) indicates that David had an active and intentional role in altering Uriah's judgment and inhibitions. The plan failed, however, because Uriah ***stayed on his couch with the servants of his lord.*** A powerful point is made here; Uriah, the drunken soldier, is more righteous than David, the sober king.

2. David Has Uriah Murdered (11:14-27)

■ **14-15** When David's ploy to get Uriah to go home failed, he was left with only one option: murder. David couched his efforts to eliminate Uriah in an elaborate scheme. David chose to send a letter with Uriah (***by hand***) with instructions to leave him vulnerable to attack on the battlefield: "Set Uriah in the forefront of the [***battle***], and then draw back from him, so that he may be struck down and die" (v 15 NRSV). Unknowingly, Uriah essentially carried his own death warrant to the man who would execute David's orders.

It is also ironic that kings in ancient times would generally employ battlefield strategies that ensured success over his enemies. In this context, however, David believed that the death of one of his men signaled a victory for himself. No word is given about what Joab thought of David's command to have Uriah die on the battlefield, but it did expose David in the sense that Joab became aware of David's evil machinations.

■ **16-25** Joab followed the orders given to him by the king and he "assigned Uriah to the place where he knew there were valiant warriors" (v 16 NRSV). Not surprisingly, Uriah died while fighting the men of the city, including "some of the servants of David" (v 17 NRSV). This last phrase is significant because it indicates David not only was responsible for the death of Uriah but was also culpable for the other warriors who unwittingly became "collateral damage" in David's scheme.

David's plan unfolded as he intended, and Joab sent word back to David about "all the news about the fighting" (v 18 NRSV). Joab instructed the messenger not to worry if David became angry at the news that his men were fighting ***close to the wall*** where soldiers were vulnerable to attack (Judg 9:53). Joab knew the messenger carried the news David coveted: **your servant Uriah . . . is dead** (2 Sam 11:21). The messenger delivered the news to David as instructed, even providing an elaborate explanation why the servants of David fought so close to the wall. In delivering the message to David, however, the servant waited until the very end of his report to tell David that Uriah had died in the battle.

David's response to the battle report in vv 22-25 is recorded differently in the LXX and MT traditions. In the LXX David became indignant when he initially heard the description of the events surrounding the battle (v 22). He questioned the strategy of fighting so close to the wall of the city, even citing the case of Abimelech (Judg 9:53) as a reason why the troops should not have been stationed there. David's anger subsided when told of the news that Uriah was dead (2 Sam 11:25). David's angry reply is missing in the MT version as well as the reference to the story of Abimelech.

Although David responded calmly to the news he received (in the MT), the reader can only surmise that David felt a sense of relief realizing that this ugly affair was nearing a conclusion. David took heart when he learned of Uriah's death and even dispatched a reassuring message to Joab basically telling him to not to be *troubled* by the temporary setback and to keep pressing the attack on the city (v 25). Emboldened by this news, David even gave instruction to **encourage** Joab.

■ **26-27** The text sharply contrasts David's relief at the news of Uriah's demise with Bathsheba's grief upon learning of the death of her husband. The text indicates that no one officially told her of Uriah's death but she simply **heard that Uriah was dead** (v 26). The text makes it sound as though the report of her husband's death was a bad rumor that she heard second hand. Bathsheba's grief is indicated by the notice that she **lamented over him.** The word that is used here to convey her grief (*vatispōd*) can also be translated "wailed," which was customary behavior after the loss of a loved one.

In OT times, lamenting the dead usually lasted a period of seven days (Gen 50:10); the same period that David gave Bathsheba before sending for her and bringing her to his house. David married Bathsheba and she bore him a son. The syntax and the grammar underscore the notion that the child was David's, not Uriah's. Moreover, the birth announcement of a son heralded a potential successor to David. The son born to David, however, would never grow old enough to become a candidate for the throne.

3. Nathan Confronts David (12:1-15a)

■ **1-4** David's actions toward Bathsheba and Uriah were called *an evil thing* by the writer of this text. Chapter 12 represents God's response to David's impropriety in ch 11. In a somewhat humorous manner, the writer of this text remarks that **Yahweh sent Nathan to David** (v 1). It was noted in ch 11 that David was notorious for sending people to do his dirty work: whether to arrange his meeting with Bathsheba or the death of Uriah. Here, God sent a prophet to confront David. The text reads that Nathan **came to David,** which was also true of Bathsheba (11:4) and Uriah (11:7). On this occasion, however, the king never sent for Nathan as he had for Bathsheba and Uriah. The text does not contain a preface to Nathan's arrival; rather, he went to the king unexpectedly and immediately told a parable. This literary construction would indicate that the message he came to deliver was an urgent one.

The story/parable that Nathan recounted would have used images and props from daily life so that the listener would have been drawn into the story. Much like the parables of Jesus (Matt 13:31-32; 18:23-25; Mark 4:1-9; Luke 10:29-37; 15:3-7, 11-32), the hearing audience would have been riveted to the details of the story, thus disarming them of defensiveness. The same was true with David since Nathan's story of the rich man, the poor man, and the lamb was intended to leave David vulnerable to the impact of its message. Nathan's parable was poignant and employed wonderful storytelling techniques. David was so drawn into the story that he did not perceive that the characters represented David (the rich man), Uriah (the poor man), and Bathsheba (the ewe lamb).

Elements of the story are also very touching. The ewe lamb, for example, is called a **daughter** because the poor man considered it to be a family member (v 3). Creative wordplays are also apparent. The word used for the **traveler** who came to visit the rich man (*'ōrēah*) sounds very similar to the name Uriah (*'ûriyyâ*). The term **came to** in v 4 is also used in conjunction with Bathsheba and Uriah earlier in ch 11 (vv 4, 7).

■ **5-6** When David learned that the rich man took the poor man's ewe, he became indignant. The text first notes that *the anger of David burned against the man much* (v 5). The language used to describe David's response is often used to illustrate Yahweh's reaction when the Israelites sinned against him. Second, David pronounced a severe judgment on the man who stole the lamb. David claimed that the man *deserved death* and the *lamb should be restored four times over for not showing compassion* (v 6).

David's response in v 6 is significant because the king in the ancient world was responsible for ensuring that justice was carried out in society. By proclaiming a judgment on the man in the parable, David unwittingly brought judgment on himself. The second part of the sentence (*the lamb should be restored four times*) is particularly noteworthy, especially as it relates to the story of David. David did pay fourfold for his actions in that he lost four sons before Solomon was made king: the baby born to Bathsheba, Amnon, Absalom, and Adonijah. It was only after the fourth son died that Solomon became king. Solomon's name is also operative since the Hebrew term for "make restitution" or "restore" (*šilēm* or *šilūmah*) is linguistically based off the same Hebrew root of Solomon's name (*šlōmōh*).

The text indicates that David would pay or make restitution for the life of Uriah with the lives of his own sons. Only after restitution was completed could there be peace. Solomon's name is also relevant since it is linguistically related to the word for peace (*šālôm*). Thus, when Solomon came to the throne there was peace because restitution had been made for David's transgressions.

■ **7-12** While David unknowingly indicted himself with the pronouncement of a sentence; Nathan made the judgment clear with the words **You are the man!** (v 7). David had been so engrossed in the narrative that he did not even realize that the story pertained to him.

Nathan's response to David highlights two important notions. First, he recounted God's gracious action toward David. Nathan reminded David that God had given David Saul's house, his wives, and the kingdoms of Israel and Judah. Even with everything that God had given David, he still did not have enough. Nathan even noted that God would have been willing to give David more had he been obedient. The second aspect of Nathan's oracle to David amounted to a judgment sentence on David and his household. The word of judgment includes the use of the word **sword** (*hereb*) in vv 9-10. David had been instrumental in cutting down Uriah by the sword of the Ammonites, now God would cause a sword to rise up on his own household.

As the story of David unfolds in the following chapters, Nathan's words prove true in that David's household is characterized by incest, murder, and insurrection. Nathan's statement in v 11, "I will take your wives before your eyes, and give them to your neighbor, and he shall lie with your wives in the sight of this very sun," speaks of the events that transpired during Absalom's revolt. Absalom had intercourse with David's concubines (secondary wives) out in the open so that everyone could see (16:20-22). This gesture signaled that Absalom had replaced David as the king.

■ **13-15a** To his credit, however, David confessed that he had **sinned against Yahweh** when he heard the words of Nathan (12:13). In the story of David, the two times he was confronted by the prophets for his sinful behavior, he humbled himself in contrition before God. This is one reason why the editor(s) of the DtrH maintained a high regard for David and considered him a faithful and righteous figure (1 Kgs 9:4; 11:4, 6, 33; 14:8; 15:3, 5, 11; 2 Kgs 14:3; 16:2; 18:3; 22:2). God, in response to David's confession, allowed David to live, but the child that was to be born would die. After Nathan delivered this news, he departed to his house.

12:7-19

4. The Death of One Child, the Birth of Another (12:15b-25)

■ **15b-19** The prophet's word regarding the child is fulfilled in this section. The text notes that **Yahweh struck the child which was born to the wife of Uriah** (v 15). The language that is used here is very similar to the plague narratives and the ark traditions where Yahweh struck people with various calamities, including death. That Yahweh would strike an innocent child indicates that the circumstances surrounding the birth of this child were sinful. It is also significant that the text does not call the child's mother Bathsheba but simply calls her the wife of Uriah. The text still envisions Bathsheba in relationship to Uriah. David **sought God on account of the young boy; he fasted, and went** *in and lay on the ground* (v 16). David engaged in this act of mourning and contrition in hopes that God would reverse the fortunes of the child.

Even though David would not eat with the elders of his house for seven days, the child still died. The servants of David were afraid to convey the news to David, thinking that David may do injury to himself. However, when David saw that the servants were whispering among each other, he perceived that something was wrong. David therefore asked the servants, **Is the child dead?** They simply responded in the affirmative: **He is dead** (v 19).

■ **20-23** With the definitive news about the child, David reversed his actions. David rose up, washed, anointed himself, and changed his clothes. The text notes that he also *went into the house of Yahweh and worshiped* (v 20). The text includes an anachronism at this point, because the term "house of Yahweh" refers to the temple. This is evidence that this narrative was written down at a time when the temple had been completed, possibly from the time of Solomon or later. The change in David's behavior perplexed his servants, but David knew that since the child died, there was nothing he could do to bring the child back to life.

■ **24-25** The narrative at this juncture moves from the death of one child to the birth of another. David **comforted** Bathsheba over the loss of the child (v 24). Thanks to David's actions, Bathsheba suffered and mourned the loss of two important people: Uriah, her husband, and a newborn son. Unlike the scenario in 11:3, Bathsheba is called David's wife (v 24*a*, **his wife**) for the first time along with the notice that *he came to her;* a reversal of "she came to him" (11:3). David **lay with her** and she *conceived and bore a son.* David gave his son the name **Solomon,** which has tremendous significance for his role in the Succession Narrative (see Introduction and comments on 12:5-6).

The conditions surrounding the birth of the two sons born could not be more different: the first was born as a result of an illicit tryst and murderous cover-up; the second through an act of tender consolation. The first child died as a consequence of David's sin; the birth of the second son received God's approbation.

The first sign that God approved of this child includes the notice that *Yahweh loved him* (v 25). The confirmation of Yahweh's favor is also highlighted in the message brought by the prophet Nathan. The son was given the name **Jedidiah**. The name **Jedidiah** literally means ***Beloved of Yahweh,*** thus underscoring the child's divine sponsorship. An explanation for the inclusion of the second name is problematic. Kings would receive a throne name upon their accession, thus it might be possible to see Solomon as the personal name and Jedidiah as the throne name. However, Jedidiah is conspicuously absent in the Solomon narrative (1 Kgs 1—11), and it occurs nowhere else in the OT. It may be better to take it as a sign of the child's favored status, as in the case of some other biblical figures (i.e., Jacob, Gen 32:28) (Gordon 1986, 260).

5. The War Against Ammon (12:26-31)

■ **26-31** The brief notice regarding the siege against **Rabbah** in v 26 continues and completes the notice about the attack in 11:1. Thus, the David and Bathsheba affair is set within the larger context of Israel's war against the Ammonites. In this phase of the battle, Joab fought the Ammonites and took Rabbah, which is called "the royal city" (NRSV; i.e., the capital).

The text underscores the notion that Joab led the troops in battle and brought them to the brink of victory. Joab sent word to David that he should be the one to conquer the city lest Joab be given credit for the triumph and the city would be named after him. David gathered the people and fought against Rabbah and ***took it*** (v 29). Although David is given credit for the conquest, it was Joab who essentially laid the groundwork for David's success.

David subsequently took ***the crown of Milcom off his head*** and **it was placed on David's head** (v 30). Milcom was the chief deity of the Ammonites, and the crown would have been worn by a cult statue of Milcom. Placing Milcom's crown on David's head commemorated David's triumph and symbolized his dominion over the people there. The crown was impressive by any standards; it weighed **a talent of gold** (roughly seventy-five pounds) and contained "a precious stone" (v 30 NRSV). David also put the citizens of the city to work with **saws** and **iron picks and axes** and to the "brickworks" (v 31 NRSV). David most likely had them involved in tearing down the city's fortifications, thus ensuring that it would not be a threat to David or his kingdom in the future.

FROM THE TEXT

1. The story of David, Bathsheba, and Uriah reveals that David's indiscretion came about as a result of some bad choices that culminated in one major catastrophe. First, David remained at home in the comfort of his palace while his army went off to fight in battle. As the king, David's main responsibility entailed leading his troops into war against Israel's enemies. David's dereliction of duty placed him in a situation he never should have been in.

Second, when David learned of Bathsheba's identity and that she was the wife of Uriah, he should never have pursued the matter any further. David, however, wantonly dismissed this information and disregarded the feelings of the people involved in order to pursue his own lustful desires. As king, David had plenty of his own concubines and wives available to him, and he could have attained more if his heart desired. Instead of being content with what he had, however, he coveted a person who belonged to another.

It is significant to note that the course of events in David's life could have been completely different if he simply would have been where he was supposed to have been in the first place. Even though he was remiss in his duties and stayed in Jerusalem, he did not have to compound the situation by making another bad choice. Thus it was a chain of events that snowballed into a bad situation.

The same principles hold true in modern life. We can make a bad situation worse by compounding a series of smaller mistakes. Instead of recognizing our failures, seeking forgiveness, and making restitution when they first occur, we often try to cover up our initial transgression by committing more sin. How many friendships, marriages, and business/work relationships, for example, could have been rescued had the offending party simply owned up to the mistake and sought to be restored. We often hear the phrase "If only he [she] would have been honest with me from the beginning" then the situation could have turned out differently. Unfortunately, arrogance, fear, or shame prevents us from admitting wrongdoing from the onset, thus deceitfully keeping the indiscretion hidden from those it would hurt.

The same principle holds true in other scenarios as well. How many wonderful opportunities in life have been squandered because of the failure to confront destructive behaviors from the onset: dishonesty, laziness, drug addiction, alcoholism, unhealthy eating habits, lack of financial discipline, or a stubborn unwillingness to take advice or listen to wise counsel? Left unchecked, even smaller, less egregious actions can lead to pain, heartache, and regret.

2. We also learn from David that kings (and leaders in general) have the ability to abuse their power. Even good kings, when entrusted with complete authority, can become infatuated with power and disillusioned to think that they can use that power unabated. It is significant that David's personal troubles and moral failures only occur after he made his residence in Jerusalem as the unquestioned leader of the people of Israel.

On his path to the throne, David relied upon God for his strength and looked to God for direction. As David reached the apex of his political journey, his attitude and perspective changed dramatically. In ch 8 David exhibited the desire to expand his power and influence through a series of conquests. Whereas in ch 8 David's focus was on the conquest of nations, ch 11 includes David's conquest of individuals. David's quest for power appears to have been insatiable as he attempted to subdue nations and the people he governed. As the king exercised his power in selfish and cruel ways, the people he governed were hurt in the process. This is evident not only in the story of David and Bathsheba but also in the narrative when David took a census. David took a census in order to increase the power of the king and the state, but in the end it was the people who suffered for David's actions (2 Sam 24:1-17).

3. Even though David was the supreme ruler of the land, he was neither above God nor above his law. David still had to answer to God and when he transgressed God's law, God sent the prophet to confront him. Even though David committed this sin in secret, God was aware of his wrongdoing and brought it to light.

To David's credit, when the prophet Nathan confronted David about his sin, David confessed his wrongdoing. Even though God forgave David, he would still have to face the consequences of his sin. As the story of David unfolds, the reader is aware that David paid a heavy price both personally and professionally for the adultery and murder he committed. A number of David's children died, his family was beset by all manner of dysfunction and strife, and his control of the kingdom was threatened as Absalom fomented a revolt against his father. All of this was in response to the word of the prophet who warned him of the trouble that would come about for his actions. Even though God loved David and caused him to prosper, God could not allow his behavior to go unpunished.

Through David's example we learn the important lesson that we reap what we sow (Gal 6:7-9). Even though we serve a gracious and forgiving God, God does not always spare us the consequences of our actions. These consequences are often reminders of our past and the harsh penalty sin metes out to its victims. Being justified does not necessarily mean that we will not bear the marks of poor decisions made. God can forgive the thief, for example, but the thief still has to face incarceration. God can forgive the income tax cheater, but the IRS will still complete the audit and levy a fine. God can forgive the drunken driver but not bring the innocent victim back to life. God can forgive the cheating spouse, but it does not ensure that the marriage will be restored. Even as we face the consequences of our sin, however, God can be at work in lives to bring healing and hope. God can teach us new lessons about his love and grace, and he gives us the strength to move beyond a past that tries to rob us of a future.

D. The Rape of Tamar and Murder of Amnon (13:1—14:33)

BEHIND THE TEXT

These two chapters are taken together based on literary and thematic grounds. The opening phrase in 13:1, ***and it happened after*** indicates a new chapter in the life of David, and a series of *vav* conjunctives that run throughout ch 14 indicate these two larger units belong together. Moreover, the opening phrase in 15:1 delineates another unit that takes up the narrative regarding Absalom's revolt against David. The material in chs 15—19 therefore serves as a fitting complement for the events that are recorded in chs 13—14.

In these two chapters, the conditions are presented that ultimately led to the rise of Absalom as the chief antagonist to his father. Chapter 13 relates how Amnon raped his half-sister, Tamar, and Absalom's and David's reactions toward Amnon. Absalom not only became angry at Amnon for raping his sister, but he also hatched the scheme that would take his brother's life.

David, on the other hand, became angry at Amnon for his actions but did not take any disciplinary action against him. These texts portray David as a weak father who failed to discipline his own son and thus provided the impetus for Absalom to take revenge on Amnon.

The text also implicates David in that he inadvertently contributed to the situation that would lead to Absalom's revolt. Not only did David's inaction stoke Absalom's anger against David, but David's willingness to allow his son to return home gave Absalom the opportunity to gather a following and foment a rebellion against his father. Thus, chs 13—14 must be taken together as the basis for Absalom's rebellion (chs 15—19) in that they provide the essential causes for it.

IN THE TEXT

1. Opening Scene (13:1-5)

■ 1 These first five verses provide the context for the following narrative. As mentioned above, 13:1 opens a new literary unit with the phrase, **and it happened afterwards.** Although the text does not distinguish which episode is referred to by this statement, the canonical setting indicates that this unit is intended to occur after the David and Bathsheba incident. These opening words may indicate an undisclosed period of time had elapsed, but the fact that they are placed right after David's affair with Bathsheba and Uriah's murder indicate the ideological/theological intentions of the editor(s) responsible for the shaping of these texts. By placing it in this literary context, the Deuteronomistic Historian(s) intended to show that the events that happen in chs 13—19 are directly related to David's adultery and murder, and thereby confirm the prophetic statements of Nathan in 12:10.

These opening verses also introduce the main characters of the narrative. In this chapter, the text focuses on David's children and the internal confusion within his own family. David's son **Absalom** (which means "my father is peace") is mentioned first, but only briefly. Although he does not appear in the story until later (v 20), the narrator takes special care to draw attention to him since he has a profound effect on David's story. Absalom is called the **son of David**, and his mother was Maacah, the Geshurite princess and daughter of Talmai (2 Sam 3:3).

It should be noted here that Maacah was a Canaanite woman, which was contrary to legislation that forbade intermarriage with foreigners (Deut 7:1-4). This provides evidence that the Deuteronomistic texts forbidding or outlawing intermarriage with non-Israelites were a later development than the time of David. Even so, the text bears out that the son of a Canaanite woman brought personal pain and anguish to David.

Absalom is said to have a sister, **Tamar**, who is essentially called **beautiful**. The text says nothing about her character but refers only to her appearance, which is so critical to the plotline of the story. Like his sister, Absalom will be noted for his nice looks (14:25).

The text introduces **Amnon** last. He is mentioned only in relationship to Tamar; he *loved her.* Tamar was the half-sister to Amnon, since he was the son of Ahinoam (2 Sam 3:2). As we have mentioned elsewhere, Ahinoam may have been the former wife of Saul (see comments on 1 Sam 25:43-44; 27:3). If true, then it would indicate that blood ties to the house of Saul existed within David's own household. Moreover, David's complex family arrangement had an important bearing on the succession to the throne, because Amnon was the oldest son and he was in line to follow David. Thus, it was conceivable that someone connected to the line of Saul could have regained the monarchy.

This fact has tremendous implications for how we are to understand the political ramifications of David's family and the unfolding drama in the following chapters. The story of Amnon and Tamar/Absalom pits two different family units against each other: the children of Ahinoam on one hand and the children of Maacah on the other.

■ **2-5** The text also reports that Amnon was *depressed* to the point of *making himself sick* on account of Tamar (v 2). The second verb is a reflexive (*lĕhithḥalōt*), which indicates that Amnon brooded over Tamar to the extent that he made himself physically ill. Amnon was also troubled because Tamar was a **virgin** and *there was nothing he could do* to change his circumstances. Biblical law prevented a son from sleeping with his (half) sister (Lev 18:9), but this legislation likely postdated the time of David (Alter 1999, 268). As a virgin, Tamar may have been chaperoned, making it difficult for Amnon to carry out his carnal intentions. The term for virgin (*bětūlâ*), however, can also mean a young woman of marriageable age (Gordon 1986, 262). Amnon may not have been looking for a long-term relationship with her, only a one-time dalliance (2 Sam 13:15). Both interpretive options remain possible.

Amnon received help and advice from **Jonadab,** Amnon's cousin and the son of **Shimeah,** David's brother (v 3). Little is known about Jonadab except that he is called *very wise* (*mě'ōd ḥākām*). The language implies that Jonadab was **shrewd** or "crafty" (NRSV); the type of person who is "resourceful." His advice to Amnon: pretend to be sick and ask your father to have Tamar feed you, which provided a pretext so that he could be alone with Tamar without David knowing his real intentions.

2. Amnon Rapes Tamar (13:6-22)

■ **6-10** Amnon took Jonadab's counsel and feigned illness. When David came to visit him, Amnon requested that Tamar come and *make cakes* for him so that he could eat from her hand (v 6). Amnon's inability to sit up would be proof that he was sick. In response to Amnon's request *David sent to the house of Tamar* (v 7). The king once more "sends" for someone to do his bidding (see ch 11); in this case, it was his daughter Tamar. The reference to

Tamar's house raises questions about the manner in which David's family was organized in the palace complex. Tamar will go to Absalom's house at the behest of David (***Go to the house of your brother Amnon and make for him food*** [v 7]). It appears not only that David's children had quarters different from the king's but also that the various families were situated in different residences within the royal dwellings.

The manner in which David ordered Tamar to serve Amnon indicates that she was treated like one of the servants. When Tamar came to Amnon's house, he was **lying down** (v 8). Like his father before him, a troubled situation involving a sexual scandal started with someone lying down (11:2). The text goes to great lengths to talk about the food that she prepared for her brother. Tamar ***took the dough and kneaded it, and made cakes before his eyes, and baked the cakes*** (13:8). The careful description about the food preparations intimates that Amnon had the opportunity to ogle his sister lustfully before he physically touched her. When Amnon **refused to eat** the food, he ordered all those that were in the room to leave (***get out!***). The verb here is a causative command (*hōṭi'û*), underscoring his sordid intentions (v 9).

■ **11-14** With the room cleared, Amnon gave the order for Tamar to bring the food into the bedroom so that he could eat from her hand. The conditions were ripe for him to enact his scheme. When Tamar brought the cakes to him, Amnon **grabbed her** and ordered her to "come, lie with me" (v 11 NRSV). The language employed in this verse is significant. The first verb (*vayaḥăzeq*) is a causative followed by a Hebrew preposition with a feminine pronoun (*bâ*). This construction connotes the idea that Amnon seized her with brute force, as when a man molests a woman. Thus the text indicates that he preyed upon her.

The second half of the verse utilizes two commands: "come" and "lie with me." Tamar was not only seized but also ordered to lie down with him. The text, with the use of two commands, strongly indicates that Tamar was not a willing participant in this affair but was being forced to do something against her will. This phrase also recalls the Joseph novella when Potiphar's wife tried to get him to sleep with her against Joseph's wishes (Gen 39:7).

Tamar's remarks in 2 Sam 13:12 indicate the severity of Amnon's actions: ***Do not force me because such a thing is not done in Israel; do not do this foolish thing.*** The word for ***force*** (*'ānah*) can mean to humble through cohabitation (i.e., raping her), thus degrading her. The word for ***foolish*** (*nebālâ*) can also imply something that is disgraceful, especially according to Israel's standards. Some even translate this as "vile" (NRSV) or "wanton folly" (RSV). The language that is utilized here also echoes the story of the rape of the Levite's concubine (Judg 19:23).

Since Amnon was bent on raping her, Tamar made the proposal that Amnon should speak to the king because "he will not withhold me from you" (2 Sam 13:13 NRSV). This response may appear confusing at first to the modern reader. If David gave Amnon permission to marry Tamar, would the union between the two family members somehow be legitimate? It may also be possible to consider that Tamar was using this invitation as a ploy of her own in order to get out of a difficult situation. Considering that she did not have a physical advantage over Amnon, this "proposal" provided her an opportunity to free herself from Amnon's advances.

Tamar's suggestion went unheeded, for Amnon was **unwilling to listen to her** (v 14). The construction in Hebrew can also be rendered "obey" or "hearken to" (KJV). Although it can be utilized in one's relationship to God (1 Sam 15:1), it can also be used in reference to human relationships. Unwilling to harken to her request, Amnon **was stronger than her and he lay with her** (v 14). The language is specific and connotes that the action was committed against her will, thus constituting rape.

■ **15-19** Amnon's love for Tamar was soon changed into severe contempt. Amnon ordered her to get out, but Tamar refused initially. Tamar's response reflects legislation that a young man was required to marry a virgin that he raped (Exod 22:16; Deut 22:28-29).

Tamar's unwillingness to leave required Amnon to have her forcefully removed from his presence. Tamar was "escorted" out and the door to Amnon's room was bolted after her. Amnon's language to his servant in 2 Sam 13:17, **Send out please this (one) out of my presence,** reflects his brutal treatment of Tamar by not specifying her name but by referring to her almost as an estranged person (i.e., **this [one]**).

Amnon's actions not only embarrassed and disgraced him but also brought shame on Tamar. As a result of her grief, Tamar **put ashes on her head** and **tore the ornamented robe** (*kĕtōnet hapasîm*) that she was wearing and went out of the room "crying" (NRSV). Interestingly, Joseph is the only other figure in the OT to have a "multicolored robe" (*kĕtōnet hapasîm*), which was torn and soaked in blood (Gen 37:29-33). We can probably assume that Tamar's tunic was also stained, since she was a virgin (Deut 22:13-21).

■ **20-22** It was only after Tamar had been raped and humiliated that her brother Absalom enters the story. The text does not indicate a time element here, but the grammar of 2 Sam 13:20 insinuates that Absalom conversed with his sister immediately after the incident with Amnon. Absalom most likely observed her disheveled appearance and knew what had just taken place. His question, "Has Amnon your brother been with you?" assumes that he knew something of a sexual nature transpired (v 20 NRSV). Absalom instructed her to keep quiet about the incident and Tamar remained a desolate woman in her brother's house. David, meanwhile, heard of Amnon's actions and became angry over the report. The language would indicate that he was livid or extremely upset (he was **greatly incensed**) over what happened (v 21). Yet, he did nothing to punish his son. Absalom, however, **hated** Amnon for violating his sister (v 22*b*). He would take action against Amnon in light of David's failure to provide discipline.

3. Absalom's Revenge (13:23-39)

■ **23-27** The text indicates that there is a considerable gap between v 22 and v 23. The events of v 23 pick up **two years** after Amnon's rape. No indication is provided as to what happened during that period, but the reader may conclude that Absalom's anger simmered for two years while he concocted a way to get revenge on his half-brother.

At the end of the two years, Absalom invited David to join him for the ***sheep shearing festival*** (v 24). Although sheepshearing could include hard work, it also included a time of merrymaking and carousing (v 28). David rejected Absalom's request to join him in the festivities even though his son "pressed him" to go (v 25 NRSV). Absalom took this opportunity to express his desire to invite Amnon to go in place of David. Whether Absalom seized this opportunity only after David refused to go or whether he had this planned out before is difficult to say. Absalom may have anticipated David's response in light of the fact that they did not share a close father-son bond.

The sheepshearing feast was scheduled to take place at a town named **Baal Hazor** (v 23). This city lay about twenty miles north of Jerusalem in the central hill country. If Absalom had premeditated revenge on his mind, this gave him the opportunity to isolate Amnon and carry out his plan. David did not understand why he would invite Amnon to the festival. David's question, ***Why would he go with you?*** probably indicates that relations between the two sons were strained or even acrimonious as a result of the previous events (v 26). Absalom, however, "pressed" David on the issue and David ***sent Amnon with him.*** The language here may indicate that Amnon may not have wanted to go originally but David made him go with all the king's sons (v 27). David here appears either naive or careless in sending Amnon with Absalom considering their personal histories. The results would be tragic for Amnon.

■ **28-29** The following scene opens with Absalom giving instructions to his servants at the feast. Although the Hebrew text does not provide much information about it, the LXX says that "Absalom made a feast like the feast of a king." 4QSam^a includes the phrase, "Absalom prepared a royal feast." The repast would have included much drinking and carousing, and Absalom's plan depended on Amnon becoming drunk. Absalom gave the order to his servants that when "Amnon's heart is merry with wine" then they were supposed to strike him down (v 28 NRSV). The servants carried out the order of Absalom and killed Amnon. Whereas David tried and failed to cover his mistake by getting Uriah drunk (11:13), Absalom succeeded in atoning for Amnon's crime through excessive celebration.

■ **30-33** The false report that Absalom killed all the king's sons reached David. Accordingly, David responded with grief by tearing his garments and lying on the ground. Jonadab, the uncle of Amnon, tried to calm David saying that ***only Amnon died, for it was determined by Absalom from the day that his sister was raped*** (v 32). Jonadab's statement raises an interesting question. How did he know that only Amnon died and not the other brothers? David did not know this information based on his reaction to the news. It may indicate that Absalom somehow made his plan known to Jonadab beforehand. Was this therefore a plan to annihilate Amnon from the beginning? Was Tamar "set up" by her own brother in order make him the next eligible candidate for the throne? Or was Absalom only seeking revenge on Amnon for the rape of his sister, and David, for not disciplining Amnon appropriately? Although tantalizing questions in and of themselves, providing sufficient answers remains difficult.

■ **34-39** After the murder of Amnon, Absalom fled to King Talmai of Geshur. Absalom returned to his grandfather and the land of his mother's birth. He stayed there for **three years,** a considerable amount of time (v 38). It is noteworthy that after Absalom returned from Geshur he fomented the revolt against David. In this respect, Absalom resembled Jeroboam I, who also took refuge in a foreign territory only to come home and take part in a rebellion against the house of David (1 Kgs 12:20-33). Was Absalom plotting the coupe while taking residence with his grandfather? Was Talmai possibly involved with the plan to overthrow David? Although the text does not say this, it does raise strong possibilities however.

4. Absalom Returns to Jerusalem (14:1-24)

The opening of ch 14 connects well grammatically with the end of ch 13. Two pieces of information here are vital. One, the text notes that Absalom stayed with Talmai for three years (2 Sam 13:38). Two, David consoled himself with the death of Amnon (13:39). The Hebrew text is somewhat difficult to translate in 13:39 since it appears to be missing a word. Reconstructions based on some LXX manuscripts and 4QSam^a read 13:39a as, **and the spirit of David the king pined to go out to Absalom.** The latter half of v 39 then reads, **because he was comforted over Amnon because he died.** The verb for comfort here (*niḥam*) can mean "to repent or console oneself." These two vital pieces of information thus indicate that Absalom was located far from home and that David "came to terms" with Amnon's death. The end of ch 13 sets the stage for Absalom's return in the following verses.

■ **1-11** Absalom's return was mediated through a third party, David's general Joab. Joab called upon a **wise woman** from the city of Tekoa as the agent to facilitate the reconciliation (v 2). Tekoa was a small city not far from Jerusalem, the same city from which the prophet Amos hailed (Amos 1:1). Whether or not Tekoa was known as a center for fostering Israelite wisdom tradition remains up for debate (Isbell 1977, 213 ff.). Although not a sage, the woman could "discern, articulate, and practice life outside the categories of bureaucratic perception" (Brueggemann 1990, 292). Joab instructed the woman to dress up as a mourner and deliver a specific message to the king. Joab, however, **put the words in her mouth** (2 Sam 14:3). The last phrase may indicate that the "wisdom" actually derived from Joab and not from the woman (see v 19).

The woman claimed to be a **widow** and presented David the story of two brothers. She recounted that the brothers were standing in a field when one of the brothers struck and killed the other. Not only does the situation the woman described parallel Absalom's, but the issue of fratricide and the phrase **in the field** also recalls the narrative of Cain and Abel (Gen 4:8). The woman also noted that the family members rose up against the other brother so that they could avenge the life of the one that was killed. However, killing the surviving son would also wipe out the only remaining descendant of the family ("quench . . . one remaining ember" [v 7 NRSV]). The woman's plight was identical to the one transpiring in David's household.

David was so engrossed in the woman's tale that he did not realize she was speaking of the king's son (for similar reaction see 12:1-7). When David heard the woman's request, he reassured her that no one else would be destroyed and that her son's life would be spared. By rendering this judgment, David also preserved the life of Absalom. As in the story of Cain and Abel, the offender would not experience retribution for his actions (Gen 4:14-15).

■ **12-24** In giving his verdict, however, David also indicted himself. The oldest son who was banished from the kingdom would be allowed to return home to Jerusalem without the possibility of revenge being taken on him. The king ordered Joab to bring Absalom home; David would not escort his son (2 Sam 13:21). Joab's role in both facilitating the meeting with David and mediating Absalom's return is intriguing. Why did he have such a vested interest in Absalom's well-being? Did he have something personal to gain from Absalom's return? Joab's response to David in v 22 (that David had "granted the request of his servant" [NRSV]) implies that bringing Absalom home was a personal favor. Joab's efforts may point to his future political aspirations (see below).

Joab traveled to the territory of Geshur to retrieve Absalom. Although David allowed his son to return home, he did not permit him to come into the king's presence. Even though David permitted Absalom's return, he was essentially ostracized and remained nonexistent to the king (vv 28-33).

5. David Forgives Absalom (14:25-33)

■ **25-27** Within the context of Absalom's return, the text includes statements about Absalom's physical appearance in v 25: ***There was not a man in all Israel to be greatly praised for his beauty, from the sole of his foot to the top of his head there was no blemish.*** These details, although they may appear out of place, may give an indication why Joab decided to sponsor Absalom. Absalom had a tremendous reputation among the people, and the fact that he had **three sons and a daughter** indicated the potential for a dynasty if he became king after David. The emphasis on Absalom's physical attributes, however, reminds the reader of King Saul who, though physically gifted, turned out to be a colossal failure. The text seems to anticipate a similar fate for Absalom as well.

■ **28-33** Although Absalom was allowed to return to Jerusalem, he did not have contact with his father for **two years** (v 28). Since Absalom was barred from David's presence, he sought Joab's help in arranging a meeting with his father. Absalom had to resort to setting Joab's field on fire in order to get his attention. It is curious that Absalom had to utilize such tactics since he lived in proximity to Joab (i.e., their fields bordered each other). Does this suggest that Absalom was essentially confined to "house arrest" by David?

Absalom's actions succeeded in gaining Joab's attention. Joab inquired, "Why did your servants set fire to my field?" (v 31 JPS). Absalom revealed the true intentions of his actions; he wanted to find out why David had allowed him to return. Absalom had been ostracized by David, and he wanted to understand the reason why David shunned him. It would have been better for Absalom to have remained in Geshur than to be ignored by his father. Absalom also believed he was innocent in the matter of Amnon: "If there is guilt in me, let him kill me" (v 32). In Absalom's mind the death of Amnon was justified and should not have been the reason why he should remain alienated from David.

Persuaded by Absalom's plea, Joab went to David on his behalf. David summoned Absalom, who then came before David **with his face to the ground.** The text never records a conversation between David and Absalom; it only includes the notice that ***David kissed him*** (v 33). This gesture, by all accounts, indicated that David had forgiven Absalom, yet they remained estranged from each other.

14:28-33

FROM THE TEXT

The story of David's family problems reminds the reader that sin and disobedience have serious consequences. The events that unfolded among David's children are understood to have stemmed from David's affair with Bathsheba and the murder of Uriah. David's family was beset by issues of rape, murder, and rebellion. The narrative, however, implicates David for the disastrous events that took place in his family.

First, the children of David mimicked or emulated the behavior of their father. Amnon's desire to have a woman he was not supposed to have reminds the audience of David's desire to obtain Bathsheba, even if it meant using cruel tactics to get what he wanted. David exhibited a poor example for his children to follow. Amnon was born while David was in Hebron, so he would have been a young man by the time David came to Jerusalem. Amnon had many years to observe his father and watch the example that he set for his sons. By all accounts, David made a poor impression on his children and they, in turn, perpetuated the same mistakes that David had made. It is ironic that David could exercise control over the people he governed, but he could not manage his own family.

Second, David also created the conditions that led to Absalom's rebellion. The text makes it clear that David never adequately punished Amnon for his criminal treatment of Tamar. Because David did not address the situation, it opened the door for Absalom to get revenge on his brother. Thus by David's inaction, he allowed the situation to fester (for two years), which allowed Absalom's anger toward Amnon to continue to boil and gave him ample time to plan Amnon's murder.

If David would have addressed these issues when they first happened, a terrible situation could have been averted. David's attitude toward Absalom also created the conditions that inspired a rebellion against David. After Absalom murdered Amnon, Absalom was basically dead to David. The strained relationship is evident in that he went back to his mother's family and stayed there for three years. It was only through the mediation of Joab and the wise woman of Tekoa that Absalom was allowed to return to Jerusalem.

Even when Absalom lived in Jerusalem, David ostracized him and did not have contact with him for two years. Absalom was screaming for the attention of his father, and he even asked Joab why David ignored him. David only **summoned** Absalom, like a servant and not a son, after Joab interceded for Absalom. David never went running to meet him as he returned as the father did in the story of the prodigal son (Luke 15:11-32). Even when Absalom presented himself before David, the text never portrays a warm and emotional reconciliation between David and Absalom, only that David "kissed" his son. David may have "forgiven" Absalom, but the scene lacks the sense of genuine reparation of a broken relationship. Thus, it should come as no surprise to the reader that Absalom lacked deep respect and love for David and instead harbored bitterness and ill will. The revolt he fomented against David made that evident.

E. David's Flight from Jerusalem and His Return (15:1—19:43)

BEHIND THE TEXT

These chapters are taken together because they are bound by two major themes: David's flight from Jerusalem and David's return. In these narratives, the life of David comes full circle. Absalom fomented a revolt against David that drove him away from the capital city (ch 15), and David was escorted back into the land at its end (ch 19). In between these two fixed points, the text follows David as he and his supporters took refuge in the Transjordan, and Absalom as he asserted his newfound authority in the capital city his father vacated.

Throughout the narrative David was given support by those who remained faithful to him, even helping David overthrow Absalom and regain the throne. David also had his detractors who ridiculed and taunted him at one of the lowest points in his life. Absalom had his share of supporters as well who rallied around him and backed his coup. Absalom also sought to destroy his father but was later cut down by David's general. With the death of Absalom, the revolt was squelched and the door for David to return was opened.

On his return home, David showed his gratitude to those who remained loyal and gave him succor during his flight from Absalom. He even pardoned those who had hurled insults at him during his exile. The text indicates that not everyone was happy with Davidic kingship, as is evidenced by the revolt, but in the end they had to accept the fact that David would remain the king.

IN THE TEXT

1. Absalom Usurps the Throne (15:1-37)

■ **1-6** Absalom began his revolt against David by first establishing his political credentials among the populace. Absalom accomplished this by taking on the pomp and circumstance of kingship. He then raised questions about the efficiency and the ability of David's administration to administer justice among the people. Absalom's usurpation began openly as he **got a chariot and horses and had fifty men run in front of him** (v 1). Absalom's use of the chariot, horses, and the running escort signified his claim to royal status. David's son Adonijah would also try to gain power in a similarly high-handed fashion (1 Kgs 1:5).

Absalom would also get up early and **stand by the road to the gate** leading into the city (v 2). In ancient times, the city gate represented the place where business and judicial activity took place, and thus anyone having a dispute would have his case decided there. Absalom's plot to turn the people against his father also included raising dissatisfaction among those looking to find justice at the gate. Even though Absalom decided that an individual had a claim that was worthy to be heard by someone from David's administration (v 3), he reminded the people that **no one was from the king** to hear the case. It is not clear whether David was just negligent in his duties as king, or if he simply gave preference to the people of Judah and basically dismissed those from the northern tribes of Saul's kingdom. Absalom's inquiry, **What city are you from?** and the response, **Your servant is from one of the tribes of Israel,** may indicate the latter was true (v 3). Absalom only agitated the situation further by stating, **If I was appointed judge in the land, any man who had a complaint would come to me and I would give him justice and righteousness** (v 4). By highlighting the shortcomings of David's kingship, Absalom gradually created doubts in the minds of the people about David, reminded them why they should be dissatisfied with his leadership, and thereby set the stage for his takeover.

Absalom also gained favor with the people by the way he treated those seeking justice: he **put out his hand, took hold** of them **and kissed** them (v

5). This amounted to a sign of respect and a gesture of friendliness; the kind of personal touch that they were not receiving from David. Absalom's plan achieved success since he **stole the heart of all the people of Israel** (v 6). The Hebrew grammar is significant here, because in some contexts the word can mean "to deceive" (Gen 31:20, 26). If this reading applies, it brings new meaning to Absalom's intentions in that the text implies he was using the people as pawns for his own benefit.

■ **7-12** Absalom's revolt, although only in its infancy at this juncture, included a secondary strategy. Absalom sought permission from David to go to Hebron to **fulfill a vow** when he was in Geshur, his mother's home territory (v 7). Although the text never records this vow, Absalom claimed that he needed to return to Hebron and worship Yahweh. This was a ruse orchestrated by Absalom so that he could join with the people of Hebron against David. Hebron represented Absalom's birthplace (3:3) and David's old capital.

The people in Hebron appeared to be dissatisfied with David as well, and they may have harbored ill will toward the king for moving his capital to Jerusalem. Since they knew Absalom and supported his cause, they joined with him and looked to him as their king. Absalom also took with him **two hundred men** from Jerusalem. These men were **innocent** and did not know of Absalom's intentions (v 11). The unsuspecting men may have lessened any suspicions that Absalom's trip to Hebron may have raised. It is also possible that Absalom intended to use them as hostages to influence their families in Jerusalem once the coup took place.

Absalom also enlisted the support and counsel of David's adviser Ahithophel. Ahithophel was from the city of **Giloh,** a town in the hill country of Judah (Josh 15:51). Ahithophel most likely supported Absalom and his rebellion in light of how David treated his granddaughter and Uriah earlier (2 Sam 11). Any chance to get revenge on David would have been welcomed. The text is clear that Absalom enjoyed the backing of many important and influential people. By all indications, the **rebellion** against David was popular and the **people following Absalom increased** (v 12).

■ **13-18** The political revolt that Absalom instigated was strong enough that David had to leave the capital. One of David's messengers informed the king that **the hearts of the Israelites were going after Absalom** (v 13). How David came to realize these catastrophic events at this time remains unclear. Does this hint at negligence on David's part to monitor adequately his political enemies? Or was the revolt concealed so carefully that David only became aware of it when it was too late?

The strength of the revolt is indicated by David's command to his servants who were with him: **Get up and let us flee because there will not be any of us who will escape Absalom. Hurry, lest he will overtake us and bring disaster down on us and strike the city with the edge of the sword** (v 14). David's household, officials, and bodyguard left the city in anticipation of

Absalom's takeover. David did leave **ten concubines** behind to watch over the house (v 16). David was also accompanied by **six hundred Gittites** or people from Gath. David had been a vassal of Achish (1 Sam 27), the king of Gath, and no doubt David developed strong relations with members of the Philistine city (2 Sam 6:10-11).

■ **19-23** In addition to David's household and officials mentioned in the previous verses, David was joined by other individuals who showed their loyalty to the king. One such individual was **Ittai the Gittite** whom David encouraged to go back and remain in the city (v 19). Ittai was also from the city of Gath and may have been in charge of six hundred Gittites who followed with David. Ittai was a **foreigner,** only one of many foreigners in David's service. He would later command a third of David's troops in the battle against Absalom (18:2). Ittai refused David's proposal to return to the city, ***Wherever my lord the king may be, whether for death or for life, there also will your servant be*** (v 21). Ittai's response mirrors that of Ruth (Ruth 1:8-17), who vowed her loyalty to Naomi. David accepted his position as a sign of great faithfulness. Interestingly, there is a play on words based on his name. Ittai (*'tay*) is similar linguistically to the phrase "with me" (*'ti*) in Hebrew. Thus, even his name signifies his loyalty to David.

As David and his entourage moved out of Jerusalem, "the whole country wept" (v 23 NRSV). This statement appears to be hyperbole since Absalom was supported by a growing number of the populace as well as people close to David. The king then "crossed the Wadi Kidron" (NRSV), which included the valley separating the City of David and the Mount of Olives on the eastern side of Jerusalem. The Kidron Valley was regarded as the boundary of the city in the time of David (1 Kgs 2:37).

■ **24-29** In addition to Ittai, David also received help from his two priests: Abiathar and Zadok. The Hebrew text represents some difficulty in vv 24-29 because it appears that the presence of Abiathar is a later insertion into the text. In v 24 the statement ***and Abiathar came up*** occurs after the phrase ***and they set the ark of God down*** (referring to Zadok and the Levites). Certain LXX manuscripts omit the latter phrase entirely, which implies the statement about Abiathar has been secondarily added. Moreover, v 25 refers to Zadok in the singular (***return***) and in v 27 David talks to Zadok only (***see and go back***), but the following statement in v 27 (**your son Ahimaaz**) has a singular possessive suffix even though the last phrase (**your two sons with you**) has a plural possessive ending. Moreover, even though Abiathar and Zadok are named in v 29, the verb ***carry back*** is in the singular. Scholars would argue that the main narrative therefore had Zadok as the main subject here, and the references to Abiathar were added later (Mauchline 1971, 273).

It is significant that of the two priests listed here, only Zadok would remain in the service of the Davidic king after the death of David. Solomon banished Abiathar and promoted Zadok as the main priest after he solidified his reign (1 Kgs 2:27). References to the Levites in 2 Sam 15:24 also show signs that this is a secondary insertion (1 Sam 6:15). It is doubtful that they enjoyed official standing at this time.

The Levites are accredited with the transportation of the ark (Num 3:31). There is no indication in this context that David asked that the ark be transported with him. Since the ark was a symbol of God's presence and power, the priests may have brought it with them as a sign of God's presence with David and as an aid in battle if Absalom followed him. However, Israel's faith in the efficacy of the ark as a cult symbol may have been shaken as a result of the defeat of the Israelite armies at Ebenezer (1 Sam 4:4-11). In light of this, David may not have believed in the ability of the ark to protect him. Moreover, he may have sent the ark back to Jerusalem as an indication of his belief that God, not the ark, would act on his behalf.

■ **30-31** David "went up the ascent of the Mount of Olives" (NRSV) just east of the city, heading eastwardly in the direction of the Jordan and the wilderness (17:16). The text portrays the march of David and his caravan almost like a funeral procession. David went up *crying* with his head **covered** and with *bare feet*, all signs that indicate a mourning ritual (Jer 14:3; Ezek 24:17; 1 Sam 4:12; 2 Sam 19:4). These verbs are also participles, thus underscoring the continuing disappointment, shame, and humiliation David experienced. The news that David's adviser **Ahithophel** also conspired with Absalom was no less troublesome. David's only response at this low point in his life was to trust God to work in these difficult circumstances: *may the Lord turn the counsel of Ahithophel into foolishness* (v 31). Ahithophel would provide Absalom with sound instruction later (17:1-4), but Absalom would foolishly disregard it.

■ **32-37** David was also joined by **Hushai** who came to offer sympathy and to offer help. The LXX even calls him "a friend of David." David, however, saw another useful purpose for his services; he could function as a spy for David to keep him informed of Absalom's intentions and to confuse the counsel of Ahithophel. David encouraged him to tell Absalom, "I have been your father's servant in time past, so now I will be your servant" (v 34 NRSV). Even in exile, David showed his wily, shrewd side as a politician and strategist. David's advice eventually paid off, since it was Hushai that provided the counsel that ultimately led to the defeat and death of Absalom.

2. David's Adversaries (16:1-23)

■ **1-4** Unlike the previous section where David received aid from his supporters, these verses recount various individuals who opposed David. In vv 1-4, **Ziba** the servant of Mephibosheth met David as he proceeded "a little beyond the summit" (NRSV) of the Mount of Olives. Ziba brought David "two hundred loaves of bread, one hundred bunches of raisins, one hundred of summer fruits, and one skin of wine" (NRSV) for the king and his household to eat and a couple of *saddled donkeys* to ride (v 1).

Ziba's kindness and generosity to the deposed king is contrasted markedly in this section with Mephibosheth's disloyalty to David. David asked Ziba, "Where is your master's son?" (NRSV). It is interesting that David mentioned "your master's son" in reference to Jonathan, who was long since dead. Ziba implied that Mephibosheth saw Absalom's revolt as an opportunity for the kingdom to return to Saul's household and therefore he returned to Jerusalem. In making this declaration he portrayed Mephibosheth as an ungrateful traitor. The reader, however, does not know if Ziba was lying to David or if he told the truth about Mephibosheth. Mephibosheth later refuted these remarks and suggested that Ziba's words amounted to slander (19:24-30). David took Ziba at his word and rewarded his loyalty by transferring Mephibosheth's property to Ziba. In doing so, Ziba inherited everything that belonged to Mephibosheth. Ziba's intentions are hard to gauge here, but he did benefit handsomely for "squealing" on Mephibosheth.

■ **5-8** When David came to **Bahurim,** a village on the eastern slope of the Mount of Olives, he was met by **Shimei son of Gera.** The text notes that Shimei, like Mephibosheth, came from "the family of the house of Saul" (NRSV). Although Shimei is never mentioned before this point in the story of David, he was probably from the Matrite clan to which Saul belonged (1 Sam 10:21). Shimei confronted David *cursing continuously.* The verb that is used in this context (*mĕqallēl*) is a participle form that connotes ongoing action, in other words "he really let him have it." Shimei showed his contempt for the deposed king by *throwing stones* at him and his servants and hurling serious charges against him. Shimei called David *a man of blood* (i.e., a **murderer**) and a **scoundrel.**

Shimei's use of the term **scoundrel** (*habbĕlīaʿal*) is similar to the word used for Eli's sons (1 Sam 2:12)—a derogatory term of the highest order. It is evident by his words that Shimei held David accountable for "the blood of the house of Saul" (v 7 NRSV). Shimei's remarks were not out of bounds considering the people associated with the house of Saul who died on David's path to the throne: Saul and Jonathan (1 Sam 31; 2 Sam 2); Abner (2 Sam 3); Ish-Bosheth (2 Sam 4); in addition to the seven sons and grandson of Saul's that David allowed the Gibeonites to slaughter (2 Sam 21). Shimei understood David's troubles to be his just desserts for the crimes he committed against Saul's family.

■ **9-14** In the midst of Shimei's accusations, **Abishai son of Zeruiah** came to David's defense with a forceful response: "Let me go over and take off his head" (v 9 NRSV). Abishai's zealous response is not surprising considering his temperament (1 Sam 21:6-8) and his position among David's trusted warriors (2 Sam 23:18-19). David, however, restrained the enthusiasm and intentions of Abishai, noting that if Shimei was cursing David, it was because God allowed it to happen. David's response was not one of apathy but one of trust in God's providence. What could he do if God brought this calamity upon him?

It is significant to note, however, that David never considered how his own actions contributed to his difficulties, especially as they related to the whole Amnon-Tamar affair (ch 13).

Shimei persisted in his relentless criticism of David as he followed him on **the hillside opposite** the road that David and his servants traveled. He continued to throw rocks, fling dust, and curse David as he proceeded outside the vicinity of the city. David and the people with him eventually came to the Jordan, ***panting*** (v 14). No doubt the entire affair was physically and mentally exhausting. The verbal form here (*'āyēphim*) indicates extreme weariness or exhaustion. While at the Jordan, David refreshed himself.

■ **15-23** The narrative at this juncture reverts back to the city of Jerusalem where ***Absalom and all the Israelites returned*** (v 15). Absalom was also joined by David's former adviser, Ahithophel. As a supporter of Absalom, Ahithophel functioned as Absalom's political adviser. Absalom looked to David's former counselor for advice: ***What will we do?*** In his first act as adviser, Ahithophel instructed Absalom ***go into*** [sleep with] ***your father's concubines who were left to guard the house*** (v 21).

A modern audience may not understand the wisdom of this statement. The symbol of a king's power and prestige was tied to the harem of concubines or wives that belonged to the king (1 Kgs 11:1). Having intercourse with David's concubines would have sent a clear message to the people of Jerusalem that Absalom had taken over the reins of power. Such an act would have also been interpreted as an insult and an affront to David, thereby making Absalom and the people supporting him ***odious to David.*** The people would have understood that the possibility of reconciliation between Absalom and David was remote. Thus, **the hands of** *the one with Absalom* **would be strengthened.** The people could support Absalom wholeheartedly and without fear knowing that Absalom would not betray them.

Concubines

A concubine was a marital companion of inferior status to a wife. In biblical times, a concubine bore children for her mistress's husband (Gen 35:22) when the legal wife was barren (Gen 16). If the primary wife later gave birth to her own children, they took over the inheritance of the offspring of the handmaiden (Gen 21:12). Israelite law provided safeguards for the rights of Hebrew girls sold as handmaidens (Exod 21:7-11). At times the concubine relationship could partake of many aspects of a regular marriage. A concubine did not always reside in her husband's home (Judg 19:2), but this was not always the case (Judg 19—20). The spouse of a concubine was called the son-in-law of her father, who was the father-in-law. Royal concubines were standard among the kings of Israel and Judah, as in other kingdoms of the ancient world (Song 6:8-9). They were clearly distinguished from the king's wives (2 Sam 5:13; 1 Kgs 11:3; 2 Chr 11:21). To lie with the king's concubine was tantamount to usurpation of the throne (2

Sam 3:7; 16:21-22; 1 Kgs 2:21-24). Royal concubines were usually in the care of a eunuch (2 Kgs 9:32; Esth 2:14). The descendants of concubines were generally classed as subsidiary tribes (Gen 22:24; 36:12) especially among the Abrahamic groups (Gen 25:6; 1 Chr 1:32). Some of the clans in Israel were the offspring of concubines (1 Chr 2:46; 7:14).

Absalom followed the advice of Ahithophel. A tent was pitched for Absalom on the roof (presumably of the king's palace) and ***Absalom slept* with his father's concubines in the sight of all Israel** (v 22). This brash and bold maneuver solidified Absalom's claim to power among the people; it was evident that David no longer ruled the kingdom. The language is significant because the phrase **his father's concubines** uses a possessive that indicated that Absalom slept with the concubines that belonged to David. The takeover was complete and the words of Nathan were fulfilled (12:11). Ahithophel provided sound advice so that his instruction to Absalom was likened to ***the word of God.*** The text does not mean to say that this was a word from God, but it was a very shrewd political move.

3. The Counsel of Hushai (17:1-29)

■ **1-4** Even though the Hebrew text and English translations create a new chapter break here, these verses follow more closely with the end of ch 16. In this section, Ahithophel provided further political counsel to Absalom. Ahithophel advised Absalom that he should be allowed to take ***12,000 select men*** (i.e., warriors) and pursue David (v 1). Ahithophel reckoned that David would be weary and discouraged (lit., ***slack of hands***) after being ousted from the capital and traveling all day toward the Jordan region. If Ahithophel and his men could attack at this strategic moment, it would provide a devastating blow to any hopes of David's resurgence.

Ahithophel planned only to kill David and bring the rest of David's followers back ***as the bride returns to her husband*** (a reading based on a reconstruction from the LXX). This is a poignant metaphor since it indicated that the people of Israel legally and rightfully belonged to Absalom, just as a bride is wedded to her husband. Ahithophel's plan assumed that if David was killed, then his supporters would transfer their allegiance to Absalom. This scenario is similar to what happened to David after the death of Ish-Bosheth (2 Sam 5).

■ **5-10** Even though Ahithophel's advice "pleased Absalom and . . . the elders of Israel" (NRSV), Absalom also sought Hushai's counsel on Ahithophel's plan (v 4). It is noteworthy that Absalom would trust the word of his father's former adviser over that of Ahithophel, who had been loyal to him from the beginning. Absalom's faith in Hushai is even more confusing considering that he called into question Hushai's loyalty to David earlier (16:16-18). This may indicate Absalom was rather naïve and lacked sound political acumen.

According to Hushai, Ahithophel's idea was not a practical one. Hushai argued that David and his men were mighty warriors and enraged "like a bear robbed of her cubs in the field" (v 8 NRSV). Moreover, David was a **man of war** (i.e., a seasoned warrior) who would not stay out in the open where he was vulnerable to attack, but would hide in "the pits, or in some other place" (NRSV) where he would have been hard to find and would have enjoyed the tactical advantage. David's time spent surviving in the wilderness hiding from Saul no doubt provided him with the survival skills he would draw upon at this time in his life. Hushai indicated that Absalom's men would be at a disadvantage in the presence of such a cagey individual, and any loss of life accrued on the part of Absalom's men would cause the others to become faint of heart; even the ***valiant warrior, who has the heart of a lion, will surely melt with fear*** (v 10).

■ **11-14** Hushai also offered a plan of attack. Unlike Ahithophel, who proposed an aggressive approach, Hushai suggested that Absalom wait until all Israel would be gathered to Absalom, **from Dan to Beersheba** (v 11). As David's operative, Hushai pushed a plan that benefited David by giving him time to escape, refresh, and regroup. Moreover, the plan required that Absalom and his troops go to David, thus putting him and his troops in a vulnerable position. A large army would not be feasible in rugged terrain where David could strategically position his own men. Hushai's advice essentially amounted to Absalom's death warrant. Absalom, amazingly yet foolishly, agreed to this tactic. In many respects, Absalom's actions resembled those of Solomon's foolish son, Rehoboam, who unwisely rejected sound counsel for imprudent advice (1 Kgs 12:8). In both cases the results of following wrong advice were disastrous.

■ **15-20** Hushai relayed the advice he gave to Absalom to the two priests who had remained in Jerusalem, Zadok and Abiathar. The priests carried their message to their two sons, Jonathan and Ahimaaz, at **En Rogel**. En Rogel was a spring at the confluence of the Wadi Hinnom and the Wadi Kidron near Gihon, the main spring that supplied Jerusalem with water. Jonathan and Ahimaaz devised a system of communication with David whereby they would pass the information to a young girl who would then deliver the message to David.

On one occasion, ***a young boy*** saw them and reported it to Absalom. Jonathan and Ahimaaz left there and were hidden in a well by the wife of an unnamed man of **Bahurim.** Because the woman spread a covering over the opening of the well and placed grain upon it, the two remained concealed when Absalom's servants came to the woman and inquired of the whereabouts of the two young men. Even though the servants of Absalom searched, they could not find them. Such was the risk that the young men took in supporting David at this tumultuous time.

■ **21-23** Because the two escaped they were able to tell David of the counsel that Ahithophel provided Absalom. The two advised David and his troops to ***arise and cross over quickly*** (both commands in Hebrew). David and the people with him crossed the Jordan **by daybreak.**

When Ahithophel saw that Absalom did not follow his advice, he understood that his actions would be construed as treason should David survive and return to Jerusalem. As a result, Ahithophel went home to his city and hung himself. The text notes that he was buried in the tomb of his father. The death of Ahithophel is significant because it represented the first major blow to the political fortunes of Absalom. By following the advice of Hushai, Absalom began to sow the seeds of his own destruction.

■ **24-26** David and the people with him came to **Mahanaim** on the other side of the Jordan in the territory of Gilead (v 24). The name literally means "two camps," and it once served as the capital of Saul's son, Ish-Bosheth (2:8). Paradoxically, Ish-Bosheth's old capital functioned as David's temporary headquarters during Absalom's revolt. David was able to find support by the people of this region because of his kind treatment of Mephibosheth (9:7).

The text also notes that Absalom set **Amasa** over the army. Amasa is described as the son of **Jether *the Ishmaelite*** and **Abigail** the sister of Zeruiah (v 25). This would theoretically make Amasa a kinsman of David by marriage and thus a Judahite. Later, after the revolt was suppressed, David placed Amasa in charge of the army (19:13), possibly to placate Absalom's Judahite supporters.

■ **27-29** The chapter closes out with three individuals who brought David and his troops food: **Shobi, Makir,** and **Barzillai.** In one shape or form, these men shared an important relationship to David. Shobi was the son of Nahash, and a member of the Ammonite royal family (10:2); Makir was originally a supporter of Saul who extended hospitality to Mephibosheth (9:4); and Barzillai was a faithful supporter whom David invited to live with him after he returned to Jerusalem (19:31-39).

4. The Death of Absalom (18:1-33)

■ **1-2** David up to this point had executed a defensive battle strategy. In this chapter, David adopted a more aggressive campaign against Absalom and his forces. Although it is unclear how many troops David had with him, like Gideon (Judg 7:16) and Saul (1 Sam 11:11) before him, David divided his troops into three camps. **Joab** led one group; **Abishai,** the brother of Joab, the second; and **Ittai** the third. The men David entrusted to this task had demonstrated bravery and loyalty on various occasions. David's battle stratagem gave his warriors flexibility in the art of guerilla warfare, utilizing the terrain and unconventional tactics against Absalom's conscript militia.

■ **3-5** David's troops would not allow the king to join the battle. David represented a high value target, whose life was **worth ten thousand** of his own men (v 3). David stayed by the city and sent help as needed. Even though David did not accompany his men into battle, he did order that his commanders were to "deal gently" (NRSV) with Absalom. David's orders do not appear to be wise ones. He essentially asked the men who were putting their lives at risk for him to show kindness to his arch rival. This command not only disrespected the men fighting for David but also conveyed weakness in the face of a dangerous adversary.

■ **6-8** David's men went out to battle near **the *forests* of Ephraim.** The reference to these forests only occurs here, but it probably included a wooded region on the east side of the Jordan. In addition, the term can be defined as a "thicket," which included a "mixture of trees and tangled undergrowth in craggy terrain" (Evans 2003, 215). This territory may have been settled by Ephraimites earlier as they branched out from the central hill country in the Cisjordan region. Fighting Absalom's troops in this forested and treacherous area definitely provided David's men ample cover to fight an unconventional style of warfare. The strategy worked well as **twenty thousand men** of Israel fell at the hands of David's servants. The text captures the ingenuity of this battle plan by stating that "the forest ***devoured*** more victims that day than the sword" (v 8 NRSV). David's men definitely used the rugged terrain to their advantage.

■ **9-15** Not only did David's men enjoy success against Israel's troops, but the battle eventually claimed Absalom's life as well. In a cruel twist of fate, the long hair for which Absalom became so famous (14:26; Josephus, *Ant.* 10.10.2) also led to his personal downfall. As Absalom's mule went under ***the network of branches of the great oak tree*** his head became caught in the tree so that he hung suspended "between heaven and earth" (v 9 NRSV). Even though Absalom hung vulnerably from the tree, David's men, aware of the command he gave them concerning Absalom, would not harm him. Joab, however, proposed a reward to the one who killed him: "ten pieces of silver and a belt" (v 11 NRSV).

Joab's invitation to kill Absalom went unheeded. One of the men defended himself stating that if he had killed Absalom then Joab "would have stood aloof" (v 13 NRSV). This statement presents an interesting view into the character of Joab in that he would not have given the reward to the man but, instead, would have stood back and allowed David to have him executed. The soldier, and possibly the other troops, knew that Joab could not be trusted. In light of the soldier's reluctance to kill Absalom, Joab seized the opportunity for himself and thrust "three spears . . . into the heart of Absalom" (v 14 NRSV). In killing Absalom, however, Joab defied David's command.

■ **16-18** Upon Absalom's death, Joab called a halt to the fighting. The men with Joab took Absalom's body and threw it into a great **pit in the forest** (v 17). Stones were heaped over Absalom's body, thus signifying the tragic end of his political ambitions. Verse 18 is generally understood to be an editorial insertion explaining the pillar that stood in **the King's Valley.** This valley lay about half a mile north of the Damascus Gate in Jerusalem (Mauchline 1971, 287). The monument commemorated the fact that Absalom did not have a son. The notice in v 18 stands in contrast to 14:27, which lists three sons of Absalom.

Two explanations are possible for this tension: Absalom's sons had already died in the fight against David's warriors, or the present verse preserves a variant tradition regarding the history of Absalom's family.

■ 19-23 The news of Absalom's death was brought to David. **Ahimaaz, the son of Zadok** volunteered to deliver the message that "the LORD has delivered him from the power of his enemies" (v 19). Ahimaaz, who functioned as a courier previously (15:36; 17:17), was anxious to "carry tidings to the king" (NRSV). Joab prevented Ahimaaz from delivering the message to David. Joab may have been looking out for Ahimaaz's safety considering that David showed a tendency to kill the bearers of bad news (1:15; 4:12). Joab may have also worried that Ahimaaz would tell David that Joab killed Absalom. David was not happy with Joab when he killed Abner (3:28). How would David react knowing that Joab disobeyed a direct order?

Joab instead selected a foreigner, a **Cushite** (someone from southern Egypt such as Ethiopia or Nubia), to tell David the news of Absalom's death. If David had the potential to kill the messenger, it was better to send a stranger than his trusted servant. Ahimaaz picked up on Joab's concerns but asked to be allowed to run ahead. Ahimaaz's respect and loyalty to David overshadowed his own concerns for his safety. This is evident from his response: **Whatever happens, I will go** (v 22). Joab allowed him, possibly thinking that the Cushite would reach David first.

■ 24-27 David waited expectantly to hear news of the battle. He "was sitting between the two gates of the city" (NRSV) so that he could be the first to greet any messenger arriving from the battle scene (v 24). In addition, a lookout was situated on the roof of the gate so that he could spot any messengers in advance and relay the information to David immediately. The lookout **raised his eyes and saw** a solitary figure running toward the city (v 24). Since soldiers usually traveled in groups, the sight of a lone figure often signaled that a courier was bringing "tidings in his mouth."

The watchman also noticed a second runner who **ran** like **Ahimaaz son of Zadok** (v 27). David knew that Ahimaaz was **a good man** and thus brought "good tidings" (NRSV). Although Ahimaaz got off to a later start, he was able to beat the Cushite to the city. Either Ahimaaz took a shortcut to the city by the way of the plain (v 23) and thus outmaneuvered the Cushite, or he was simply faster and able to outrun him (which is suggested by vv 27-28). His excitement in bearing good news may have also propelled him past the other messenger.

■ 28-32 The syntactical construction of v 27*b* and v 28 creates the sense that Ahimaaz's report immediately followed David's proclamation that Ahimaaz brought good news. Moreover, the syntax indicates that Ahimaaz **called out,** almost with impatience and anticipation, to David in order to get his attention just before he arrived at the city. His brief but timely word as he approached David said it all: **All is well!** Ahimaaz's brief message to David included the word šālôm, a wordplay on the name Absalom itself (*’bšālôm*) and a prelude to David's inquiry regarding the well-being (šālôm) of his son in v 29.

Ironically, it was anything but peaceful with Absalom, whose name literally means "father of peace." Ahimaaz's answer to David also intimated that he clearly understood Joab's concerns in reporting Absalom's death. Ahimaaz never told David about Absalom's fate except that God had "delivered . . . the men who raised their hand against my lord the king" (v 28). David did not raise his hand against Saul and God protected him, but the people who had raised their hand against David died in the attempt. Ahimaaz's response also bordered on gibberish when read literally: *I saw a great crowd to send the servant of the king, Joab, and your servant, and I do not know what* (v 29). Alter notes that this incoherent language is not due to a textual corruption but is an incoherent and nervous response to a question that Ahimaaz dare not answer (1999, 309). When David realized he would not get the whole story from Ahimaaz, he turned to the Cushite for the pertinent information. The Cushite relayed the news of Absalom's death to David but in an indirect manner, thus softening the blow: *May the enemies of my lord the king be like the lad* (v 32).

■ 33 The MT inserts a syntactical and chapter break at this juncture of the story so that the reader is left in some suspense over David's reaction to the news of Absalom's death. Will David turn on the Cushite and have him killed as he did with the Amalekite? Modern English translations provide the answer to this question before chapter 19 begins (v 33). David did not respond in anger but with extreme grief. The text notes that he *trembled* and he *cried*. David could only respond by repeating the now famous phrase: **My son Absalom! My son, my son Absalom!** Many readers may find in David's words an almost pathological and incomprehensible response.

How could David show such remorse over a defiant son whose rebellion literally cost him control of the kingdom? Some may argue that the love of a father transcended the reckless actions of a rebellious son, no matter how much they may hurt the parent individually. However, David's reaction may point to his own failures as a father. It was his lack of firm discipline in Absalom's life that allowed him to become so reckless and dangerous. The note about David's desire that he should have died in place of his son (v 33) may even hint at David's culpability in Absalom's destruction. David's anguish could also be the result of the culmination of a series of bad events that transpired in his life after his affair with Bathsheba. He had one son die at birth, another son killed by Absalom, and now the death of a third son. It is possible that this last event proved too much for David to bear.

5. David Returns to Jerusalem (19:1-43)

■ 1-4 The different textual divisions found in the MT and modern translations also have ramifications for interpretation and emphasis. Since modern translations refer to David's lament in 18:33, the focus on the opening unit of chapter 19 is on Joab's rebuke of David in vv 5-8a. However, in the MT, David's lament is found in 19:1 (as opposed to 18:33) and thus presents a more sympathetic portrait of the king in that it focuses on David's grief.

The news reached Joab that **David was crying and mourned over Absalom** (v 1). The combination of the two verbs is intended to underscore David's grief. The first verb is a participle (*bōkaeh*) showing that David continued to cry over Absalom's death. The second is a reflexive (*vayit'abēl*), which underscores the mourning that David experienced personally. In essence, the grammar signifies that David was so consumed with his own grief that he did not give thought to how it affected the warriors who fought for him. Once David's personal (selfish?) display of grief became known to his men, it had a devastating effect on them. The troops understood that David **was in pain over his son,** and this became an insult to the people who defended him and risked their lives for him. Instead of this being a time of joy and celebration, the **troops stole away into the city.** David made his men feel ashamed, like those **who flee in battle would steal away** in cowardice (v 3). As a result, the victory that day was turned into **a time of** mourning (v 2), and David only compounded matters by covering his face and crying out: **My son Absalom! O Absalom, my son, my son!** (v 4).

■ **5-8** In light of David's behavior, Joab came to the king's house to rebuke him face-to-face. Joab bluntly stated that David **put to shame** all those who had saved his life, as well as the life of his sons, daughters, wives, and concubines (v 5). Joab also accused David of loving those who hated him and hating those who loved him. By his own actions, David had made it appear that his **commanders and officers** meant nothing to him and that if Absalom were still alive he would be pleased (v 6). Joab, not fearing any reprisal from the king, then ordered David with a series of three quick but direct commands in v 7: **Arise, go out, and speak to the heart of your servants.** This last phrase could be translated as to "speak kindly" (NRSV) or to **encourage** your servants.

Joab threatened David that if he did not speak good words to his men and repair the damage that David caused, **not a man will spend the night with you** (v 7). Joab had the power to encourage the army to abandon David and thus leave the king powerless. This situation would "be worse for you than any disaster that has come upon you" (NRSV). Joab's words intimated that if David did not fix the situation that another rebellion, one led by him, would be on the horizon. David heeded Joab's advice but only in part. Instead of speaking to the troops, **the king rose up and sat at the gate** while **all the people came to him** (v 8).

The image here of David is not one of a grateful, victorious leader, who spoke enthusiastically to his men. Rather, this image recalls the portrait "of a man beaten to a pulp, who can barely stand, and does only the minimum requested or expected of him" (Alter 1999, 213). Even though beaten down,

David survived and Absalom did not. The death of Absalom sent the men of Israel (i.e., Absalom's troops) fleeing to their home territories. The Israelites would have to decide their future and their leader now that their hopes were crushed in Absalom's defeat.

■ **9-10** The material in this section addresses the issue of Israel's future political leadership. What would the Israelites who had backed Absalom do now that the political coupe had failed? The text notes in v 9 that ***all the people were deliberating*** over the prospects of submitting themselves to David's rule. The verb that is used in this context (*dîn*) is passive and thus can be read as "quarreling" (GNT, NASB) or "contending" (YLT) ("disputing" [NRSV]). The text conveys the notion that the people "were at strife" (RSV) over this issue. The text also leaves the impression that the Israelite tribes tried hard to convince themselves that turning to David amounted to a good choice: ***The king rescued us from the power of our enemies, he delivered us from the power of the Philistines, and now he has fled from the land before Absalom*** (v 9).

According to this line of reasoning, the northern tribes based their decision on David's ability in the past to "save" them from their oppressors. They did not base their decision on their own feelings toward David nor on how they would fare under his rule. Their approach was utilitarian, pragmatic, and shortsighted. It may have benefited them in the short-term, but it would hurt them in the long run.

■ **11-15** While the Israelite tribes deliberated over their decision, David either ignored or took for granted Israel's support, and he turned his attention to garnering the favor of the people of Judah. He understood that people from his home territory sponsored Absalom and that any hopes for his reinstallment depended on rapprochement with the tribe of Judah. In light of this, David sent his two trusted priests, Abiathar and Zadok, to act as his go-betweens and pave the way toward reconciliation (v 11).

David commanded his priests to do two important things. First, they were to remind the people of Judah that **you are my brothers,** "you are my bone and my flesh" (v 12 NRSV). David shared a close relationship with them since and they were like family to him. David hailed from the tribe of Judah and therefore enjoyed a closer personal relationship with them. Second, they were to send a message to the general of Absalom's deposed army, Amasa. They were to tell him that David considered him to be like family even though he had led the opposition forces. They were also to relay to Amasa that David offered to make him commander over his army in place of Joab (v 13). Joab's reaction is not recorded here, but the reader can assume he was not delighted with David's choice to elevate the commander of the opposing forces.

David's strategy paid off, and he ***inclined the heart of every man of Judah as one man*** (v 14). It remains unclear whether David swayed the hearts of the men or Amasa did. The NRSV inserts Amasa here, while the JPS sets the name Amasa within brackets. The NIV simply reads **he won over the hearts of all the men of Judah,** thus leaving the issue unclear.

Nevertheless, this plan did bode well for David, as they sent back this message with a unified voice: ***Come back, you and all your servants!*** (v 14). The verb is an imperative so that the impression is given that the people wanted David to return and anticipated his homecoming.

As David came to the Jordan, **Judah** met David at **Gilgal** (v 15). The symbolism of this cannot be overlooked, considering how Gilgal served as an important stopping point as the Israelites prepared to enter into Canaan (Josh 4—5) and the people renewed the kingship during the days of Saul (1 Sam 11:14). David's crossing the Jordan near Gilgal invites the reader to consider his return and the reestablishment of the Davidic monarchy in light of these important events. Judah ***brought David*** or escorted him across the Jordan into the land, thus symbolizing the end of David's exodus from Jerusalem.

■ **16-23** The rest of the chapter is concerned with various individuals who met with David as he crossed over into the land of Israel. In this section (vv 16-23) and the next (vv 24-30), two individuals associated with the house of Saul met with David on his return to Jerusalem. **Shimei,** who defiantly cursed David and threw stones at him when he left Jerusalem (16:5-14), now displayed humility and contrition as he readied to meet David. Shimei essentially begged David to forgive him in light of how he treated the king earlier. The text notes that he **hurried** or ***hastened*** to greet the king and along with him came a ***thousand men of Benjamin*** (vv 16-17).

The thousand men were not with Shimei when he cursed David, but they did hail from Saul's tribal territory. It is possible that they were concerned David would take revenge on them as well. Shimei also **fell** before David and begged him to forgive him for how he treated the king earlier (vv 18-19). He essentially pleaded with David to ***not consider*** his ***guilt*** nor **remember** how he had ***done wrong*** on the day David left Jerusalem (v 20).

David's warrior, Abishai, saw in Shimei's vulnerability an opportunity to gain revenge on David's enemy. Abishai's response in v 21, ***Will not Shimei be put to death because he cursed the Lord's anointed?*** provided a rational justification for death since the king, the Lord's anointed, was considered sacrosanct (1 Sam 24:6-7). Although an understandable response, it essentially concealed his desire to get personal revenge on Shimei. David disassociated himself from Abishai, however, by saying, "What have I to do with you, you sons of Zeruiah?" (2 Sam 19:22 NRSV). David's response is intriguing since he uses the plural "sons" even though he is addressing Abishai. David's remarks appear to be aimed at Joab, Abishai's brother, as well since cutting people down characterized his modus operandi.

David's plan did not include retribution; **you shall not die** (v 23). David sealed his promise with an **oath,** which was binding on him for the rest of his days. David's response to Shimei in this context was not only merciful but also politically shrewd and pragmatic. It would have been difficult for him to have secured the loyalty of the Benjamites had he ordered Shimei to be killed on the spot.

David did not forget about Shimei, however, but let the matter lie until he was on his deathbed when Solomon took the reins of power. It was then, after David's throne had been firmly secured among the people of Israel, that David reminded Solomon how Shimei treated him on that fateful day he left Jerusalem and instructed him not to hold him guiltless. In essence, David charged Solomon to kill Shimei ("you will know what to do to him" [1 Kgs 2:9]), thus "technically" keeping the oath he made to Shimei.

■ **24-30** In addition to Shimei, **Mephibosheth, the grandson of Saul** (a reading based on the LXX, the MT reads **the son of Saul**), also came to greet David. Mephibosheth came to David with a disheveled appearance: **He had not dressed his feet, trimmed his moustache, and his clothing had not been washed** (v 24). Mephibosheth's unkempt exterior symbolized an act of mourning on behalf of David during Absalom's revolt and was intended to be taken as a sign of his loyalty to the king. David's question in v 25, "Why did you not go with me?" (NRSV), was an attempt to square the information Ziba had provided him earlier (16:1-4) with Mephibosheth's alibi in 19:26-27. Mephibosheth relayed to David that Ziba **deceived** him. Mephibosheth had planned to saddle a donkey and ride it so that he could join David. Since Mephibosheth was lame, he claimed he did not have time to get ready to go meet David, thus providing Ziba the opportunity to go ahead of him and **slander your servant to my lord the king** (v 27).

Mephibosheth's language in v 27 employs a wordplay since the word for **slander** (*rāgal*) is nearly identical to the word for "foot"/"feet" (*regel*), thus drawing attention to Mephibosheth's handicap and Ziba's attempt to disparage him. Mephibosheth's plea also included strategic language in which he consistently referred to himself as **your servant,** he called David **an angel of God,** and he recalled David's generosity toward him after the death of Saul and Jonathan, his father.

David appeared to be unable to distinguish whether Ziba's or Mephibosheth's story was the true one. As a result, he altered his earlier decision (16:4) and allowed both to lay claim to the property that David had granted to Ziba earlier. Instead of abiding by the decision, Mephibosheth relinquished his portion of the field, thus showing his loyalty to David and his gratitude **that my lord the king has come to his home in peace** (v 30).

■ **31-40** David was greeted last by his old friend **Barzillai,** who had provided for him while he stayed at Mahanaim (17:27-29). David did not forget about Barzillai's kindness to him and offered to return the favor by inviting him to come to Jerusalem with him, where David would **provide** for him (v 33). Barzillai declined David's offer by essentially claiming that he was too old to be able to enjoy life at David's court, and he did not want to be a **burden** to

David. Barzillai did offer to cross over the Jordan a little ways with David and requested that **Kimham,** possibly his son (1 Kgs 2:6), be able to cross over with David and stay with the king (2 Sam 19:36-37). David agreed to fulfill Barzillai's wishes out of the king's great respect for his friend: **Kimham shall cross over with me, and I will do for him** *what is good in your eyes, and all that you have requested of me* **I will do for you** (v 38). When David crossed over the Jordan, he **kissed Barzillai** and he ***blessed him,*** two signs of David's affection and reverence for his faithful ally.

As David crossed the Jordan, Kimham and all of the people of Judah went with him. The text makes a point to note that only **half the *people* of Israel** were present (v 40). This last note insinuates that not all the people of Israel supported David nor did they wish to see him return as king. Already the text is raising the issue that trouble would lay ahead for the house of David.

■ **41-43** David had not returned to Jerusalem before signs of intratribal squabbles appeared to be brewing. All the men of Israel came to David with a complaint. They wanted to know why it was that **our brothers, the men of Judah,** have "stolen you away, and brought the king and his household over the Jordan" (v 41 NRSV). The accusation by the men of Israel is interesting for a couple of reasons. First, the language "stolen you away" is similar to the language used to describe the manner in which Absalom had enticed the people of Israel away from David (v 41). Now they were using the same words against the men of Judah. Second, the Israelites were careful to call the Judahites **our brothers,** thus making this appear to be the kind of conflict that arises in a family. Later on, when the northern tribes became dissatisfied with Davidic rule, they disassociated themselves from the king's family, arguing they had no "share" in the house of David (1 Kgs 12:16).

19:31-43

FROM THE TEXT

The story of David's flight from Jerusalem during Absalom's rebellion draws out a number of important ideas. First, David shared much of the blame for Absalom's rebellion in that he failed to deal adequately with the situation with Amnon (2 Sam 13) and in the manner he treated Absalom (ch 14). Because David was lax as a father in disciplining his children and in setting a good example for them, he reaped a harvest of pain, humiliation, and suffering as a result. Furthermore, the people found in Absalom an individual who would provide them the type of leadership they were searching for, because David and his administration were negligent in their dealings with the population. Thus, not only was Absalom dissatisfied with the way his father treated him, but the people were discontent with Davidic rule as well. These factors created the conditions that fostered the rebellion and David's political setback.

Second, in spite of the rebellion that drove David from office, God remained true to the covenant promise that he made to David. Throughout the text the reader is led to wonder if David's time as king of Israel was finished as he left Jerusalem with no guarantee that he would come back. Even though David faced great opposition and the situation remained bleak, in the end, David regained his throne and control of the kingdom. In the process, we are reminded that God did not let any of his promises to the king fall. As God proved so many times throughout the history of his people, God remained dependable and fulfilled his word to those with whom he makes a covenant.

Third, in the story of Absalom's rebellion we also learn the value of friendship and loyalty. Even though David had his detractors, David still had a circle of people who remained faithful to him. At many points in the narrative, various individuals put their lives on the line for David (17:15-21), helped confuse the plans of his enemies (17:5-11), brought nourishment and help during times of need (17:27-29), and fought for him in order to protect him (18:1-18). David's return to Jerusalem and the restoration of his kingdom would not have been possible without the assistance of others. It is also true that in times of adversity we find out who our true friends are. David realized who his true friends were and showed his gratitude to them for their faithfulness (19:31-40).

Fourth, we also learn that David extended mercy and forgiveness to his enemies instead of vengeance and revenge. Throughout the narrative David faced various forms of opposition from those who did not support him and thought bad of him. Absalom disrespected his father in that he organized his rebellion right under his father's nose. When David left Jerusalem in humiliation, people such as Shimei hurled insults at him and cursed him. Even David's counselor, Ahithophel, turned on him and sought his demise. According to the text, David never entertained the thought of "getting even" with his enemies.

In the war with Absalom, David ordered his troops not to hurt his son. The news of Absalom's death did not bring David satisfaction; rather, he expressed an outburst of emotional hurt and pain. When momentum swung back in David's favor and it became obvious that the rebellion was over, he did not seek to repay the people who wanted to harm him. Even though Abishai, for example, wanted to destroy Shimei for his contemptible actions toward David, he would not allow Abishai to harm him. David even extended kindness to Mephibosheth, who appeared to betray David during the revolt (16:3). This was an especially powerful gesture considering that Mephibosheth had possibly returned evil in spite of David's previous kindness to him (ch 9). Thus, through David's example we learn that forgiveness, not vengeance, accomplishes God's redemptive work in the world.

F. The Revolt of Sheba (20:1-26)

BEHIND THE TEXT

Chapter 20 can be broken down into two major sections: vv 1-22 relate to the revolt of Sheba; vv 23-26 include a revised roster of David's chief officials. The revolt of Sheba indicated that the intertribal rivalries and dissensions that fostered Absalom's rebellion were not completely stamped out. Although Sheba received some support for the separatist movement, he did not enjoy political backing from all the northern tribes. The dispute that is recorded in vv 1-22 seems to have been provoked by disagreements between representatives from Judah and Israel at the end of ch 19 (Birch 1998, 1350). David had to deal with rebellious leaders like Sheba in order to reunify his kingdom. The picture of the political discontent that is preserved in ch 20, however, reminds the reader that the final years of David's reign were not ones of tranquil contentment.

Scholars are in agreement that the list of David's officials (vv 23-26) has been inserted into the text. Disagreement arises as to whether the registry is simply a variant of the list found in 8:15-18 (McCarter 1984, 435) or whether there were two lists—one dating to an earlier part of David's reign (8:15-18) and one deriving from a later stage (20:23-26) (Anderson 1989, 243-44; Mettinger 1971, 7). In light of the differences between the lists, the latter opinion seems more likely.

IN THE TEXT

■ **1-2** Even though David returned to Jerusalem with his kingship intact, trouble still awaited him. Absalom's rebellion had been effectively quelled, but a new revolt was in the making. The text opens in v 1 with the reference to **Sheba son of Bicri, a Benjamite.** Sheba is unknown up to this point, but he was among the Bicrite clan and, more importantly, from the same territory as King Saul. Thus, his sympathies lay with the northern tribes and Saulide rule, not David.

Sheba is called a ***scoundrel***, utilizing the same language in reference to Eli's sons (*bĕliya'al*) in 1 Sam 2:12. The fact that he is called "good-for-nothing" (TM) here is an indication that this text has a distinctly Judean view and derives from circles that are pro-Davidic in perspective. Sheba did not support Davidic rule and thereby instigated a revolt among the tribes of Israel with his call to rebellion in v 1: **We have no *portion* in David, no *share* in Jesse's son! Each man to his tent, O Israel!** These words also anticipate the northern tribes' response when they broke away from David's house at the time of Rehoboam (1 Kgs 12:16). Sheba's call to protest resonated among the people of Israel, and they followed Sheba while the people of Judah remained loyal to David.

■ **3** David returned to his house in Jerusalem. One of his first orders of business included locking up the **ten concubines** who were left behind at the time of Absalom's rebellion. Since Absalom had already "gone into" his father's concubines, David put them **under guard** and **provided for them,** but he did not ***go in to them*** (i.e., have sexual relations). The text notes that the concubines remained under guard **till the day of their death, living as widows.** Although David provided for their daily needs, they lived in celibacy in order to prevent any other man from marrying them and to insulate David from the embarrassment that Absalom's revolt must have caused him.

■ **4-13** The text in vv 4-22 returns to the matter of Sheba's revolt. David appears to have acted quickly in order to put a stop to the rebellion before it could grow in momentum. David looked to Absalom's former general, **Amasa,** to gather up the men of Judah (v 4). The urgency of David's request is apparent since David gave him **three days** to assemble the men. For reasons unknown, Amasa delayed in getting the troops together and the appointed time passed. As a result, David turned to his trusted warrior **Abishai** along with David's servants to pursue Sheba (v 6).

Although David did not consult Joab for this mission, Joab's men went with Abishai in search of Sheba (v 7). In addition, David's personal bodyguard, **the Kerethites and Pelethites,** joined the rest of the warriors in quelling the coupe. Amasa joined up with the small army at "the large stone that is in Gibeon" (v 8 NRSV). The text never tells the reader how Amasa reached the warriors, but Joab, who had been in disguise, was there to greet him. When Amasa inquired about the well-being of Joab, the latter approached Amasa to kiss him and then struck him with a sword in the belly so that "his entrails poured out on the ground" (v 10 NRSV). At this point in the narrative, Joab killed three important men associated with David: Abner (2 Sam 3:27), Absalom (18:14), and Amasa (20:10). Joab may have committed these murders with impunity since only he knew the truth about Uriah. Since only a few people had information about Uriah's murder, Joab was able to hold this information against David and not fear any recrimination from the king. Solomon, on the other hand, eliminated Joab when he succeeded David as king (1 Kgs 2:28-34).

■ **14-22** Sheba traveled through the northern country and came to the city of **Abel Beth Maacah** (v 14). This was a town located about twelve miles north of Lake Huleh near the city of Dan. Although Sheba started the revolt against David it appears as though it did not gain significant strength. Among all the Israelite people, only the Bicrites (Sheba's own clan) supported the movement. Joab's forces came to the city and besieged it. First they set up a siege ramp and then began to batter the wall down.

With the city under duress, **a wise woman** called out to Joab and inquired about the efficacy of destroying the Israelite city (v 16). The destruction of the town would likely have inflamed passions against David for "swallow[ing] up the heritage of the LORD" (v 19 NRSV). This also represents the second occasion when Joab had interactions with a woman who was called wise (see 14:2). On the first occasion he utilized the woman from Tekoa to secure the return of Absalom. On this occasion, he relied upon the advice of a wise woman to apprehend David's enemy. Joab provided the reason for the siege by indicating that Sheba had revolted against David and now took shelter behind the city's walls. Joab pressed negotiations with her: "Give him up alone, and I will withdraw from the city" (v 21 NRSV). Joab's request was reasonable to the wise woman. She returned to the people of the city and persuaded them to give up Sheba. The people cut off Sheba's head and threw it to Joab. The woman's instruction proved to be sound after all: she helped save the city and she prevented Joab from committing unnecessary violence against fellow Israelites. With the rebellion essentially over, Joab blew the trumpet and the troops dispersed from the city and went home.

■ **23-26** With order restored, the text includes a brief notice about David's administrative staff. The placement of David's officers at this juncture is logical considering that David's kingship had been restored. As in ch 8, the list of officers appears after David solidified his hold on the kingdom. The list of the administrative team in these verses is very similar to the one in 8:15-18.

Some important differences do exist, which indicates that David's cabinet changed over time. **Adoniram** is listed as the officer in charge of **forced labor.** Under David and then Solomon, both foreigners (1 Kgs 9:13-21) and Israelites (1 Kgs 5:13-17) alike were conscripted for the king's service projects. Being pressed into the king's service became very unpopular and was one of the major causes of the schism of the united monarchy (1 Kgs 12:16). Adoniram would later be killed by the very people he oversaw (1 Kgs 12:18).

Ira is listed as a ***priest of David*** and appears to have replaced David's sons (2 Sam 8:18). Ira hailed from Havvoth Jair in Gilead (Num 32:41; Deut 3:14), and he did not appear to enjoy the same status as Zadok and Ahitub in cultic matters. **Sheva** is a variant of the name Seraiah (2 Sam 8:17). For **Abiathar** see comment on 2 Sam 8:17.

FROM THE TEXT

This unit reminds us that God's people are not immune from the criticisms and hostilities of those who oppose us. Even though David represented God's anointed leader among the people, and God had restored David's monarchy after a tumultuous revolt, David still faced opposition from his detractors, especially from those loyal to Saul's household. This instance from David's life illustrates the point that even as believers, we may be living in God's will, demonstrating a holy life, and carefully abiding by God's instruction, yet have people come across our path who are antagonistic toward us and actively challenge us. Being a follower of God does not ensure that we will be popular with everyone.

The lives of Joseph, Moses, Daniel, Jesus, and Paul attest to the fact that people of great faith and obedience can face all manner of abuse, persecution, and adversity, even when it is unwarranted. Their examples also teach us that our faith in God and our commitment to living by God's holy principles may even be the reason why certain people despise us. During these times it is important to keep in mind that just because we face unfair treatment by others does not indicate that we are living outside the center of God's will. It is imperative that we fix our gaze upon God and not get distracted by those who hurl insults at us, trust in God's providential care to sustain us, and not seek revenge upon those who treat us wrongly. In this way we can live out God's purpose in our own life and reflect the character and example of Christ to our world.

V. THE APPENDICES (21:1—24:25)

BEHIND THE TEXT

Chapters 21—24 stand in a unique position within the overall structure of Samuel. On the one hand, they represent the formal closing of the book, yet on the other, they form their own distinct literary unit. For a long time, scholars viewed this unit as an "intrusive" appendix that basically interrupted the Succession Narrative in 2 Sam 9—20 and 1 Kgs 1—2 (Birch 1998, 1354). Because scholars initially deemed this material superfluous, they did not think that it had any significant bearing on the interpretation of Samuel. This view has changed in more recent times as scholars have read and evaluated these chapters in light of the final, canonical shaping of Samuel. Analysis of chs 21—24 has revealed that they form a chiastic structure (Budde 1902, 304; Childs 1979, 273-75):

A 21:1-14: a narrative on the expiation of Saul's guilt
  B 21:15-22: a list of heroes and their deeds
    C 22:1-51: a song of thanksgiving for Yahweh's deliverance
    C' 23:1-7: a song in celebration of God's promise to David
  B' 23:8-39: a list of heroes and their deeds
A' 24:1-25: a narrative of the expiation of David's guilt

Based on the above diagram, the reader can detect that chs 21—24 have been arranged in a very careful and deliberate manner by the editor(s) of Samuel. These materials form a concentric ring in which two songs of praise and thanksgiving (22:1-51; 23:1-7) are framed by two accounts of David's heroes and their accomplishments (21:15-22; 23:8-39), and then conjoined with two narratives based on the theme of expiating the guilt of Saul and David (21:1-14; 24:1-25).

The arrangement of these chapters contains a basic logic that becomes apparent upon closer inspection. Chapter 24 corresponds with 21:1-14 based on their common "punishment" theme for royal abuses that took place under the Israelite king (Anderson 1989, 282). The lists of David's warriors in 21:15-22 and 23:8-39 have been paired together in order to portray David as both a leader of heroic men and one who relied upon their help in times of distress. The setting of David's song of thanksgiving (22:1-51) is appropriate considering that it is preceded by two dangerous, but unsuccessful, revolts against David (chs 15—20) and by the four giants episode (21:15-22). Finally, the poetic text of 23:1-7 functions as a kind of last will and testament of David as he recalled God's promise to him and anticipated the perpetuation of the Davidic dynasty after his death.

The canonical arrangement of chs 21—24 also has important interpretive and theological significance. At the "heart" of this chiasm (C, C') God's covenant faithfulness is emphasized. This is evident in the fact that God came to David's rescue, delivered him from trouble, and gave him victory over his enemies. God's faithfulness was also at the core of the covenant God established with David and the basis upon which David could trust that his desires for the dynasty would come to fruition. The "fringes" of the chiasm (A, A') present a different message altogether. Whereas the center of the chiasm speaks well of God's character, the outer ridges raise concerns about human kings and their tendency to misuse the authority God entrusted to them. In the case of Saul, it speaks of his brutality in slaying the Gibeonites without justifiable cause (21:1-14). With regard to David, it points to his desire to build up the power of the king and the state by taking the census. Brueggemann has rightly pointed out that ch 24, for example, reveals a king beset by self-serving arrogance and autonomy (1988, 383).

In terms of their transmission history, chs 21—24 were various independent, and originally unrelated, materials that were combined together by the final editor(s) of Samuel. The first of these textual units, 21:1-14, is based on a tradition that appears out of place from a chronological perspective. Both the events of ch 9 and Shimei's cursing of David (16:7 ff.) presuppose that the killing of the seven sons of Saul had already taken place (Hertzberg 1964, 381). The events of ch 21 thus fit better at the beginning of David's reign rather than at the end. The story may have been taken from its original context (before ch 9) during the transmission process and subsequently placed after ch 20 by the final compiler(s). In doing so, the final editor(s) of Samuel maintained the theme of David's dispute with members of Saul's family, a theme that occurs prominently throughout the story of David.

Second Samuel 21:15-22 consists of four short episodes that occur during the Philistine wars. In each of these accounts, the opponent is a man of unusual size and, in some cases, physical description. These texts may have originated from archives in which notable deeds were put down into writing and formed the "Book of the Wars of the LORD" (Num 21:14) (Hertzberg 1964, 386). Like 21:1-14, this material does not seem to fit the literary context and may have been originally connected with the reports of David's battles with the Philistines in 2 Sam 5:17-25, for example. The accounts of 21:15-22 may have been inserted after ch 20 by the final compiler(s) because the last war waged by David was recorded in ch 20. Attempts by scholars to explain the reasoning for its placement at the end of Samuel "will probably not succeed," however (McCarter 1984, 451).

The poetic text of 22:1-51 parallels, in many respects, Ps 18. Because the psalm comes down to us in two versions, it is likely that they originated from a single version of the poem. The divergences that do exist are "scribal in origin and correspond to the categories of change that take place in the transmission of any ancient text" (McCarter 1984, 473). The song is a thanksgiving hymn, and as such, bears many of the characteristic hallmarks of a psalm of this genre (i.e., introduction, call for help, description of deliverance, reference to God's righteousness, a confession, etc.). This psalm is generally considered to be quite old, most likely stemming from the time of the early monarchy, and had its origins in a cultic setting (Hertzberg 1964, 392-93).

The poetic text of 23:1-7 is presented as the "last words" or "last will" of a dying man. As such, the passage forms a parallel with the last words of Jacob (Gen 49) and Moses (Deut 33). However, 2 Sam 23:1-7 is depicted as a prophetic oracle and not as a formal blessing (Evans 2003, 240). Outside of v 1, which appears to be an editorial insertion, the poem is believed to trace back to the early monarchical period. Evidence for an early dating of this text is based on parallels with the Balaam oracles of Num 24, which are recognized as ancient, as well as the "king under the image of the sun" motif (vv 3*b*-4) found in Egyptian literature of the Middle Kingdom (McCarter 1984, 484). Moreover, the poem also speaks of the royal house of David as a living institution and not as an object of a futuristic messianic hope. This would indicate that it corresponds to the monarchical period and not a later time.

The litany of David's warriors in 23:8-39 is concerned with two elite groups within David's army: the Three (vv 8-12) and the Thirty (vv 13-39). The list appears to have expanded as David's power grew. The first ten warriors after Asahel (v 24) come from the territory of Judah and from towns within a close radius of Bethlehem. The next ten hail from the northern portion of Israel and probably joined David after he established control over Saul's former kingdom. The three warriors in vv 33-35 are from southern Judah. To these twenty-three warriors the Three were added along with Abishai, Benaiah, Asahel, and Joab, thus bringing the total number to thirty. This most likely represented the original roster of David's mighty men (McCarter 1984, 500). The men in vv 36-39 represent replacements, as a number of them came from east of the Jordan or were of non-Israelite origin.

Scholars express different opinions about the literary history of ch 24. Some argue that the chapter is more or less a unified whole with some secondary (vv 10, 17) additions inserted (Smith 1929, 387). Others isolate more extensive Deuteronomistic revisions throughout (Veijola 1975, 340-57). A number of scholars argue that this text is the compilation of larger, independent traditions (Dietrich 1972, 42; Schmid 1970, 241-50; Rupprecht 1977, 5-9). Within this model three narrative blocks have been conjoined: vv 2, 4b-9 recount David's census (leaving vv 1, 3-4a as redactional supplements); vv 11-15 include Gad's visit with David (v 10 is a later addition); and vv 16, 18-25 consist of an altar etiology (v 17 is a secondary insertion) (Rupprecht 1977, 10-15).

Although modern scholarship has tended to reduce the chapter into various elements, a canonical reading of the text shows a logical structure exists. David's census causes God to send the prophet Gad to David; Gad proclaims judgment on David for his actions; the people suffer a plague because of the king; David purchases a threshing floor upon which he can offer sacrifices. Initial observations on the overall flow of the chapter reveal that the events are driving toward a purposeful end, which culminate with the purchase of the threshing floor.

IN THE TEXT

1. David and the Gibeonites (21:1-14)

■ 1 The chapter opens with the notice that **there was a famine *in the land*.** Extended dry periods were not uncommon in the land of Canaan (Gen 12:10; 26:1), however, the famine referenced here appears to be especially harsh, it lasted ***three years.*** The people of the ancient world understood famine to be a sign that the gods/goddesses they worshipped were angry and thus withheld rain. David was no different, and he ***inquired of Yahweh*** as to the cause of the drought. The text does not mention that he utilized priestly channels in order to communicate with God; it appears he sought God directly. It is also not clear where David made inquiry, but a high place was located in Gibeon (1 Kgs 3:4-5). Considering the Gibeonites are the main subject in the following verses, this seems like the most plausible option.

Yahweh provided the explanation for the famine: "There is blood-guilt on Saul and on his house, because he put the Gibeonites to death" (NRSV). This statement recalls the episode in Josh 9 when Joshua and the Israelites spared the Gibeonites from slaughter. The Israelites subjugated the Gibeonites and they became servants ("hewers of wood and drawers of water" [Josh 9:21 KJV,

NRSV]) to the Israelites. They appear to have been employed in the service of the sanctuary at Gibeon. Because the Israelites made a covenant with the Gibeonites (Josh 9:15), they were obligated to protect them (Josh 10:1-15). Instead of protecting them, the text claims Saul was responsible for killing them. The text never recalls, however, an incident when Saul took mortal action against the Gibeonites, thus breaking the treaty. Either the material that recorded the massacre was lost, or it is possible that the killing is associated with the slaughter of the priesthood at Nob (1 Sam 22:6-23).

■ **2-6** When David received his answer he called the Gibeonites together. The text provides a parenthetical note in v 2*b* stating that the Gibeonites were not Israelites but a remnant of the **Amorites,** members of the pre-Israelite inhabitants of the land. This notice is likely a secondary insertion into the text to clarify the identity of the Gibeonites and to explain Saul's actions toward them (Caird 1953; Smith 1929). Both pieces of information would have been helpful to later readers.

David appeared ready to assist the Gibeonites in any way he could (v 3): ***What can I do for you? With what shall I cover over that you may bless the heritage of Yahweh?*** David asked the victims of this brutal act how the crime should be atoned for and what should be done to those responsible. As king, David was responsible for overseeing and maintaining justice in society, and he was endued with the power to carry it out. The Gibeonites provided David with their request in v 6; they asked that **seven** of Saul's **descendants** be killed as reparations for the Gibeonites Saul murdered. The Gibeonites' request for justice was commensurate with the crime committed against them. They did not seek gold or silver as payment from anyone in Saul's family, nor did they seek to ***put to death anyone in Israel*** (v 4). They sought blood in response for the blood that Saul shed. The execution of Saul's descendants was in line with tribal membership while seven is chosen because it was deemed to be holy (Hertzberg 1964, 383).

The method of their desired execution was unclear. The term used in v 6 is based on a word (*yāqaʿ*) whose meaning is ambiguous. The NIV translates it as **exposed** while others read "impale" (NRSV, JPS). Considering the following prepositional phrase, ***before Yahweh,*** it is probably best read as "impale." Either way, it was intended to be a painful and humiliating punishment. This was to take place ***at Gibeah of Saul, the chosen of Yahweh.*** Modern commentators read "Gibeon" instead, based on a reconstruction of the text from the LXX. This makes sense in light of the fact that a high place was located in Gibeon.

David's response to the Gibeonites in v 6 was laconic and direct: **I will give them.** The execution of Saul's family members was fair, considering the crime occurred when Saul was king. This would have satisfied the Gibeonites' desire for retribution, but it was not excessive enough that it would have engendered harsh feelings among the Israelites. David also benefited from the death of Saul's family members, since this would have eliminated the opportunity for anyone from Saul's house to resurrect his old monarchy. The move essentially strengthened David's grip on the kingdom.

■ **7-9** Of the remaining male descendants in Saul's family only **Mephibosheth** was allowed to live (v 7). The text notes that David **spared** Jonathan's son, because of the oath that had been established between Jonathan and David (1 Sam 20:12-17). The term used here also includes the notion of having compassion on someone, such as when Pharaoh's daughter displayed compassion toward Moses and spared his life (Exod 2:6).

David took the two sons of **Rizpah,** who was Saul's concubine (2 Sam 3:7-11), **Armoni and Mephibosheth,** as well as the **five sons** from Saul's oldest daughter, **Merab** (v 8). The MT actually reads "Michal" here, but other texts indicate that Michal was barren (2 Sam 6:23) and that Adriel was her husband (1 Sam 18:19). The name Merab is also attested in ancient textual traditions such as the LXX, the Peshitta, and the Targums. Thus "Merab" is preferred.

The text continues to show David's active involvement with this process: he spared Mephibosheth, took the sons of Rizpah and Merab, and then "gave them into the hands of the Gibeonites" to be executed (2 Sam 21:9 NRSV). It is no surprise why Shimei who was associated with the family of Saul cursed David as a murderer and a scoundrel during Absalom's revolt (16:6-7).

The Gibeonites *impaled them on the hill before Yahweh* in the *first days of the harvest, at the beginning of barley harvest* (v 9). The sons were executed at the time of the barley harvest (April-May) in the month of Ziv. Ziv corresponded to the second month of the agricultural year according to the Canaanite calendar (McCarter 1984, 442) and is mentioned in conjunction with the construction of Solomon's temple (1 Kgs 6:1, 37).

Some scholars have argued that this chapter shows evidence of David's assimilating Canaanite worship practices by having the members of the family of Saul executed at this particular time of the year. The king was responsible for the fertility of the land, and sacrificing the members of Saul's household would ensure that the rains would return (Kapelrud 1955, 116-17; 1959, 299). Others, however, have shown that the real focus here centers on the issue of exacting punishment for treaty violations, an issue that is mentioned in other ancient cultures (Fensham 1964, 20). In avenging the crime, the burden of guilt for a crime committed in the past would not be transmitted to the present generation.

■ **10-14** Rizpah, the mother of two of the sons, watched over the bodies of the deceased "from the beginning of the harvest until rain fell" to protect them from the wild creatures (v 10 NRSV). Rizpah's vigil lasted for months, from April or May all the way through the summer (Hamilton 2004, 361). This was contrary to the law in Deut 21:22-23, which prohibited a corpse to remain on the stake overnight. The presence of rain indicated that David's attempt to make reparations for the death of the Gibeonites was successful. The text notes that "God heeded supplications for the land" (v 14b NRSV); the drought ended now that Saul's crime had been atoned for.

The caring efforts of Rizpah did not go unnoticed. David was told what she had done in caring for the bodies of Saul's descendants. David was so moved by her actions that he took the bones of Saul and Jonathan from the people of Jabesh Gilead (1 Sam 31:12-13), and they were gathered with the bones of those who were impaled. The bones were returned to the land of **Zela** and placed in the tomb of Saul's father **Kish**.

2. David's Men (21:15-22)

■ **15-17** These verses recount four short episodes in which David and his men fought Philistine giants. The first account (vv 15-17) begins with the statement "the Philistines went to war again with Israel" (v 15). The placement of this opening battle account is curious and out of place. Is it intended to follow ch 20, which recounts David's most recent battle, or does it connect better with 2 Sam 5:17-25, which narrates David's last battle with the Philistines? The manner in which these traditions have been assembled makes answering that question with any certainty a difficult task.

The text makes reference to **Ishbi-Benob,** who is called "one of the descendants of the giants" (v 16 NRSV). The term used here (*rāpâ*) to describe Ishbi-Benob is similar to the "Rephaites" who are also noted for their great size (Gen 14:5; 15:20; Josh 12:4; 13:12). The description of his spear is also similar to the story of Goliath (1 Sam 17:7), though the spear of Ishbi-Benob is half as heavy (**three hundred shekels**) and made out of **bronze**. The text notes that Ishbi-Benob was intent on killing David, but David was in no shape to fight this warrior (***David was weary*** [v 15b]). Abishai, David's nephew by his sister Zeruiah (1 Sam 26:6; 2 Sam 2:18), came to David's aid and ***struck the Philistine and attacked him*** (21:17).

The text highlights David's vulnerability here; he is in no shape to fight and he has to rely on the assistance of one of his warriors to spare him from harm. Although David has been nothing less than a stellar fighter up to this point in the text, in vv 15-17 he is depicted as one who is prone to frailty and weakness. It appears David became a liability to his warriors, and they did not want to take the risk of losing him. They commanded David not to go out to battle anymore, lest **the lamp of Israel** be extinguished.

■ **18-22** Three brief battle reports are included in vv 18-22 to round out the chapter. In the first account, **Sibbecai** killed one of the giants named **Saph** at **Gob**. The location of the town Gob is unknown; it is only mentioned here and in v 19. Sibbecai is called a **Hushathite;** he hailed from the town of Hush, which was located southwest of Bethlehem (2 Sam 23:27; 1 Chr 4:4). He is listed as one of David's "thirty" warriors (2 Sam 23:27).

The second account in v 19 states that **Elhanan . . . the Bethlehemite** killed **Goliath the Gittite.** The similarities to David's battle with Goliath (1

Sam 17) is undeniable, including the reference to Goliath's spear, ***whose shaft was like a weaver's beam*** (1 Sam 17:7). Different arguments have been set forth in order to explain the parallels between this verse and the account of 1 Sam 17. One, Elhanan who is also the "son of Dodo" (2 Sam 23:24) was an alternative name for David. Two, the much more famous David eventually replaced Elhanan in the story over the course of time. Third, the name Goliath became secondarily associated with the anonymous Philistine David killed. Fourth, the Chronicler notes that Elhanan killed Lahmi (1 Chr 20:5), thus preserving the original account of the story. No clear-cut answer exists, but the second and third options seem most plausible.

The third account in vv 20-21 shifts the battle scene to the Philistine city of **Gath** where **Jonathan son of Shimei, David's brother** killed a Philistine with **six fingers on each hand and six toes on each foot.** The relationship between the Jonathan listed here and Jonathan the son of Shammah the Hararite from the list of thirty (2 Sam 23:33) is unclear. The former is associated with Bethlehem and its surroundings, while the latter is not. The latter is listed as Jonathan the son of Shammoth the Harorite in 1 Chr 11:24.

3. David's Song of Thanksgiving (22:1-51)

■ **1** This verse corresponds to the heading of Ps 18. It indicates that this song was a response for deliverance from David's enemies including **the hand of Saul.** No specific occasion is mentioned here, but David's flight from Saul in the wilderness may be hinted at here.

■ **2-4** Various metaphors are employed in these verses that depict God as a shelter in a time of distress. A number of the metaphors recall particular incidents by the words chosen (Baldwin 1988, 287). God is called **my rock** (v 2), for example, which described David's situation in 1 Sam 23:25-28. The term **my fortress** recalls 1 Sam 22:4; 24:22, and Jerusalem itself (2 Sam 5:7). The phrase **God . . . my rock** (22:3*a*) is also similar to 1 Sam 24:2. Thus, David recalled past experiences when God saved him from his enemies as the basis for his confidence that God would come to his aid again (v 4).

■ **5-7** The words here recall moments when David was being assailed by various opponents. The threats were so severe that the **waves of death** confronted him and the "cords of Sheol" (NRSV) entangled him. It was in these moments of opposition, however, that David ***called upon Yahweh*** and God wonderfully heard his voice and cry.

■ **8-16** In response to David's cry, God marshaled the forces of nature in order to rescue his servant. The imagery in these verses is also reminiscent of the manifestations of power that God demonstrated at Sinai (Exod 19:9, 16-20). The text indicates that God, who has all power over nature, would move heaven and earth to answer the call of the one in distress.

■ **17-20** David was on the receiving end of God's intervention into his affairs. God "drew [him] out of the mighty waters" (JPS) and ***delivered him from his*** *enemies.* God brought him to "a broad place" (NRSV) where he was safe and now he could live in peace.

■ **21-25** The Lord delivered David because his actions were just and right, especially toward Saul. David had "kept the ways of [*Yahweh*]," and "from his statutes I did not turn aside" (vv 22*a*, 23*b* NRSV). David did not take revenge on Saul but waited upon the Lord to vindicate him. Now that vindication had come, he could safely conclude that he was right with God (Ps 66:18-19). David was **blameless** before the Lord and therefore the Lord **rewarded** him accordingly.

■ **26-31** God's interactions with people are in direct proportion to their own character. God is loyal to those that are loyal to him, blameless to those who are blameless, and pure to those who are pure. To the crooked or corrupt, however, God shows himself as **shrewd.** God works to bring the haughty down, but the humble (i.e., the afflicted) he delivers. With God on his side, David could "leap over a wall" or "crush a troop" (v 30 NRSV) because God **is a shield for all who take refuge in him** (v 31).

■ **32-36** In response to all of God's saving action, the writer asks in v 32, ***Who is God but Yahweh?*** Yahweh proved to be a rock to David, "girded [him] with strength" (v 33 NRSV), and "set [him] secure on the heights" (v 34 NRSV). God provided "the shield of [his] salvation, and [God's] help made [him] great" (v 36 NRSV).

■ **37-43** Because of God's help David was able to destroy his enemies and strike them down until they were unable to rise again. God provided strength for the battle and God made David's assailants ***sink under*** him (v 39). Even when his enemies cried out to God, he would not listen to them and there was no one to save them. Because God had abandoned his enemies, David was able to beat them like **the dust of the earth** and ***crushed them and stamped them down like the mire of the streets*** (v 43).

■ **44-46** The establishment of David's monarchy may be the background for these verses. God delivered David from strife ***with my people.*** This may possibly refer to the latter portion of David's reign when there were plenty of occasions for strife. God kept David as **the head of *the* nations** (v 44*b*) and people who he did not know "served" (v 44*c* NRSV) him. Foreigners came **cringing** to him (v 45*a*), they "obeyed" him (v 45*b* NRSV), and they "came trembling out of their strongholds" (v 46*b* NRSV; see 2 Sam 8:1-14).

■ **47-50** In light of all God had done for David, the last portion of the song culminates with adoration and praise. David acknowledged that ***Yahweh lives*** and that God, the rock of his salvation, is the one who gave him vengeance over his enemies and exalted him over his adversaries. Because of this, David will extol Yahweh **among the nations** and sing praise to his name.

■ **51** David celebrated the link between God and king. God was a "tower of salvation" (NRSV) to his anointed one and God showed "love to his anointed" (NRSV). God's love also extended to David's descendants, the members of the dynasty that God promised to the king (2 Sam 7).

4. David's Last Words (23:1-7)

■ **1** David's last words are presented as an **oracle**. Although the oracle has been ascribed to David, it is doubtful whether these reflect his actual last words. The poetry is ancient, however, and could date to the early monarchical period. In giving his last will and testament, David resembles the great heroes from Israel's past who also gave significant speeches before their death: Jacob (Gen 49), Moses (Deut 32—34), and Joshua (Josh 23—24). David's words signal the formal closing of an important era in Israel's story, but they also point to the future in that they presuppose the eternal covenant God made with David's family (2 Sam 23:5).

■ **2-4** David is presented as a prophet as well as a poet in this section. He notes in v 2 that *the spirit of God speaks through me, his word is upon my tongue.* David's prophetic utterance centers on the subject of righteous leadership. He notes that the person who rules "justly" (v 3 JPS, NRSV) rules also with the **fear of God.** The ruler who reigns in righteousness and with a concern for justice is comparable to "the light of morning, like the sun rising on a cloudless morning" (NRSV). Both the king and the people benefit from this type of leadership. It brings blessing like "the rain on the grassy land" (NRSV).

■ **5** David indicated that his house resembled the just rulers of the previous verses ("is not my house like this?" [NRSV]). He recalled the **everlasting covenant** that God made with him and understood it to be a binding legal contract ("ordered in all things and secure" [NRSV]). It follows then, that since David sought to rule justly, that "all [his] help and . . . desire" (NRSV) would be brought to fruition according to the promise God made to David.

■ **6-7** The picture of the godly leader is contrasted with the ungodly. The "godless are all like thorns that are thrown away" (v 6a NRSV). The godless are judged worthless and have to be discarded because they oppose God's cause and they are dangerous. "They cannot be picked up" (v 6b NRSV) but have to be touched with **the shaft of a spear** or *iron bar* (v 7a). Left alone, the godless choke the growth of all that is good, therefore they have to be consumed by fire.

5. The Mighty Men of David (23:8-39)

The list of David's mighty men is organized into three separate sections: notices regarding the Three (vv 8-12), accounts of the heroic deeds of Abishai and Benaiah (vv 18-23), and the registry of the Thirty (vv 24-39).

■ **8-12** The first section pays attention to the valiant deeds of **Josheb-Basshebeth, Eleazar,** and **Shammah** (v 8). Josheb-Basshebeth is called the **chief of the Three** and a **Tahkemonite.** The place name is likely a variant of the reading in 1 Chr 11:11 where he is called a Hacmonite. He is credited with killing **eight hundred men** at one time.

Eleazar, **son of Dodai the Ahohite,** was with David "when they defied the Philistines" (v 9 NRSV). This last phrase is defective and should be read "when the Philistines defied them at Pas-dammim" (McCarter 1984, 490).

This reading is based on a reconstruction from the LXX and 1 Chr 11:13. The text notes that Yahweh was able to bring about a ***great victory*** against the Philistines through his efforts.

The last of the Three mentioned, **Shammah son of Agee,** fought against the Philistines on "a plot of ground" (v 11 NRSV) at the town of **Lehi.** Lehi is mentioned as the place where Samson struck a thousand Philistines with the jawbone of a donkey (Judg 15:9-19). The text again notes that Yahweh brought about a ***great victory*** through him.

■ **13-17** These verses recount a separate episode related to David's battles with the Philistines in 2 Sam 5:17-21. In this context, David and his men were at **the cave of Adullam** (2 Sam 23:13; see 1 Sam 22:1). The Philistines were encamped in **the Valley of Rephaim,** in the neighborhood of Jerusalem severing David's connections in the direction of Israel (Hertzberg 1964, 405). The Philistines also had set up a **garrison** in David's hometown of **Bethlehem.**

In the middle of this report the text notes that David **longed for** some **water from the well** that was in Bethlehem by the city gate (v 15). Then "the three warriors broke through the camp" (v 16 NRSV) and drew the water and brought it back to David. David subsequently threw the water on the ground, unable to drink it knowing that his men put their lives at risk. David's words in v 17, ***Yahweh forbid that I should do this,*** underscores the sincerity and conviction with which David decided to forgo the water his soldiers provided at their peril. The pouring of the water was a type of ritual sacrifice that emphasized the specialness of their gift to David (Evans 2003, 242).

■ **18-23** These verses recount the exploits of two of David's mighty men: **Abishai** (vv 18-19) and **Benaiah** (vv 20-23). Abishai held the rank of "chief of the Thirty" (NRSV). Abishai was the brother of **Joab,** David's main general, and the nephew of David (1 Chr 2:16). He is remembered in the text for his bravery, killing **three hundred men** with **his spear.** David, at times, did not always agree with Abishai (1 Sam 26:8 ff.; 2 Sam 3:39; 16:9 ff.; 19:21 ff.), but there was no denying his loyalty to David. He even appears to have saved David's life (2 Sam 21:17). Although he enjoyed success and counted among the Thirty, he never attained a position among the Three.

The text records Benaiah as an ***active man.*** He hailed from **Kabzeel** in southern Judah (Josh 15:21) and was remembered as "a doer of great deeds" (2 Sam 23:20a NRSV). The text recalls two of these deeds: "he struck down two sons of Ariel of Moab" (v 20b NRSV). The term for Ariel (*ʾariʾēl*) can also be translated as "lions of God." In light of the following statement, he "went . . . and killed a lion in a pit" (v 20c NRSV), a number of scholars have opted for this reading (Hertzberg 1964, 406). The short notice that "snow had fallen" (NRSV) is probably included to hint at the notion he tracked a lion who was down in a pit. Benaiah was also a great hand-to-hand warrior, killing an Egyptian (***a nice looking man***) who had spear in his hand. Benaiah was able to snatch the spear out of his hand and then killed him with his spear. Like Abishai, he was **renowned among the thirty** but did not attain to the level of the Three.

Benaiah was put in charge of David's **bodyguard.** David's bodyguard consisted of the Kerethites and Pelethites, warriors who originated from the Aegean region. The bodyguard played an important role in David's reign, especially at the end of his life when it was time to coronate Solomon as David's successor (1 Kgs 1:32-40).

■ **24-39** These verses include the long registry of the Thirty warriors. As it stands, vv 24-39 provide a list of thirty names yet the last statement in v 39 reads: **thirty-seven in all.** In order to correctly arrive at the number thirty-seven, scholars believe that the following names should be included: Joab, Abishai, Benaiah, and the Three. This still leaves thirty-six names. Part of the problem lies in the text itself. Verse 32 is obscure and it references **the sons of Jashen.** It is possible that all of the sons may not be listed here. If that is the case, then it may account for why the numbers do not add up correctly.

6. David's Census, the Plague, and the Threshing Floor (24:1-25)

■ **1-9** This unit opens with the interesting statement in v 1: *and the anger of Yahweh again flared up against Israel.* These words indicate that Yahweh was angry with the Israelites on a previous occasion. Which occasion is being referred to here? Some scholars note that this statement refers back to the events in 2 Sam 21:1-14, a situation when Yahweh was angry with the Israelites over Saul's harsh treatment of the Gibeonites. In both cases, a serious transgression was committed by a king, a holy place was included, and in each case a disastrous situation led to some form of blessing (Hertzberg 1964, 426). Another explanation may be associated with reference to Uriah in the verse that immediately precedes this chapter (23:39). The reference to Uriah reminds the audience of his murder and thus serves as the pretext for God's anger against Israel. Although both solutions remain possibilities, a definitive answer to this question remains elusive.

In response to this statement, the text notes in v 1 that Yahweh **incited David** to take a census: "Go, count the people of Israel and Judah" (NRSV). The term "incite" (*sût*) implies that God instigated David to take the census. But why would God tell David to take a census that led to David's disobedience (v 10) and a plague (vv 11-17). Answers to this question are varied in number and difficult to determine with certainty. One solution is to see v 1 as a later editorial statement added to three originally independent narratives about a census, a plague, and a threshing floor (see Behind the Text). This editorial remark provides a theological rationale for why a census David had taken resulted in divine sanction.

A second suggestion includes the idea that David was God's vehicle by which he punished Israel (Evans 2003, 245). Thus, God incited David to take the census so that God could mete out punishment for a sin/crime (unknown in this context) the Israelites committed and assuage God's anger.

Third, this verse has to be seen within the overall narrative flow of the chapter. God incited David to take the census in order to instigate the plague that ultimately led to the purchase of a threshing floor and the construction of an altar. Thus, the narrative moves from David's disobedience to atonement.

Fourth, the problem with the census may be associated with the manner in which it was conducted and David's reason for taking it (see below).

The other issue relates to God's responsibility for the census. If God incited David to take it, does this not imply that God bore responsibility for the consequences that followed? At this time in Israelite thought and belief, all phenomena, both good and bad, were ascribed to God. Therefore, even though the census was not considered a good thing, the impetus for taking emanated ultimately from God. Although this is a difficult concept for modern readers to understand, the ancient mind categorized the source of good and evil in this manner. This understanding changed over time, however, as good and evil were assigned to different sources/beings. This is one reason why, for example, the cause of the census was attributed to "Satan" (*sāṭān*) in 1 Chr 21:1. Although the Satan in Chronicles is not the NT form of Satan or the devil, it does show that the Chronicler was unwilling to assign temptation to Israel's God.

The text notes in 2 Sam 24:2 that **the king** ordered **Joab and the commanders of the army** to go count the people. It is interesting that David is called **the king** as he barked the command to his official. The grammar appears to be drawing attention to his office and the power he wielded as the top official in Israel. The census David ordered was to be a thorough one in which all the people **from Dan to Beersheba** were counted. Thus David would **know how many *people* there are.** The phrase **from Dan to Beersheba** is formulaic and implies the whole country of Israel from north to south; top to bottom. Ironically, this phrase is used in reference to Samuel's trustworthiness as a prophet (1 Sam 3:20). In this context it magnifies the extent of David's sin.

Joab raised concerns in 2 Sam 24:3 about David's desire to count the people: **Why does my lord the king want to do *this*?** Joab's question hinted at the impropriety of the census. In Chronicles, Joab's resistance to David's order is more defiant in that he failed to carry out the census in full (1 Chr 21). The reason for Joab's apprehension is understandable in light of the reason why a king would take a census. It is generally understood that a census was taken for two reasons: (1) it served as a basis for levying taxes and (2) for registering men for military service (Bright 1981, 198). In light of v 9, it seems reasonable to assume that David took the census in order to determine the number of fighting men he had at his disposal.

Various references in the OT indicate that numbering the troops before a time of war constituted customary practice (Num 1:2-3; Josh 8:10; Judg

7:3; 20:17 ff.; 1 Sam 11:8; 15:4; 2 Sam 18:1; 1 Kgs 20:15, 27; 2 Kgs 3:60). The evidence, however, seems to indicate that David ordered his census in a time of relative peace since it took over nine months to complete (2 Sam 24:8) (Yarchin 2000, 326). Taking a census in a time of peace would have made the people uneasy and aroused suspicions among the relatively independent tribes of the early monarchy (Keil and Delitzsch 1967, 502-3; McKane 1963, 302). Joab's response to David's order reveals this concern.

In spite of Joab's reluctance, the word of the king "prevailed against Joab and the commanders of the army" (v 4 NRSV). In the end, David was going to push his plan even when his commanders counseled against this logic. Joab and the men carried out the census in vv 5-9.

The geographical route depicts the extreme borders of David's territory. The census party went east of the Jordan near **Aroer** (v 5), continued north into the direction of **Gilead** and **Kadesh** (v 6). Then it moved westward toward **Dan** and the **fortress of Tyre** in the northwest (v 7). Finally it traveled south into the **Negev of Judah** at **Beersheba** (v 7). The route indicates the thoroughness with which Joab and his men carried out the census. It not only took them nine months to complete but also included every eligible person, including non-Israelites (v 7). The text appears to be indicating that no one remained out of David's reach. Joab then reported the tabulation of fighting men available: ***800,000 men of Israel*** and ***500,000 men of Judah.***

■ 10 After the census was completed the text notes that ***the heart of David struck him.*** David felt guilt over the census, and his conscience reminded him of the wrong he committed. But what did David do wrong? Part of the problem may have been the manner in which the census was taken. According to ancient law (Exod 30:11-16), a ransom had to be paid to God after a census was taken. Everyone who was entered into the records had to pay a half shekel as an offering to Yahweh. If the money was not paid according to the law, then a plague would descend on those who were enrolled. This is the reason, for example, that Josephus cites as the cause of the plague in this context (*Ant.* 7.13.1).

The census, however, also points to a larger, more troubling issue. By taking the census, David sought to expand the power of the king and the state. David's actions border on hubris in that he attempted to exert and magnify his authority above God's dominion. In essence, David pursued a policy of centralized control over the people of Israel. In the process, however, David no longer represented the shepherd leader who brought deliverance to Israel, but a warrior king who endangered the people's well-being (Yarchin 2000, 357).

David's guilt prompted him to humbly confess his wrongdoing before Yahweh. David acknowledged that he **sinned greatly** and asked God to ***remove the guilt of your servant*** (v 10). The term for "sin" (*ḥāṭāʾ*) used here is one of the most common terms for sin in the OT. It generally conveys the idea of "missing the mark," thus indicating that one has fallen short of God's standards. The term for "guilt" (*ʿāvôn*) speaks to the consequences of the sin committed or the punishment the sinned deserved. David also commanded that God **take away** the guilt/punishment that his sin incurred. David's response demonstrated his belief in God's ability and willingness to atone for the sin he committed.

■ **11-17** God responded to David's supplication through the agency of the prophet **Gad.** Gad is called "David's seer" (NRSV), which indicates that he functioned as the king's personal religious adviser who mediated God's message when needed. Little is known of Gad, but he provided words of instruction to David earlier in his life (1 Sam 22:5). Gad revealed to David that God *held three things over him* and that he should choose one of the following options as a punishment for the census he had taken (2 Sam 24:13): one, **three years of famine;** two, David would have to flee **three months** from before his foes; or three, a "pestilence" (NRSV) would come upon the land that would last **three days.** Although the three punishments appear to be personally directed toward David (i.e., famine on **your land,** foes will **pursue you,** a pestilence will come upon **your land**) the text bears out that ultimately it was the people David governed who bore the brunt of David's sin. Overwhelmed by the options Gad presented to him (*I am greatly distressed*), David could not decide his fate and thus placed the decision *into the hand of Yahweh* (v 14). David believed he fared better in the hands of God who might show mercy on him.

The text makes it clear that Yahweh decided to send "a pestilence on Israel" (NRSV). The pestilence afflicted all of the territory included in the census: **from Dan to Beersheba.** The pestilence also took a heavy toll on the people of Israel in that **seventy thousand** people died from it (v 15). God did not permit Jerusalem to be destroyed and restrained the angel who **stretched out his hand** toward the city. It is ironic that even though the directive for the census emanated from David in the city of Jerusalem, both the capital and the king were spared while the people throughout David's kingdom perished. The *angel of Yahweh* was by **the threshing floor of Araunah the Jebusite** when the pestilence stopped (v 16). In the ancient world, threshing floors represented places where divine activity took place (Ahlstrom 1961, 113-27; see also comment on 6:6). Araunah's threshing floor would be no different in that David offered sacrifices on this spot, and it later served as the location of the Temple Mount in the time of Solomon (see below).

When David witnessed the destruction, he remonstrated in 24:17 over the fact that his actions ("I alone have sinned" [NRSV]) brought disaster upon unsuspecting and innocent people (*what have these sheep done?*). David arrived at the conclusion that the king and people were inextricably bound; the king's decisions had serious repercussions over those he ruled. David pleaded that the punishment should be directed against him and his family instead.

■ **18-25** The events following the census and plague took place at the threshing floor of Araunah, the subject of vv 18-25. The prophet Gad instructed David to erect an altar on the site so that David could offer sacrifices in order to atone for his sin and restore proper order between God and Israel. Before David could erect an altar, he had to purchase the threshing floor from Araunah, which belonged to him. Araunah was a **Jebusite**, a member of the city of Jebus before David took the city (2 Sam 5:6-12), and thus a Canaanite.

The name Araunah is non-Israelite and may derive from the Hurrian word *ewrine*, meaning "lord" (Gordon 1986, 320). Some scholars have taken this to refer to his title. In v 16 the name Araunah appears with the definite article, evidence that is often used to support this conclusion (Hoffner 1973, 225). Not all scholars are in agreement with this position, however. Instead of a title, Araunah may have been a person of significant status within the Canaanite city. In v 23 the translation may read, **all this Araunah the king gives,** suggesting that he functioned as the king of the city at the time David conquered Jebus. If so, David allowed him to live in honorable retirement after he had taken the city from the Jebusites (Gordon 1986, 321).

Araunah suggested in v 22 that David **take** the land and he offered him **oxen** and **threshing sledges** and ***the yokes of the oxen*** for the sacrifice as well. Although Araunah offered to ***give*** these items to David, he refused and offered to pay **fifty shekels** for the threshing floor and the oxen. By making payment for the threshing floor, David ensured that the land would be legally owned by an Israelite and not a Canaanite.

In negotiating for this precious property, David resembled Abraham when he purchased the cave of Machpelah as a burial plot for Sarah (Gen 23). In both cases, the process of naming a price for the plot of land and then making a precise payment for the stated amounted constituted an ancient bill of sales (Tucker 1966, 77-84). Like the cave of Machpelah, the land that was purchased would serve an important role in the life of the people of Israel. The threshing floor that David acquired became the foundation for Solomon's temple (1 Chr 21:28—22:1). The altar that David built and the sacrifices he made on that site foreshadowed the temple that Solomon would erect and the offerings that would be made there.

Second Samuel ends with the note that God accepted David's burnt offerings and fellowship offerings and answered his prayer for the land. The end of the plague signaled the restoration of David, the penitent sinner, to favor and fellowship with God.

FROM THE TEXT

Throughout this last section of Samuel a number of important theological points are made that can be applied to our own journeys of faith.

1. As mentioned above (Behind the Text), the canonical arrangement of chs 21—24 underscores the faithfulness and dependability of God. As David's song of thanksgiving highlights, God is a refuge and a rock whom we can call upon in times of distress and turmoil. It is significant that many of the verbs in the first portion of the psalm (vv 1-4) are passive in nature. The writer un-

derscores the idea that in times of adversity and opposition, God will work on our behalf and it is our responsibility to simply trust God and wait while he works out our salvation before our eyes. It is during those moments of confusion and chaos that our minds and hearts can remain at rest because we know that God is our defense.

The text also notes that as Lord of creation, God has all the resources at his disposal to give us aide to comfort us and sustain us in the midst of dire circumstances. Although the writer uses creative imagery and hyperbole to illustrate God's mastery over creation at times (vv 8-16), the point is powerfully made that God will do everything within his power to work on our behalf.

Not only does God have the power to deliver us from our enemies and set us on a broad place, but God can also free us from our fears and anxiety and give us the strength to endure seasons of hardship. The writer also affirms that God is capable of reversing our fortunes and turning our misfortunes into times of victory. We are reminded that God humbles the proud (v 28) and can elevate the position of the lowly and weak.

2. The list of David's warriors in 21:15-22 and 23:8-39 remind us that friendship is invaluable and we rely on the assistance of others in life. Even someone as great and successful as David had close friends who supported him and carried his burdens in times of weakness. As we have witnessed throughout his story, not only did David come to the throne as the result of the assistance of his friends, but also they cared for him in his darkest moments.

As David's life began to crumble around him (i.e., chs 15—20), his friends cared for him, watched out for him, and even put their lives on the line for him. The text of 22:15-17, in particular, intimates that there were times when David grew weary and his warriors had to fight for him. Likewise, in our times of discouragement and weakness, the friendship of others can be a healing agent that comforts us in times of pain, encourages us when we feel like giving up, and provide us wisdom and guidance when we do not know which course of action to follow.

Friendship is a gift from God. We are created to be in community and not live in isolation. The old maxim remains true: no person is an island unto himself or herself. When God created the man in the garden, for example, God realized that it was not good for the man "to be alone." The man required human fellowship and contact, the type of social and emotional nourishment that other parts of the created order could not afford him.

In the NT, Paul's friends and companions were indispensable to him and the mission to which God called him. Paul relied on his companions to travel with him as he carried the gospel message throughout the Mediterranean world (Acts 13:13; 14:11; 15:40; 16:3). Others provided companionship and moral support during times of persecution (Acts 16:16-40; Rom 16:7). Still others visited Paul in prison while he languished in a Roman jail (Acts 28:30). Paul also had to rely upon the generosity and charity of others to meet his own needs (Phil 4:16-18) and the needs of believers in various churches (1 Cor 16:1; 2 Cor 8-9; Gal 2:10). If great men such as David and Paul required the assistance of others, how much more do we?

3. The last portion of Samuel (ch 24) provides a necessary critique on kingship and leadership in general. Throughout the last chapter of Samuel, we are reminded that even though God selects leaders to guide and give direction to a community of individuals (both religious and secular), leaders are still mortal and remain under the jurisdiction of God's authority. When David ordered that a census of the Israelites be taken, his desire to exalt the power of both the king and the state became apparent. David essentially put his faith in the resources at his disposal rather than in God. By taking the census, David forgot the important principle that his power to rule derived from God and not from the army he was able to assemble. As David attempted to assert his authority as king independently from God, he illustrated the temptation that leaders fall prey to when they are given great responsibility and endowed with power.

The same tendencies exist among leaders in modern times, including pastors and others who have ecclesiastical responsibilities. God anoints and calls various people to provide leadership over his church, the body of Christ. Sadly, even Christian leaders can become enamored with their prominent positions and the power that is inherent within them. Like David, they forget that they are called to be humble servants whose primary task is to provide caring and edifying direction to God's people. They try to lead without God's help, often relying on their own initiative and imagination, pushing their own agenda, and at times, abusing the power that God has entrusted to them. The allure of being in a position of responsibility can even become a narcissistic pursuit in which the glare of being in the spotlight becomes intoxicating and a boost to one's ego.

The results of failed leadership can be devastating. As the story of David and the census reveals, there is a direct correlation between the actions of the leader and the effects on the people within the group/community. The people in the community are the ones who unwittingly and innocently bear the brunt of a leader's misguided choices and actions. The people of Israel, for example, faced a terrible pestilence because of David's actions and his own hubris. Similarly, the community of faith can be torn apart by scandals, factions, and painful conflicts because the leaders have not functioned as the shepherds of God's people. The life of David thus serves as a fitting warning of how even the best of leaders can go astray when they forget what their true purpose and role is within the life of the church.

4. Although the story of David and the census is catastrophic in one sense, it also proclaims the main theme of Scripture: God has always and continues to act redemptively toward the problem of human sin. The books of Samuel could have ended on a note of despair because of David's sin; however, the general trajectory of this narrative moves from one of human disobedience

to one of atonement and restoration. David's sin resulted in pain and heartache for the Israelite people, but it culminated in the purchase of a threshing floor where offerings could be made on his behalf.

In the midst of this narrative, we are reminded that God has always provided the means by which sin could be atoned and thus reverse the harmful effects that it has in the life of a person and on a community. The property that David purchased not only served as the place of atonement for David's sin but also would become the foundation of the temple, the main religious site where the Israelites would present their atonement offerings as well.

In viewing the narrative from this perspective, the story of David and the threshing floor represents just one episode in the overall story of "salvation-history" that encompasses the whole of Scripture. The meta-narrative of God's redeeming grace runs through the story of the people of Israel and the prophets, culminates in the life, death, and resurrection of Jesus, and reverberates throughout the message of Paul and the early church. It is a message that continues to be heralded today and into eternity.

We are also reminded that the mercy and forgiveness David received was predicated on his response to his own guilt and the word from God through the prophet. To David's credit, each time that he was confronted by the prophet with regard to his disobedience, he responded in humble contrition (2 Sam 12:13; 24:10, 17), took responsibility for his actions, and confessed his wrongdoing. This is one of the enduring images that David leaves the reader of the text. Even though God chose David to lead the Israelite people and he became one of the most impressive kings of Israel's past, he was not perfect. Like us, he was prone to bouts of spiritual weakness and he committed his share of moral blunders.

However, David's greatness is witnessed in the fact that when he transgressed God's authority, he was still able to acknowledge his dependence upon God and his need for forgiveness. Psalm 51, a psalm that tradition ascribed to David after his affair with Bathsheba and murder of Uriah, eloquently recalls his desire to be cleansed from sin and for God to create a clean heart within him (v 10). David's willingness to humble himself before God stands in sharp contrast to his son, Solomon, whom the text never records confessing his sin before God (1 Kings 11:1 ff.). In David, then, the example of how to respond in genuine sorrow and repentance for one's sin and God's readiness to meet human sin with his mercy and forgiveness is forever preserved.

www.ingramcontent.com/pod-product-compliance
Lightning Source LLC
Chambersburg PA
CBHW082103250426
43661CB00079B/2624